황용 선생의
못 잊게 해줄게 수험 영단어

황용 선생의 **못 잊게 해줄게 수험 영단어**

초판 1쇄 인쇄 2012년 04월 23일
초판 1쇄 발행 2012년 04월 30일

지은이 l 황 용
펴낸이 l 손형국
펴낸곳 l (주)에세이퍼블리싱
출판등록 l 2004. 12. 1(제2011-77호)
주소 l 서울시 금천구 가산동 371-28 우림라이온스밸리 C동 101호
홈페이지 l www.book.co.kr
전화번호 l (02)2026-5777
팩스 l (02)2026-5747

ISBN 978-89-6023-790-2   53740

영어가 한국어와 친구였어?

중독주의!!

· 국내 최초 영어권의 단어 사용정도를 랭킹으로 수록한 진정한 우선순위 단어집
· 강력하고 재미있는 암기법으로 암기 효과 급상승
· 수능, NEAT, 공무원, 편입, 각종 공인시험대비 핵심어휘 약 1만 개 수록

황 용 지음

황용 선생의
못 잊게 해줄게
수험 영단어

ESSAY

영어실력은 어휘력이다! 수험독자들은 '어떻게 하면 효율적으로 단어 공부를 할까?' 고민하고 있다. '어떻게 하면 비교적 쉽게 단어를 가르쳐 줄까?' 하는 고민 끝에 그간의 강의와 공부 경험을 바탕으로 이 교재를 만들었다. 아울러 주요 시험 출제 단어(수능, 공무원, 편입, TOEFL, TOEIC, TEPS)와 빈출 단어에 대한 철저한 분석, 실제 영어권에서 이 어휘가 얼마나 쓰이는지 한국 최초로 빈출 순위를 수록하는 효율성을 제공하였다. 예를 들어 현대 원어민들이 주로 쓰는 86,800단어 중 3만 등 이내에 쓰이는 단어들은 원어민들이 상당히 자주 쓴다. 그만큼 각종 시험에 등장할 확률이 높은 단어라는 뜻이다.

수십 년이 지난 아직도 중학교 물상선생님이 저자에게 가르쳐준 주기율표가 기억나는 것은 무슨 이유일까? 그만큼 기억에 남도록 인상 깊게 외우는 방법을 가르쳐 주었기 때문일 것이다. 내가 그동안 공부했던 방식대로 단어가 기억에 오래 남도록 외우는 방법을 기록해 놓았다. 이 책을 한 번만 보지 말고 적어도 여러 번 반복하라. 이것이 내가 미국에서 학업 할 때 좋은 성적을 거둘 수 있었던 나만의 어휘공부 방식이다. 이 책에 실려 있는 어휘를 충분히 소화하게 되면 대학입시를 비롯한 다른 수험대비 영어 학습에서도 좋은 결과를 거둘 수 있을 것이다. 영어 시험에서 어휘를 잡으면 거의 다 잡은 것이다. 영어교육의 처음과 끝은 사실은 어휘교육이다. 결국 언어실력의 차이는 어휘 차이라는 것이다. 이 교재가 완성되기까지 미국에서 많은 시간 고생하면서 도움을 아끼지 않은 사랑하는 아내에게 감사의 마음을 전한다. 그리고 많은 조언을 아끼지 않은 사랑하는 제자 신효영, 박순현, 신세영 군에게도 감사의 마음을 전한다, 그리고 누구보다 나를 창조하신 하나님께 감사를 드린다. 이 책으로 공부하는 수험 독자들에게 영어 어휘 학습의 좋은 안내자가 될 수 있다면 더 큰 보람이 없겠다.

미국 New York, Buffalo에서   지은이   황 용

University at Buffalo

Applied Linguistics

Ⓡ 책의 왼쪽에 보면 이 표시(Ranking)와 함께 실제 원어민이 어느 정도 이 어휘를 사용하는지 순위를 적어 놓았다. 예를 들어 777/86800이라면 현대 영어를 쓰는 원어민이 86,800 어휘 중 777번째로 사용한다는 뜻이다. 약 3만 등 이내의 단어들은 원어민들이 상당히 빈번히 쓰고 중요한 어휘들이기 때문에 시험에 출제될 가망성도 높다고 할 수 있다.

Ⓣ 각 단어 오른쪽에 있는 이 표시는 그 단어를 암기하는 Tip이다. 단어 암기는 어떤 방법이든 짧은 기간에 암기만 할 수 있다면 이것은 좋은 방법이라 할 수 있다. 흔히 사용하는 etymology(어원)에 의한 방법과 말을 만들어서 외우는 방법 두 가지를 사용하였으나 되도록 쉬운 방법을 쓰려고 노력하였다. 특히 한국어와 발음이 비슷함을 이용하거나 어려운 것은 말을 만들어서 하는 암기법을 수록하였다. 여러 번 읽어보면 입에 익어서 보다 단어를 빨리 암기하는 데 큰 도움을 얻을 수 있을 것이다.

▶ 기타 표시들

빈출어휘, 기출어휘 표시와 나올 가망성이 높은 어휘, 예문, 반의어, 유의어, 중요한 파생어들을 표시하였다. 유의어, 반의어는 애매한 경우 기록되지 않은 것이 많으며 예문은 직접 해석해 보시는 것이 좋으므로 해석을 달지 않았으니 참고하길 바란다.

각 단어들 옆에 체크가 두 개 있는 것은 빈출어휘, 하나있는 것은 기출어휘, 무표시는 앞으로 나올 가능성이 있는 중요 어휘이다.

그리고 책 뒷부분에 어원 편 정리가 있으니 활용하기 바란다.

▶ 단어 학습 활용법

어떤 언어학자의 연구에 따르면 모르는 단어를 약 25회 정도 반복했을 때 겨우 한 단어를 암기한다고 한다. 우리의 목표는 덜 보고 많이 외우는 것인데 다음과 같은 원칙을 준수해야 한다.

1. 반드시 규칙적으로 학습하라(하루에 목표량을 정하고 꾸준히 학습하라).

2. 일주일후에 외웠던 단어를 다시 반복 학습하고 다시 한 달 후에 또 반복 학습하라. 진도만 나가는 것은 의미가 없다. 정확히 외우도록 반복하라.

Contents 차 례

A

abandon
[əbǽndən]
® 5863/86800

v. 단념하다
❶ 도박으로 없(ab)앤(an)돈(don) 단념하다
⑨ give up, surrender
⑩ This bicycle was abandoned years ago.

abide
[əbáid]
® 15122/86800

v. 머무르다, 약속을 지키다
❶ 어버이(abide)다 하면 함께 **머무르며**(같이살며) 그분들의 말씀
에 **따른다**
c.f) abide by: ~에 따르다
⑩ We had to abide in Buffalo.

abnormal
[æbnɔ́:rməl]
® 8128/86800

adj. 비정상적인
❶ norm은 기준이라는 뜻인데 여기에 접두어 Ab(혹은 a - 어원편
참조)가 붙어서 **반대, 이탈**의 뜻을 나타내는 경우가 있다. 여기
서는 정상적인 것의 이탈이므로 **비정상적인**
⑨ exceptional, anomalous ⑭ normal, ordinary
⑩ The results of the blood test were abnormal.

aboard
[əbɔ́:rd]
® 7255/86800

ad. prep. 배, 비행기, 열차, 버스를 타고
❶ a는 에어플레인 줄인 것+b는 버스 줄인 것(oard - 한국말로 읽
으면 오르다): **비행기나 버스타고**
⑩ Welcome aboard flight OZ135 to Seoul.

abolish
[əbáliʃ]
® 10502/86800

v. 없애다, 철폐하다
❶ 없(ab) 애(o) 리(li) 쒸(sh) - 내가 꼭 **없애리** 쒸
⑨ get rid of, do away with, eliminate
⑩ She likes abolishing the death penalty.

aboriginal
[æbərídʒənəl]
® 순위 외/86800

adj. 원래의, 원주민의
❶ ab(아빠)+original(원래의): 원래의 아빠이므로 그대로 **원래의**
⑨ primitive ㉒ aboriginality: 원시성
⑩ Do you remember the aboriginal state of this object?

abound
[əbáund]
[R] 16343/86800

v. **풍부하다**
[T] abound를 빨리 읽으면 **오버한다**가 됨. 오버하는 사람은 대개 자기만의 정서가 **풍부하다**
[유] teem
[파] abundance: 풍부
[예] I live in a region where snow abounds.

abreast
[əbrést]
[R] 20085/86800

ad. **옆으로 나란히**
[T] **옆으로(abrea)+st(서다)** - 천천히 발음해보면 한국 말 **옆으로 서다**가 된다
[유] side by side
[예] We were swimming two abreast.

✔ **abroad**
[əbrɔ́:d]
[R] 2542/86800

ad. **해외로**
[T] **ab(분리, 이탈의 뜻)+road (길)**: 우리 집 앞과 이탈된 **해외**
[예] I sometimes go abroad in winter.

✔ **abruptly**
[əbrʌ́ptli]
[R] 6123/86800

ad. **갑자기**
[T] **갑자기** 복권에 당첨되니 **아 부럽다리! (abruptly)**
[유] Suddenly, all of a sudden, on a sudden, all at once
[파] abrupt: 갑작스런, 뜻밖의
[예] Abruptly, he won megamillion dollars.

✔ **absence**
[ǽbsəns]
[R] 1785/86800

n. **부재(출석하지 않음)**
[T] 나 어제 **없어써(absence): 부재**
[반] presence [파] ***absent***: 부재의 ***absently***: 방심하여
[예] A new manager was appointed during my absence.

absent-minded
[ǽbsənt-máindid]
[R] 순위 외/86800

adj. **멍한, 건망증 있는**
[T] **absent(없는** - 발음은 없는 이지만) + **mind(정신)** 두 단어 합치면 **정신이 없는**
[예] Her absentminded husband forgot their anniversary.

A

absolute
[ǽbsəlù:t]
[R] 2813/86800

adj. **절대적인**
[T] 이 길 밖에는 **없어루트(absolute** - 루트는 길로 이해): 이 길 밖에 없다면 이 길이 **절대적인**
[반] relative [파] ***absolutely***: 절대적으로
[예] She absolute faith in her judgment.

absolve
[æbzάlv]
[R] 43833/86800

v. **용서하다, 책임을 면하게 하다**
[T] **아부잘보(absolve): 아부하고 잘 보**이면 **용서해 줄게**
[유] forgive, pardon, excuse
[예] God already absolved us of a sin.

absorb
[æbsɔ́:rb]
[R] 8165/86800

v. **흡수하다**
[T] **아빠 술봐(absorb)** - 아빠가 술 보고 빨리 **흡수하다**. 술을 좋아하시나 봐 ^^
[유] imbibe, soak [파] ***absorption***: 흡수
[예] Plants absorb carbon dioxide.

abstract
[æbstrǽkt]
[R] 3977/86800

adj. **추상적인**
[T] 사전에도 **없었더래(abstract)**. 사전에도 없었다면 뜻이 아주 **추상적인**
[유] ideal, metaphysical
[반] concrete, nonabstract [파] ***abstraction***: 추상
[예] Love and faith are abstract concepts.

absurd
[æbsə́:rd]
[R] 7262/86800

adj. **말이 안 되는, 불합리한, 모순된, 어리석은**
[T] 일본이 한국 **앞서다(absurd)**니 **말이 안 되는**
[유] foolish, ridiculous [반] realistic, reasonable
[예] What an absurd opinion!

abundance
[əbʌ́ndəns]
[R] 9690/86800

n. **풍부함**
[T] **아빤 돈써(abundance)**: 그래도 가정에서 **아빠가 돈쓰**기에는 경제 사정이 **풍부함**
[유] plenty, affluence [파] ***abundant***: 풍부한
[예] Here were Buffaloes in abundance.

abuse
[əbjúːz]
ⓡ 2733/86800

n. v. 남용, 학대하다
❶ ab(반대, 이탈)+use(이용하다): use가 잘 이용하는 것이라면 ab가 붙어서 분리, 이탈의 뜻을 나타냄. 따라서 **잘못 사용하다, 학대하다** 의 뜻
예 Many children had been physically abused in Africa.

academic
[ækədémik]
ⓡ 2093/86800

adj. 대학의, 학구적인
❶ 아까(aca) (배운건)데(de) 미(my - 수우미양가의 미)야?, 공부와 관련된 단어임 - **학구적인**
파 *academy*: 학(술)원
예 I only care about love. I have no interest in academics.

accelerate
[æksélərèit]
ⓡ 12535/86800

v. 가속화하다
❶ 차를 빨리 가게하려면 액서레이더(accelerate)를 밟아야 함
ⓢ speed, quicken, hasten ⓐ decelerate
예 The rate of economic growth has continued to accelerate.

accentuate
[ækséntʃuèi]
ⓡ 29708/86800

v. 강조하다, 액센트를 붙이다
❶ accent(악센트)+ate(동사, 형용사어미): 액센트 찍다, 강조하다
ⓢ emphasis, stress 파 *accent*: 강조
예 The mayor accentuated the quality of life.

accept
[æksépt]
ⓡ 1046/86800

v. 받아들이다
❶ 어서 **오셉(accept)**: 어서 오세요 하면서 **받아 들이다**
ⓢ take ⓐ decline, refuse, reject, turn down
파 *acceptable*: 받아들일 수 있는
예 Do you accept credit cards?

access
[ǽkses]
ⓡ 921/86800

n. 접근, 통로, 입구
❶ ac(접두어 ad의 변형으로 '쪽으로'의 뜻) cesss는 go의 뜻. 따라서 어느 쪽으로 가다이므로 **접근**, 혹은 내가 좋아하는 연예인을 보면 **악써서 (access) 접근** 하다로 암기
파 *accessible*: 접근하기 쉬운
예 I have Internet access at the UB library.

A

accident
[ǽksidənt]
[R] 1607/86800

n. **사고**
[T] 사고 나서 **아악(ac)** 비명 **쓰던(cident)?**
[유] misfortune
[예] She was injured in an accident at school.

acclaim
[əkléim]
[R] 16763/86800

n. v. **환호, 갈채를 보내다**
[T] 유명연예인이 내가 싸인 해줄까? 하자 **와~ 그레욤!!(acclaim)** 하며 학생들이 **환호하다**
[유] applaud
[예] I have acclaimed her beautiful performance.

accommodate
[əkάmədèit]
[R] 5646/86800

v. **편의를 도모하다, 숙박시키다, 사람을 수용하다, 화해하다**
[T] 죄수를 **아 감옥에다(accomodate)수용하데,** 어제 싸우던 애들 **아까뭐 데이트(accomodate)**하던데: **화해하다,** 이밖에 **편의를 도모하다**의 뜻도 있음
[파] *accommodation*: 숙박시설, 편의
[예] Over 5000 people can be accommodated on the resort.

accompany
[əkʌ́mpəni]
[R] 7605/86800

v. **동반하다**
[T] **company는 친구, 동료** 아닌가? **동반하다** 대개 ac(ad)가 들어간 단어는 뒷단어가 뜻을 좌우
[예] She will accompany me to the store.

accomplish
[əkάmpliʃ]
[R] 16976/86800

v. **달성하다**
[T] **아 깜깜(accom)**(한데)(문제) **풀어서**(plish) 목표 달성했어
[유] perform, achieve, carry out, fulfill
[파] *accomplishment*: 성취
[예] We have two ways to accomplish this task.

accord
[əkɔ́:rd]
[R] 6427/86800

v. **주다, 일치하다, 허용하다**
[T] cord는 마음 이라는 뜻(어원 편 참조) 따라서 ~**로(ac) 마음(cord)을 주다,** 즉 허용하다의 뜻
c.f) *according to*: ~에 따르면
[예] My hobby and his interests do not accord.

accordingly
[əkɔ́:rdiŋli]
ⓡ 3863/86800

adv. 따라서
① 아고딩이니?(accordingly), 그래서(따라서) 대학갈려고?
ⓢ therefore, consequently, hence, so
예 He knew his limitations and acted accordingly.

account
[əkáunt]
ⓡ 613/86800

n. 계산, 계좌
① 어(ac)! 카운트(count - 셈하다): 계산
c.f) account for: 차지하다, 설명하다
    accountant: 회계사
예 I closed bank accounts last week.

accrue
[əkrú:]
ⓡ 19862/86800

v. 저절로 생기다, 이자가 붙다
① 이자가 억으루(accure)붙다
예 He will get back any interest that have accrued.

accumulate
[əkjú:mjəlèit]
ⓡ 13480/86800

v. 축적하다
① ac(~에)+cum(쌓다 - 어원편참조)+ate(동사형 어미)cum은 쌓는다는 말: 축적하다
예 Evidence of his guilt is accumulating.

accuracy
[ǽkjərəsi]
ⓡ 4864/86800

n. 정확성
① (눈이) 애꾸라서(accuracy) 정확성이 필요함
ⓢ precision, accurateness
파 accurate: 정확한
예 The experiment is performed several times to ensure accuracy.

accuse
[əkjú:z]
ⓡ 13871/86800

v. 고소하다
① 건드리면 악(ac)!(하면서) 고소(cuse) 할거야
ⓢ charge, indict
예 She was accused of lying on the employment application.
(그녀는 입사원서에 거짓말한 것으로 고소되었다.)

✔ **accustomed**
[əkʌ́stəmd]
[R] 7381/86800

adj. **익숙한**
[T] ac(~에) + **갔었담(custom)**: 갔었던 곳에 **익숙한**
[예] She felt uncomfortably full, as she was not accustomed to eating so much.

✔ **ache**
[eik]
[R] 12797/86800

v. **쑤시다, 아프다**
[T] **ache(아이쿠)! 아프다**
[유] hurt, pain
[예] After I played soccer, my body ached for two days.

✔ **achieve**
[ətʃíːv]
[R] 1515/86800

v. **달성하다, 얻다**
[T] **얻쥐! 봐(achieve)**: (바라는 걸)**얻쥐** 두고 **봐**
[파] *achievement*: 성취, 업적 *achiever*: 성취자
[예] At last, I achieved my goal.

✔ **acid**
[ǽsid]
[R] 2051/86800

adj. **맛이 신, 신랄한, 산성의**
[T] **아(a) 시다(cid) - 맛이 신**
[유] sour, acidic
[예] I washed windows with an acid solution of vinegar and water.

✔ **acknowledge**
[æknάlidʒ]
[R] 5355/86800

v. **인정하다, 승인하다, 감사표시하다**
[T] 1등으로 **인정하니, 애가(좋아서) 난리지(acknowledge)**
[유] admit, agree [반] deny
[예] I readily acknowledged my mistake.

✔ **acoustic**
[əkúːstik]
[R] 9395/86800

a. **청각의, 전자 장치를 안 쓴**
[T] acoustic guitar(전자 장치를 안 쓴 기타)
[예] He can play acoustic guitar better.

acquaint
[əkwéint]
[R] 38654/86800

v. **알려주다, 숙지시키다**
[T] **알고 있다(acquaint)**: 천천히 읽으면 발음이 **알고 있다**(어퀘인트)와 비슷함
[유] familiarize, introduce [파] acquainted: 알고 있는
[예] This class is designed to acquaint students with the region's most important writers.

✔ acquire
[əkwáiər]
[R] 4305/86800

v. **얻다**
[T] **얻과이어(acquire): 얻다**(발음이 비슷)
[유] gain, get [반] lose
[예] I acquired a good reputation about the project.

✔ acreage
[éikəridʒ]
[R] 27973/86800

n. **평수, 면적**
[T] 평상시 **면적** 단위로 **에이커**란 말을 자주 쓴다
[파] acre(에이커): 4,046.8 제곱미터
[예] What acreage is your estate?

acrid
[ǽkrid]
[R] 26685/86800

adj. **매운, 쓴, 얼얼한**
[T] **매운탕**을 냄비**에 끓이다(acrid): 매운**
[예] Acrid smoke rose from the chimney.

✔ active
[ǽktiv]
[R] 1411/86800

adj. **능동적인**
[T] act(행동) + ive(형용사형 어미): **능동적인**
[반] inactive, passive [파] *activation*: 활성 *activity*: 활동
[예] We are active members of our church.

✔ actually
[ǽktʃuəli]
[R] 338/86800

adv. **실제로**
[T] act(행동) + ly(형, 부사형 어미): **실제** 행동하는
[유] In fact, As a matter of fact
[파] *actual*: 현실의 *act*: 행위 *action*: 행동 c.f) *actor*: 배우
[예] Actually, I'd rather spend the evening at home.

acute
[əkjú:t]
[R] 3885/86800

adj. **날카로운, 급성의, 심각한**
[T] **어 끝이(acute)** 날카로운, 끝이 날카로우면 대개 **급성**이고 **심각한** 상태
[유] keen, sensitive, sharp [반] obtuse
[예] I had acute pain in my shoulder.

✔ adapt
[ədǽpt]
[R] 7054/86800

v. **적응시키다, 각색하다**
[T] 나는 성격이 좋아서 **어데붙어도(adapt) 적응**을 잘한다
[유] adjust
[예] She adapted the novel for movies.

A

✔ add
[æd]
℞ 1250/86800

v. 더하다
❶ 애 도(add) - 애도 더해라
㊀ plus ㊁ abate, bate, deduct
㈎ *addition*: 추가 *additional*: 추가의
㈄ Add one spoon of sugar to the coffee.

✔ addictive
[ədíktiv]
℞ 10577/86800

adj. 중독성의
❶ add(더하다) + tive(형용사형 어미): ~에 더해있는, 더해져 **붙어** **있는**
㊀ adherent ㈎ addict: 중독시키다, 중독자
㈄ The robber is an alcohol addict.

✔ address
[ǽdres][ədrés]
℞ 1459/86800

n. v. 연설, 연설하다, 편지 보내다, ~라 부르다
❶ 편지 **어디로써**?(address): 편지, 또 니가 **연설** 때 얘(이아이도) **들었어**(address): 연설
㈄ How can I address you?

adept
[ədépt][ǽdept]
℞ 16504/86800

adj. n. 숙련된, 달인
❶ 내가 영어 가르쳐줄까? **아 넵둬**(adept), 넵두라는 말은 자기도 **숙련**되어있다는 말
㊀ expert, authority: 달인
㊁ amateur, inexpert, nonexpert: 비전문가
㈄ He's an adept in homework.

✔ adequate
[ǽdikwit]
℞ 2754/86800

adj. 적당한, 충분한
❶ 돈이 없는데 **어디 꿀 데**(adequate)?(적당한데) 없소?
㊀ sufficient, enough
㈄ This cell phone is adequate to my needs.

adhesion
[ædhíːʒən]
℞ 14561/86800

n. 부착, (의견의)고수
❶ **어디 헤어젼**(adhesion)? 내가 붙여줄게, 어디 헤어져 닳은데 있니? 부착해 줄게
㊀ bond, cling ㈎ adhere: 고수하다 adhesive: 부착의
㈄ He adhered to his plan.

adjacent
[ədʒéisənt]
ⓡ 6702/86800

adj. 인접한, 이웃의
❶ <u>아저씬(adjacent) 이웃의</u> 사람
㈜ adjoining, bordering ⓐ distant
예 My house is adjacent to Buffalo downtown.

adjunct
[ǽdʒʌŋkt]
ⓡ 23190/86800

n. 부속물, 보조자
❶ ad(~에) + junct(쩍)<u>붙어있는 부속물</u>
㈜ aid, appendix, supplement
예 Massage therapy can be used as an adjunct along with the medication.

✔ adjust
[ədʒʌ́st]
ⓡ 6631/86800

v. 조정하다, 순응하다
❶ 새로 이사 간 곳에 <u>adjust(아저씨)하면서 그 곳에서 적응할 분 위기를 조정하다</u>
㈜ regulate, modify
예 I adjusted the volume on the radio in my car.

administer
[ædmínistər]
ⓡ 10744/86800

v. 관리하다, 경영하다, 다스리다, 집행하다
❶ <u>어디 民(admin)(백성)이 있었다(ister)면 다스려야 함</u>
㈜ administered: 주어진
예 The assistant will administer the test.

✔ admire
[ædmáiər]
ⓡ 8320/86800

v. 감탄하다
❶ <u>아들 말이여(admire)!하며 효심에 감탄하다</u>
㈜ esteem, respect
파 *admirable*: 감탄할만한 *admirer*: 찬미자
예 I admire the way you handled such a touchy situation.

✔ admit
[ædmít]
ⓡ 2630/86800

v. 허락하다
❶ <u>어디 밑(admit)어 보자며 허락하다</u>
㈜ acknowledge, agree, allow ⓐ deny
파 *admission*: 입장, 입학
예 This baseball ticket admits two people.

A

admonition
[ædməníʃən]
Ⓡ 40513/86800

n. 훈계, 경고
❶ mon은 지켜보고 있다는 뜻(어원편 참조), ~로(ad) + 지켜(mon) + 봄(tion - 명사형 어미)
㉮ advice, counsel, monition
㉠ She offered words of advice and admonition.

✔ adolescence
[ædəlésəns]
Ⓡ 11921/86800

n. 청소년기
❶ 청소년기엔 얘도 레슨(adolescence) 받고 다른애도 레슨받고, 공부하느라 바쁘네
㉮ minority, nonage ㉯ *adolescent*: 청춘의, 미숙한
㉠ He struggled through his adolescence.

✔ adopt
[ədápt]
Ⓡ 3654/86800

v. 채택하다, 입양하다
❶ 고아원서 아기를 골라서(채택해서) 입양하니 애답다(adopt)
㉠ We adopted a child from Korea.

adorn
[ədɔ́:rn]
Ⓡ 30629/86800

v. 꾸미다
❶ 부부동반 모임에 남편이 안 꾸미고 온 아내를 보고 한마디 하자 부인이 하는 말 - 아~ 돈(adorn)이 있어야 꾸미지? ㅋㅋㅋ
㉮ decorate, beautify ㉰ deface
㉠ Her paintings adorn the walls.

✔ adult
[ədʌ́lt]
Ⓡ 2010/86800

n. adj. 성인, 다 자란
❶ 다 자란 아들(adult - 발음이 아들과 비슷)
㉮ grown - up, mature ㉰ adolescent, immature
㉯ *adulthood*: 성인기, 성인임
㉠ We need to approach this in an adult way.

✔ advantage
[ædvǽntidʒ]
Ⓡ 1399/86800

n. 유리함, 이로움
❶ 어디 번티(번영한 티) 지?(advantage) - 유리
㉮ profit, benefit ㉰ disadvantage
㉯ advancement: 진보 advantageous: 유리한
　　advance: 진보하다, 나아가다
㉠ He has the advantage of me.

✔ advent
[ǽdvent]
ⓡ 8200/86800

n. 출현, 도래, 재림
❶ 어디 빈터(advent)가 있어야 예수님이 **출현**하시고 **재림**하시지
예 We witnessed the advent of computer.
  (우리는 컴퓨터의 출연을 목격했다.)

adventure
[ædvéntʃər]
ⓡ 5270/86800

n. 모험
❶ ~로(ad) + 가다(vent - 가다의 뜻 어원편 참조) - 무조건 가는 것 이므로 모험
예 Life is an adventure in forgiveness.

adversary
[ǽdvərsèri]
ⓡ 17584/86800

n. 적, 상대방
❶ 내가 벌서는 중인데 **얘 두 벌서리**(adversary)? **상대방**도 벌을 서리?
ⓨ enemy, antagonist, foe, opponent
ⓑ friend
예 His political adversaries tried to prevent him from winning the nomination.

adverse
[ædvə́:rs]
ⓡ 6316/86800

adj. ~에 거스르는, 불리한, 반대의
❶ 얘두 벌 서(adverse)? 선생님 말씀 **거스리는**
ⓨ negative, opposed, disadvantageous, unfavorable
ⓑ advantageous, favorable, friendly
예 I'm not adverse to continuing the debate.

✔ adversity
[ædvə́:rsəti]
ⓡ 22210/86800

n. 역경, 불운
❶ **얘 두 벌섰지**(adversity): 같이 벌서면 **불운**
예 He fell in adversity.

✔ advertise
[ǽdvərtàiz]
ⓡ 11166/86800

v. 광고하다
❶ 광고해서 **얘도 (돈)벌었다제**(advertise)?
파 *advertisement*: 광고
예 They are advertising the new edition of the book.

A

advocate
[ǽdvəkit][ǽdvəkèit]
Ⓡ 7853/86800

n. v. 옹호자, 변론하다
Ⓣ ad(~로) + voc(목소리 - 어원편 참조) + ate(형용사, 동사형어미): ~로 목소리를 내다: 옹호자, 변론하다. vocal 이 가수와 관련되는 걸 기억
㊒ exponent, advocator, proponent
예 He advocated higher salaries for teachers.

aeronautics
[ὲərənɔ́:tiks]
Ⓡ 33244/86800

n. 항공학
Ⓣ aero(공기, 비행기) + ics(학문 명칭): 항공학
예 In order to build a functioning airplane, you need to have a vast knowledge of aeronautics.

aesthetic
[esθétik]
Ⓡ 6365/86800

adj. 미학적인, 예술적인
Ⓣ 예술쎄틱(aesthetic) - 발음하면 비슷함
㊒ beautiful, attractive, beauteous, artistical
반 homely, ill - favored, plain,
예 We hired Susan as our interior decorator because she has such a fine aesthetic sense.

✔ **affair**
[əfέər]
Ⓡ 2937/86800

n. 일
Ⓣ 아빠 일(affair) - 아빠가 하는 일도 일이죠
㊒ thing
예 After the war, the government focused on its own domestic affairs.

✔ **affect**
[əfékt]
Ⓡ 2042/86800

n. v. 감동, 정서, 영향을 끼치다
Ⓣ af(~에) + fec(영향 주다, 만들다 - 어원편 참조): ~일을 만들다, 영향주다
㊒ influence, sway
파 *affective*: 감정적인 c.f) *affection*: 애정
예 Cold weather affected the crops.

affiliation
[əfiliéiʃən]
Ⓡ 16940/86800

n. 입회, 가입, 제휴
Ⓣ 입휠(입회) 리(affili) + ation - 명사형어미)
㊒ association, membership
예 Whatever their political affiliation, they believe there is no one quite like him.

affirm
[əfə́:rm]
® 20883/86800

v. 확언하다, 긍정하다
❶ af(~에, 로) + firm(굳게 하다): 확언하다
㊦ assert ㊨ deny ㊙ affirmative: 긍정적인
㊟ We cannot affirm that this painting is genuine.

✔ afflict
[əflíkt]
® 39727/86800

v. 괴롭히다
❶ 괴롭히면 아프릭(afflict - 아프다고!!!!)
㊦ distress, agonize, anguish
㊟ The disease afflicts an estimated two million people every year.

affluence
[ǽflu(:)əns]
® 19310/86800

n. 풍부, 풍요
❶ af(~로) + flu(흘러 넘침) + ence(명사형어미): 흘러넘칠 정도로 풍요로움
㊦ wealth
㊟ This affluence of new students is straining an already crowded school system.

✔ afford
[əfɔ́:rd]
® 2225/86800

v. ~할 여유가 있다, 주다
❶ 아빠(af) + ford(포드)차도 살 여유가 있다
㊦ offer, provide
㊟ The country can't afford another drought.

✔ afterward
[ǽftəwərd]
® 45762/86800

adv. 뒤에, 나중에
❶ after(뒤) + ward(~쪽으로, 영어단어에 ~ward가 붙으면 ~쪽으로라는 뜻)
㊦ after, later ㊨ ahead
㊟ He found out about it long afterward.

✔ agent
[éidʒənt]
® 2327/86800

n. 대리인
❶ 나 없으면 대리인은 얘 이젠(agent)
㊦ representative, deputy ㊙ *agency*: 대리 기관
㊟ Our agent in Hong Kong will ship the merchandise.

A

aggravate
[ǽgrəvèit]
ⓡ 29489/86800

v. 악화시키다, 화나게 하다
❶ 애 끓어 봤데(aggravate) - 애 간장 끓으면 건강 **악화되고 화나죠**
⑪ irritate
㉠ A headache can be aggravated by too much exercise.

✅ aggressive
[əgrésiv]
ⓡ 4425/86800

adj. 공격적인
❶ 아! 그래서씨바(aggressive) - 말이 **공격적인** 사람들 싸울 때보면 이야기 듣다가 그래서 씨바
⑪ combative 파 *aggressively*: 공격적으로
㉠ He started to get aggressive and began to shout.

agile
[ǽdʒəl]
ⓡ 23037/86800

adj. 기민한, 경쾌한
❶ 애절(agile)한 마음에 그녀 전화 받을 때 **기민한, ag는 기민한** (어원편 참조)
⑪ graceful, featly, light, quick and active
⑭ awkward, clumsy
㉠ Leopards are very fast and agile.

agitation
[ǽdʒətéiʃən]
ⓡ 11553/86800

n. 동요, 불안, 흥분
❶ 얘기 떼선(agitation) - 아이를 유산해서 **동요, 불안**
⑪ storm, unrest, nervousness
㉠ She left in great agitation.

agonize
[ǽgənàiz]
ⓡ 순위외/86800

v. 괴롭히다, 괴로워하다
❶ 애고 놔줘(agonize)! 괴로우니까
⑪ afflict, anguish
㉠ He who will not economize will have to agonize.

✅ agrarian
[əgréəriən]
ⓡ 14185/86800

adj. 농업의
❶ 영어에 **agr이 들어가면 땅 + ian(사람이나 형용사 어미): 땅에 관한, 농사의**
⑪ agricultural, farming 파 *agriculture*: 농업
㉠ The government of Brazil announced that agrarian reform had been a success.

✅ ahead
[əhéd]
🅡 1633/86800

adv. ~ 앞에
❶ 앞(a)에 + 머리(head): 머리 앞에 이므로 결국 ~**앞에**
예 Please walk ahead of me.

✅ aid
[eid]
🅡 1202/86800

v. n. 돕다, 도움
❶ A이다(aid) - 성적이 A이다, A를 맞으면 GPA(평균)올리는데 **도움 됨**
㊌ abet, help, assist
예 Fortune cannot aid those who are lazy.

✅ aim
[eim]
🅡 1601/86800

n. v. 목표, 겨누다
❶ 성적 목표는 A임(aim)
㊌ goal
예 He aimed at the target but missed it.

airborne
[ɛ́ərbɔ̀:rn]
🅡 12277/86800

adj. 공중에 떠있는
❶ 공중에 떠있는 에얼(공기) 본(airborne)적 있니?
㊌ aloft
예 Once the plane was airborne I loosened my seat belt.

✔ aircraft
[ɛ́ərkræ̀ft]
🅡 1669/86800

n. 항공기
❶ air(공기, 항공기) + craft(비행기, 선박, 기술): 항공선박 즉 비행기
예 We'll travel Canada by aircraft.

aisle
[ail]
🅡 11791/86800

n. 통로
❶ 我일(아일 - 내가 다닐) (aisle) 통로
예 Once we got inside the stadium we walked down the aisle to our seats.

akin
[əkín]
🅡 12583/86800

adj. (서술적 용법에 쓰여서) 친족의, 동족의
❶ 친족이기에 아낀(akin)!
㊌ affiliated, related, allied
파 be akin to: ~에 가깝다, 유사하다
예 Foxes are closely akin to dogs.

A

alarm
[əlɑ́:rm]
ⓡ 3823/86800

n. v. **경보, 경보하다**
❶ 알람(alarm)이 울려 걱정하는, all(모두) + arm(무기로) 혹은 알람 시계 생각 All to the **arm**s가 alarm으로 줄은 것임
ⓢ frightened ⓐ reassured
판 alarming: 놀라운, 걱정스러운
예 He didn't mean to alarm me.

alert
[əlɔ́:rt]
ⓡ 5092/86800

adj. v. **방심 않는, 기민한, 경계시키다**
❶ 정신이 일어(alert)난 - 깨어있는 **방심 않는**
ⓢ watchful: 정신 바짝 차린, alarm: 경보하다
예 The radio alerted coastal residents to prepare for the hurricane.

✔ algebra
[ǽldʒəbrə]
ⓡ 20250/86800

n. **대수학**
❶ 수학 **대수**만 나오면 난 **잊어버려(algebra)**
c.f) Arithmetic
예 I am a leaner of elementary algebra.

alien
[éiljən]
ⓡ 6067/86800

adj. n. **외국의, 이질적인, 외국인**
❶ **외일이언(alien - 외인일리언): 외국인 일리언**
ⓢ foreign, nonnative ⓐ domestic, native
예 It's completely alien to her tastes.

alight
[əláit]
ⓡ 13340/86800

v. **(탈 것에서) 하차하다**
❶ 사람이 **하차하니** 차가 **어!라이트(alight)한** (가벼운)
ⓢ get off ⓐ board, get on
예 Many tourists alighted from the bus.

✔ alike
[əláik]
ⓡ 5439/86800

adj. adv. **같은, 마찬가지로(똑같이)**
❶ 나도 **마찬가지로 아이 라이크(alike) 유**
ⓢ similar, akin ⓐ differently
예 He thinks all politicians are alike.

allegiance
[əlíːdʒəns]
ⓡ 9310/86800

n. 충성심
❶ 어우르쟌쑤(allegence) - 어울린다는 말은 함께한다는 뜻이므로 팀의 단결을 통해 **충성심**을 가지고 있다는 말
ⓢ loyalty, fidelity, faithfulness
ⓐ disloyalty, faithlessness
ⓔ Both candidates are working hard to convince voters to switch allegiances.

alleviate
[əlíːvièit]
ⓡ 13827/86800

v. 덜다, 경감하다
❶ 엘리베이터(alleviate)를 타는 것은 **부담을 덜기** 위한 것
ⓢ allay, ease ⓐ aggravate, exacerbate
ⓔ I have to find ways to alleviate my stress.

✔ alliance
[əláiəns]
ⓡ 3066/86800

n. 동맹, 협정
❶ 모두(all) + i(나)가 + 되는 것(ance - 명사형 어미)은 동맹
ⓢ union, league 파 *ally*: 동맹하다, 동맹국
ⓔ We need to form a closer alliance between U.S and Korea.

allocate
[ǽləkèit]
ⓡ 11699/86800

v. 할당하다, 지명하다
❶ 그 돈이 다 **얼로갔데(allocate)?** - 어디로 돈이 **할당 되었냐는 뜻**
ⓢ allot, assign, designate ⓐ misallocate
ⓔ We need to find best ways to allocate our foods.

allot
[əlát]
ⓡ 32564/86800

v. 할당하다
❶ 골 랏(all ot)!: 땅을 **분배하니** 골랏(발음 비슷)
ⓢ allocate, assign
ⓔ Each speaker will be allotted 15 minutes.

✔ allow
[əláu]
ⓡ 876/86800

v. 허용하다
❶ 하라 우(allow) - 발음이 하라 우 - **허용하다**
ⓢ permit, approve, grant ⓐ ban, forbid, prohibit
ⓔ No smoking allowed in this area.

alloy
[ǽlɔi]
Ⓡ 15359/86800

n. v. 합금, 혼합물, 혼합하다
❶ **오라이!(alloy** - 오라는 말은 함께 **합하자**는 말)
Ⓢ admixture, blend, mix, amalgam, amalgamation
예 This table is made up of aluminum alloy.

allure
[əlúər]
Ⓡ 35811/86800

v. 매혹하다, 사로잡다
❶ **어! 누워** 하며**(allure) 매혹하다.** 혹은 영어의 **lure(누워)는 유혹하다**의 뜻임
Ⓢ charm, enchant
예 I was so allured by my sister's friend that I asked her for a date.

✔ **almost**
[ɔ́:lmoust]
Ⓡ 274/86800

adv. 거의
❶ **all(모두) most(대 부분) - 거의**
Ⓢ all but, nearly, about: 약
예 Analysts said that the price of gasoline rose by almost 20 percent.

✔ **alone**
[əlóun]
Ⓡ 739/86800

adj. adv. (서술적용법으로 쓰여) 홀로, 다만 ~뿐
❶ **홀론(alone) - 역시 발음상 홀로**
Ⓢ single
예 Please leave me alone.

✔ **aloud**
[əláud]
Ⓡ 7074/86800

adv. 소리 내어
❶ **어 라우드(aloud)** - 뒷단어(loud)의 뜻만 생각. a만 접두어로 붙은 단어는 뒷단어가 뜻을 나타내는 경우가 많다
Ⓐ silently, soundlessly, voicelessly
예 I read the magazine aloud.

✔ **alter**
[ɔ́:ltər]
Ⓡ 4457/86800

v. 바꾸다
❶ **올타(alter)**하고 **바꾸다**
Ⓢ change, modify Ⓐ fix, set
예 Alcohol can alter a person's mood.

alternative
[ɔ:ltə́:rnətiv]
®1192/86800

n. adj. 양자택일, 대안, 대신의
❶ alter(바꾸다)만 봐도 대체한다 뜻 임을 알 수 있음
⊛ option, selection, substitute
㈜ alternate: 번갈아 하는, 교대하다
   alternately: 교대로(=one after another)
㈖ You have the alternative of study or working.

altitude
[ǽltətjù:d]
®11386/86800

n. 고도
❶ alto(알토)는 높은 소리이므로 altitude는 높은 상태, **고도**
⊛ height, elevation c.f) attitude: 태도 aptitude: 적성
㈖ She find it difficult to adjust to the city's high
   altitude.

altogether
[ɔ̀:ltəgéðər]
®3006/86800

adv. 전부, 완전히
❶ all(모두) + 같이(together): 모두 같이 이므로 **전부**
⊛ entirely, in total ⊕ incompletely, partially, partly
㈖ I had an altogether new idea about the project.

amaze
[əméiz]
®29829/86800

v. 깜짝 놀라게 하다, ~에 놀라다
❶ 어매! 이제(amaze) 큰일 났네, 어떤 일이 **깜짝 놀라게 하다**
⊛ surprise, astonish, astound
㈖ It amazes me that he got summa cum laude.

ambassador
[æmbǽsədər]
®6479/86800

n. 대사, 사절
❶ 아입대사다(ambassador) - 나는 대사(배사가 대사와 발음 비슷)다
⊛ agent, delegate
㈖ U.S president met Korean ambassador.

ambiguity
[æ̀mbigjú:əti]
®7892/86800

n. 애매함
❶ ambi(양쪽 - 어원편 참조) + guity(명사형): 양쪽다 인 것 같은 **애매함**,
   혹은 **안비교했디**(ambiguity) - 안 비교해서 **애매함**, 이런 식으로 기억
⊛ obscurity, uncertainty
⊕ clarity, clearness, obviousness
㈜ *ambi*valent: 불안정한 *ambi*dextrous: 양손잡이의
   *ambi*dextrous: 복장이 남녀 공통의
㈖ She has to avoid ambiguity in her speech.

28

ambition
[æmbíʃən]
[R] 5783/86800

n. 야심
[T] 양쪽을(ambi) 다 가짐.(야심) 혹은 MB선 - 대통령 되신 야심
[유] goal, aspiration, yearning, longing
[예] Congressman was my ambition.

amenable
[əmí:nəbəl]
[R] 14825/86800

adj. 순종하는
[T] 아멘(amen) + able(~할 수 있는) 아멘하며 순종하는
[유] willing, suited [반] unamenable, unwilling
[예] Whatever you decide to do, I'm amenable — just let me know.

amiable
[éimiəbəl]
[R] 15854/86800

adj. 상냥한
[T] 시아버지가 며느리를 애미야 (하고)상냥하게 불(amiable)러요
[유] friendly, affable, kind - hearted
[반] ill - natured, ill - tempered
[예] I knew my instructor as an amiable person.

amid
[əmîd]
[R] 6664/86800

prep. ~사이에, 한복판에
[T] a(하나) + mid(중간): 하나가 중간에 있으므로 ~사이에
[유] among, amidst
[예] It was hard to recognize you amid all the people.

among
[əmʌ̀ŋ]
[R] 404/86800

prep. ~가운데서, ~사이에서
[T] 아 멍(among)한 가운데 영어시간 지났네
[예] Among many friends, I like Sam.

amount
[əmáunt]
[R] 634/86800

n. 총계, 총액, 양
[T] 아 마운트(amount) - 산(mount)으로 쌓을 정도의 양
[예] I'll give you the whole amount in five - dollar bills.

ample
[ǽmpl]
[R] 8077/86800

adj. 풍부한, 넓은
[T] 암 플(ample - ple은 full로 생각하면) 암세포가 풍부한
[유] abundant, plentiful [반] bare, minimal, spare
[파] amplify: 확대하다, 증가하다
amplification; 확대 amplitude: 폭, 풍부
[예] I didn't have ample money for Canada trip.

amuse
[əmjú:z]
[R] 18306/86800

v. **즐겁게 하다**
[T] **어! 뮤직(amuse)**을 들려주며 즐겁게 하다
[유] entertain
[파] ***amusing***: 재미있는(=humorous)
amused: 즐거워하는 amusement: 즐거움, 오락
[예] I amused my friends with witty conversation.

analogy
[ənǽlədʒi]
[R] 7389/86800

n. **유사**
[T] **아나로그(analogue)** 시계는 바늘로 대충 **유사**하게 시간을 봄 따라서 어낼러지는 대충, 반면 디지털 시계는 정확한 시간을 보여줌
[유] likeness, resemblance
[예] There is analogy between U.S and Korea.

analysis
[ənǽləsis]
[R] 740/86800

n. **분해, 분석**
[T] **어(a)(칼)날로 씻어서(nalysis) 분해** 함 - 발음해 보면 어 날로 씻어서 해부할 때 보면 칼 날로 분해
[파] ***analyze***: 분석하다 ***analyst***: 분석가
[예] New York Times published an analysis of the Korean tension.

ancestor
[ǽnsestər]
[R] 14064/86800

n. **조상**
[T] **an(앞서) + cest(간 - 어원편 참조) + or(사람)**
[유] antecedent, forefather [반] descendant(=descendent)
[파] ancestry: 가계, 혈통(lineage)
[예] It is reported thar the ancestor of Japan is Koguryo.

anchor
[ǽŋkər]
[R] 10050/86800

n. v. **닻, 고정시키다, 정박하다**
[T] 9시 뉴스 **고정 앵커(anchor)**라는 말에서 **고정시키다** 혹은 배가 **안가(anchor)** - 배가 안가는 것을 닻을 내린 것 때문
[예] The ship has a kedge anchor.

ancient
[éinʃənt]
[R] 2008/86800

adj. **고대의**
[T] 고대(고대 다니는)의 **애인 시원타**(ancient)
[유] antique, old, outdated [반] modern, new, recent
[예] I studied both ancient and modern history in University.

anecdote
[ǽnikdòut]
[R] 20297/86800

n. 일화
[T] 아내가 도운(anecdote) 이야기, 일화
[유] story, tale
[예] I told her several humorous anecdotes about my childhood.

✔ **angle**
[ǽŋgl]
[R] 3666/86800

n. 각도, 앵글 족
[T] 카메라 앵글(angle) - 트라이 앵글(각도)
[예] I took the angle of the mountain.

anguish
[ǽŋgwiʃ]
[R] 10402/86800

n. v. 심한 고통, 심히 고통스러워하다
[T] 내가 운것이(anguish)고통 때문이었어
[유] pain, agony [반] delight, comfort, relief
[예] I experienced the anguish of poverty when I was young.

✔ **ankle**
[ǽŋkl]
[R] 7245/86800

n. 발목
[T] 발을 윤 클(ankle)이다. 발목을 삐어서
[예] I sprained my ankle yesterday.

✔ **anniversary**
[æ̀nəvə́:rsəri]
[R] 4212/86800

n. 기념일
[T] anni, annu은 년을 나타냄
anni(1년) + verse(돌다 - 어원편 참조): 1년마다 돌아오는 기념일
[파] annually: 해마다
[예] He celebrated the tenth anniversary of their marriage.

✔ **announce**
[ənáuns]
[R] 6576/86800

v. 발표하다
[T] 아나운서(announcer)는 뉴스를 발표한다
[유] declare, report [파] *announcement*: 알림
[예] He announced his marriage.

✔ **annoy**
[ənɔ́i]
[R] 17775/86800

v. 괴롭히다, 애태우다
[T] 어느 놈 이(annoy) 우리 아이를 괴롭히니?
[유] harass [반] comfort, calm, soothe [파] *annoyance*: 성가심
[예] In summer, mosquitoes annoy people in Korea.

anonymous
[ənánəməs]
ⓡ 6352/86800

adj. 익명의, 알려지지 않은
❶ an(반대의 뜻) + onym(이름 - 어원편 참조) + ous(형용사어미): 이름 없는
⑨ unknown, unidentified, unnamed ⑪ named
㉠ The anonymous donor gave his kidney to a patient.

antagonist
[æntǽgənist]
ⓡ 28395/86800

n. 반대자, 적수
❶ 같은 배를 안타고 있었다(antagonist): 적수, 반대자
⑨ contestant, enemy, opponent, foe
⑪ ally, friend
㉠ Korea is the antagonist of Japan in technology.

antarctic
[æntá:rktik]
ⓡ 11364/86800

adj. 남극의
❶ ant(반대 - 어원편 참조) + arctic(북극의)
⑨ south pole ⑪ arctic
㉠ He played a role in Antarctic exploration.

antecedent
[æntəsí:dənt]
ⓡ 24242/86800

n. 선조
❶ ante(전에) + cede(오다) + ent(사람): 전에 온 사람 - 선조
⑨ predecessor, forerunner, ancestor
⑪ descendants, offsprings
㉠ My antecedents moved to Buffalo in 1905.

anthem
[ǽnθəm]
ⓡ 15397/86800

n. 국가, 성가, 축가
❶ 안쌈(anthem - 앉아있음) 안되는 노래 - 국가
㉠ The band played the national anthem of Korea.

✔ anthropology
[ǽnθərəpálədʒi]
ⓡ 9111/86800

n. 인류학, 인간학
❶ 인간이 산다는 것이 참 안쓰러버(anthropo)
㉠ When I was in college, my major was anthropology.

antibiotic
[æntibaiátik]
ⓡ 17603/86800

n. adj. 항생물질, 항생 물질의
❶ anti(반대, 저항) + bio(살아있음): 항생
㉠ Penicillin is an antibiotic.

A

anticipate
[æntísəpèit]
ℝ 8749/86800

v. 기대하다
🅣 **안티 씹혔데(anticipate):** 안티 씹히길(안티가 없어지길) **기대하다**
🅢 expect
🅔 I eagerly anticipated my girl friend's arrival.

antidote
[æntidòut]
ℝ 20357/86800

n. 해독제, 대책
🅣 **anti(반대) + dote(독 - 발음이 독과 비슷함): 해독제**
🅢 medicine, remedy, cure
🅔 Good jobs are the best antidote to general crime.

antipollution
[æntipəlúːʃən]
ℝ 순위외/86800

n. adj. 공해 방지, 공해방지의
🅣 **anti(반대) + pollution(오염): 공해 방지**
🅔 New York state passed antipollution laws.

antiquity
[æntíkwəti]
ℝ 13835/86800

n. 태고, 고대
🅣 **한(an) 태고(tiqui):** 한나라 태고 시대
🅢 ancient times 🅐 modern times 🄟 *antique*: 고대의
🅔 Indian lived here in remote antiquity.

antiseptic
[æntəséptik]
ℝ 24375/86800

adj. n. 방부의, 무균의, 방부제
🅣 **anti(반대) + septic(셉 티): 셀수없는티 막는: 무균의 방부의, 무균의**
🅢 a food preservative: 방부제
🅔 This food has no antiseptic.

apart
[əpáːrt]
ℝ 2805/86800

adv. 따로, 떨어져서
🅣 **a(한) + part(부분):** 전체에서 한 부분만 보면 **따로 떨어져** 있음
🅢 near 🄟 apart from: ~은 제외하고 *apartment*: 아파트
🅔 New York and Seoul are thousands of miles apart.

apathetic
[æpəθétik]
ℝ 29430/86800

adj. 냉담한, 무관심한
🅣 **a(반대, 이탈) + pathy(마음, 감정):** 마음이 가지 않는, 냉담한, 무관심한
🅢 unfeeling, cool
🅔 I am becoming apathetic about my girl friend.

apology
[əpáləʤi]
ⓡ 9220/86800

n. 사과
❶ 앞으로 절(apology) 대 안할게 하며 사과하다
[파] *apologize*: 사과하다
[예] Please accept my apology.

apparatus
[æpəréitəs]
ⓡ 6579/86800

n. 기구
❶ 아빠랑(appara) (기구) 탔어(tus): 물론 여기서의 기구는 아니지만
ⓢ appliance, device
[예] The fire fighter Department has excellent fire - fighting apparatus.

apparel
[əpǽrəl]
ⓡ 36141/86800

n. 의복
❶ 상처난 앞 팔을(apparel) 옷으로 가려야
ⓢ clothing, attire, clothes, garment
[예] The department strore had a sale on summer apparel.

apparent
[əpǽrənt]
ⓡ 1928/86800

adj. 명백한
❶ 친아버지인지 DNA검사하고 나서 그 결과가 **아빠란다(apparent) 애비단다(evident) 애비였어(obvious) 그리어(clear) 파터(아빠)다(patent)**
ⓢ evident, obvious, patent, clear ⓐ obscure
[파] *apparently*: 겉으로 보아
[예] The solution to the calculus problem was apparent.

appeal
[əpíːl]
ⓡ 918/86800

v. n. 호소하다, 상고하다, 매력
❶ 앞빌(appeal - 앞에서 빌면서)호소하다
[파] appealing: 매력적인
[예] The president appealed to the people about the tax cuts.

appear
[əpíər]
ⓡ 924/86800

v. 나타나다, ~인듯하다
❶ 앞에(appear)나타나다
ⓢ emerge, come out, show up, turn up
ⓐ disappear [파] *appearance*: 출현
[예] She appeared very late in the party.

A

appetite
[金pitàit]
Ⓡ 7675/86800

n. 식욕
❶ 식욕이 좋아 늘 **입이타잇(appetite)** - 입이 타이트하다 입이 꽉
  차있다는 뜻 뭐 먹느라고
㊦ hunger, emptiness
㊕ appetizer: 식욕을 돋우는 음식
㊁ I have no appetite for lunch because of headache today.

✔ applaud
[əplɔ́:d]
Ⓡ 20466/86800

v. 박수갈채 하다, 칭찬하다
❶ **앞으로도(applaud)**잘해주길 바라면서 **박수치다**
㊦ cheer
㊁ They applauded wildly at the end of the match.

✔ application
[æplikéiʃən]
Ⓡ 1021/86800

n. 적용, 지원, 지원서
❶ **지원하려면 앞으로 가이소(application)**
㊕ apply: 적용하다, 응용하다, 약을 바르다, 지원하다
㊁ Please fill out this application form.

✔ appoint
[əpɔ́int]
Ⓡ 6914/86800

v. 임명하다, 지명하다
❶ ap(~로) point(가리키다): 임명발표에서 **지명하다**
㊦ nominate, name ㊨ dismiss, discharge, fire
㊕ *appointment*: 약속
㊁ She was appointed professor of linguistics at UB.

✔ appreciate
[əprí:ʃièit]
Ⓡ 3487/86800

v. 감사하다, 감상하다, 진가를 인정하다
❶ **앞**(에서 눈물) **뿌려서(appreciate) 감사하다**
㊕ *appreciation*: 감상, 감사 *appreciative*: 감상하는
  appreciatively: 감사하게도
㊁ I really appreciated the information you gave me.

✔ approach
[əpróutʃ]
Ⓡ 601/86800

v. n. 접근하다, 방법
❶ **앞으로 춰(approach)!**하면서 기차가 **접근하다**
㊦ near, move toward, close
㊨ back, recede, retreat, withdraw
㊁ Now, we're approaching Kenmore avenue.

appropriate
[əpróupriit]
[R] 871/86800

adj. 적절한
[T] ap(~에) + proper(적절한) + ate(동사, 형용사형 어미): ~에 적절한
[유] suitable, apt, applicable, fit
[반] improper, inapplicable
[예] This movie is not appropriate to teen - age people.

approve
[əprú:v]
[R] 6797/86800

v. 승인하다, 허가하다
[T] ap(~에) + prove(증명하다): ~에 대해 증명해주다
[유] accredit, authorize
[반] decline, deny, disapprove
[파] *approval*: 승인
[예] My parents approved my plan to visit Niagara Falls.

approximate
[əprɑ́ksəmèit]
[R] 10735/86800

a. v. 근접한, 가까워지다
[T] **아빠라서 메이트(approximate)처럼 가까운** 아빠라서 메이트(친구)처럼 가까운
[예] Your report is approximate to the truth.

aptitude
[ǽptitù:d]
[R] 20298/86800

n. 습성, 경향, 적성
[T] **아파트(apt) 어떠대? (itude):** 한국 사람들은 아파트 선호 **경향**
[유] fitness
[예] I have a special aptitude for applied linguistics.

arbitrary
[ɑ́:rbitrèri]
[R] 6688/86800

adj. 임의대로, 무작위로
[T] 집에서는 **아비들이(arbitrary) 임의대로** 한다 - 아버지가 맘대로 한다는 말
[유] random, without order
[반] methodical, nonrandom, orderly, organized, systematic
[예] I made a completely arbitrary decision.

arbor
[ɑ́:rbər]
[R] 54370/86800

n. 수목
[T] **수목** 드라말(드라마를) **볼(arbor)누나**
[유] tree
[파] arboreal: 나무에 사는
[예] The fifth of April is Arbor Day in Korea.

A

archaic
[ɑːrkéiik]
ⓡ 13695/86800

adj. **고대의**
❶ **고대에 대해 알게 있는(archaic)가?**
⑨ antiquated, old fashioned, ancient
⑩ University at Buffalo needs to update its archaic computer systems.

✔ architecture
[ɑːrkətèktʃər]
ⓡ 3315/86800

n. **건축, 구조물**
❶ 아아크(arch - 아치형, 혹은 우두머리) + 宅(tec - 집 택) + 지어(ture): 아치형 집 지어 - **건축**
⑩ Mr. Kim studied architecture in University.

arctic
[ɑ́ːrktik]
ⓡ 7797/86800

adj. **북극의**
❶ **북극에서 물은 얼까틱(arctic)? 북극서 물 얼지?**
⑭ antarctic
⑩ Upstate New Yorker suffer an antarctic temperature in winter.

ardent
[ɑ́ːrdənt]
ⓡ 17397/86800

adj. **열렬한**
❶ 모든 것을 **알**려고하**던(ardent) 열정적인** 학생
⑨ passionate, fervent, enthusiastic, eager
⑭ dispassionate, emotionless
⑩ At last I confessed my ardent love to her.

arduous
[ɑ́ːrdʒuəs]
ⓡ 17495/86800

adj. **힘드는, 분투하는**
❶ 미국에서 학기 성적을 **R줬어(arduous)**: 공부가 **힘든**, 미국에서 성적 R은 resign을 줄인 말(학생스스로 점수가 안 나올 것 같거나 개인 사정으로 미리 그만 둠)
⑨ hard, difficult, strenuous ⑭ easy
⑩ I went through an arduous teaching internship program.

✔ argue
[ɑ́ːrgjuː]
ⓡ 2363/86800

v. **논쟁하다, 주장하다**
❶ **알구(argue)떠드는 거야?**
⑨ claim ㉙ *argument*: 논의
⑩ She argued over our marriage.

arid
[ǽrid]
® 14384/86800

adj. 건조한, 불모의
❶ 어리다(arid)아직 불모(털이 안남)의, 불모의 땅은 건조한
⊕ anhydrous, dry, barren
예 There are a lot of arid area in Middle East.

✔ arise
[əráiz]
® 2941/86800

v. 일어나다, 발생하다
❶ 뒷 단어 rise(일어나다)를 생각하자
⊕ turn out, emerge
예 Difficult problems arise daily in our lives.

arithmetic
[əríθmətik]
® 10596/86800

n. 산술
❶ 어려서(arith) 한 메써메틱(metic - 수학): 어릴 때 한 수학은 산수
⊕ calculation, computation
예 We learned arithmetic in elementary school.

✔ arm
[ɑ:rm]
® 1112/86800

n. v. 팔, 무기, 무장시키다
❶ 옛날에는 무기가 없어서 팔(arms)로 싸웠음
예 They were walking arm in arm.

✔ armrest
[á:rmrèst]
® 77186/86800

n. 팔걸이
❶ arm(팔) + rest(휴식): 팔이 쉴 곳은 팔걸이
예 Armrest is the part of a chair that supports the arm.

✔ aromatic
[ærəmǽtik]
® 15689/86800

adj. 향긋한
❶ aroma(향) + tic(형용사 형 어미) aroma therapy(방향 요법)를 생각하자
⊕ flavorful, fragrant, perfumed 파 aroma: 향기
예 I gave aromatic flowers my girl friend on Valentine's day.

arouse
[əráuz]
® 14912/86800

v. 일깨우다, 감정을 자극시키다
❶ 어라 우제?(arouse - 어라 울지?)감정을 자극해서
⊕ wake, awake, excite, stimulate ⊕ lull
예 Hassan trial aroused a lot of New Yorker's interest.

A

✤ arrange
[əréindʒ]
ℝ 3915/86800

v. 정돈하다, 배열하다, 준비하다
❶ **어라인제(arrange) 정돈 좀 하자**
㋲ fix, set, settle ㋴ disarrange, disorder
c.f) array: 배열하다, 차려입다
㋹ *arrangement*: 배열, 정리
㋋ I arranged my stuff on school desk.

arrest
[ərést]
ℝ 3991/86800

v. 체포하다
❶ **걸렸었다(arrest) - 어레스트**인데 자꾸 발음하면 그런 것도 같다
㋲ apprehend ㋴ discharge, release
㋋ Amherst police arrested the murder suspect.

✔ arrogant
[ǽrəgənt]
ℝ 9614/86800

adj. 무례한, 거만한
❶ 말이 **애로간(arrogant - 어린애로 알고 말한) - 상대방에게 무례한**
㋲ rude, impolite, haughty ㋴ meek, gentle
㋹ *arrogance*: 거만
㋋ Chris is very arrogant guy in school.

✤ article
[áːrtikl]
ℝ 1514/86800

n. 물품, 논설, 기사, 조항
❶ 아마 **일(숫자) 일 걸**(article - 알리클을 발음하면 일일걸 비슷함): **조항**에 번호를 붙여 일, 이, 삼
㋲ item, object, essay, composition, paper, theme
㋋ I read an exciting article in New York Times.

✤ artifact
[áːrtəfækt]
ℝ 44614/86800

n. 공예품
❶ **art(예술품) + fact(만듦): 공예품**
㋲ object
㋋ The King's tomb contained many peculiar artifacts.

✤ artificial
[àːrtəfíʃəl]
ℝ 4295/86800

adj. 인공적인
❶ **art(예술) + fic(만들다) + ial(형용사 어미): 예술은 사람이 만드는 것, 인공적인**
㋲ manmade ㋴ artless, natural
㋋ Pepper paste contains no artificial flavor.

artillery
[ɑ:rtíləri]
® 8649/86800

n. 대포, 포병대
❶ 대포 알들이(artillery)적진으로 날아가요
유 guns, cannon
예 Robert was a first lieutenant in the artillery.

artisan
[ɑ́:rtəzən]
® 23859/86800

n. 장인
❶ artis(예술품) + an(사람): 만드는 사람, 장인
유 craftsman, skilled worker
예 I bought two baskets made by local artisans.

ascend
[əsénd]
® 25501/86800

v. 올라가다, 상승하다
❶ 점수 올라가니까 주변에서 어 쎈데(ascend)!
유 arise, rise 반 descend, dip, drop, fall
파 ascent: 오르기, 승진, 향상
예 The eagles ascended into the sky.

ascertain
[æ̀sərtéin]
® 10798/86800

v. 확인하다
❶ (봉투를)어서 떼(ascerta) 안(in)에 있는 걸 확인해라
유 find, find out 반 miss, overlook
예 Fall semester's course registration information can be
ascertained by UB students with a computer.

ascribe
[əskráib]
® 27590/86800

v. ~탓으로 돌리다
❶ 어서 꺼라(ascribe) 하며 공부 안하는 것 TV 탓으로 돌리다
유 attribute
예 He ascribed his fault to family problem.

ashamed
[əʃéimd]
® 6643/86800

v. (서술적으로 쓰여) 부끄러운
❶ 아! 수염(ashamed) 하며 부끄러워하는, 혹은 What a shame!!
을 기억할 것
유 shamed 반 shameless, unashamed
파 ashamedly: 부끄러워서
예 I was ashamed to show my house.

A

ashore
[əʃɔ́:r]
® 9549/86800

adv. 해안에
❶ 해안에 있으면 **아! 쉬원(ashore):**
[예] I went ashore to see sunrise.

✔ aside
[əsáid]
® 2723/86800

adv. 곁에, 옆으로 떨어져서
❶ **Side가 옆인 것을 기억하자.** 대개 a만 앞에 붙은 서술단어들은 a를 뺀 나머지 만 알면 단어의 뜻을 알 수 있다
[예] Please stand aside. I'm in a hurry.

✔ aspect
[ǽspekt]
® 2321/86800

n. 외모, 측면
❶ a(~에, ~로) + spect(보다 - 어원편참조): **보이는 것**
⊕ phase, side
[예] What is the aspect of the problem that interests you most?

✔ aspire
[əspáiər]
® 18556/86800

v. 열망하다
❶ (꽃이)**어서 피래(aspire)** 하면서 **열망하다**
⊕ desire eagerly 펴 *aspiration*: 열망
[예] I aspired to be a member of National Assembly.

assail
[əséil]
® 55703/86800

v. 공격하다, 추궁하다
❶ **어서(as) 미사일(sail)로 공격해**
⊕ attack ⊖ defend
[예] The prime minister of Italy was assailed by the media.

assault
[əsɔ́:lt]
® 3917/86800

v. 공격하다, 습격
❶ 어 **쏠테(assault)** 야?: 어 총으로 쏠 테야? **공격하다**
⊕ attack, raid ⊖ defend
[예] He was arrested for assaulting a college student.

✔ assemble
[əsémbəl]
® 12413/86800

v. 모으다
❶ 아 센 불(assemble) 때려면 나무 **모아야** 한다
⊕ collect, gather ⊖ break up, disperse, split
펴 *assembly*: 집회, 국회
[예] Children like to assemble interesting toys.

assert
[əsə́ːrt]
ⓡ 9066/86800

v. 주장하다, 단언하다
❶ 어(a)! 섯다(ssert)고 주장하다
⊕ maintain, declare, claim, affirm
㉠ I assert that Mr. Hassan is guilty.

assess
[əsés]
ⓡ 3457/86800

v. 평가하다
❶ 사람의 가치를 as(어서) + sess(세어서) 평가하다
⊕ evaluate, estimate
㉠ My house was assessed at five hundred thousand dollars.

✅ asset
[ǽset]
ⓡ 4235/86800

n. 자산, 이점
❶ AS(as)받을 것이 세트(set)로 있음 - 자산이 많은 가봐
⊕ advantage, resource, benefit
㉠ English ability is a beautiful asset to me.

✅ assign
[əsáin]
ⓡ 13394/86800

v. 할당하다, 배정하다
❶ 너에게 할당된 것이야. 어서 사인(assign)해
⊕ allot 파 *assignment*: 할당, 임명, 과제
㉠ The teacher assigned us 50 math problems for homework!

✅ assist
[əsíst]
ⓡ 3604/86800

v. 돕다
❶ 스포츠의 assist생각 - 어시스트는 도움주는 것
⊕ help, aid ⊖ hinder, frustrate
파 *assistant*: 보조자
㉠ Teaching assistant assisted me with my homework.

✔ associate
[əsóuʃièit]
ⓡ 6235/86800

v. 연합시키다, 관련시키다, 동료
❶ associate(어서오시엿) - 어서 오시라고 인사하는 것은 자기와 함께하자는 말로 같이 연합하자, 관계를 맺자는 뜻이다
⊕ join, unite, company
⊖ break up
㉠ He no longer wish to be associated with girl like her.

A

assortment
[əsɔ́:rtmənt]
[R] 16636/86800

n. 구분, 분류
[T] as(~에) + sort(종류)별로 모아놓다
[유] classification, grouping
[예] This book has a wonderful assortment of English words.

assume
[əsjú:m]
[R] 2446/86800

v. 가정하다, ~인 체하다
[T] 아줌마(assume)인체 하다
[유] suppose, presume [파] ***assumption***: 가정
[예] I assumed he like New York but he moved to Boston.

assure
[əʃúər]
[R] 7234/86800

v. 보증하다, 확신시키다, 보험 들다
[T] as(~에) + sure(확실한): 역시 a 빼고 뒷 단어만, 확신시키다
[유] guarantee [파] ***assuredly***: 확실히
[예] I assured him that everything would turn out all right.

asthma
[ǽzmə]
[R] 9481/86800

n. 천식
[T] 천식은 아주마(asthma)니 기침한다
[예] I was an asthma sufferer for a long time.

astonish
[əstániʃ]
[R] 54989/86800

v. 깜짝 놀라게 하다
[T] 어 스타니?(astonish) - 스타가 나타나 깜짝 놀라게 하다
[유] amaze, surprise, astound, startle
[예] My girl friend's sudden appearance astonished me.

astrology
[əstrálədʒi]
[R] 23402/86800

n. 점성술
[T] astro, aster(별 - 어원편 참조) + logy(이론, 학문, 말): 점성술
[예] She believes in astrology.

astronaut
[ǽstrənɔ̀:t]
[R] 29914/86800

n. 우주 비행사
[T] astro(별) + naut(항해하는 사람): 우주 비행사
[예] China will sent astronauts to the moon sooner or later.

✔ astronomy
[əstránəmi]
® 13927/86800

n. 천문학
❶ astro(별) + nomy(학문, 법): 별에 관한 학문 - **천문학**
파 *astronomer*: 천문학자 *astronomical*: 천문학의, 천체의
예 He is interested in Astronomy observation.

✔ athlete
[ǽθli:t]
® 13726/86800

n. 운동선수
❶ 힘도 쓰고 애써야 돼(athelete): **운동 선수**는 힘도 쓰고 애쓰고
파 *athletic*: 운동의
예 Athletes from around the Asia will be competing at the Asian Games.

✔ atmosphere
[ǽtməsfiər]
® 2092/86800

n. 대기, 분위기
❶ atmo(어때 뭐?) + sphere(지구, 공): **지구는 어때 뭐?(지구 공기, 분위기가 어때?)**
유 air
예 North Korea often creates a tense atmospheres.

✔ atomic
[ətámik]
® 6616/86800

adj. 원자의
❶ a(반대, 이탈의 의미) + tom(쪼개다): **쪼갤 수 없는**
파 *atom*: 원자
예 Atomic bomb dropped on Japan during second world war.

✔ attach
[ətǽtʃ]
® 8168/86800

v. 붙이다, ~에 들러붙다
❶ 오늘 학교에서 **어땠지?(attach)** 하며 친구가 **들러붙다**
유 add 반 detach
예 I attached application file to the e-mail.

✔ attack
[ətǽk]
® 1072/86800

v. 공격하다
❶ 어! 태클(attack) 걸어 **공격하네**
유 assail, assault 반 defend, guard
예 The United states will attack north Korea if they use nuclear weapon.

attain
[ətéin]
® 11951/86800

v. 성취하다, 달성하다
❶ 얻데인(attain) - 얻다, 달성하다
㊤ achieve, reach, accomplish, gain, obtain
㋨ You can attain your goal unless you give up.

attempt
[ətémpt]
® 882/86800

v. n. 시도하다, 시도
❶ 해보니 어 땜?(attempt): 해보다, 시도하다
㊤ endeavor, strive, try
㋨ I attempted to solve two difficult calculus problems with my friend.

attend
[əténd]
® 2740/86800

v. 출석하다, 시중들다
❶ 너 그 학교 다녀보니 어떤데(attend)?: 출석하다
㉣ *attendant*: 수행자, 출석자
㋨ I'm attending Yong Moon High School.

attention
[əténʃən]
® 715/86800

n. 주의, 돌봄
❶ 주의 깊게 보니 영어 샘 어떠션(attention)?
㊤ awareness, consciousness, watchfulness ㊦ inattention
㋨ You need to pay more attention in English study.

attest
[ətést]
® 35392/86800

v. 증명하다
❶ at(~에) + test(시험보이다): 증명하다
㊤ confirm, verify, certify, authenticate ㊦ disprove
㋨ I can attest that I am not guilty.

attic
[ǽtik]
® 9530/86800

n. 다락방, 아테네식의
❶ 요즘은 다락방 없디(attic)
㋨ Attic is the space or room at the top of a building.

attire
[ətáiər]
® 27343/86800

n. 의복
❶ 어 (멋진) 타이야(attire), 타이(tie)도 의복
㊤ apparel, clothing, clothes, costumery, dress
㋨ I like neatly attired girls.

attitude
[ǽtitjùːd]
Ⓡ 1706/86800

n. 태도, 자세
❶ 우리아이 **태도 어때**(attitude)**튜터?**: 선생님(튜터)우리 아이 태도 어때요?
㊎ posture: 자세
예 She's friendly and has a good attitude.

attorney
[ətə́ːrni]
Ⓡ 9157/86800

n. 대리인, 변호사
❶ 죄지어서 **아 떠니**(attorney)? 걱정 마 변호사 있으니까?
㊎ lawyer
예 I will become an attorney at law in New York State.

attractive
[ətrǽktiv]
Ⓡ 1975/86800

adj. 매력적인
❶ 내 **매력**이 **어때 티비**(attractive) 나올만 하지?
㊎ charming, appealing, fascinating, alluring
파 *attract*: (주의, 흥미를) 끌다 *attraction*: 끄는 힘, 매력
예 An attractive girl greeted me in front of my friend's house.

attribute
[ǽtribjùːt][ətríbjuːt]
Ⓡ 8803/86800

n. v. 속성, ~의 탓으로 하다
❶ 애들이(attri)**뷰티**(bute) (애들의 **속성**), **아들**(attri)이 **부티**(bute) 나서 호강(호강을 아들 탓으로 돌리다)
㊎ property, characteristic, trait, nature: 속성, ascribe, impute: ~의 탓으로 하다
예 She attributed her mistakes to the English teacher.

audience
[ɔ́ːdiəns]
Ⓡ 1859/86800

n. 청중, 관객
❶ aud(듣다) + ence(명사형 어미): **청중**
파 *auditory*: 청각의
예 The audience was respectful of the speaker's opinion.

authentic
[ɔːθéntik]
Ⓡ 7994/86800

adj. 진짜의
❶ 옷엔 **틱**(authentic) 하고 **진짜** 메이커가 박힘
㊎ genuine, real, veritable, bona fide
㊙ bogus, counterfeit, fake, false
예 She prepared a very authentic Korean meal.

A

author
[ɔ́:θər]
[R] 2323/86800

n. v. **작가, 저자, 집필하다**(write)
[T] **좀(au - 한자로 나) 써(thor):** 내가 썼어=**저자**
[유] writer
[파] authorize: 인가하다, 권한을 부여하다
[예] I enjoyed the book, but I can't remember the name of the author.

authority
[əθɔ́:riti]
[R] 525/86800

n. **권한, 권위, 당국**
[T] 돈? **좀(au** - 한자로 내가) **쓰랬지(thority)?:** 내가 맘대로 하는 **권한**
[예] Who has the authority to get into the class?

autobiography
[ɔ̀:təbaiɑ́grəfi]
[R] 12332/86800

n. **자서전**
[T] **auto(스스로) + bio(인생) + graphy(쓰기):** 풀어보면 자기 인생 이야기 즉 **자서전**
[예] I read her autobiography last year.

autograph
[ɔ́:təgræ̀f]
[R] 21099/86800

n. v. **서명, 서명하다**
[T] **auto(스스로) + graph(쓰다): 서명**
[유] signature, John Hancock
[예] I got Justin Bieber's autograph in Time Square.

automation
[ɔ̀:təméiʃən]
[R] 13488/86800

n. **자동**
[T] **auto(스스로) + mation(만듦): 자동**
[파] *automatic*: 자동의 *automatically*: 자동으로
[예] Guitars made by automation are usually cheaper than hand - made ones.

autonomy
[ɔ:tɑ́nəmi]
[R] 4615/86800

n. **자치권**
[T] auto(스스로) + nomy(관리하다 - 어원편 참조) 혹은 **어떤 놈이 (autonomy)** 우리 **자치**를 막어?
[유] independence, free will, self - determination
[반] heteronomy
[예] The politician focused on our individual autonomy.

✓ available
[əvéiləbəl]
[R] 319/86800

adj. **이용 가능한**
[T] **avail(5 배 일** - 다섯 배 일의 쓸모가 있다) + able(~할 수 있는): 쓸모가 있는, **이용 가능한**
[파] avail: 쓸모가 있다, 도움이 되다
[예] Are there any available facilities in this fitness center?

avenge
[əvéndʒ]
[R] 29797/86800

v. **원수를 갚다**
[T] 양식 축낸 것 **복수해서 없앤 쥐(avenge)**
[유] revenge
[반] forgive
[예] He avenged his father.

✓ average
[ǽvəridʒ]
[R] 1032/86800

n. **평균**
[T] 맨날 **평균**내서 혼내니 **애버리지(average):** 시험 **평균**으로 혼내면 애를 버린다는 말
[예] His work has been above the average.

avert
[əvə́:rt]
[R] 18583/86800

v. **위험을 피하다**
[T] **어! 벌(이)다(avert):** 벌이 오면 **피하다**
[유] prevent
[예] I averted an accident on my way to school.

aviation
[èiviéiʃən]
[R] 7263/86800

n. **비행, 항공술**
[T] **avi(날다) + tion**(명사형 어미)**: 비행**
[유] flight
[예] He is a best pilot in the field of aviation.

avid
[ǽvid]
[R] 22118/86800

adj. **열성적인**
[T] **업이다(avid)** - 직업이라고 생각하면 **열성적인**
[유] enthusiastic, eager, ardent, dedicated
[반] uneager, unenthusiastic
[예] I am an avid admirer of Hollywood movies.

A

✔ avoid
[əvɔ́id]
ⓡ 1298/86800

v. 피하다
❶ 어렸을 때는 "공부해라"하는 **어버이(avoid) 피하다**
㊌ elude, evade, stay away from
㊎ confront, face
㊍ *avoidable*: 피할 수 있는
㊐ She keeps avoiding me.

✔ await
[əwéit]
ⓡ 11020/86800

v. 기다리다
❶ a는 빼고 **wait만 생각하면 기다리다**
㊌ wait for
㊐ He is still awaiting an answer.

✔ awake
[əwéik]
ⓡ 5580/86800

v. adj. 눈뜨다, 각성시키다, (서술적으로 쓰여) 깨어있는
❶ a는 빼고 **wake를 생각**
㊌ alert, aware ㊍ *awaken*: 깨우다
㊐ I awoke at five in the morning everyday.

✔ award
[əwɔ́:rd]
ⓡ 649/86800

v. n. **수여하다, 상**
❶ 아카데미(Academy) 어워드(award) 생각하면 아카데미 상
㊌ present: 수여하다, reward: 상
㊐ The president awarded a gold medal to winner.

✔ aware
[əwéər]
ⓡ 938/86800

v. 깨닫다, 인식하다
❶ 너 그거 **알아? '어 외워(aware)'** - 응 외운다는 말은 알고 있다는 뜻
㊌ know, realize
㊎ unaware, unconscious
㊍ *awareness*: 인지
㊐ Are you aware that English is important subject?

✔ awe
[ɔ:]
ⓡ 10954/86800

n. v. **경외심, 두려움, 두렵게 하다**
❶ 교회가면 **오(awe)!주님** 하면서 **경외심을 갖음**
㊍ awful: 무서운, 심한 *awfully*: 무섭게
㊐ I have a feeling of awe to God.

✓ awesome
[ɔ́:səm]
[R] 13052/86800

a. 멋진, 두려운
[T] 그녀는 **옷 삼(awesome - 옷 이 참) 멋진**
[예] I want to go out with that awesome dude.

✓ awkward
[ɔ́:kwərd]
[R] 5141/86800

adj. 서툰, 어색한
[T] 발표하는데 **서툴러서 웃고하다(awkward)**
[유] unskillful, unhandy, inexpert [반] adept, adroit
[파] *awkwardly*: 서투르게
[예] I am awkward at English vocabulary.

bachelor
[bǽtʃələr]
[R] 12249/86800

n. 미혼남자, 학사
[T] **결혼 전**에 내 사랑 **바치오러(bachelor):** 결혼 전 남자의 사랑을 생각
[유] unmarried man c.f) spinster
[예] I am a bachelor for years, and then finally married.

✓ backward
[bǽkwərd]
[R] 9447/86800

adv. 뒤쪽의, 역행하는
[T] **back(뒤) + ward(쪽으로): 뒤쪽으로**
[유] back, rearward [반] ahead, forward
[예] Please step backward.

baggage
[bǽgidʒ]
[R] 11838/86800

n. 수화물
[T] **수화물** 보고 너 **백(bag)이지(baggage)**?
[유] luggage
[예] I had to check the baggage in before boarding.

✓ balance
[bǽləns]
[R] 1158/86800

n. v. 균형, 은행 잔액, 균형을 잡다
[T] **밸런스(balance - 균형)**를 잘 맞춰야지, **은행잔액**도 부족하지 않게
[유] equilibrium [반] imbalance, nonequilibrium, unbalance
[예] I lost my balance and fell down the stairs.

✓ ball
[bɔ:l]
[R] 1363/86800

n. 공, 무도회
[T] **볼(ball)**만한 **무도회**
[예] Am I all set for the masked ball?

balloon
[bəlúːn]
🅡 9497/86800

n. 기구, 고무풍선, 부풀다
❶ 에드 **벌룬(balloon)**생각: 광고용으로 제작한 공중에 떠있는 **풍선**
예 I blew up a balloon.

ballot
[bǽlət]
🅡 7003/86800

n. 투표, 투표용지
❶ 투표 안하는 사람 **벌러(ballot)**서 **투표하다**
유 vote
예 They cast their votes in a secret ballot.

ban
[bæn]
🅡 3064/86800

v. 금지하다
❶ **반(ban)대** 하다
유 forbid, prohibit, prevent, bar 반 allow, let, permit
예 University at Buffalo has banned smoking in all school buildings.

bandage
[bǽndidʒ]
🅡 17345/86800

n. 붕대
❶ **분대지(bandage)? - 붕대지?**
예 I applied a bandage on the cut.

banish
[bǽniʃ]
🅡 23668/86800

v. 추방하다
❶ **반(ban)대하는 이씨(ish)**를 추방하다
유 deport, displace, exile
예 The United States banished illegal immigrants from the country.

bankrupt
[bǽnkrʌpt]
🅡 8666/86800

n. v. 파산자, 파산한, 파산시키다
❶ **bank (은행) + rupt(깨다 - 어원편 참조)**: 돈 빌려준 은행을 깸
예 As a lawyer, she specialized in working with bankrupts.

✔ **banner**
[bǽnər]
🅡 10385/86800

n. 깃발
❶ Star Spangled banner(성조기), **플럭(flag)이는 깃발에 배 너(banner)**: 국기가 나오면 애국심에 몸가짐을 바로 가진다, 배 나온 사람보고 배 넣고 국기에 대한 경의를 표하자는 뜻
유 flag, colors, pendant
예 The national flag of America is star spangled banner.

51

✓✓ **bar**
[bɑ:r]
[R] 1293/86800

n. v. 술집, 막대기, 방해하다, 변호사
[T] 바(bar - 술집)에 못 들어가게 **변호사가 막대기로 막다**
[예] There are age limits at bars.

✓ **bare**
[bɛər]
[R] 3772/86800

adj. v. 벌거벗은, 벗기다
[T] 베어(bare - 천천히 읽으면 베어 (벗어) 비슷하게 발음된다.)
[유] naked, nude, undressed
c.f) *barely*: 겨우, 거의~아니다
[예] I covered my bare arms with my long shirt.

✓ **bargain**
[bá:rgən]
[R] 6439/86800

n. 매매, 떨이
[T] 바겐(bargain) 세일(sale - 매매)
[유] deal
[예] When is a bargain day of the department store?

barley
[bá:rli]
[R] 10210/86800

n. 보리
[T] 보리(barley)
[예] Cereals are composed of oats and barley.

✓✓ **barn**
[bɑ:rn]
[R] 5806/86800

n. 헛간
[T] 반(barn)지하 헛간
[예] We a big barn for two horses.

barometer
[bərámitər]
[R] 23106/86800

n. 기압계, 척도
[T] 바로(baro) + 측정하다(meter)
[유] standard: 기준, benchmark: 척도, criterion: 기준
[예] Barometer is used to measure temperature.

✓ **barren**
[bǽrən]
[R] 12488/86800

adj. 불임의
[T] 배란(barren)이 안 되는, **불임의**
[유] infertile, sterile, unproductive
[반] fertile, fruitful
[예] He sowed seed in a barren field.

✔ **barrier**
[bǽriər]
® 5086/86800

n. 장벽
❶ 막대기(bar)가 이어(rier)져 있다고 생각하면 **장벽**
⊛ obstacle, barricade
예 The car race track was surrounded with barriers to protect spectators.

✔ **barter**
[bá:rtər]
® 21862/86800

v. 물물교환하다
❶ **물물교환 받다(barter)**
⊛ exchange, bargain, trade
예 We were bartering at the flea market.

✤ **base**
[beis]
® 1115/86800

n. adj. 바닥, 토대, 비천한
❶ 야구의 **base**(1루, 2루, 3루)**는 바닥, 토대**임을 생각
⊛ basis, foundation ⊕ head, top
퍄 basis: 기초, 근거 basically: 기본적으로 basement: 지하실
예 This case is based on his testimony.

bay
[bei]
® 2839/86800

n. v. **만, 개가 짖다**
❶ 배 나온 사람 생각, 배(bay)가 나온 곳이 있다면 들어간 곳은 **만**
예 San Francisco Bay is located in California U.S.

✤ **beach**
[bi:tʃ]
® 2587/86800

n. 물가, 해안
❶ 속이 비치(beach)는 해안
⊛ coast, seaside, shore
예 I plan to go to Palm beach in summer.

bead
[bi:d]
® 21520/86800

n. 구슬, 염주알
❶ 스님이 염주알 돌리며 빌다(bead)
예 She bought a necklace which is composed of wooden beads.

✔ **beam**
[bi:m]
® 6396/86800

n. v. 대들보, 광선, 빛이 나다
❶ H beam(빔), 레이저 빔 등 흔히 쓰이는 단어를 생각할 것
예 The Moon shed its beams upon the school.

B

bean
[biːn]
® 10861/86800

n. 콩
❶ 발음 비 + ㄴ(bean) - 콩 비지 ㄴ 을 줄인 것
[예] Don't spill the bean.

bear
[bɛər]
® 1772/86800

n. v. 곰, 낳다, 나르다, 자세를 취하다
❶ 애를 베어(bear)낳다, 나무를 베어(bear) 나르다, 공부하는 자세가 베어(bear)있다
[예] I was born and raised in Ohio.

beard
[biərd]
® 7422/86800

n. 턱수염
❶ 오늘 면도하다 **턱 수염을 베었다(beard)**
c.f) moustache: 멋있다 씨 - 콧수염
　　　whisker: 위스킬 - 위에서부터 기른 구레나룻
[예] He grew a beard and mustache.

beast
[biːst]
® 7565/86800

n. 짐승, 동물
❶ 사람과 **비슷한(beast)짐승**
⊕ brute
[예] Did you see beauty and beast?

beat
[biːt]
® 1808/86800

v. 치다, 쳐부수다
❶ 음악의 **beat**, 비트가 강한 음악
⊕ hit, pound, strike
[예] Sometimes, I beat a drum to reduce stress.

beckon
[békən]
® 45317/86800

v. 부르다, 신호하다
❶ 배 큰(beckon): 배가 커서 배부르다고 **신호하다**
⊕ signal
[예] I beckoned a waiter to order foods.

bedridden
[bédrìdn]
® 43634/86800

adj. 누워만 있는
❶ 베드(bed - 침대)에 리던(ridden - 있던) 사람, 누워만 있는
⊕ confined to bed
[예] My grandmother was 89 and bedridden.

B

✔ beforehand
[bifɔ́:rhæ̀nd]
ⓡ 9275/86800

adv. 미리
❶ 손쓰기(hand) + 전(before): 미리
⊕ previously, earlier
예 I'd like to make reservations beforehand.

beggar
[bégər]
ⓡ 17756/86800

n. 거지
❶ 배가(beggar) 고픈 거지
예 We provide meal for hungry beggars.

✔ behalf
[bihǽf]
ⓡ 5817/86800

n. 측, 편
❶ behalf-B(be)가 half(절반)이므로 A편, B편 중 B편이 절반, 어쨌든 편, 측면 belong의 T에서 담고 있다
c.f) in behalf of: 위하여, on behalf of: 대신에
예 The ambassador came on behalf of the President.

✔ behave
[bihéiv]
ⓡ 4763/86800

v. 처신하다
❶ 말로 말고 **행동을 보여봐(behave)**
⊕ conduct 파 *behavior*: 행동 *behavioral*. 행동의
예 I behaved like a child for a long time!

behold
[bihóuld]
ⓡ 19634/86800

v. 보다, 바라보다
❶ 보(be) 호(hol) 다(d): 보다
⊕ gaze upon, view, look at, see
예 People who have beheld the beauty of Mountain Kumkang never forget it.

✔ belong
[bilɔ́:ŋ]
ⓡ 4149/86800

v. 속하다
❶ 어머니는 아기를 **배롱(belong - 배로)**담고 있다, 속하다
파 belongings: 소유물
예 He doesn't belong in our school.

✔ beloved
[bilʌ́vid]
ⓡ 8215/86800

adj. 가장 사랑하는
❶ love를 생각하면 쉽게 생각날 것 임
⊕ cherished, precious ⊛ unbeloved
예 I was beloved by all students when I was in Korea.

below
[bilóu]
[R] 690/86800

adv. ~**아래에**
[T] be를 빼고 **low를** 생각하면 쉽게 기억 가능
[유] beneath, under, underneath [반] up
[파] beneath: ~아래에
[예] Temperature of Buffalo often drops below zero in winter.

bend
[bend]
[R] 5763/86800

v. **구부리다**
[T] 좋은 **변**(벼는)**다(bend)** 고개를 **구부린다**
[예] He bent the knee.

beneficial
[bènəfíʃəl]
[R] 5627/86800

adj. **유익한**
[T] **bene, bon(좋은 - 어원편 참조) + fic(만드는 - 어원편 참조):** 좋은 것을 만드는 - 유익한
[유] profitable
[반] harmful
[파] *benefit*: 이익, ~에게 이롭다 benevolence: 자비
[예] Regular exercise is beneficial to all students.

besides
[bisáidz]
[R] 3527/86800

prep. ~**외에**
[T] A사이즈 **외에 B 사이즈**
[유] In addition to~: ~이외에
[예] There are other ways to go to UB North campus besides cars.

bestow
[bistóu]
[R] 27957/86800

v. **주다, 수여하다**
[T] 이게 **비수다(bestow)**하면서 칼을 **주다**
[유] grant, award, give
[예] The gold medal was bestowed upon the winner.

bet
[bet]
[R] 3339/86800

n. v. **내기, 내기를 걸다**
[T] 노름에서 **베팅(betting)** 생각
[유] gamble, stake
[예] A: Are you sure? B: I'll bet.

B

betray
[bitréi]
ⓡ 14215/86800

v. 배반하다, 누설하다
🅣 비틀어 이(betray)야기 해서 **누설하다**
🅔 You betrayed me by revealing my secrets to other students.

✔ **beverage**
[bévəridʒ]
ⓡ 27831/86800

n. 음료수
🅣 배부르지(beverage)? 밥 먹은 후 **음료수** 마시면서 하는 말
🅢 drink
🅔 The price of the value meal includes a beverage and nugget.

beware
[biwéər]
ⓡ 10470/86800

v. 조심하다, 경계하다
🅣 비와여(beware)! 조심하세요
🅢 cautious
🅔 Beware that you should not make mistakes in college entrance exam.

bewilder
[biwíldər]
ⓡ 75423/86800

v. 당황하게 하다
🅣 비가 와일드(bewilder)하게 와서 **당황하게하다**
🅢 puzzle, confuse, perplex
🅔 My parent's sudden attitudes bewilder me.

✦ **beyond**
[bijánd]
ⓡ 837/86800

prep. ~의 저쪽에, ~을 지나서
🅣 비온뒤(beyond) 즉 비가오고 **(시간이) 지나서**
🅔 The high school is just beyond those supermarkets.

✦ **bias**
[báiəs]
ⓡ 5549/86800

n. adj. 편견
🅣 나를 둘(bi)로 보았어(bias) - **편견**을 가지고
🅢 one - sidedness, partiality, prejudice
🅑 impartiality, neutrality, objectivity
🅔 Our English teacher has a bias against poor students.

bid
[bid]
ⓡ 2566/86800

v. 명령하다, 인사하다
❶ 빌어(bid)!하고 **명령하다**
㉮ order
㉑ The captain bid retreat for rearrangement.

✔ bilingual
[bailíŋgwəl]
ⓡ 14551/86800

a. n. 두 나라 말을 하는, 2개 국어 하는 사람
❶ bi(둘) + lingua(말): **두 개의 말을 하는**
㉑ We want a fluent bilingual speaker.

✔ bill
[bil]
ⓡ 711/86800

n. 계산서, 지폐, 법안, 부리, 계산하다
❶ 계산하려면 **계산서 달라고 빌(bill)어야**
㉑ I sent him a bill for the work I had done.

✔ bind
[baind]
ⓡ 8690/86800

v. 묶다
❶ 바인드(bind)노트 아세요? 여러 장을 **묶어 놓은** 노트 말입니다
㉮ tie ㉯ untie
㉑ The police bound the suspect with a rope.

✔ biography
[baiágrəfi]
ⓡ 8109/86800

n. 전기
❶ bio(인생, 삶) + graphy(씀): 인생에 대해 쓴 것이므로 **전기**
㉮ memoir
㉑ I read a new biography of Admiral Lee, soon seen.

✔ bitter
[bítər]
ⓡ 3629/86800

adj. ad. 쓴, 쓰게
❶ 비루(bitter - 맥주의 비루라고 생각)**는** 맛이 **쓴**
㉮ acrid ㉯ sweet
㉑ Beer has a bitter taste.

bizarre
[bizá:r]
ⓡ 6827/86800

adj. 이상한
❶ **이상한 곳**(범죄 많은 나라)에서 미국가면 **비잘(bizarre - 비자)**받아야
㉮ exotic, odd, strange ㉯ realistic, reasonable
㉑ She wore a bizarre outfit.

B

❤ blame
[bleim]
ⓡ 3061/86800

v. 비난하다
❶ 불이 임(blame)할 것이다(벌을 받을 것이다)고 **비난하다**
ⓢ criticize, censure, condemn
ⓐ extol, praise
예 I don't blame you. Everybody can make mistakes.

❤ blank
[blæŋk]
ⓡ 4596/86800

a. n. 공백의, 공백
❶ blank space(흰 공간) - 공백, blank - 흰(어원)
예 Fill in the blank.

❤ blanket
[blǽŋkit]
ⓡ 6517/86800

n. 담요, 덮는 것
❶ 추우면 **불나게(blanket)** 팔리는 **담요**
ⓢ cloak, cover, covering,
예 You may need another blanket tonight on account of weather forecast.

blast
[blæst]
ⓡ 6381/86800

n. v. 강풍, 폭파하다
❶ 강풍이 불었었다(blast)
ⓢ wind
예 The bomb blast killed dozens of people in Middle East.

bleak
[bli:k]
ⓡ 7757/86800

adj. 쓸쓸한, 황량한
❶ 애인을 버리고(bleak) 오는 분위기(이별하느라)는 **쓸쓸한**
ⓢ desolate, gloomy, cheerless
ⓐ bright, cheerful, cheering
예 Bleak wintry days will ends soon.

❤ bleed
[bli:d]
ⓡ 18900/86800

v. 피를 흘리다, 마음아파하다
❶ 피를 뿌리다(bleed)
ⓢ shed ⑭ *blood*: 피
예 My nose bled because of overwork.

✓ **blend**
[blend]
[R] 7693/86800

v. **혼합하다**
[T] 술 브랜디(blend와 발음 비슷한 brandy)를 생각할 것, 브랜디가 소다수를 혼합한 것이므로 혼합하다
[유] combine, mix, compound
[반] break down, break up, separate, unmix
[예] This food blended traditional and modern tastes.

✓ **bless**
[bles]
[R] 10341/86800

v. **축복하다**
[T] **God bless you, 갓 블레 슈.** 미국인들이 축복하면서 많이 하는 말을 생각해보세요. 재채기해도 God bless you라고 합니다
[유] give a benediction [반] curse
[예] God has blessed Korea for a long time.

blink
[bliŋk]
[R] 18175/86800

v. **눈을 깜빡거리다**
[T] **불 윙크(blink)** 하면서 **눈을 깜빡이다**
[유] wink
[예] I blinked my eyes when the light flashed.

✓ **bliss**
[blis]
[R] 13185/86800

n. **더 없는 행복**
[T] 욕심을 **버려서(bliss)더 없는 행복**을 느낌
[예] Bliss is supreme happiness.

✓✓ **block**
[blɑk]
[R] 2301/86800

n. v. **덩어리, 한 구획, 억제하다**
[T] 길 물을 때 몇 **블록(block - 구획)** 떨어져 있다고 종종 듣지요
[예] Go down two more blocks.

✓✓ **bloom**
[blu:m]
[R] 10467/86800

n. v. **개화, 꽃이 피다**
[T] **꽃이 피어서** 보라고 **부름(bloom)**
[유] blossom, flower [파] ***blossom***: 꽃, 꽃이 피다
[예] Many flowers were just beginning to bloom.

✓✓ **blow**
[blou]
[R] 2945/86800

v. n. **불다, 휘날리다, 타격**
[T] 바람이 **불어와(blow)** 태극기가 **휘날리다**. 권투나, 격투기 중계에서 레프트 블로우(blow - 타격)를 날리다
[예] The wind is blowing harder outside.

B

✔ **blunder**
[blʌ́ndər]
[R] 19448/86800

n. 큰 실수
[T] 불난다(blunder)면 큰 실수하는 것
[유] mistake, error
[예] Your first blunder is to ignore my opinion.

blurred
[blə:rd]
[R] 10885/86800

adj. 희미한, 흐릿한
[T] 바람이 불었다(blurred) 그래서 먼지에 시야가 희미한
[유] dim, indistinct
[예] The tears in my eyes blurred the words on the page.

blush
[blʌʃ]
[R] 15249/86800

v. 얼굴을 붉히다, 부끄러워하다
[T] 얼굴이 부(끄)러셔(blush) 붉어진
[유] flush
[예] I always blush when I meet female students.

boast
[boust]
[R] 11913/86800

v. 뽐내다
[T] 져스틴 비버를 보았었다(boast)고 뽐내다
[유] speak proudly
[예] She boasts about her son's admission to Harvard University.

bold
[bould]
[R] 5929/86800

adj. 대담한
[T] 간이 부었다(bold): 대담한
[유] brave, daring, audacious
[예] Sam was a bold and fearless explorer.

✔ **bomb**
[bɑm]
[R] 3155/86800

n. v. 폭탄, 폭격하다
[T] 폭격기가 부암(bomb)소리내면서 폭격하다
[예] Arabic terrorists planted a bomb near the subway station.

✔ **bond**
[bɑnd]
[R] 3259/86800

n. 올가미, 유대 관계, 채권
[T] 본드(bond)는 접착 따라서 붙들어매고 속박함
[파] bondage: 속박
[예] Non - visa travel program helped to strengthen the bonds between U.S and Korea.

book
[buk]
ⓡ 357/86800

n. v. 책, 예약하다
➊ **부킹(booking)은** 사람을 만나려고 예약하는 것
㊉ reserve: 예약하다
㉿ booklet: 소책자
㉦ I booked two seats at the UB basket ball game.

boost
[bu:st]
ⓡ 4210/86800

v. 끌어올리다, 인상하다
➊ 여배우가 **벗었다(boost)고** 출연료 **인상하다**
㊉ increase, raise, elevate
㉦ Private Univ. managed to boost their students by cutting tuitions.

booth
[bu:ɵ]
ⓡ 9937/86800

n. 오두막, 작은방
➊ 전화 **부스(booth)는** 작은 방
㉦ I'm looking for a telephone booth near here.

border
[bɔ́:rdə:r]
ⓡ 2494/86800

n. v. 가장자리, 경계, 접경하다
➊ **국경을** 잘 지켜 **보다(border)**
㊉ edge, bound, boundary, brim, margin, rim
㉦ Sheldon grew up in Malaysia, near the Indonesian border.

bore
[bɔ:r]
ⓡ 5235/86800

v. 구멍을 파다, bear의 과거, 지루하게 하다
➊ **구멍 판** 부분에 물 **부으래(bore)**
㉦ The landlord didn't return security deposit because I had bored a hole in the wall.

bosom
[búzəm]
ⓡ 16712/86800

n. 가슴
➊ 신체의 일부 중 가슴 부분은 **부었슴(bosom)**
㊉ breast
㉦ Practice makes perfect, which we should keep in our bosom.

B

bother
[báðə:r]
® 3730/86800

v. 괴롭히다, 귀찮게 굴다
❶ 이것 좀 **봐줘(bother)!**하며 **귀찮게 굴다**
㉮ disturb, intrude ㉯ calm, soothe, tranquilize
㈜ bothersome: 성가신
㈀ Sorry for bothering you.

bottom
[bátəm]
® 1366/86800

n. 바닥
❶ **바담(bottom)은 바닥**과 발음이 비슷
㉮ base ㉯ top
㈀ I respects Abraham Lincoln from the bottom of my heart.

bough
[bau]
® 27275/86800

n. 큰 가지
❶ 한국 산수화를 보면 **바우(bou)위에 나무 큰 가(gh)지**가 늘어져 있다는 사실을 생각해 볼 것
㉮ branch, limb c.f) *branch*, twig: 가지
㈀ A lot of tree boughs fell on the street during the snowstorm.

bound
[baund]
® 2037/86800

v. adj. 튀다, 경계를 짓다, ~로 향하는
❶ 공이 **바운드(bound)하다**
㉮ spring: 튀다, border, edge: 경계 짓다
㈜ boundless: 한없는 *bounce*: 공이 튀다
㈀ Buffalo is bounded on the north by Ontario Canada.

bow
[bou][bau]
® 5422/86800

n. v. 활, 머리를 숙이다
❶ 당신을 우러러 **봐유(bow)**하며 **머리 숙이다**
㈀ I bowed my head to the crowd.

bowl
[boul]
® 3716/86800

n. 사발
❶ punch bowl(강원도 양구의 6.25격전지) Super bowl의 bowl도 사발
㈀ He and I ate the same bowl.

brace
[breis]
🄬 14441/86800

n. v. 버팀대, 지지하다
❶ 버팀대를 부러서(brace) 지지가 약해지다
🄯 support
🄴 I braced my family with small income.

branch
[bræntʃ]
🄬 1858/86800

n. 가지, 부문
❶ branch(부랜치 - 부러진 가지로 이해)
🄯 bough
🄴 Where can I find a branch office of A?

brand
[brænd]
🄬 5189/86800

n. v. 상표, 상표를 붙이다
❶ 어떤 브랜드(brand - 상표)를 원하나?
🄯 trademark
🄴 What brand is this shoes you are wearing?

breach
[bri:tʃ]
🄬 3023/86800

n. 깨트림, 위반, 침해
❶ 담배피지 말라는데 여기 불있지(breach)?: 담배피지 말라는데 피워서 불있지? 위반
🄯 violation
🄴 Shooting in D.M.Z is obviously a breach of the piece treaty.

breadfruit
[brédfrù:t]
🄬 86061/86800

n. 빵나무의 열매
❶ Bread(빵) + fruit(열매)
🄴 Breadfruit is a large round tropical fruit.

break
[breik]
🄬 1090/86800

n. v. 파괴, 틈, 휴식시간, 깨트리다
❶ '깨트리다'라는 뜻은 아실테고 깨트리면 틈이 생기고 Winter Break(겨울방학)라는 말로보아 휴식시간이라는 뜻도 있다는 것 기억할 것
🄴 I broke two cups by mistake yesterday.

breakdown
[bréikdàun]
🄬 5396/86800

n. 고장
❶ 컴이 브레이크(break)가 걸려 다운(down) 됨
🄯 malfunction
🄴 The factory has had frequent equipment breakdowns.

B

breakthrough
[bréikərù:]
® 8975/86800

n. 돌파구, 큰 발전
❶ 안 좋은 것을 (break)깨트려 + (through - 여기저기): **큰 발전**
⊕ advancement, enhancement, improvement
⊛ setback
예 To study English education at U.B was a major breakthrough in my life.

breast
[brest]
® 4912/86800

n. 가슴
❶ 신체 일부 중 **가슴이 불었었다(breast)**
예 Breast of chicken is secret ingredient of this food.

breath
[breθ]
® 1972/86800

n. 숨, 호흡
❶ 불어서(breath) 호흡 하게 해준 응급환자
⊕ animation 파 breathless: 숨 가쁜 *breathe*: 호흡하다
예 She climbed the mountain out of breath.

breathtaking
[bréθtèikiŋ]
® 14378/86800

adj. 깜짝 놀랄만한
❶ breath(숨을) + taking(가질 만 한): 숨은 생명이므로 **깜짝 놀랄만한**
⊕ remarkable, astonishing, ⊛ unexciting
예 The view of the Niagara Falls was breathtaking.

breed
[bri:d]
® 4428/86800

v. 새끼를 낳다, 기르다
❶ 새끼를 낳으려고 배가 **부르다(breed)**
⊕ hatch, raise, reproduce
예 He is breeding cattle after he retired the company.

breeze
[bri:z]
® 5672/86800

n. 미풍
❶ 미풍(부드러운 바람)이 **불었지(breeze)**
⊕ wind
예 The gentle breeze reminds us of spring.

brevity
[brévəti]
® 25170/86800

n. 간결성
❶ 브라벗디(brevity)? 집에서는 **간단히** 편하게
⊕ briefness, conciseness ⊛ length
예 I modified my speech for brevity.

bribe
[braib]
[R] 17617/86800

n. v. **뇌물, 매수하다**
[T] **뇌물** 받았다고 **불어 입(bribe)**으로
[유] backhander(구어에서 뇌물이라는 뜻)
[예] We don't bribe police cops to avoid a traffic violation ticket.

✔✔ **brick**
[brik]
[R] 4550/86800

n. **벽돌**
[T] **불이(brick)** 좋아야 잘 굽히는 **벽돌**
[예] There few house which is made up of bricks in western New York.

✔ **bride**
[braid]
[R] 6577/86800

n. **신부**
[T] **bri**ght(밝은) 한 **d**ress(드레스)입은 신부
[반] bridegroom
[예] I returned from Buffalo with my lovely new bride.

bridle
[bráidl]
[R] 17320/86800

n. v. **굴레, 고삐, 굴레를 씌우다, 속박하다**
[T] **속박하는** 하인들 그만 **부려들(briddle)**
[유] halter
[예] The horseman drew bridle to rest the horse.

✔✔ **brief**
[bri:f]
[R] 1902/86800

adj. **간결한**
[T] **브리(brief)핑은 간결하게**
[유] concise, succinct, short [반] complex, complicated
[예] His brief mention surprised all students.

✔✔ **bright**
[brait]
[R] 1844/86800

adj. **빛나는**
[T] **불 나잇(bright - 불이 나는) - 빛나는**
[유] radiant, brilliant, shining
[반] dim, dull, unbright, unbrilliant
[파] ***brighten***: 빛내다 ***brightness***: 빛남, 밝음
[예] February 20, 2011 was a bright, sunny and warm day.

✓ **brilliant**
[bríljənt]
[R] 2814/86800

adj. **빛나는**
[T] **불 일리언(brilliant):** 불이 일어나 빛나는
[유] radiant, shinning [반] unbright, unbrilliant
[파] ***brilliantly***: 번쩍번쩍
[예] Robert gave her a brilliant diamond.

brim
[brim]
[R] 20539/86800

n. **모자의 테, 가장자리**
[T] 샌드위치 만들 때 식빵 **가장자리**는 **버림(brim)**
[유] edge
[예] I often wore a wide - brimmed New York Yankees hat.

brisk
[brisk]
[R] 11127/86800

adj. **활발한**
[T] **불이서(bris - 불이 섰 구(k):** 불이 섰다는 말은 **활발한** 상태
[유] lively, energetic, active [반] inactive, inanimate
[예] Brisk voices can be heard in our school playground.

brittle
[brítl]
[R] 11907/86800

adj. **깨지지 쉬운**
[T] 조심해서 **부려틀(brittle).** 틀이 **깨지기 쉬우니까**
[유] weak, fragile, frail, breakable
[예] As she get older my mother's bones become increasingly brittle.

✓ **broad**
[brɔ:d]
[R] 1963/86800

adj. **넓은**
[T] 체중이 **불었다(broad)**는 말은 체형이 넓다
[유] wide [반] narrow
[파] breadth: 넓이 broaden: 넓히다
[예] When I was young, my wish was to live in a broad house.

✓ **broadcast**
[brɔ́:dkæ̀st]
[R] 5331/86800

v. **방송하다**
[T] **불렀다(broad) 게스트(cast).** 좋은 방송하려고
[유] air [파] ***broadcasting***: 방송(의)
[예] World cup soccer games were broadcast from Seoul.

brochure
[brouʃúər]
Ⓟ 7393/86800

n. 안내책자
❶ **안내 책자** 만들어 관광객 **부르쇼(brochure)**
Ⓢ leaflet, pamphlet, booklet
예 The government of New York state made a tourist guide brochure.

broil
[brɔil]
Ⓡ 순위외/86800

v. 고기를 굽다
❶ **불로 일(broil)**해야 하는 **고기 굽기**
Ⓢ grill
예 The restaurant cook broiled a steak for a customer.

bronze
[brɑnz]
Ⓡ 5282/86800

n. 청동
❶ 올림픽에서 **브론즈(bronze)** 메달은 동메달
예 She won a bronze in skiing.

brood
[bruːd]
Ⓡ 16714/86800

n. v. 한배에서 난 새끼, 한 떼, 알을 품다
❶ **한배의 새끼** 때문에 배 **부르다(brood)** - 배속에 새끼가 들어 있으면 배가 부를 수밖에
Ⓢ litter
예 The blackbird flew back and forth to its brood.

brook
[bruk]
Ⓡ 9283/86800

n. v. 작은 냇가, 참다
❶ 물이 **불룩(brook)**하면 그때부터 물이 아니라 냇가
Ⓢ stream, creek
예 That brook. has tiny fish.

broom
[bru(ː)m]
Ⓡ 14652/86800

n. 빗자루
❶ 바람 **불음(broom)** ! 낙엽 때문에 **빗자루** 필요
c.f) broomstick: 빗자루
예 I swept the backyard with the broom.

✓ brow
[brau]
Ⓡ 8329/86800

n. 눈썹, 이마
❶ 시원한 **눈썹**과 이마 **보라우(brow)**
예 He wore his hat low over his brow.

B

✔ **browse**
[brauz]
® 19482/86800

v. n. 여기저기 구경하다, (풀, 잎)을 뜯어먹다, 어린 잎
❶ 브라우스(browse)를 사려고 여기저기 구경하다
㊤ look through: 대충 훑어보다
㈜ I'm just browsing.

bruise
[bru:z]
® 18921/86800

n. 타박상, 멍
❶ 팔이 **부러져(bruise)** 멍들고 **타박상**
㈜ I had a bad bruise on my arm after I fell.

✔ **bubble**
[bʌ́bəl]
® 10627/86800

n. 거품
❶ 밥을(bubble)하면 밥이 끓느라 **거품**이 인다
㈜ When the water boils, add Ramen.

✔ **bud**
[bʌd]
® 12371/86800

n. v. 싹, 봉오리, 싹이 트다
❶ 봄에는 새싹이 내 벗(bud)
㈜ budding: 싹트는
㈜ The bush has many buds but no flowers yet.

Buddhism
[búːdizəm]
® 19570/86800

n. 불교
❶ Buddha(부처) + ism(주의, 학설, 종교)
㈜ Many people believe in Buddhism in Asia.

✔ **budget**
[bʌ́dʒit]
® 1240/86800

n. 예산
❶ **예산**이 **빠듯(budget)**함
㈜ What's the average monthly budget for a family of three?

✔ **buildup**
[bíldʌp]
® 47281/86800

n. 증대
❶ build(쌓아서) + up(위로)올리면 증대
㊤ increase, expand
㈜ The build - up troops makes war seem more likely.

bulk
[bʌlk]
® 4038/86800

n. 크기, 대부분
❶ 발 크(bulk) 기: 발의 크기
Ⓢ majority 파 bulky: 큰
예 The great bulk of American people are very kind.

✔ bull
[bul]
® 4609/86800

n. 황소
❶ 뿔(bull) - 시카고 불스, 혹은 뿔(bull)난 황소
예 Chicago bulls was largely dependent on Michael Jordan.

bulletproof
[búlitprù:f]
® 79811/86800

adj. 방탄의
❶ bullet(불이 - 총이) 나오는 것을 proof(막는)
c.f) waterproof: 방수의
예 All president's car has bulletproof windows.

✔ bump
[bʌmp]
® 12097/86800

n. v. 충돌, 충돌하다, 마주치다
❶ 뻥(bump)하고 충돌하다
파 bumpy: (길 따위가) 울퉁불퉁한
예 I bumped into my ex-girl friend on my way to home.

bumper
[bʌ́mpəər]
® 15540/86800

n. 자동차 완충기
❶ 자동차 밤바(bumper)가 완충기 역할을 하는
예 The bumper of my car was slightly dented.

✔ bunch
[bʌntʃ]
® 6082/86800

n. v. 떼, 다발, 다발로 묶다
❶ 생일에 꽃다발 받지(bunch)?
Ⓢ bundle
예 He bought a bunch of flowers on her birthday.

bundle
[bʌ́ndl]
® 8605/86800

n. 묶음
❶ 요즘 돈을 다발로 번다(bundle)?
Ⓢ bunch
예 She purchased a bundle of banana to make salad.

70

✓ **burden**
[bə́:rdn]
[R] 3455/86800

n. 짐
[T] 내가 **벗은(burden) 짐**
[유] load
[예] Put down your heavy burden.

✓ **burr**
[bə:r]
[R] 24872/86800

n. 기계의 윙윙거리는 소리, r의 진동 음
[T] burr하고 발음해보면 r이 진동한다. 벌의 윙윙 거리는 소리
[예] She burrs her r's.

burrow
[bə́:rou]
[R] 14589/86800

n. 굴, 피난처, 우리
[T] **벌 로(burrow)** 꽉찬 **굴**
[유] den
c.f) shelter: 쉴 터, 피난처
[예] Foxes live in burrow during winter.

✓ **burst**
[bə:rst]
[R] 3535/86800

v. 폭발하다, 갑자기~하다
[T] **발사다(burst)!** 하자 폭탄이 **폭발하다**
[유] explode, blow
[예] The snowstorm caused the pipes to burst.

✓ **bury**
[béri]
[R] 7598/86800

v. 매장하다
[T] 사람 **발이(bury)** 흙을 다져 **매장하다**
[유] entomb, inhume [반] exhume
[예] The war hero was buried in the National cemetery.

✓ **bush**
[buʃ]
[R] 2629/86800

n. 관목, 수풀
[T] **수풀** 속에서 토끼가 **부쉬(bush)**럭 거림
[예] Don't beat around the bush.

bustle
[bʌ́sl]
[R] 17237/86800

v. 떠들어대다, 북적거리다
[T] **버슬(bustle - 버스를)**타려고 사람이 **북적거리다**
[유] buzz [파] bustling: 부산한, 떠들썩한
[예] He bustled about his marriage.

✔ **butterfly**
[bʌ́tərflài]
[R] 9583/86800

n. 나비
[T] **나비야**! 번데기 **벗어(butter)**서 **플라이(fly)**해
[예] Butterfly is a kind of insects.
(나비는 일종의 곤충이다.)

buzz
[bʌz]
[R] 9666/86800

v. 벌이나 기계가 윙윙거리다, 소란 떨다
[T] **버즈(buzz-버스)**가 나타나자 먼저타려고 소란 떨다
[예] Bees were buzzing around the flowers.

by-product
[bai-prάdəkt]
[R] 60450/86800

n. 부산물
[T] **by**(옆에 나온) + **produce**(생산물): **부산물**
[예] Online clime is by - product of computer revolution.

✔ **cabin**
[kǽbin]
[R] 6591/86800

n. 오두막, 선실
[T] 엉클 톰스 **캐빈(cabin):** 탐 아저씨 **오두막**
[유] cottage
[예] I was born in a cabin built of logs.

✔ **cafeteria(cafe)**
[kæ̀fitíəriə]
[R] 24783/86800

n. 식당
[T] **카페튀어리어(카페가 튀어야) 좋은 식당**
[예] We're supposed to meet in the fancy cafeteria.

cage
[keidʒ]
[R] 6961/86800

n. 새장, 우리
[T] 새가 하는 말 - **새장**에서 나**가야지(cage)!**
[예] Korean students are confined in school like cages.

calamity
[kəlǽməti]
[R] 27682/86800

n. 재난, 불행
[T] **칼에 미쳐(calamity)** - 칼 쓰면 **불행**
[유] catastrophe, mischance, mishap, disaster
[예] Yi, Yi predicted calamity of Josun beforehand.

calculate
[kǽlkjəlèit]
[R] 6902/86800

v. 계산하다
[T] 숫자를 **갈켜레이(calculate) - 계산하게**
[유] reckon, compute
[예] She needs to calculate how long it will take her to drive to long island.

calf
[kæf]
[R] 9581/86800

n. 송아지, 장딴지
[T] **C**(ow - 카우)의 어린피(**a - 어l - 린f - 피**)는: 카우의 어린피 **송아지**
[예] What is the age of calf?

calm
[kɑ:m]
[R] 3205/86800

a. 조용한, 잔잔한, 진정시키다
[T] **깜(calm)**깜해지면 시끄럽게 하다가도 **조용한**
[예] He is as calm as a bishop.

canal
[kənǽl]
[R] 4050/86800

n. 운하
[T] **물로 가네(canal)?** 물로 가는 물 길 - 운하
[예] Some people want to stop the president's canal construction policy.

cancel
[kǽnsəl]
[R] 7665/86800

v. 취소하다
[T] 캔 **술(cancel)** 을 너무 마셔 수업 취소하다
[유] call off, discontinue [반] continue, keep
[파] *cancellation*: 취소
[예] The instructor canceled phonetics class.

cancer
[kǽnsər]
[R] 2397/86800

n. 암
[T] **간 - can(에) 술(cer)**가면 **암**
[예] Eating garlics may help reduce the risk of cancer.

candidate
[kǽndidèit]
[R] 2530/86800

n. 후보자
[T] **cand(흰) + ate(사람, 형용사, 동사 어미): 흰 옷**후보들이 흰옷을 입은데 서 유래, 혹은, **간디(candi)**는 위인후보자 **되었데(date)**
[유] applicant, applier [반] noncandidate
[예] Five candidates applied for congressman.

candle
[kǽndl]
Ⓡ 8219/86800

n. 초
❶ **초를 켠들(candle)** 방이 밝아지지 않는다
예 Can I light a candle?(초를 켜도 될까요?)

cane
[kein]
Ⓡ 11720/86800

n. 지팡이
❶ **지팡이**로 맞고 **깨인(cane)**버릇없는 학생
㊌ walking stick
예 The old man rapped the gate with his cane.

capability
[kèipəbíləti]
Ⓡ 7530/86800

n. 능력
❶ 내 **능력**으로 빚을 **갚아부렀지(capability)**
㊌ ability ㊗ disability
㋻ *capable*: 유능한
c.f) *capacity*: 수용능력, 용량
예 His capability was unquestionable.

cape
[keip]
Ⓡ 7108/86800

n. 갑, 곶, 봉
❶ **갑(cape):** 읽어보면 한국말처럼 **갑**
예 I went to the very tip of the cape. in order to catch best fish.
The Cape of Good Hope(희망 봉)

capital
[kǽpitl]
Ⓡ 718/86800

n. adj. **수도, 자본, 대문자, 주요한**
❶ 빌려간 내 **자본 갚아들(capital)**, cap(머리)
㋻ capitalism: 자본주의 capitalize: 자본화하다, 대문자로 쓰다
예 The capital of Korea is Seoul.

Capitol
[kǽpitl]
Ⓡ 26346/86800

n. 국회의사당
❶ **cap(머리)** + **i(가)** + **tol**(똘똘이 돌아가야 할) **국회의사당**, 각 지역의 머리들(대표들)이 토론하러 올 **국회의사당**
㊌ statehouse: 주 의사당
예 The capitol of Korea is located at YoYido.

capricious
[kəpríʃəs]
® 27028/86800

adj. 변덕스러운
❶ 왔다 **변덕스럽게 갔버리셨어(capricious)**
ⓢ unpredictable
예 He's such a capricious boss I never know how he'll react.

C

✔ captain
[kǽptin]
® 1887/86800

n. 대장, 선장
❶ cap(우두머리) + 탄(tain): 선장, 대장이 탄
ⓢ commander
예 The airplane captain has turned on the "fasten seat belt" sign.

caption
[kǽpʃən]
® 16096/86800

n. 페이지 기사의 표제, 제목
❶ 제목을 보게 **페이지 깝쇼(caption)**
ⓢ title, subtitle
예 The caption on the picture says "This year's contest winners."

captivate
[kǽptəvèit]
® 66649/8680

v. 마음을 사로잡다
❶ Capti(깨쳐) + vate(빼앗다): 다른 사람을 깨쳐 마음을 사로잡다
ⓢ fascinate charm, attract ꤨ captivity: 감금, 사로잡힘
예 Her speech captivated me.

capture
[kǽptʃər]
® 5615/86800

n. v. 포획, 포획하다
❶ Cap(머리) + ture(쥐): 머리 쥐 잡게(포획)
ⓢ catch, grab ꤨ release
예 The police captured the suspect of murder.

carcass
[ká:rkəs]
® 24549/86800

n. 시체
❶ 칼(cal) 갔어(cass): 죽은 시체
ⓢ cadaver, corpse
예 The carcass of the dead horse was found along the dirt road.

care
[kɛər]
®️ 355/86800

n. v. 걱정, 돌봄, 주의, 조심하다
❶ 아기가 깨어(care) 돌봄, 혹은 아기가 자꾸 깨어(care)**걱정**
⊕ carefulness, anxiety
파 *careless*: 부주의한 *carelessly*: 부주의하게
carelessness: 부주의 *careful*: 조심하는
carefully: 주의깊게
예 Take care!!!

career
[kəríər]
®️ 1327/86800

n. 직업, 경력, 생애
❶ 요즘 애들은 직업을 가리어(career) - 또 빛나는 캐리어(career - 경력)라는 말 하죠? 이건 경력이라는 뜻
⊕ vocation, calling, work, livelihood
예 He sought a career as a lawyer.

cargo
[káːrgou]
®️ 7780/86800

n. 짐, 화물
❶ 짐들은 화물칸으로 가고(cargo)
⊕ load, freight
예 The ship was carrying a cargo of crude oil.

carpenter
[káːrpəntər]
®️ 11679/86800

n. 목수
❶ carpen(갈 판 - 판을 연장으로 갊) + ter(사람): 판을 연장으로 가는 목수
예 Carpenter can make good looking tables and chairs.

carriage
[kǽridʒ]
®️ 4339/86800

n. 마차, 운반
❶ 옛날에는 마차가 카(car - 차) 지(riage)? 옛날에는 마차가 차 지
⊕ wagon
예 Her carriage went out of control on the road.

carrot
[kǽrət]
®️ 13372/86800

n. 홍당무
❶ 어디가? 당근 캐러(carrot)가
예 The chef chopped some carrots for Mexican foods.

C

✔ carry
[kǽri]
Ⓡ 1009/86800

v. **나르다**
❶ 짐을 나르는 배우(Jim carry): 짐 캐리가 짐을 나른다구?
⊕ convey, transport, transmit
c.f) carry on=continue: 계속하다 *carrier*: 나르는 사람(것)
[예] This car cannot carry more than five people.

✔ cart
[kɑːrt]
Ⓡ 7123/86800

n. **손수레**
❶ 마트에 가면 입구에서 **카트(cart - 손수레)**를 끌고 감
[예] In order to borrow a shopping cart, we have to pay 25 cents.

✔ carve
[kɑːrv]
Ⓡ 17450/86800

v. **새기다, 조각하다**
❶ 조각을 **칼로베(carve)** 서 **새기다**
⊕ sculpt, sculpture
[예] He carved her name on her tombstone.

✔ case
[keis]
Ⓡ 195/86800

n. **경우, 시례, 사건, 사실, 산자, 문법의 격**
❶ 이거 case(상자)에 담아주세요. **This is not the case**(이것은 사실이 아니다)
[예] The police studied the case of the missing child.

✔ cash
[kæʃ]
Ⓡ 1204/86800

n. **현금**
❶ 수표 **깨셔(cash)!: 현금**으로 바꾸라는 말
[예] Our supermarket accepts only cash.

✔ cashier
[kæʃîər]
Ⓡ 23155/86800

n. **현금 출납원**
❶ 큰 돈 **깨 셔(cashier)** - 출납원이 하는 말
[예] The job of cashier is job is to receive money in a shop, bank, restaurant, etc.

✔ cast
[kæst]
Ⓡ 2360/86800

v. n. **던지다, 계산하다, 주조하다, 주조**
❶ 수류탄 **까서던(cast)지다**. 어원적으로 cast는 던지다 임
⊕ throw
[예] He cast a fishing net to catch salmon.

castle
[kǽsl]
[R] 1853/86800

n. 성
[T] 아파트 광고에 롯데 **캐슬(castle)은** 집이 **성** 같이 좋다는 말)
[유] palace
[예] Lotte castle is not a real castle.

casual
[kǽʒuəl]
[R] 4680/86800

adj. 우연한, 일시적인
[T] **일시적인** 잠에서 **깨주얼(casual)!!!!**
[유] unexpected [반] planned
[예] I prefer casual wear to formal suit.

catastrophe
[kətǽstrəfi]
[R] 12832/86800

n. 큰 재난
[T] **끝에서 도로 피(catastrophe):** 다시 끝에서 피가? 결국 **큰 재난**
[유] tragedy, disaster [반] triumph
[예] The oil spill in west sea was an environmental catastrophe.

✔ **categorize**
[kǽtigəràiz]
[R] 36134/86800

v. 분류하다
[T] category(범위) + ize(~화 하다): 반으로 나누다
[유] classify [파] *category*: 범주, 부류
[예] The books are categorized into beginner and advanced.

✔ **caterpillar**
[kǽtərpìlər]
[R] 21510/86800

n. 애벌레, 무한궤도
[T] **애벌레** 징그럽다 **갖다버려라(caterpillar)**
[예] Caterpillar is a small, long animal with many legs, which feeds on the leaves of plants.

cathedral
[kəθí:drəl]
[R] 3703/86800

n. 성당
[T] 일요일 날 집에 있지말고 **성당**가서 신부님 말씀 들어. **가서 들어(cathedral)!!!**
[예] Buffalo has several old cathedrals in downtown.

✔ **cattle**
[kǽtl]
[R] 3562/86800

n. 소 떼
[T] **카우(ca) + 들(ttle):** 카우들이므로 소떼
[예] I saw a herd of cattle.

cause
[kɔ:z]
[R] 754/86800

n. v. **원인(이유), 초래하다**
[T] **꼬시(cause)**는 것은 **원인,** 꼬신 결과 사고를 치니까
[유] reason [반] result, effect
[파] cause and effect: 원인과 결과
[예] What is the cause and effect of this accident?

caution
[kɔ́:ʃən]
[R] 5802/86800

n. v. **조심, 경계 조심시키다**
[T] 이상한 장사꾼이 사람들 **꼬션(caution - 꼬셔) 조심**해
[유] watchfulness, carefulness
[파] cautious: 조심스런
[예] She drove with extreme caution.

cave
[keiv]
[R] 6004/86800

n. v. **동굴, 굴을 파다**
[T] 갑 **갑해(cave) 동굴**은
[예] We can see bats in caves.

cease
[si:s]
[R] 6990/86800

v. **그만두다**
[T] 나쁜 짓 손 **씻어(cease) 그만 두다**
[유] stop [반] continue
[파] cease - fire: 휴전, ceaseless: 끊임없는
[예] A.J wright ceased operations this year.

ceiling
[sí:liŋ]
[R] 3830/86800

n. **천장**
[T] **천장 씌워랑(ceiling)**
[예] The apartment has low ceilings.

celebrate
[séləbrèit]
[R] 5593/86800

v. **축하하다**
[T] 지방작가 **설로 불러(celebra -** 서울로 불러) 상 받는 것 **축하하다**
[유] commemorate c.f) celebrated: 유명한
[예] She celebrated my birthday by giving me a present.

celebrity
[səlébrəti]
[R] 12732/86800

n. **유명인사**
[T] **유명인사**를 보자 난 **설레버렸디(celebrity)**
[예] The trial made her quite a celebrity.

cell
[sel]
ⓡ 1852/86800

n. 독방, 세포, 전지
❶ 내가 **살(cell)** 독방
예 The robber was in the police station's cell overnight.

cellar
[sélər]
ⓡ 9109/86800

n. 지하실
❶ 지하로 물이 **셀라(cellar)**
⊕ basement 예 I cleaned out from cellar to attic.

cemetery
[sémətèri]
ⓡ 8481/86800

n. 공동묘지
❶ **사람들이(삶들이)(cemetry) 묻혀있는 곳, 공동묘지**
⊕ graveyard: 묘지
예 Many of the soldiers who died in the Korean war are buried in a national cemetery.

census
[sénsəs]
ⓡ 6905/86800

n. 인구조사
❶ **인구를 셌었어(census)**
⊕ population count
예 We have a census in this country every ten years.

centennial
[senténiəl]
ⓡ 62715/86800

adj. 백주년의
❶ cent(백) + enn(1년 이상의 년) + ial(주로 형용사형 어미)
⊕ hundredth anniversary
예 The centennial games start every 100 years.

center
[séntər]
ⓡ 11154/86800

n. v. 중심, 중심을 두다
❶ 삼성동 무역 **센터(center)**
⊕ hub, heart
파 *central*: 중심의 *centrality*: 중심 *centralize*: 중심에 모으다
예 Myongdong is the center of Seoul Korea.

centigrade
[séntəgrèid]
ⓡ 28109/86800

adj. 섭씨의
❶ **센티(centi)를** 다르게 발음하면 **썹티**
⊕ Celsius c.f) Fahrenheit: 화씨
예 Korea is using Centigrade in the weather forecast.

ceremony
[sérəmòuni]
ⓡ 4729/86800

n. 의식
- ❶ 골 넣은 선수가 **쎄레모니(ceremony)** 혹은 교회에서 주는 **세례모니(ceremony - 세례의식)**로 기억
- ⊕ ritual: 종교적 의식(=rite)
- 예 The wedding ceremony will be held in United baptist church.

certain
[sə́:rtən]
ⓡ 430/86800

adj. 확실한, 어떤
- ❶ C를 빼고 발음하면 **어떤(ertain)**
- 파 *certainly*: 확실히 *certainty*: 확실성
- 예 It is certain that he is rich.

certificate
[sərtífəkit]
ⓡ 3286/86800

n. 증명서
- ❶ 확실(certi)하게 + 만들어(fic) 주는 것: **증명서**
- ⊕ credential
- 예 I earned my teaching certificate at UB.

challenge
[tʃǽlindʒ]
ⓡ 1502/86800

n. 도전
- ❶ UFC **도전자**는 챔피언 벨트를 언제 **찰른지(challenge)**
- 파 *challenging*: 도전적인
- 예 I will take up his challenge.

chamber
[tʃéimbər]
ⓡ 3261/86800

n. 방, 침실
- ❶ **방**에서 잠만 자는 **잠보(chamber)**
- ⊕ bedroom
- 예 After watching movie, he retired to his chamber.

changeover
[tʃéindʒòuvər]
ⓡ 28545/86800

n. 전환, 대체
- ❶ change(전환) + over(끝) - 앞 단어만 보고
- ⊕ conversion
- 예 The changeover to the new taxation system has created a lot of problems.

chant
[tʃænt]
Ⓡ 13114/86800

v. n. 노래 부르다, 노래
❶ 그는 술 췬다(chant) 면 노래를 부른다
예 I heard the chant of a bird in the morning.

chaos
[kéias]
Ⓡ 5000/86800

n. 혼돈, 무질서
❶ 무질서가 깨였어(chaos)
㊂ disorder ㊀ order 파 chaotic: 무질서한
예 The loss of electricity in winter caused chaos.

character
[kǽriktər]
Ⓡ 1196/86800

n. 특성, 문자, 등장인물
❶ 캐릭터(character - 등장인물)의 성격이 어떠냐는 둥, 캐릭터 상품 뽀로로 라는 둥, 사회에서 많이 쓰는 말을 기억
파 characteristic: 특징 *characterize*: ~의 특색을 이루다
characterization: 특정 짓기
예 All characters in this novel were very funny.

charge
[tʃɑ:rdʒ]
Ⓡ 990/86800

v. 짐을 싣다, 책임지우다, 충전하다, 고발하다
❶ 무거워라, 나 대신 이것 좀 차지(charge)?하며 부담 지우다
c.f) *charity*: 자비
예 The police charged John with a murder crime.

charm
[tʃɑ:rm]
Ⓡ 5546/86800

n. 매력, 마력
❶ 참(charm - 매력있는) 한 색시 소개시켜 줄까?
㊂ fascination, attraction
예 Miss Kim has many charms.

charter
[tʃɑ́:rtər]
Ⓡ 3824/86800

n. 선언서
❶ 선언서를 차트(Charter)로 만듦
예 Do you know the charter of the UN?

chase
[tʃeis]
Ⓡ 5380/86800

v. 쫓다
❶ 차 사서(chase) 쫓아다니다
㊂ follow, pursue
예 The sheriff are chasing the con man.

✔ chat
[tʃæt]
® 5890/86800

v. 잡담하다, 이야기하다
❶ 채팅(chatting)하다는 말을 통해 **이야기하다**는 뜻 임을 알 수 있음
⊕ converse
㈜ *chatter*: 지껄여대다, 지껄임 *chatty*: 수다스러운
㈒ We had a pleasant chat over the telephone.

✔ cheat
[tʃi:t]
® 12610/86800

v. 속이다, 부정한 짓을 하다
❶ 시험시간에 **치팅(cheating - 컨닝)은 부정한 짓**을 하는 것
⊕ deceive
㈒ Jacob cheated in a final English grammar examination.

✔ check
[tʃek]
® 1413/86800

n. v. 수표, 계산서, 점검, 저지하다, 점검하다
❶ 이메일 좀 **체크(check)** 할게라는 말에서 체크는 **점검하다, 수표**라는 뜻도 있죠
㈒ I want to pay by check.

✔ cheek
[tʃi:k]
® 4444/86800

n. 뺨, 볼
❶ 뺨을 짝(cheek)때리다
㈒ I kissed my baby on the cheeks.

✔ cheer
[tʃiər]
® 8364/86800

n. 갈채, 환호
❶ 술 잔을 부딪치며 **환호**하면서 **취얼스(cheer - 취했어?)!**
⊕ applause, bravo
㈘ catcall, depress
㈜ *cheerful*: 기분 좋은
  cheerfully: ~좋게
  cheering: 갈채, 원기를 돋우는
  cheerless: 기쁨이 없는
㈒ The cheers of the fans filled the stadium.

✔ chemistry
[kémistri]
® 4250/86800

n. 화학
❶ **가만히 있었더니(chemistry)**화학은 가만히 있으면 되는**(化)** 학문
㈒ I just failed my chemistry test.

cherish
[tʃériʃ]
ⓡ 23699/86800

v. 소중히 하다
ⓣ 니가 **제일이야 쒸(cherish)**하면서 **소중히 여기다**
ⓢ appreciate, esteem ⓐ disdain, despise
ⓟ cherished: 소중한=valued, prized
ⓔ I will cherish every waken moment.

chest
[tʃest]
ⓡ 2613/86800

n. 가슴
ⓣ **체해서 답(chest)**답했다 **가슴이**
ⓢ bosom, breast
ⓔ He has a broad chest.

chew
[tʃuː]
ⓡ 14742/86800

v. 씹다
ⓣ **츄잉(chewing) 껌(gum)**(씹기 껌)
ⓢ chomp, crunch
ⓔ You're not allowed to chew gum in class.

chief
[tʃiːf]
ⓡ 886/86800

n. adj. 우두머리, 주요한(major, principal, leading)
ⓣ **치프(치일높프 - cheif): 제일 높은 우두머리**
ⓔ The chief engineer on the project.
　 He has many concerns, chief among them his health.

childhood
[tʃáildhùd]
ⓡ 3332/86800

n. 유년시대
ⓣ **child(철드 - 철들어야 함 - 어린이) + hood(시절, 시대)**
ⓟ childish: 어린애 같은, 유치한
　 childlike: 어린애다운, 천진난만한
ⓔ Both men had unhappy childhoods.

chilly
[tʃíli]
ⓡ 13957/86800

adj. 쌀쌀한, 으스스한
ⓣ **아! 추워리(chilly)**
ⓢ brisk, cool, crisp ⓐ warm
ⓟ chill: 차갑게 만들다(=cool)
ⓔ It's a little chilly outside.

C

chimney
[tʃímni]
Ⓡ 9292/86800

n. 굴뚝
❶ 산타야! 굴뚝에서 **춥니?(chimney)**
예 Santa went down the chimney.

✔ chin
[tʃin]
Ⓡ 5062/86800

n. 턱
❶ 니가 **친(chin) 턱**
㊋ jaw
예 My dog likes being scratched under his chin.

chip
[tʃip]
Ⓡ 4588/86800

n. 잘라낸 나뭇조각, 토막
❶ 산골 집에 **첩첩(chip)히** 쌓인 **나무토막**
㊋ flake, fragment
예 Wood chips were spread over the ground between the plants.

chisel
[tʃízəl]
Ⓡ 21422/86800

n. 끌, 정
❶ 딱딱히 굳은 **치즐(chisel)** 갈아 줄 끌
예 Chisel marks can be seen.

✤ choice
[tʃɔis]
Ⓡ 826/86800

n. 선택
❶ 나는 이것이 **좋아서(choice)선택**했어
㊋ option, alternative, decision
예 The child had no choice about going to school.

choke
[tʃouk]
Ⓡ 16934/86800

v. 질식시키다, 질식하다
❶ 질식해서 **쪽크(choke)** 늘어지다
㊋ suffocate, smother
예 Chew your food well so you don't choke.

✔ chop
[tʃɑp]
Ⓡ 10512/86800

v. n. 도끼로 찍다, 절단하다, 절단
❶ 고기를 **자르려** 손으로 **잡다(chopped)**
㊋ cut, fell
예 Chop (up) the onions and carrots roughly.

chore

✔ **chore**
[tʃɔːr]
® 24000/86800

n. 허드렛일
❶ 다른 일 없으면 허드렛 일이나 **죠!(chore)!**
⊕ errand
例 The children were each assigned different household chores.

chronicle

chronicle
[kránikl]
® 1134/86800

n. 연대기, 기록, 설명
❶ chroni(시간) + cle(글) - 시간을 기록한 글
⊕ 설명: account
例 I read a chronicle of the American Civil War.

chubby

chubby
[tʃʌbi]
® 25233/86800

adj. 뚱뚱한
❶ 살이 **첩첩이(chubby)** 쌓인 - 뚱뚱한
⊕ plump
例 He was always chubby as a child.

circle

✔ **circle**
[sɔ́ːrkl]
® 2761/86800

n. 원
❶ 써클 혹은 싸이클(cycle, circle)은 전부 **원**
⊕ ring, hoop ⊕ square
例 She drew a circle around the correct answer.

circuit

✔ **circuit**
[sɔ́ːrkit]
® 3489/86800

n. 순회
❶ circu(원 - 써클에서 나온 말) + it(가다): 원으로 빙빙 돌다, 순회
⊕ circulation, rotation 派 *circulate*: 순환하다
例 It takes a year for the Earth to make one circuit around the sun.

circumstance

✔ **circumstance**
[sɔ́ːrkəmstæns]
® 10035/86800

n. 상황
❶ circum(원) + st(서있다, stand의 줄임) + ance(명사형 어미): 주변에 둘러 서 있는 것(환경)
⊕ condition, situation
例 Do not judge his behavior without considering every circumstances.

circumvent
[sə̀:rkəmvént]
ⓡ 26343/86800

v. 회피하다
ⓣ 둘러(circum) + 가다(vent) - **회피하다**
ⓨ avoid ⓑ confront
ⓔ We circumvented the problem by using a different program.

cite
[sait]
ⓡ 15776/86800

v. 인용하다, 언급하다
ⓣ 연인이 서로 좋아하는 **사이다(cite)고 말하다**
ⓨ mention, refer to ⓑ plagiarize
ⓔ He cited the constitution in his defense.

✔ **citizen**
[sítəzən]
ⓡ 5626/86800

n. 시민
ⓣ **시티가 준(citizen) 것, 시민 증**
ⓨ resident, townsman
ⓟ *city*: 도시 *citizenship*: 시민권
ⓔ She was a United States citizen but lived most of her life abroad.

✔ **civil**
[sívəl]
ⓡ 1189/86800

adj. 시민의, 예의바른
ⓣ 시볼(civil): **시를 볼 사람은 시민**
ⓨ civic, civilian
ⓟ *civilization*: 문명 *civilized*: 문명화된
ⓔ They got married in a civil ceremony at city hall. She was barely civil to me.

✔ **claim**
[kleim]
ⓡ 895/86800

v. 주장하다, 목숨을 앗아가다
ⓣ **주장하려면 목소리가 크래임(claim)**
ⓨ assert, declare ⓑ deny, retract
ⓔ She claimed that he was telling the truth.

✔ **clap**
[klæp]
ⓡ 20375/86800

v. 찰싹 때리다, 박수치다
ⓣ 큰 **랩(clap)소리에 박수치다**
ⓔ I clapped my hands in appreciation.

clarify
[klǽrəfài]
℗ 7511/86800

v. 분명히 하다, 밝히다
❶ Clear(분명한) + ify(만들다) - 분명하게 하다
⊛ elucidate
예 Can you clarify exactly what it is you're proposing?

clasp
[klæsp]
℗ 21866/86800

v. 꽉 잡다
❶ 글라스(glass로 생각) 입(clasp)을 꼭 잡다
⊛ hold, grasp, fasten ⊕ unfasten, loose
예 She clasped her son in her arms.

classification
[klæ̀səfikéiʃən]
℗ 4946/86800

n. 분류
❶ class(반)으로 + fication(만 듦): fic, fac은 만들다는 뜻, factory (만드는 곳, 공장)를 생각해 볼 것
⊛ arrangement, assortment
파 *classify*: 분류하다
예 Do you understand the system of classification used in biology?

clay
[klei]
℗ 5093/86800

n. 진흙
❶ 옛날에는 진흙으로 그림을 그려이(clay)
예 Clay roof tile was also found.

clergyman
[klə́:rdʒimən]
℗ 16466/86800

n. 성직자
❶ 성직자들은 나쁜 거 하지 말라고 그러지 마(clergyman)! 하는 말 많이 함
⊛ minister, pastor
예 He was a teacher at Oxford University and a clergyman as well.

clerk
[klə:rk]
℗ 4405/86800

n. v. 사무원, 점원, 점원으로 일하다
❶ 글을(clerk) 쓰는 사무원
예 He is a town clerk of New York state.

C

✔ client
[kláiənt]
® 1685/86800

n. 소송 의뢰하는 고객
❶ 억울해서 제발 **승소**하게 해달라고 **크라이(cli)** + **하면서 언(ent -** 몸이 얼은) 사람
예 Mr Black has been a client of this firm for many years.

✔ cliff
[klif]
® 5138/86800

n. 절벽
❶ **걸리(cliff)**는게 없으면 **절벽**은 오르기 힘들어
⊕ bluff, crag
예 Standing at the edge of the cliff, we watched the waves crash on the shore far below.

cling
[kliŋ]
® 12684/86800

v. 매달리다, 고수하다
❶ 어떤 일에 **끌리(cling)**면 그 일에 **매달린다**
⊕ adhere, stick
예 The wet paper clings to the glass.

clinic
[klínik]
® 5393/86800

n. 진료소
❶ 나 **진료**받았는데 **크리니(clinic)?**(깨끗하니?)
예 The clinic is offering free screening for diabetes.

✔ clipping
[klipiŋ]
® 24342/86800

n. 자르기
❶ 끌립!(clip-뭘 자르는 소리)
⊕ trim
예 I'm always clipping recipes out of magazines.

closet
[klázit]
® 18479/86800

n. 벽장, 화장실
❶ **닫아야 하는 곳(closet)**
예 The sheets and blankets are in the hall closet.

clout
[klaut]
® 19204/86800

n. 영향력
❶ **영향력 클 아웃(clout)** - 내가 아웃되면 팀에 끼치는 영향력이 클
⊕ influence
예 She used her political clout to have another school built.

clown
[klaun]
ⓡ 13163/86800

n. 시골뜨기, 익살꾼
❶ 꼴 나은(clown)시골뜨기 - 좀 보기좋은 촌놈
ⓢ comedian, joker
예 Those big shoes make you look like a clown!

clue
[klu:]
ⓡ 6592/86800

n. 단서
❶ 사건을 끌르(clue - 푸는)는 단서
ⓢ evidence, indication
예 Police are still looking for clues in their search for the missing girl.

clump
[klʌmp]
ⓡ 18236/86800

n. 덩어리
❶ lump만 봐도 덩어리, 큰넘(clump) - 큰 놈은 큰 덩어리
ⓢ bunch
예 There is a clump of bushes at the edge of the field.

clumsy
[klʌmzi]
ⓡ 11581/86800

adj. 솜씨 없는
❶ 꼴 없지(clumsy): 꼴이 안 나는, 솜씨 없는
ⓢ inexpert, tactless, awkward, cumbersome
예 He is very clumsy and is always breaking things.

cluster
[klʌstər]
ⓡ 7251/86800

n. v. 떼, 한데 모이게 하다
❶ 작은 돈 굴려서 떼(cluster)로 모이게 하다
ⓢ bunch, batch, gather, concentrate, group
예 Have a look at the cluster of galaxies in this photograph. People clustered around the noticeboard to read the exam results.

coal
[koul]
ⓡ 2002/86800

n. 석탄
❶ 커울(coal)이면 추워서 석탄을 때야 함
예 His face is as black as a coal.

C

coalition
[kòuəlíʃən]
ⓡ 3719/86800

n. 연합
❶ 함께(co) + 모두(al)로 + tion(명사형 어미) 만듦
㊦ alliance
㊤ The groups united to form a coalition.

coarse
[kɔːrs]
ⓡ 9627/86800

adj. **조잡한, 거친**
❶ **조잡한 꼴새(coarse) -** 조잡한 꼴 좀 봐
㊦ crude, rough, harsh
㊤ The beach had rough, coarse sand.

❧ coat
[kout]
ⓡ 2774/86800

n. v. **층, 뒤덮다**
❶ **코트(coat)는** 추워서 **층층이** 덮는 것
㊦ 뒤덮다: cover
㊤ That wall needs another coat of paint.

✔ cocoon
[kəkúːn]
ⓡ 29437/86800

n. **누에꼬치**
❶ 엊그제 **누에꼬치**였는데 많이 **컸군(cocoon)**
㊤ The insects spin a cocoon.

codify
[kádəfai]
ⓡ 52542/86800

v. **법전으로 편찬하다, 요약하다**
❶ **(codify - 가둬 파일) -** 사람을 가둘 수 있는 요약된 파일은 법전
㊦ 분류하다(classify, categorize)
㊤ The author tries to codify important ideas about language.

coffin
[kɔ́ːfin]
ⓡ 5639/86800

n. **관**
❶ **관**에 넣으면 **갑 갑한(coffin)**
㊤ Coffins are said to be the preferred sleeping places of vampires.

cognitive
[kágnətiv]
ⓡ 6267/86800

adj. **인식의**
❶ co(함께) + gn(알다) + tive(형용사형 어미) 혹은, gn(그니 - 알고 있니)만 봐도 알 수 있음
㊤ Some of her cognitive functions have been impaired.

✓ cohesion
[kouhí:ʒən]
Ⓡ 11730/86800

n. 결합
[T] 코 헤젼(cohesion)? 내가 붙여줄께
[유] unity
[파] *coherent*: 응집력 있는, 조리가 있는(logical)
cohesive: 결합력 있는(adhesive) ↔ released: 떼어놓은
[예] The lack of cohesion within the party lost them votes in the election.

✓ coin
[kɔin]
Ⓡ 6140/86800

n. v. 동전, 주조하다
[T] 코인(coin - 동전)
[유] 주조하다(invent, create)
[예] That machine doesn't take coins.

coincide
[kòuinsáid]
Ⓡ 9560/86800

v. 일치하다, 동시에 발생하다
[T] co(함께) + incident(일어나기 쉬운): 동시에 발생하다
[유] occur, happen
[예] Our vacations coincided this year.

collaboration
[kəlæ̀bəréiʃən]
Ⓡ 5778/86800

n. 협동, 합작
[T] col(함께) + labor(노동) + tion(명사형 어미)
[유] cooperation, efforts together
[예] This dictionary is a collaboration of many minds.

collapse
[kəlǽps]
Ⓡ 3561/86800

v. 붕괴하다
[T] col(함께) + lapse(실수하다 - 어원편 참조) 혹은 col(함께) + lapse(없어지다)
[유] disintegrate, fall
[예] The roof collapsed and buried the crowd.

✓ colleague
[káli:g]
Ⓡ 4929/86800

n. 직장의 동료
[T] col(함께, 영어의 com, con, col, cor, co 등은 함께라는 뜻) + league(함께하는 동맹) 따라서 함께하는 그룹 즉, 동료
[유] companion, co - worker, partner
[예] A colleague of mine will be speaking at the conference.

C

✔ collect
[kəlékt]
® 3317/86800

v. 모으다
❶ 이것저것 **골랐다(collect) - 모으다**
⊕ gather, accumulate
㉠ *collectible*: 모을 수 있는 *collection*: 수집
㉢ The professor collected the students' exams.

collective
[kəléktiv]
® 3502/86800

n. 집단, 공동체
❶ collect(골라 냈다 - 골라낸 집단)
⊕ gathering, group
㉢ I have a collective identity because I have a bunch of friends at school.

collide
[kəláid]
® 27016/86800

v. 충돌하다
❶ 차가 가다가 클라데(collide - 차가 큰일났다는 것은 **충돌했다는 말**)
⊕ bump into, hit each other
㉢ The two vans collided at the crossroads.

colonize
[kálənàiz]
® 64298/86800

v. 이주시키다
❶ 따로 **이주** 시키게 **골라 놔줘(colonize)**
⊕ inhabit
㉢ Sir! we need to colonize the west colonies!!

✔ colony
[káləni]
® 6559/86800

n. 식민지
❶ 누가 나라를 **식민지로 갈랐니(colony)?**
⊕ settlement
㉠ colonial: 식민지의 *colonist*: 식민지 개척자
㉢ Many Western nations are former European colonies.

✔ colorful
[kálərfəl]
® 6621/86800

adj. 다채로운
❶ color(색깔) + full(꽉 찬)
⊕ interesting
㉠ *colorless*: 무색의 *color*: 색 *colored*: 착색한
㉢ I wore a colorful outfit.

colossal
[kəlásəl]
® 17733/86800

adj. 거대한
❶ 집이 커어설(컸어)(colossal) - 거대한
⊕ immense, huge, enormous
例 He saw a colossal statue of the town's founder.

column
[káləm]
® 3314/86800

n. 기둥, 신문의 특정 기고란
❶ 신문에는 황 용 선생의 **칼럼(column - 기고)** 혹은 **그럼(column)** 넌 우리 회사의 **기둥**이야
⊕ pillar: 기둥, article: 신문기사
例 She writes a weekly column for the paper.

✔ combat
[kámbæt]
® 5132/86800

n. 전투
❶ 함께(com) 배트(bat)휘두름: 싸움
⊕ warfare, battle
例 He was killed in combat.

❖ combine
[kəmbáin]
® 4791/86800

v. 결합하다, 연합하다
❶ 함께(com) + 둘(bi) + 인(ine): 둘을 하나로 묶음, 연합하다
⊕ associate, unite
파 *combination*: 조화 *combined*: 결합한
例 They combined the two companies.

comet
[kámit]
® 16896/86800

n. 혜성
❶ 꼬마(comet)별, 혜성
例 Billy likes to look for comets.

❖ comfort
[kámfərt]
® 2880/86800

n. 위로, 위안
❶ com(함께) + fort(불): 날을 그리며 위안 삼다, 함께 볼 날을 그리며 위안 삼다
⊕ consolation, solace
⊕ irritation
파 *comfortable*: 편안한 *comfortably*: 안락하게
　 comforting: 위안이 되는
例 Her presence was a comfort to him.

C

✔ command
[kəmǽnd]
ℝ 2424/86800

v. 명령하다
➊ **가만 둬(command)!** 라고 **명령하다**
⊕ govern, rule ⊖ obey
예 The captain commanded his men to attack.

commanding
[kəmǽndiŋ]
ℝ 9412/86800

adj. 당당한
➊ **command(명령하고 있는) + ing: 당당한**
⊕ forceful
예 He has a very commanding voice.

commemorate
[kəmémərèit]
ℝ 16957/86800

v. 기념하다
➊ **함께(com) + 기억(memo) + ate(동사형 어미)**
⊕ celebrate
예 The festival commemorates the town's founding.

commend
[kəménd]
ℝ 16132/86800

v. 칭찬하다, 추천하다
➊ 의사가 **잘 꾸멘(e)다(commend)고 추천, 칭찬하다**
⊕ praise, extol: 칭찬하다, recommend: 추천하다
예 His poetry is highly commended by other writers.

✔ comment
[kάment]
ℝ 1909/86800

v. n. 언급하다, 언급
➊ **노코멘트(comment): 유명인이 안 좋은 소문에 시달리다 기자가 물어보면 노코멘트!!!!**
⊕ commentary, remark
파 *commentary*: 시사 해설, 주석
예 He refused to comment on the decision of the court.

✔ commercial
[kəmə́:rʃəl]
ℝ 1275/86800

adj. n. 상업의, 상업 광고방송
➊ 광고방송 나오는데 꼬마 심부름 시키면, 엄마! **가만 있얼(commercial)! 하면서** 화를 냄. 꼬마에게 상업광고가 재미있어서
⊕ business, mercantile 파 commerce: 상업
예 Their music is too commercial.

95

commission
[kəmíʃən]
® 972/86800

n. v. 위임, 수수료, 임명하다, 위탁하다
① com(함께) + mission(임무): 함께 임무를 수행 - **임명, 위탁,** 아마
그 일을 해결하려면 코미션(commission - 수수료) 좀 줘야 할 거야
⊕ fee: 수수료; authorize, empower: 위임하다
c.f) *commit*: 범죄 저지르다, 위임하다 *commitment*: 범행, 위임
예 She gets a commission for each car she sells.
She was commissioned in the Navy as a captain.

committee
[kəmíti]
® 505/86800

n. 위원회
① 커 미팅(committee), 미팅이 크면 **위원회**
⊕ board, cabinet
예 We're waiting for recommendations from the advisory
committee.

commodity
[kəmádəti]
® 7519/86800

n. 상품
① 상품들 보면 꼬마 좋지(commodity)
⊕ goods, products, article of trade
예 Oil is a commodity in high demand.

common
[kámən]
® 528/86800

adj. 흔한
① 고만(common)고만한 사람은 **흔하지**
⊕ communal, ordinary
⊕ rare, unusual
파 commonplace: 평범한 것, 평범한 *commoner*: 평민
예 "Smith" is a common name.

commonality
[kàmənǽləti]
® 31835/86800

n. 평민, 보통시민(=commonalty)
① common(보통)al + ity(추상명사)
예 Commonality means ordinary people.

commonwealth
[kámənwèlθ]
® 4752/86800

n. 연방, 공화국
① 우리는 평민(commom)이 잘사는(wealth)공화국
예 What is The british commonwealth?

communism
[kámjənìzəm]
® 7308/86800

n. 공산주의
❶ 함께(com) 무너짐(munism): 공산주의
예 After the fall of Communism, many citizens find themselves happy to have their religious freedoms back.

community
[kəmjú:nəti]
® 399/86800

n. 사회, 단체
❶ comm(함께) + unity(하나됨): 단체, 사회
㊌ society
예 Many communities are facing budget problems.

commute
[kəmjú:t]
® 30869/86800

v. 통근하다
❶ 코 밑에(commute - 가까운데)를 통근하다
예 He commutes to work by train.

compact
[kəmpǽkt]
® 5025/86800

adj. v. 간결한, 압축하다
❶ 콤팩트 디스크(C,D)는 간결하게 압축해 놓은 것
㊌ 간결한: brief, concise
압축하다: compress, squeeze
예 The drill has a compact design.
The snow had compacted into a hard icy layer.

company
[kámpəni]
® 209/86800

n. 회사, 동료
❶ 너희 회사 껌 파니(company)? 혹은 com(함께) pan(빵)을 먹는 + y(집합체)
㊌ 회사: corporation, enterprise
동료: companion, comrade
예 The company is based in Paris.

compare
[kəmpéər]
® 3727/86800

v. 비교하다
❶ com(함께) + pare(빼어) - 껌 빼어 이 껌 저 껌 비교하다
㊌ contrast
㊟ comparable: 비교할만한(similar, equivalent)
comparative: 비교의 *comparison*: 비교
예 Dekker's plays cannot compare with Shakespeare's.

compartment
[kəmpáːrtmənt]
Ⓡ 10250/86800

n. 구분, 칸막이
❶ 함께(com) + part(부분) + ment(명사형어미): 칸막이를 함께 해 놓음
유 booth, cell room
예 The refrigerator has a separate compartment for meats.

compass
[kámpəs]
Ⓡ 9816/86800

n. v. 주위, 한계, 나침반, 제도용 컴퍼스, 둘러싸다
❶ 컴파스(compass)로 한 바퀴 돌리면 둘러싸짐
예 The discussion went beyond the compass of my brain.
An old stone wall compasses their property.

compassion
[kəmpǽʃən]
Ⓡ 9624/86800

n. 연민, 동정
❶ com(함께) + passion(마음, 열정): 마음을 함께한 것은 연민
유 charity, pity, sympathy 반 enmity, harshness
예 He felt compassion for the lost child.

✔ compel
[kəmpél]
Ⓡ 18648/86800

v. 강요하다
❶ 껌 빼(compel)라고 강요하다
유 force, constrain 반 coax
예 His disregard of the rules compels us to dismiss him.

✔ compensate
[kámpənsèit]
Ⓡ 7799/86800

v. 갚다, 보상받다
❶ 빚을 갚았었데(compensate)
유 recompense, reimburse 파 *compensation*: 배상
예 Victims of the crash will be compensated for their injuries.

✢ compete
[kəmpíːt]
Ⓡ 4431/86800

v. 경쟁하다
❶ 불량배들이 com(서로) + pete(팼데), 이권 경쟁하다
유 contest, contend 반 yield, surrender
파 *competent*: 유능한 competently: 유능하게, 솜씨있게(adeptly)
competition: 경쟁, *competitive*: 경쟁의
competence: 적성, 능력, *competitively*: 경쟁하여,
competitiveness: 경쟁
예 Thousands of applicants are competing for the same job.

C

✔ compile
[kəmpáil]
ⓡ 17657/86800

v. 편집하다, 수집하다
- ❶ com(함께) + pile(파일) 로 만들다, 편집하다
- ㉮ put together, collect, gather
- 예 We're compiling some facts and figures for a documentary on the subject.

complacency
[kəmpléisənsi]
ⓡ 14086/86800

n. 만족
- ❶ com(껌씹으며) + placency(풀어 쓴 C): 시험 볼 때 자기는 껌 씹으며 대충푼게 성적이 C 나와 만족스러움
- ㉮ satisfaction ㉵ complacent: 자기만족의
- 예 The public was lulled into complacency.

✪ complain
[kəmpléin]
ⓡ 5719/86800

v. 불평하다
- ❶ 자본이 없어 **껌팔아 인(complain)제** ㅠㅠ 하며 신세를 **불평하다**
- ㉮ criticize, protest ㉵ complaint: 불평
- 예 He works hard but he never complains.

complement
[kámpləmənt]
ⓡ 7860/86800

n. 보충
- ❶ com(함께) + pl(풀이) + ment(먼): 함께 풀이해도 답이 먼, **보충이 필요**
- ㉮ supplement
- 예 A good wine is a complement to a good meal.

✪ complete
[kəmplí:t]
ⓡ 770/86800

v. 완성하다
- ❶ 함께(com) 풀었다(plete), 풀이를 완성하다
- ㉮ finish
- ㉵ *completion*: 완성 *completely*: 완전히, 전적으로(entirely)
- 예 Complete the sentence with one of the adjectives provided.

✪ complex
[kəmpléks]
ⓡ 1077/86800

adj. n. 복잡한, 복합물(group of buildings)
- ❶ com(함께) + plex(겹겹히 한): 복잡한, 복합물
- ㉮ elaborate, involved
- ㉵ *complicate*: 복잡하게 하다 *complexity*: 복잡성
- 예 The situation is more complex than you realize.
  A complex of protein molecules.

✔ compliment
[kámpləmənt]
ⓡ 11337/86800

n. 칭찬, 증정
❶ 껌을 뿌리면(compliment)서 증정, complement와 철자 i 가 다른데 칭찬해주면 아이(i) 좋아 로 기억할 것
ⓢ commendation, tribute
ⓐ criticism
파 *complimentary*: 칭찬의
예 I take it as a compliment when people say I look like my mother.

comply
[kəmplái]
ⓡ 5528/86800

v. 명령이나 요구에 따르다
❶ 함께(com) + 플라이(ply)하자는 요구에 따르다
ⓢ conform, obey
ⓐ disobey, resist
예 They asked him to leave and he complied.

✔ component
[kəmpóunənt]
ⓡ 3509/86800

n. 구성성분
❶ 함께(com) + 놓여짐(pon) + (ent): 함께 놓여진 것
ⓢ element, part
파 *compose*: 구성하다, 작곡, 작문하다
   composed: 작곡된(written, created)
   composition: 합성(make up), 혼합물, 화해
   composer: 작곡가
예 He sells spare computer components.

✔ compost
[kámpoust]
ⓡ 10450/86800

n. 혼합물, 퇴비
❶ 껌에 뭘 부었었다(post) - 껌에 뭘 혼합
예 The movie is a compost of love and friendship.

compound
[kəmpáund]
ⓡ 6165/86800

v. 혼합시키다, 화해하다
❶ 함께(com)넣어서(혼합시켜서) 파운드(pound) 케익을 만듦
ⓢ combine, mix
예 Most tires are made of rubber compounded with other chemicals and materials.

✔ comprehend
[kὰmprihénd]
[R] 13754/86800

v. **이해하다, 포함하다**
[T] 함께(com) + 풀이(ple) + 한다(hend): 이해하다
[유] understand
[파] *comprehension*: 이해 *comprehensive*: 포괄적인
[예] I fail to comprehend their attitude.
The course will comprehend all facets of Japanese culture.

compress
[kəmprés]
[R] 28081/86800

v. **압축하다, 요약하다**
[T] 함께(com) + 압박을 가하다(press)
[유] condense
[예] He compressed the air in a closed chamber!

comprise
[kəmpráiz]
[R] 9130/86800

v. **포함하다, ~로 이루어지다**
[T] 함께(com) 풀어져(prise)(놓여져) 이루어지다
[유] consist of, be made up of, be composed of
[예] Each army division comprised 4,500 troops.

compromise
[kάmprəmὰiz]
[R] 4155/86800

v. **타협하다**
[T] 함께(com) + promise(약속하다) - 타협하다
[유] adjust, agree
[예] Well, you want $400 and I say $300, so let's compromise at/on $350.

compulsory
[kəmpʌ́lsəri]
[R] 4861/86800

adj. **강제적인**
[T] **껌 뺐어라(compulsory)**하며 강제적인
[유] forced, mandatory, obligatory, requisite
[반] optional
[파] compulsion: 강제
[예] Wearing seat belts in cars is compulsory by law.

computation
[kὰmpjutéiʃən]
[R] 21248/86800

n. **계산**
[T] 컴퓨터는 원래 계산기였던 것이므로 computation은 계산
[파] compute: 계산하다(=calculate)
[예] Methods used for the computation of taxes.

✔ conceal
[kənsí:l]
[R] 9165/86800

v. 숨기다
[T] 큰 실(conceal)수 숨기다
[유] cover, hide [반] expose, reveal
[예] He concealed the gun under his coat.

conceit
[kənsí:t]
[R] 29539/86800

n. 자부심
[T] 큰(con) 시(ceit)에서 산다는 자부심
[유] pride
[반] humility
[예] The conceit of that man is incredible!

conceive
[kənsí:v]
[R] 12001/86800

v. 느끼다, 상상하다
[T] 큰 집에(conceive)산다고 상상하다
[유] think
[예] I think my uncle still conceives of me as a four - year - old.

✔ concentrate
[kánsəntrèit]
[R] 3118/86800

v. 집중하다
[T] 함께(con) + 중심, 가운데(cent):
[유] focus
[파] *concentration*: 집중
[예] I can't concentrate on my work with all that noise.

✔ concept
[kánsept]
[R] 1610/86800

n. 개념
[T] 요즘 유행하는 컨셉(concept)이라는 말 TV에서 많이 듣는데 개념이라는 뜻
[유] idea, notion [파] *conception*: 개념
[예] It is very difficult to define the concept of beauty.

✔ concern
[kənsə́:rn]
[R] 981/86800

v. 염려하다, 관련 있다
[T] 간섭(concern)하는 것은 관련있고 염려하기 때문
[유] affect, involve 관련있다
[파] *concerning*: ~에 대하여 *concerned*: 걱정하는
[예] I am concerned about his health.
The water shortage concerns us all.

concise
[kənsáis]
® 15859/86800

adj. 간결한
❶ 끈 사이즈(concise)는 간결한 게 좋다
⊕ brief, succinct 파 concisely: 간결하게
예 Make your answers clear and concise.

☙ conclude
[kənklúːd]
® 5434/86800

v. 결론짓다
❶ con(함께) clude(닫다), 결론을 함께 짓다. include는 안에 놓고
닫다 이므로 포함하다. exclude는 밖에 놓고 닫다 이므로 제외
하다
⊕ complete, end, finish 반 begin
파 conclusive: 결정적인(decisive, definitive, final)
   conclusion: 결말(end)
예 Before I conclude, I'd like to thank you all for coming.

concomitant
[kɑnkɑ́mətənt]
® 18537/86800

adj. 수반하는, 부수된, 동시에 생기는
❶ 꼼꼼히 한(concomitant) 결과, 부수적으로 생기는
⊕ 동시에 생기는(concurrent)
예 Loss of memory is a natural concomitant of old age.

concur
[kənkə́ːr]
® 26983/86800

v. 일치하다
❶ con(함께) + cur(흐르다): 일치하다
⊕ be united in
예 The new report concurs with previous findings.

condemn
[kəndém]
® 11606/86800

v. 비난하다
❶ 간댐(condemn) - 화재로 간이 데었다고 비난하다
⊕ blame
예 The film was condemned for its sexism.

condense
[kəndéns]
® 38130/86800

v. 요약하다, 응축하다
❶ 큰 댄스(condense)를 요약한 춤
⊕ concentrate, summarize 반 enlarge expand
파 condensation: 응축
예 The cooler temperatures cause the gas to condense into
   a liquid.

condition
[kəndíʃən]
ⓡ 1229/86800

n. 상태, 조건
❶ 조건은 컨디션(condition)을 봐서 결정하자
⊕ state 파 *conditionally*: 조건부로
예 Happiness is the state or condition of being happy.

conduct
[kándʌk]
ⓡ 2422/86800

n. 행동
❶ 큰 덕(conduct)이 있는 행동
⊕ behavior 파 *conductor*: 전도체(transmitter)
예 I couldn't help being surprised at his conduct.

confederate
[kənfédərit]
ⓡ 43605/86800

n. 동맹국
❶ 적이 쳐들어 오면 함께(con) 패더래이(federate - 연합, 동맹)
⊕ ally, confederacy
예 We welcome the Confederate army.

confer
[kənfə́:r]
ⓡ 13384/86800

v. (칭호, 학위를) 수여하다, 베풀다, 의논하다
❶ 나중에 이 돈 갚어(confer)하면서 돈을 주고 베풀다
⊕ award, bestow 파 *conference*: 회의
예 An honorary doctorate was conferred on him by
　　Edinburgh University.
　　I should like some time to confer with my lawyer.

confess
[kənfés]
ⓡ 9442/86800

v. 고백하다
❶ 간 빼서(confess) - 간 뺀다는 일상용어는 속에 있는 것을 다
　고백한다는 뜻
⊕ reveal, disclose
예 I must confess that I haven't read the book.

confide
[kənfáid]
ⓡ 21625/86800

v. 터놓고 이야기하다, 위임하다
❶ 조직원들이 이번에는 큰 판이다(confide)라고 터놓고 이야기하다
⊕ disclose, divulge, reveal
파 confidential: 신임하는, 비밀을 터놓는
　　confidence 신뢰, 자신감 *confident*: 확신하는, 자신 있는
예 She confides in no one but her husband.
　　She confided her jewelry to her sister.

configuration
[kənfigjəréiʃən]
® 6886/86800

n. **구성, 배열, 형태**
❶ con(함께) + figure(모양): 함께 모양이 형성된 구성
㉮ 배열: arrangement, 형태: shape
㉠ The basic configuration of the building is that of a geodesic dome.

✔ **confine**
[kənfáin]
® 15094/86800

v. **한정하다**
❶ 함께(con)끝(fin)을 정하다 - **한정하다**
㉮ limit
㉠ Confine your efforts to finishing the book.

confinement
[kənfáinmənt]
® 15252/86800

n. **감금**
❶ con(함께) + fin(끝, 한계) + ment(명사형 어미): 함께 끝을 정해 놈
㉮ captivity
㉠ The dog was kept in confinement until it was determined to be healthy.

✔ **confirm**
[kənfə́:rm]
® 3517/86800

v. **확인하다**
❶ 함께(con) + 굳게(firm) **확인하다**
㉮ verify
㉠ Flights should be confirmed 48 hours before departure.

✔ **conflict**
[kánflikt]
® 1744/86800

v. **충돌하다**
❶ 함께(con) 염산 **뿌리(flic)**며 **충돌하다**
㉮ contest, struggle
㉯ agree
㉣ conflicting: 상반되는(contrary, opposing)
㉠ My class conflicts with my going to the concert.

✔ **conform**
[kənfɔ́:rm]
® 8060/86800

v. **순응하다, 합치하다**
❶ 큰(con) 형식(form)에 **순순히 응하다**
㉮ meet
㉠ Most teenagers feel pressure to conform.
The list conforms with the contents of the trunk.

confound
[kənfáund]
® 31319/86800

v. 혼동하게 하다
❶ con(함께) + found(찾아봐): 함께 찾으면 헷갈리지?
⊕ bewilder, perplex
예 The murder case has confounded investigators.

✔ confront
[kənfránt]
® 8860/86800

v. 직면하다
❶ 함께(con) + 마주치다(front): 직면하다
⊕ face
예 They confronted the invaders at the shore.

✔✔ confuse
[kənfjú:z]
® 11268/86800

v. 혼동하다
❶ 함께(con) 녹다(fuse): 함께 녹아있으니 혼동스럽지... 어느 것인지
⊕ puzzle, obscure
예 You must be confusing me with someone else.

congenial
[kəndʒí:njəl]
® 20747/86800

adj. 마음 맞는, 같은 성질의
❶ con(함께) + gen(타고난) + ial(형용사형 어미)
⊕ favorable, agreeable
파 congenital: 질병이 선천적인(present at birth)
예 I found the work to be congenial.

✔ congestion
[kəndʒéstʃən]
® 12020/86800

n. 혼잡
❶ 큰 재수 촌(congestion)은 재수생들로 혼잡
⊕ crowding, jam
예 The (traffic) congestion in the city gets even worse during the summer.

conglomerate
[kənglámərət]
® 14532/86800

n. 집단
❶ con(함께) + glomerate(글루모여라): 집단
⊕ assortment
예 A conglomerate is a kind of company.

✔ congratulate
[kəngrǽtʃəlèit]
®12391/86800

v. 축하하다
❶ 우승했더니 **축하한다고 큰 그릇(트로피) 주데(congratulate)**
㊀ applaud, compliment ㊁ criticize
ⓟ *congratulation*: 축하
ⓔ They congratulated him on his marriage.

---

congress
[kάŋgris]
®1867/86800

n. 의회
❶ 이 분은 **큰 그릇이여서(congress) 국회로~**
ⓟ congressman: 의회 의원
ⓔ Congress is not currently in session.

---

conjecture
[kəndʒéktʃər]
®19127/86800

n. 어림짐작
❶ con(함께) + jecture(던지기): 생각을 남과 함께 던지기 - 어림짐작
㊀ guessing, speculation
ⓔ There's been a lot of conjecture in the papers recently about the royal marriage.

✔ connect
[kənékt]
®8610/86800

v. 연결하다
❶ 줄이 짧자 줄을 **꺼내(connect) 연결하다**
㊀ join, unite
㊁ detach, separate
ⓟ *connectedness*: 연락 *connection*: 연결, 관계
ⓔ A hallway connects the two rooms.

---

connotation
[kὰnoutéiʃən]
®27959/86800

n. 함축
❶ 속에 숨겨놓지말고(**함축**) **까놓으션(connotation)**
㊀ implication ㊁ denotation: 외연
ⓔ The word "childlike" has connotations of innocence.

✔ conquer
[kάŋkər]
®16649/86800

v. 정복하다
❶ 정복자들은 간(이) **커(conquer)**
㊀ defeat, vanquish, overpower ㊁ surrender, yield
ⓟ conquest: 정복, 승리
ⓔ The city was conquered by the ancient Romans.

conscience
[kánʃəns]
® 5738/86800

n. 양심
❶ 함께(con) 아는 것(science): 누구나 있는 양심
㉦ scruples
㉣ *conscious*: 의식있는, 양심의
consciously: 의식적으로(intentionally, purposely)
consciousness: 자각, 의식
㉡ You didn't do anything wrong - you should have a clear conscience(= not feel guilty).

consensus
[kənsénsəs]
® 4622/86800

n. 일치, 합의
❶ 함께하는(con) 감각(sensus): 같은 생각 - 일치
㉦ accord, concordance
㉡ The decision was made by consensus.

consent
[kənsént]
® 2766/86800

v. 동의하다, 승낙하다
❶ 함께(con) 보내다(sent): 같은 마음으로 보내다, 동의하다
㉦ agree, assent, permit, approve
㉡ We asked her permission, and she consented.

consequence
[kánsikwèns]
® 2854/86800

n. 결과, 중요성
❶ 건강검진 결과 **간 시꺼먼스(consequence), 결과**적으로 간이 안좋음
㉦ result, effect, outcome
㉣ *consequently*: 따라서, 결과적으로
㉡ The accident was the consequence of reckless driving.

conservation
[kànsə:rvéiʃən]
® 2538/86800

n. 보존
❶ **건설 보전conservation)**, 건설한 것은 보존, 유지가 잘돼야
㉦ preservation
㉣ conservative: 보수적인
conserve: 보존하다, 유지하다(retain)
㉡ the conservation of the environment.

C

❤ consider
[kənsídər]
ⓡ 849/86800

v. 생각하다
❶ 근사하다(consider)고 생각하다
ⓢ look upon, regard, reflect on, see, think of, deem
ⓟ *considerable*: 고려할 만한, 상당한, 중요한(substantial, significant, great) *considerably*: 적지 않게,
consideration: 고려 *considerate*: 동정심 있는, 사려 깊은
ⓔ He considered the cost before buying the new car.

❤ consist
[kənsíst]
ⓡ 6132/86800

v. 구성하다
❶ 함께(con) 서(sist) 있다: 구성하다
ⓢ constitute
ⓟ consistent: 언행이 시종일관된, 일치하는
consistency: 일관성
ⓔ This cake consists mainly of sugar, flour, and butter.

console
[kənsóul]
ⓡ 13410/80000

v. 위로하다
❶ 서로(con) + 솔로(sole)라고 **위로하다**
ⓢ comfort, solace
ⓔ Only his children could console him when his wife died.

consonant
[kánsənənt]
ⓡ 16639/86800

adj. 일치한
❶ 함께(con) + 소리(son) + ant - 함께 소리난: 일치한
ⓢ agreeable, in accord, consistent
ⓔ behavior consonant with his character.

conspicuous
[kənspíkjuəs]
ⓡ 8562/86800

adj. 현저한, 뚜렷이 보이는
❶ 큰(con) 스피커였어(spicuous) 그래서 **뚜렷한**
ⓢ evident, noticeable, obvious
ⓔ In China, her blonde hair was conspicuous.

conspiracy
[kənspírəsi]
ⓡ 6609/86800

n. 공모, 모의
❶ 함께(con) 스피릿이(spiracy - 정신이) 필요한 공모
ⓢ plot, scheme
ⓟ conspire: 공모하다, 음모를 꾀하다
ⓔ I think there was a conspiracy to keep me out of the committee.

constant
[kánstənt]
® 1974/86800

adj. 변치 않는, 끊임없는
❶ 끈(con) 이 (계속) 서있는(stant): 변치 않는
⊕ continual
⊗ variable
㈜ *constantly*: 변함없이
c.f) *continuous*: 끊임없는(unbroken)
　　continuously(without interruption): 잇따라
　　continue: 계속하다
　　continual: 잇따른
　　continually: 계속적으로
㈜ All conditions during the three experiments were constant.

constitute
[kánstətjù:t]
® 5031/86800

v. 구성하다
❶ con(함께) + stitute(서있다): 함께 구성되어 있음
㈜ Eleven members constitute our society.

constrain
[kənstréin]
® 21103/86800

v. 제한하다, 억압하다
❶ 큰 스트레스(constrain) 받게 억압하다
⊕ inhibit, restrict
㈜ The country's progress was constrained by a leader who refused to look forward.

constrict
[kənstríkt]
® 57550/86800

v. 수축시키다, 억제하다
❶ 큰(con) 엄격한(strict): 크게 엄격하게 억제하다
⊕ contract, restrict
㈜ The drug causes the blood vessels to constrict.

construct
[kənstrʌ́kt]
® 5584/86800

v. 건설하다
❶ 건설트럭이라고 발음하면 건설회사 트럭은 건설하기 위한 차
⊕ build, erect, devise ⊗ destroy
㈜ *constructive*: 건설적인, 구조상의
　　construction: 건설
㈜ They plan to construct a barn behind the house.

construe
[kənstrú:]
® 27847/86800

v. 번역하다, 해석하다
❶ 어려운 말은 까서(cons) + 들어(true), 어려운 말을 **해석하라**
⊕ interpret
예 Any change in plan would be construed as indecision.

✔ **consult**
[kənsʌ́lt]
® 6260/86800

v. 상의하다
❶ 요즘 간판 보면 컨설팅(consulting)이라는 간판이 많은데 전부 **상담해준다는** 뜻
⊕ counsel, discuss
파 *consultant*: 의논상대
예 Consult your lawyer before signing the contract.

✔ **consume**
[kənsú:m]
® 11004/86800

v. 소비하다
❶ 돈 쓰고 나서 **큰 한숨(consume)**쉬다
⊕ spend, expend, use up
파 *consumption*: 소비(use) *consumer*: 소비자
예 The new lights consume less electricity.

consummate
[kənsʌ́mət]
® 26059/86800

adj. 더 없는, 뛰어난, 완전한
❶ consummate(큰 - 뛰어난 삶 이었데)
⊕ 완전한(superb, complete)
예 He's a consummate athlete.

✔ **contact**
[kántækt]
® 987/86800

n. v. 접촉, 연락하다
❶ 큰 댁(contact)에 **연락**하다
⊕ communication, touch, connection
예 For more information, contact the city's tourism office.

contagious
[kəntéidʒəs]
® 21759/86800

adj. 전염성의
❶ 전염병 옮기는 큰 돼지였어(contagious)
⊕ communicable(전달할 수 있는 의 뜻도 있음)
예 It's a highly contagious virus.

contain
[kəntéin]
[R] 2232/86800

v. **포함하다**
[T] **컨테이너(container)**를 생각하면 여러 물건들을 포함하고 담는 것
[유] include, hold
[파] *container*: 그릇, 컨테이너
[예] This glass contains water.

contaminate
[kəntǽmənèit]
[R] 36425/86800

v. **더럽히다, 오염시키다**
[T] **큰 댐이(contami) 나 때(nate)**문에 오염되다
[유] infect
[예] Be careful not to allow bacteria to contaminate the wound.

contemplate
[kántəmplèit]
[R] 10049/86800

v. **숙고하다**
[T] con(함께) + temple(절)에 가서 생각하다. 숙고하다
[유] consider
[예] He contemplated the meaning of the poem for a long time.

contemporary
[kəntémpərèri]
[R] 2216/86800

adj. n. **현대의, 당대의, 동시대의 사람**
[T] 함께(con) + 시간(tempo) + ary(형용사 어미) 당대의
[유] current, modern
[예] A magazine devoted to contemporary fashions.

contempt
[kəntémpt]
[R] 6040/86800

n. **경멸**
[T] **갓뎀(contempt** - goddamn - 욕)하면서 경멸하다
[유] ridicule, scorn
[반] admiration respect
[예] He feels that wealthy people view him with contempt because he is poor.

content
[kántent]
[R] 1678/86800

n. **내용물, 속**
[T] 함께(con) 친 텐트(tent) - 속
[유] substance [파] contentment: 만족, 안심
[예] The contents of his bag spilled all over the floor.

✔ contention
[kənténʃən]
® 9129/86800

n. 논쟁
❶ con (큰) + tention(발음 비슷하므로 tension의 긴장으로 보면) - 큰 긴장은 논쟁
㊀ controversy, debate, conflict
㉠ *contend*: 다투다, 주장하다
㉡ The matter has been settled - it's no longer in contention.

✿ contest
[kántest]
® 4834/86800

n. 시합
❶ 함께(con) + 테스트(test): 시합
㊀ competition ㉠ contestant: 경쟁자
㉡ She's won a lot of beauty contests.

✿ context
[kántekst]
® 1209/86800

n. 문맥, 배경
❶ 함께(con) + 글(text): 함께 글을 보면 문맥
㊀ setting
㉡ This small battle is very important in the context of Scottish history.

contiguous
[kəntígjuəs]
® 17058/86800

adj. 인접하는
❶ 옛날에는 함께(con) + 대구(tiguous) 였어: 옛날에는 대구 소속이어서 대구에 인접 해 있었다는 말
㊀ adjoining
㉡ Connecticut and Massachusetts are contiguous states.

✿ continent
[kántənənt]
® 5170/86800

n. 대륙
❶ 함께(con) 있다가 떼어논(tinent): 대륙
㉡ Europe and Asia are sometimes considered together to be one continent.

✔ contract
[kántrækt]
® 833/86800

n. v. 계약, 계약하다, 오그라들다
❶ 야구 선수들 함께(con) + 뛰라고(tract): 계약
㊀ expand ㉠ *contractor*: 계약자
㉡ The contract requires him to finish work by the end of the year.

contradict
[kàntrədík]
ⓡ 16278/86800

v. 반박하다
❶ contra(반대) + dic(말): 반대되는 말하다
⊛ dispute, oppose 파 *contrary*: 반대의(in confliction with)
예 How dare you contradict (me)?

contrast
[kántræst]
ⓡ 1574/86800

n. 대조
❶ 반대로(contra) + 섰다(st)는 대조
⊛ comparison, distinction
예 I observed an interesting contrast in the teaching styles of the two women.

contribute
[kəntríbju:t]
ⓡ 3465/86800

v. 기부하다, 공헌하다
❶ 우린 돈도 없는데 **기부**를 하다니 **간들이 부었데?(contribute)**
예 He contributed a large money to a fund.

contrive
[kəntráiv]
ⓡ 32539/86800

v. 고안하다
❶ **큰 드라이버(contrive)를 고안하다**
⊛ devise, invent, come up with
예 The prisoners contrived a way to escape.

controversy
[kántrəvə̀:rsi]
ⓡ 4413/86800

n. 논쟁
❶ contro(반대) + verse(말, 시, 운문): 논쟁
⊛ argument, quarrel
예 The new movie is a subject of controversy.

convenience
[kənví:njəns]
ⓡ 7534/86800

n. 편리
❶ 함께(con) + 편의(veni) + ence: 편리한
⊛ expedience, ease 파 *convenient*: 편리한
예 An elevator was available for the shoppers' convenience.

convention
[kənvénʃən]
ⓡ 2820/86800

n. 정치, 종교 집회, 관례
❶ **컨벤션(convention) 센터**
⊛ tradition 파 *conventional*: 전통적인, 형식적인
예 Where are they holding their party convention?

C

converse
[kənvə́:rs]
🅡 16480/86800

v. adj. 대화하다, 거꾸로의
❶ 함께(con) + verse(시, 운문, 말): 함께 말하다
㊋ chat, discuss 파 *conversation*: 대화
예 She's so shy that conversing with her can be quite difficult.
One must also consider the converse case.

convert
[kənvə́:rt]
🅡 6126/86800

v. 바꾸다, 개종시키다
❶ 함께(con) + 바꾸다(vert): 개종시키다
㊋ change, transform, alter
예 He converted to(= started believing in) Catholicism when he got married.

convey
[kənvéi]
🅡 6411/86800

v. 나르다, 수송하다
❶ 끈 베어(convey) 묶어서 **운반하다**
㊋ carry, transport
예 The goods are usually conveyed by sea.

convict
[kənvíkt]
🅡 17246/86800

n. v. 죄인, 유죄를 입증하다
❶ 큰 빚(convict) 진 **죄인**
㊋ criminal, prisoner ㊌ acquit
예 an escaped convict.
He has twice been convicted of robbery.

convince
[kənvíns]
🅡 6112/86800

v. 납득시키다, 확신시키다
❶ 철없는 아들이 비싼 옷을 사 달라하자 **큰 빚있어(convince)**하며 **납득시키다**
㊋ persuade
파 convincingly: 설득력 있게 (believably)conviction: 신념, 확신
예 They convinced us of their innocence.

cooperate
[kouápərèit]
🅡 14958/86800

v. 협동하다
❶ 함께(co) + 운영하다(operate): 협동하다
㊋ collaborate
파 *cooperation*: 협동
예 It will be much easier if everyone cooperates.

✔ cope
[koup]
® 2414/86800

v. n. 대처하다, 성직자가 입는 망토
❶ 코피(cope)에 대처하다
㉦ deal with
㉫ It must be difficult to cope with three small children and a job.

✔ copper
[kápər]
® 4502/86800

n. 구리
❶ 동(구리) 값퍼(copper)!
㉫ This is a container made of copper.

cordial
[kɔ́:rdʒəl]
® 26755/86800

adj. n. 마음에서 우러난, 강장제
❶ cord(마음) + ial(형용사 어미): 마음의
㉦ warm, friendly
㉫ We received a cordial greeting from our hostess at the party.

core
[kɔ:r]
® 2884/86800

n. 속, 핵심
❶ 얼굴은 코에(core)핵심이 있음
㉦ center, nucleus
㉫ The basic lack of government funding is at the core of the problem.

corporate
[kɔ́:rpərit]
® 2206/86800

adj. 단결한, 단체의, 법인의
❶ www.co.kr에서 co가 corporation(회사, 조직)
㉦ corporative
㉫ All adults take corporate responsibility for the upbringing of the tribe's children.

corps
[kɔ;rz]
® 6269/86800

n. 군단, 부대
❶ 훈련에 배가 고파서(corps) 힘든 해병대
㉫ the U.S. Marine Corps.

C

corpse
[kɔ:rps]
[R] 8040/86800

n. **시체**
[T] **골 파서(corpse)죽은 시체**
[유] cadaver, carcass
[예] We can't forget a battlefield strewn with corpses.

✔✔ **correct**
[kərékt]
[R] 1508/86800

adj. v. **바른, 정정하다**
[T] 함께(cor) + 바르게(rect) 하다
[유] faithful: 바른, reform: 정정하다
[파] *correctly*: 바르게
[예] The native guide corrected our pronunciation.

✔ **correlation**
[kɔ̀:rəléiʃən]
[R] 5671/86800

n. **상호관계**
[T] **cor(함께) + relation(관계):** 서로 간의 관계
[예] There's a high correlation between smoking and lung cancer.

✔ **correspond**
[kɔ̀:rəspάnd]
[R] 8549/86800

v. **일치하다, 응답하다**
[T] 함께(cor) 반응하다(respond): 응답하다
[유] agree, coincide
[파] correspondent: 상대방, 서신왕래자, 통신원
corresponding: 상당하는
correspondence: 일치(agreement), 통신, 편지왕래
correspondingly: 유사하게
[예] His actions do not correspond with his words.

cosmos
[kάzməs]
[R] 17804/86800

n. **우주, 질서, 조화, 코스모스**
[T] **우주**여행 **가자멋있어(cosmos)**
[유] galaxy, space: 우주
[예] the origins of the cosmos.

✔✔ **cost**
[kɔ:st]
[R] 452/86800

n. v. **가격, 비용이 들다**
[T] **코세웠다(cost)** 는데 **가격**이 얼마?
[유] expense, price
[파] *costly*: 비용이 많이 드는(expensive)
[예] That camera cost $200.

costume
[kástju:m]
ⓟ 9295/86800

n. 복장
ⓣ **가서 춤(costume) 복장**으로 갈아입어
ⓢ apparel, garment
예 The children were dressed in halloween costumes.

✔ cottage
[kátidʒ]
ⓟ 3029/86800

n. 시골집, 오두막
ⓣ 방학에 **시골집**에 **갔댔지(cottage)**
ⓢ cabin, lodge
예 We rented a cottage for the weekend.

✔ cotton
[kátn]
ⓟ 3711/86800

n. 면
ⓣ 너와 난 **같은(cotton)면**이 많아
예 This shirt is made up of cotton.

couch
[kautʃ]
ⓟ 10940/86800

n. v. 긴 의자, 눕히다, 표현하다
ⓣ 철자가 다르긴 하지만, coach가 couch(긴 의자)에 선수들을 앉히고 작전하다
ⓢ sofa: 긴 의자
예 Find yourself a place on the couch and make yourself at home.

council
[káunsəl]
ⓟ 275/86800

n. 의회
ⓣ 의원들이 **카운슐(counsel - 상담)받는방(cil - 실)**
ⓢ Assembly
파 *counsel*: 협의, 충고하다, 상담하다(advise) *counseling*: 상담
예 The city council is considering a ban on smoking in restaurants.

counteract
[kàuntərǽkt]
ⓟ 16493/86800

v. 거스르다
ⓣ **counter(반대) + act(행동하다)**
ⓢ negate
ⓐ reinforce
예 The drug will counteract the poison.

C

counterattack
[kàuntərətǽk]
ⓡ 60700/86800

n. **역습, 반격**
ⓣ 반대(counter) + 공격(attack): 역습
예 The Republicans have launched a strong counterattack against the Democrats' manifesto.

counterfeit
[káuntərfit]
ⓡ 24378/86800

adj. n. v. **가짜의, 위조품, 위조하다**
ⓣ counterfight인데 counterfeit은 가짜라고 생각
⊕ bogus, imitation, falsify
⊖ original, real, genuine
예 This watch may be a counterfeit, but it looks just like the original.

counterpart
[káuntərpà:rt]
ⓡ 8508/86800

n. **사본, 짝, 동등한 것**
ⓣ 반대되는(counter) + 부분(part): 복사를 하면 반대 부분은 사본이 됨
⊕ equivalent
예 I met the lead actress and her male counterpart.

✤ countless
[káuntlis]
ⓡ 9585/86800

adj. **무수한**
ⓣ count(세다) + less(없는): 셀 수 없는
⊕ innumerable, many
파 *count*: 세다 *counter*: 계산대
예 I've heard it played countless times on the radio.

county
[káunti]
ⓡ 888/86800

n. **군(행정구역)**
ⓣ 미국 LA의 오렌지 county, 내가 살던 곳은 뉴욕 버팔로의 Erie county
예 Texas is divided into 254 counties.

✔ courteous
[kə́:rtiəs]
ⓡ 16656/86800

adj. **정중한**
ⓣ 왕이 사는 **코트(궁전)여서(courteous)** 정중한
⊕ polite, respectful, well - mannered
파 *courtesy*: 예의바름
예 Although she often disagreed with me, she was always courteous.

covet
[kʌ́vit]
ℝ 44950/86800

v. 탐내다, 갈망하다
ⓣ **카 빛**(covet - 차가 빛)나는 것을 **탐내다**
ⓢ desire
㉠ She always coveted power but never quite achieved it.

coward
[káuərd]
ℝ 14474/86800

n. adj. 겁쟁이, 겁 많은
ⓣ **카우(소)와**(coward) 같이 **겁 많은**
ⓢ poltroon ⓐ hero ㉠ cowardly: 비겁한
㉠ He is anything but a coward.

✔ coworker
[kóuwə̀:rkər]
ℝ 순위외/86800

n. 동료
ⓣ 함께(co) + 일하는(work) + 사람(er)
ⓢ fellow worker, colleague
㉠ My coworker and I went on a business trip.

cozy
[kóuzi]
ℝ 57308/86800

adj. 편안한
ⓣ 티코(Tico)는 Tiny + Cozy를 줄인 말, 작고 편하다는 말
ⓢ comfortable
㉠ The room was warm and cozy.

crack
[kræk]
ℝ 4659/86800

n. v. 금, 흠, 일격, 틈, 부서지다
ⓣ **크랙커**(crack) 먹으면 **금**이 잘 가고 부숴 짐
ⓢ cranny, crevice: 금 break, fracture: 부수다
㉠ in a crack: 순식간에
㉠ The plate cracked when I dropped it, but it was still usable.

✔ cradle
[kréidl]
ℝ 13459/86800

n. 요람
ⓣ 요람에서 **크래! 아들**(cradle)
㉠ Cradle means small bed for a baby.

✔ craft
[kræft]
ℝ 4177/86800

n. 기능, 공예, 수공업
ⓣ 스타 **크래프트**(craft) 잘하는 것도 기능이 뛰어나야
ⓢ skill ㉠ craftsman: 숙련공
㉠ The silversmith worked with great craft.

C

cram
[kræm]
[R] 23799/86800

n. v. **혼잡, 무리하게 다져넣다, 벼락공부**
[T] 크라이(cr) + 이그잼(am) - **벼락공부** 후회하며 울면서 시험 봄 - 벼락 공부하느라
[유] crowd, jam, compress: 무리하게 다져넣다
[예] He crammed the suitcase with his clothes.

crash
[kræʃ]
[R] 3630/86800

n. v. **파멸, 추락, 소리를 내며 무너지다**
[T] **그래 씨(crash)!** 욕 하면 **파멸**하다
[유] wreck
[예] The walls crashed down around them.

craving
[kréiviŋ]
[R] 21998/86800

n. **열망**
[T] **걸려 이병(craving)** 낫고자 하는 **열망**
[예] I have a Craving for a tobacco.

crawl
[krɔ:l]
[R] 12353/86800

v. **기다**
[T] 단어를 천천히 읽으면 **크어월(기어와 crawl)**
[유] creep
[예] Does the baby crawl yet?

creature
[krí:tʃər]
[R] 4531/86800

n. **창조물, 인간**
[T] 신이 **인간**을 만들고 **그렸죠(creature)**
[파] *create*: 만들다(bring about, produce),
creative: 창조적인(inventive, original)
creatively: 창조적으로 *creation*: 창조(물)
[예] She is a charming creature.

credible
[krédəbəl]
[R] 12102/86800

adj. **신뢰할 수 있는**
[T] **그래도 볼(credible) 신뢰할 수 있는** 사람
[유] believable, reliable
[예] We've received credible information about the group's location.

credit
[krédit]
Ⓡ 1396/86800

n. v. 신용, 학점, 신뢰하다,~에게 공을 돌리다
❶ 크레디트 카드, 미국에서는 수업시간에 잘 하면 extra credit(보너스 점수)을 준다
㉙ creditable: 명예가 되는, 훌륭한
㉞ He's already got three credits in earth science.

creditor
[kréditər]
Ⓡ 8365/86800

n. 채권자
❶ 신뢰해주는 사람(creditor) - 크레디트 카드
㉯ debtor
㉞ The company couldn't pay its creditors.

creed
[kri:d]
Ⓡ 8336/86800

n. 신조, 주의
❶ 그리도(creed)믿고 있는 신조
㉔ belief: 주의
㉞ The Amish live by a strict creed that rejects many of the values and practices of modern society.

creek
[kri:k]
Ⓡ 15014/86800

n. 개울
❶ 발음을 이용하여 크릭(creek) 캐우릭(개울익)
㉔ stream
㉞ The children waded in the creek.

creep
[kri:p]
Ⓡ 10524/86800

v. 기다
❶ 기어립(creep) - 기다
㉞ Old age crept upon her.

crest
[krest]
Ⓡ 10289/86800

n. 정상
❶ 그래(cre) 정상에 섰다(st)
㉔ peak, summit
㉞ The wolf came from the crest of a hill.

crevice
[krévis]
Ⓡ 38187/86800

n. 갈라진 틈
❶ 히말라야 등반 때 크레비스(crevice - 틈)
㉔ split
㉞ Steam escaped from a long crevice in the volcano.

cricket
[kríkit]
® 2933/86800

n. 귀뚜라미, 운동이름
❶ 얘는 가을이 되면 **그렇게**(cricket) 또 우나보다
㈀ Cricket is my favourite sport.

criminal
[krímənl]
® 1994/86800

adj. n. 범죄의, 범인
❶ 야한 **그림이 널**(criminal) **범죄**로 몰았구나
㈜ illegal, unlawful ㈘ *crime*: 범죄
㈀ The way we waste this planet's resources is criminal.

cripple
[krípəl]
® 22289/86800

n. 절름발이
❶ 크립(clip - 자른) 발(ple) - 절름발이
㈀ He returned from war a cripple.

crisis
[kráisis]
® 1743/86800

n. 위기
❶ 큰 위 싯어(crisis) 건강의 **위기** 넘김
㈜ disaster, emergency
㈀ In times of national crisis, we need strong leaders we can trust.

criterion
[kraitíəriən]
® 5885/86800

n. 기준
❶ **표준**된 사람 소망하면 **그리되어리언**(criterion)
㈀ What is the criterion of moral judgement?

critic
[krítik]
® 6446/86800

n. 비판자
❶ 그리(cri) 하면 안 된다고 **틱**(tic)틱 거림
㈜ faultfinder
㈘ *critical*: 비판적인, 중요한 *criticism*: 비판 *criticize*: 비판하다
㈀ The play has been well received by the critics.

crocodile
[krákədàil]
® 17042/86800

n. 악어
❶ 커라 크다 입(crocodile) - 악어
㈀ The young girl usually drowned or was eaten by crocodiles.

crook
[kruk]
® 13397/86800

n. v. 갈고리, 굽은 것, 구부리다, 훔치다
❶ 굽어꾸(crook) - 갈고리는 굽었구
㋐ bend, curve
㋐ You should repair the crook of an umbrella handle.

crop
[krɑp]
® 4937/86800

v. 자르다
❶ 칼롭(crop) 자르다
㋐ cut
㋐ He had his hair cropped when he went into the army.

crouch
[krautʃ]
® 19161/86800

v. 몸을 구부리다
❶ 육상의 crouching 스타드 - 몸을 구부리는 스타트
㋐ I saw her coming and crouched behind a bush.

crow
[krou]
® 14425/86800

n. v. 까마귀, 까마귀가 울다
❶ 끄록 - 까옥(crow)
㋐ His face is as black as crow.

crow
[krou]
® 14425/86800

n. v. 수탉의 우는 소리, 수탉이 울다, 까마귀
❶ 꺼 쿠로(crow), 암닭은 꼬끼오, 수탉은 거꾸로
㋐ We were woken at dawn by a cock crowing repeatedly.

crowd
[kraud]
® 2287/86800

n. v. 군중, 떼 지어 모이다
❶ 구름(cloud와 발음 비슷)처럼 모여드는 군중
㋐ mass, mob
㋐ crowded: 붐비는
㋐ A crowd of about 15,000 attended the concert.

crucial
[krúːʃəl]
® 2259/86800

adj. 중요한
❶ 십자가(cru - cross와 같은 어원) + cial(형용사형 어미): 기독교인에게 십자가가 얼마나 중요한가?
㋐ important, essential
㋐ Her work has been crucial to the project's success.

✔ crude
[kru:d]
⑧ 5704/86800

adj. 조잡한, 천연그대로의
❶ 그대로데(crude): 천연 그대로의
㉮ 조잡한(roughly made),
천연그대로의(unprocessed, simple, primitive)
㉖ They built a crude shelter out of branches.

cruel
[krú:əl]
⑧ 5655/86800

adj. 잔인한
❶ 혁대를 끌러(cruel) 때림 - **잔인한**
㉮ brutal, inhuman
㉖ Don't tease him about his weight - it's cruel.

✔ crunchy
[krʌ́ntʃi]
⑧ 29791/86800

a. 으드득 깨무는 소리를 내는
❶ 과자가 **크런치(crunchy)**한
㉖ I was crunching cookies.

✔ crush
[krʌʃ]
⑧ 11260/86800

v. n. 부수다, 쑤셔 넣다, 분쇄, 반함
❶ 글루(cru - 그 쪽으루) **쑤시(sh)**다: 그쪽으로 쑤시다, 자꾸 쑤시다 보면 분쇄됨
㉮ break, smash
㉖ The package had been badly crushed in the post.

crust
[krʌst]
⑧ 9393/86800

n. 껍질, 외피
❶ 껍질을 끌렀었다(crust - 벗겼었다)
㉮ hull, shell
㉖ I don't like the crust on my sandwich.

✔ crutch
[krʌtʃ]
⑧ 26990/86800

n. 목발, 버팀
❶ 목발을 짚는 물리치료 환자에게 응원하는 소리 **그렇치!(crutch)**
㉖ I went to school on crutches.

✔ cue
[kju:]
⑧ 11952/86800

n. 단서, 연기 신호
❶ 일상생활에서 연기신호로 **cue(큐)**! 하는 소리
㉖ He gave his cue to the actors.

125

cuisine
[kwizí:n]
® 12292/86800

n. 요리법, 요리
❶ 요리하다 깨진(cuisine)그릇
예 Do you know Korean cuisine.

cultivate
[kʌ́ltəvèit]
® 15942/86800

v. 경작하다, 재배하다
❶ cul(칼) + ti(터) + vate(베엤데): 칼로 농사터 베어
㊐ farm, grow, raise
ᆵ cultivator: 경작자(farmer), *cultivation*: 경작
예 They survived by cultivating vegetables and grain.

cumbersome
[kʌ́mbərsəm]
® 15701/86800

adj. 귀찮은, 성가신
❶ 늙으면 검버섯(cumbersome) 귀찮은
㊐ burdensome
예 The application process is cumbersome and time -
  consuming.

cuneiform
[kjú:ni:əfɔ́:rm]
® 71746/86800

n. 쐐기 문자
❶ (문자가 없으니) 쐐기 문자 꾸니 폼(cuneiform) - 쐐기문자의 형
  태를 꾼다
예 The state borrowed cuneiform character.

cunning
[kʌ́niŋ]
® 11685/86800

adj. v. 교활한, 교활함
❶ 시험 시간에 교활한 커닝(cunning) 꾼
㊐ crafty, wily
예 She was cunning enough to fool me.

cupboard
[kʌ́bərd]
® 5514/86800

n. 찬장
❶ 컵오르다(cupboard) 컵이 오르내리는 곳은 찬장
예 This house has built - in cupboard.

curb
[kə:rb]
® 10554/86800

n. v. 고삐, 구속, 억제하다
❶ 날 억제하는 칼 봐(curb)!
㊐ 억제하다: control
예 The Government should act to curb tax evasion.

cure
[kjuər]
[R] 5328/86800

v. **치료하다**
[T] **귀에(cure)치료하다**
[유] heal, remedy
[예] The infection can be cured with antibiotics.

curing
[kjuəriŋ]
[R] 26963/86800

n. **치료하기, 양생(건축), 말리기(식품), 굳히기**
[T] 치료하다의 cure에서 나온 말로 건축물을 보호하거나 식품을 말리는데 쓰인다. **구하링(curing)**
[예] The term curing is used for architecture as well.

curiosity
[kjùəriάsəti]
[R] 6449/86800

n. **호기심**
[T] **호기심**이 있어서 귀를 **기울였었지(curiosity)**
[유] inquisitiveness, interest
[파] *curious*: 호기심 있는
[예] Her natural curiosity led her to ask more questions.

curl
[kə:rl]
[R] 12051/86800

v. **말다, 구불구불하다**
[T] 미용실에서 **컬(curl)**이 잘 나왔다는 말은 **곱실곱실하게 되었다**는 뜻
[유] coil, wave
[예] She curls her hair every morning.

current
[kə́:rənt]
[R] 694/86800

adj. n. **통용하는, 현재의, 조류**
[T] 굴러(cur - 어원편 참조) 다니는: **통용되는**
[유] 조류: flow of water
[파] *currency*: 유통, 통화(money) *curriculum*: 교육 과정
currently: 널리, 현재
[예] The dictionary's current edition has 10,000 new words.

curse
[kə:rs]
[R] 10927/86800

n. v. **저주, 저주하다**
[T] **가서(curse)** 죽으라고 **저주하다**
[반] bless
[예] People believe that someone put a curse on the house.

custom
[kʌ́stəm]
ⓡ 5401/86800

n. 관습
❶ **커서 또 함 (custom)** - 또 하는 것은 **관습**
ⓢ habit
㊟ customary: 습관적인, 보통의(usual, typical)
㊐ It is the custom for the bride to wear a white dress on her wedding day.

customer
[kʌ́stəmər]
ⓡ 2170/86800

n. 고객
❶ **가서 또 뭘(customer)** 사려고 하는 **손님**
ⓢ visitor
㊐ She is one of our best customers.

cute
[kju:t]
ⓡ 15489/86800

adj. 귀여운
❶ **귀엿(cute)** - 귀여운
ⓢ adorable, pretty
㊐ He's got a really cute baby.

damp
[dæmp]
ⓡ 4323/86800

adj. n. v. 축축한, 습기, 축축하게 하다
❶ **댐(dam)을 퍼(p)**내면 **축축한** 습기가 있음
ⓢ wet, humid
㊐ The grass is still damp.

dare
[dɛər]
ⓡ 4064/86800

v. 감히 ~하다
❶ 감히 어디다 갖다 **데어(dare)**?
㊟ *daring*: 대담(한)
㊐ Dare you tell him the news?

dawn
[dɔ:n]
ⓡ 3712/86800

n. 새벽
❶ 먼 **돈(dawn - 먼동)**이 트기 전
ⓢ twilight
㊐ We woke at dawn.

D

daydream
[déidrì:m]
ⓡ 39089/86800

v. n. **공상(에 잠기다), 백일몽**
❶ 낮에 꿈을 꾸지 않으므로 꾸면 daydream은 공상
ⓨ fantasy
例 I was just enjoying a daydream about winning the Nobel Prize for literature.

✔ deadly
[dédli]
ⓡ 8007/86800

adj. **치명적인**
❶ 죽을 정도면(dead) 치명적인
ⓨ fatal, lethal 파 *dead*: 죽은
例 Why did you have a deadly weapon?

✔ deaf
[def]
ⓡ 3478/86800

adj. **귀가 먼**
❶ 귀가 먹으면 뎁뎁(deaf - 답답) 함
例 He's been totally deaf since birth.

✔ deal
[di:l]
ⓡ 684/86800

n. v. **거래, 취급, 다루다, 처리하다, 거래(하다)**
❶ big deal(큰 거래)이라는 말을 생각
ⓨ bargain, contract c.f) *dealer*: 상인
例 She got a good deal on her new house.

✔ debate
[dibéit]
ⓡ 1401/86800

n. **논쟁(하다)**
❶ 어느 것이 길고 짧은 지 **대봤데(debate) - 논쟁**
ⓨ contention, controversy
例 Education is the current focus of public debate.

✔ debt
[det]
ⓡ 1885/86800

n. **빚, 부채**
❶ 대부다(debt)=빚
ⓨ liabilities ⓐ assets 파 debtor: 채무자
例 He managed to pay off his debts in two years.

✔ decade
[dékeid]
ⓡ 2650/86800

n. **10년, 10**
❶ dec은 10이라는 뜻. December, Deci liter에서 Deci 등도 마찬가지로 10의 뜻
파 decimal: 십진법의
例 It is fun to be in the same decade with you.
- Franklin D. Roosevelt

decaf
[diːkǽf]
® 순위외/86800

v. 카페인을 없앤
❶ de(부정의 뜻) + caf(카페인)
예 Let me have decaf coffee.

decay
[dikéi]
® 6884/86800

v. n. 썩다, 부패, 쇠퇴(하다)
❶ 감자 뒤(de)가 까이다(cay) - 뒷부분 **썩다**
㊐ decompose
예 Sugar makes your teeth decay.

deceive
[disíːv]
® 17474/86800

v. 속이다, 기만하다
❶ 뒤로 세봐(deceive), 부정한 돈을 몰래 뒤로 세는 것 생각해보세요—**속이다**
㊐ cheat, defraud ㊙ deceit: 속이다 deception: 속임수
예 The company deceived customers by selling old computers as new ones.

decent
[díːsənt]
® 4563/86800

adj. 점잖은, 품위 있는, 단정한, 훌륭한, 알맞은
❶ 신사가 **뒤에선(decent)** 모습이 **점잖은**
㊐ courteous, polite
예 I thought he was a decent sort of person.

decisive
[disáisiv]
® 6154/86800

adj. 결정적인
❶ D싸이즈(decide)로 **결정할** 정도의
㊐ conclusive, definitive
㊙ decisively: 결정적으로 *decide*: 결정하다 *decision*: 결정 *decided*: 결정적인
예 The fight ended with a decisive blow.

declare
[diklέər]
® 7357/86800

v. 선언하다, (세관에) 신고하다
❶ 뒷 거래 여?(declare)하고 묻자 그런 거 안 한다고 세관에 **신고하다**
㊐ proclaim, pronounce ㊙ declaration: 선언
예 America declared war on Japan in 1941.

D

decline
[dikláin]
ⓡ 2150/86800

v. 아래로 기울다, 쇠퇴하다, 거절하다
❶ 아래로(de) + 기울다(Cline)
㊋ decrease: 감소(하다) refuse, reject: 거절하다
㉔ His interest in the project declined after his wife died.

decorate
[dékərèit]
ⓡ 13530/86800

v. 장식하다
❶ 예쁘게 장식하니 **됐구려(decorate)**, 혹은 데코레이션(decoration) 케익 생각
㊋ adorn, garnish, ornament
㉔ They decorated the wedding car with ribbons and flowers.

decree
[dikrí:]
ⓡ 7657/86800

n. v. 명령, 포고, 판결, 명령하다
❶ 뒷 글이(decree) 명령, 판결 문
㊋ mandate, order
㉔ More than 200 people were freed by military decree.

dedicate
[dédikèit]
ⓡ 28374/86800

v. 바치다, 전념하다
❶ 데디(아빠)에게 케익을(dedicate) 바치다
㊋ devote ㊅ dedication: 헌납
㉔ He has dedicated his life to scientific research.

defeat
[difí:t]
ⓡ 2711/86800

n. 패배(시키다), 타파
❶ 대 패(defeat) - 크게 패배시키다
㊋ destruction, ruin ㊀ victory, triumph
㉔ Napoleon was defeated by the Duke of Wellington at the battle of Waterloo.

defect
[difékt]
ⓡ 8542/86800

n. 결점
❶ 출세하기 위해 뒷 빽(defect)이 없는 결점
㊋ shortcoming ㊅ *defective*: 결함이 있는
㉔ There are so many defects in our education system.

defer
[difɜ́:r]
® 19203/86800

v. 연기하다
❶ de(뒤로) + fer(나르다): 뒤로 나르다, 연기하다
⊕ postpone, put off, delay
예 Can we defer making a decision until 2 p.m?

✔ deficient
[difíʃənt]
® 16797/86800

adj. 부족한
❶ 뒤 빼선(deficient - 뒷 부분을 빼서) 부족한
⊕ inadequate, lacking, insufficient
⊛ adequate, sufficient
파 *deficiency*: 부족
예 His theory is deficient in several respects.

✔ define
[difáin]
® 3715/86800

v. 정의하다
❶ de(아래 혹은 부정의 의미) + fin(끝)을 내다: 뭐라고 정의하다
⊕ clarify, explain
파 *definite*: 명확한 *definitely*: 명확하게 *definition*: 정의
예 The student a term that is difficult to define in the dictionary.

defy
[difái]
® 15167/86800

v. 도전하다, 반항하다
❶ 공부 못하는 뒷 반이(defy)앞 반에 도전하다
⊕ confront, oppose, resist
파 defiance: 도전, 저항
예 Children are openly defying their teachers.

degrade
[digréid]
® 34141/86800

v. 타락하다
❶ 아래로(de) + 성적, 등급(grade): 타락하다
⊕ debase, demean, disgrace
⊛ dignify
예 He degenerated into a poor homeless.

✔ degree
[digrí:]
® 1026/86800

n. 정도, (온도·각도의) 도, 학위
❶ degree(지글이) 지글 지글 물이 끓는 온도
예 This job demands a high degree of skill.

delay
[diléi]
[R] 3004/86800

v. n. **미루다, 늦추다, 지연, 연기**
[T] **뒤로(de) + 놓다(lay):** 미루다
[유] postpone, defer, put off
[예] My plane was delayed by an hour.

delegate
[déligit, -gèit]
[R] 9960/86800

n. **대표**
[T] 국제회의에 **대표**단이 **달려갔데(delegate)**
[유] agent, representative
[예] He met the U.N. delegates from African countries.

deliberate
[dilíbərit][dilíbərèit]
[R] 5535/86800

adj. v. **신중한, 숙고하다**
[T] **대리 버려야 돼?(deliberate)신중**하게 고민 중
[유] cautious, considered, careful [파] ***deliberately***: 신중히
[예] She spoke in a clear, deliberate manner.

delicate
[délikət]
[R] 4754/86800

adj. **섬세한, 미묘한**
[T] 디자이너를 **데려갔데(delicate)** - **섬세한** 작업을 위해
[유] exquisite, fine
[예] Peaches have delicate skins which are easily bruised.

delicious
[dilíʃəs]
[R] 6549/86800

adj. **맛있는**
[T] **달았었셔(delicious):** 단 것은 **맛있는**
[유] appetizing, mouth - watering
[예] We ate a delicious cake.

delight
[diláit]
[R] 4298/86800

n. v. **기쁨, 기쁘게 하다**
[T] **뒤(de)에 + 빛을 비추다(light)**
[유] pleasure [파] ***delightful***: 매우 기쁜
[예] My sister's little boy is a real delight.

deliver
[dilívər]
[R] 4043/86800

v. **배달하다, 말하다**
[T] **배달**하려면 오토바이 타고 **달려봐(deliver)**
[유] hand, pass [파] ***delivery***: 배달, 연설
[예] The shop is delivering our new bed on Thursday.

demand
[dimǽnd]
[R] 919/86800

n. v. **요구, 요구하다, 수요**
[T] **뒤만(demand)**봐 달라고 **요구**하다
[유] requirement, requisition
[예] I demanded an explanation.

democracy
[dimάkrəsi]
[R] 2396/86800

n. **민주주의**
[T] **dem(사람들) + cracy(다스림):** 사람들이 다스리는 것이 민주주의
[예] In a democracy, every citizen should have the right to vote.

demonstrate
[démənstrèit]
[R] 3757/86800

v. **보여주다, 시위하다**
[T] **demo(데모)**한다는 말 들어봤을 텐데요 시위. 혹은 de(아래로) + monster(보여주다 - 어원편 참조)에서 기억할 수도 있을 것이다
[유] show, display
[예] The teacher demonstrated how to use the equipment.

dense
[dens]
[R] 7478/86800

adj. **빽빽한, 밀도 높은**
[T] **댄스(dense)**추기엔 클럽에 사람이 너무 **빽빽한**
[반] sparse [파] *densely*: 조밀하게 *density*: 조밀도
[예] He cut a path through the dense jungle.

deny
[dinái]
[R] 3921/86800

v. **부인하다, 거절하다**
[T] **되니(deny)**? 하고 묻자, **거절하다**
[유] refuse, forbid, reject
[반] accept
[파] denial: 부인
[예] Yes, I was there. I don't deny it.

departure
[dipά:rtʃər]
[R] 3859/86800

n. **출발**
[T] **뒷발쳐(departure) 출발하다:** 말 뒷 쪽 발을 쳐서 출발하듯이
[유] takeoff
[반] arrival
[파] *department*: 부(서) *depart*: 출발하다
[예] Our departure was delayed because of bad weather.

✔ **depict**
[dipíkt]
[R] 18293/86800

v. **그리다**
[T] de(아래에) + pict(그리다 - picture를 줄인 말)
[유] portray, represent, picture
[예] Angels are usually depicted with wings.

deplore
[diplɔ́:r]
[R] 30032/86800

v. **한탄하다**
[T] **뒷프롤(deplore** - TV프로)개탄하다
[유] grieve, lament
[반] rejoice
[예] We deplore the development of nuclear weapons.

✔ **deposit**
[dipázit]
[R] 4269/86800

v. n. **예금(하다), 보관물**
[T] de(아래에) + pos(놓다): 예치하다
[예] I deposited over $3,000 this afternoon.

✔ **depress**
[diprés]
[R] 23625/86800

v. **억압하다**
[T] do(아래로) + press(누르다), 혹은 성적 D 플러스로 성적 억압하다
[유] press, push
[파] ***depressed***: 의기소침한, 불경기의
depression: 우울
[예] These changes could depress the economy.

deprive
[dipráiv]
[R] 14426/86800

v. **빼앗다, 박탈하다**
[T] de(뒤로) + pri(**프라이드) +** ve(베): 어떤 지위를 뒤로(가지고 있던) 지위를 빼앗다, 박탈하다
[유] rob
[예] You can't function properly when you're deprived of sleep.

✔ **derive**
[diráiv]
[R] 7444/86800

v. **이끌어내다, 유래하다**
[T] de(뒤에서) + rive(일어나다): ~에서 유래하다
[유] originate, stem
[예] She derives great pleasure from playing the violin.

descend
[disénd]
® 12366/86800

v. 내려가다
❶ de(아래로) + scend(내려가다)
⑪ ascend 파 descendant: 자손 descent: 하강
예 Jane descended the stairs.

�💚 describe
[diskráib]
® 2346/86800

v. 묘사하다, 설명하다
❶ 아래에(de) + scribe(쓰다)
㊦ depict, picture, portray
파 *description*: 묘사, 설명 descriptive: 묘사적인
예 He described the painting in detail.

✅ desert
[dézərt], v.[dizə́:rt]
® 4039/86800

n. adj. 사막, 불모의, 버리다
❶ 사막에서 햇빛 쬐면 데져(desert - 불에덴다구)
㊦ barren: 불모의, abandon: 버리다
예 He was deserted by his friends and family.

✔ deserve
[dizə́:rv]
® 5939/86800

v. ~할[받을] 만하다
❶ 어디 뒤져봐(deserve)! 저사람 상 받을 만해
㊦ merit
예 After all that hard work, you deserve a holiday.

designate
[dézignèit]
® 19344/86800

v. 지명하다, 나타내다
❶ de(아래에) + sign(서명) + ate(동사, 형용사형 어미): 아래에 써서 지명하다
㊦ denote, indicate: 나타내다
예 Traditionally, the president designates his or her successor.

✅ desire
[dizáiər]
® 1869/86800

n. v. 욕구, 소망, 바라다
❶ 원하는 것 되자이어(desire)
㊦ longing, want
파 *desirable*: 바람직한
예 I desire only to be left in peace.

despair
[dispέər]
[R] 5340/86800

n. 절망(하다)
[T] **뒤에서**(또) **패어(despair)**절망하다. 앞에서 맞고
[유] desperation, hopelessness
[파] *desperate*: 절망적인, *desperately*: 필사적으로
[예] She finally gave up in despair.

D

despise
[dispáiz]
[R] 18791/86800

v. 경멸하다, 깔보다
[T] de(아래, 부정의 뜻) + spi(보다): 아래로 보다, 깔보다. spe, spi는 보다의 뜻을 가진 어원
[유] abhor, detest, hate
[예] The two groups despise each other.

despite
[dispáit]
[R] 673/86800

prep. ~에도 불구하고
[T] **뒤 스파이 도(despite)**(뒤에 스파이가) 있어도
[유] in spite of, nevertheless
[예] I still enjoyed the week despite the weather.

destiny
[déstəni]
[R] 8445/86800

n. 운명
[T] 왜 이런 **운명**이 **됐었다니(destiny)**!
[유] fate, fortune
[파] destine: 운명 짓다 *destined*: 운명 지어진
destination: 목적지
[예] You can't fight destiny.

destitute
[déstətjù:t]
[R] 25119/86800

adj. 빈곤한, 결핍된
[T] 집이 가난하게 **돼서** (열심)**뛰었데(destitute)**
[유] indigent, needy, penniless
[예] The floods left thousands of people destitute.

destruction
[distrʌ́kʃən]
[R] 3792/86800

n. 파괴, 파멸
[T] de(부정의 뜻, 아래에) + struction(섰더라) 섰다의 반대는 파괴
[유] demolition, ruin [반] construction
[파] *destructive*: 파괴적인 *destroy*: 파괴하다
[예] War results in death and widespread destruction.

✔ detach
[ditǽtʃ]
® 22906/86800

v. n. 떼어놓다, 군대, 군함을 파견하다
❶ detach(더 뗐지?): 떼다, 반의어는 attach(안 뗐지?=붙이다)
ⓔ separate ⓑ attach
ⓟ *detached*: 떨어진
ⓔ You can detach the hood if you prefer the coat without it.

✔ detail
[dí:teil]
® 1662/86800

n. 세부 사항, 상세한 설명(하다)
❶ de(더) + tail(꼬리): 더 꼬리같이 세부적인 부분을 말하다
ⓔ particulars
ⓔ They designed every detail of the house.

✔ detect
[ditékt]
® 5805/86800

v. 발견하다, 탐지하다
❶ 없어진 뒷 댁(detect - 뒷집여자)을 **발견하다**
ⓔ find
ⓟ detective: 탐정(의) *detector*: 탐지기
ⓔ Some sounds cannot be detected by the human ear.

✔ detergent
[ditə́:rdʒənt]
® 17332/86800

n. 세제
❶ 때(de) 털전(tergent) - 세제는 때를 털지요
ⓔ Detergent is a chemical substance for removing dirt from clothes.

✔ determine
[ditə́:rmin]
® 2561/86800

v. 결정하다
❶ 뒤 털 밀(determine) 겠다고 **결정하다**
ⓔ decide, conclude
ⓟ *determination*: 결심, 결단력 *determined*: 결연한
ⓔ Eye color is genetically determined.

✔ device
[diváis]
® 3275/86800

n. 장치, 고안
❶ 리바이스(청바지) 짝퉁 디바이스(device) 고안
ⓔ apparatus, gadget
ⓟ *devise*: 고안하다
ⓔ She purchased a electronic device.

devil
[dévl]
ⓡ 4802/86800

n. 악마
❶ 뒤(에서) 불(devil) 나오는 **악마**
㉛ satan, demon
㉖ He is a tricky devil, so be careful.

devoid
[divóid]
ⓡ 12810/86800

adj. ~이 결여된
❶ 100살 즈음 돼보이(devoid)는 의욕이 **결여된**
㉛ deficient, lacking
㉖ He seems to be devoid of compassion.

❖ **devote**
[divóut]
ⓡ 9995/86800

v. 바치다, 전념하다
❶ 나는 공부에 **전념할** 테니 뒤 보우(devote) - 내 뒤를 봐 달라는 말
㉛ dedicate
㉕ *devoted*: 헌신적인 *devotion*: 헌신
㉖ She devoted her life to god.

✔ **devour**
[diváuər]
ⓡ 27889/86800

v. 게걸스럽게 먹다
❶ 더! 밥을(devour)하며 게걸스레 먹다
㉖ He hungrily devoured the foods.

❖ **dew**
[dju:]
ⓡ 16333/86800

n. 이슬
❶ 이슬만 먹 듀(dew)
㉖ The grass was wet with the morning dew.

✔ **diabetes**
[dàiəbí:tis]
ⓡ 9475/86800

n. 당뇨병
❶ 당뇨병 걸리면 **다이**(die)하고 비리비리(betes)
㉖ Diabetes is a disease in which the body cannot control the level of sugar in the blood.

✔ **diagnose**
[dáiəgnòus]
ⓡ 21655/86800

v. 진단하다
❶ 의사가 **다이여 그 노우즈**(diagnose) - 그 "코는 죽는다"라고 **진단하다**
㉖ The doctor diagnosed her illness as mental disease.

dialect
[dáiəlèk]
ⓡ 11589/86800

n. 방언
❶ dia(둘, 가로질러) + lect(말): 말이 두 개 이상 여러 개, 방언, 사투리
㊦ idiom
㊐ The poem is written in northern dialect.

✔ dialog(ue)
[dáiəlɔ̀:g]
ⓡ 4842/86800

n. 대화
❶ dia(가로질러, 둘) + logue(말): 서로 오가는 말
㊐ There's very little dialogue in the film.

diameter
[daiǽmitər]
ⓡ 6017/86800

n. 지름, 직경
❶ dia(가로질러) + meter(측정한 것) - 지름
㊐ The pond is six feet in diameter.

✔ diaper
[dáipər]
ⓡ 55865/86800

n. 기저귀
❶ 애기들은 기저귀 다입어(diaper)
㊐ She changes her baby's diaper everyday.

✔ dictate
[díkteit]
ⓡ 12038/86800

v. 명령하다
❶ dic(말) + ate(동사형 어미) 하다
㊦ order, command
㊊ dictation: 받아쓰기 dictator: 독재자
c.f) *dictatorship*: 독재(권)
㊐ Tradition dictates that the youngest member should go first.

✔ diffuse
[difjú:z]
ⓡ 14406/86800

v. 퍼지게 하다, 보급하다
❶ diffuse(뒤로 퍼지게)하다
㊦ expand, disperse ㊊ *diffusion*: 보급
㊐ Television is a powerful means of diffusing knowledge.

✔ dig
[dig]
ⓡ 6674/86800

v. 파다
❶ 뒤게(di)깊게(g)파다
㊦ hollow, burrow
㊐ The dog was digging a hole to hide its bone in.

D

✔ **digest**
[didʒést, dàid-]
[R] 11680/86800

v. **소화되다**
[T] **다이제스트(digest)** - 다 이제서 트림, 소화되고
[파] ***digestion***: 소화(작용) ***digestive***: 소화의
[예] Sit still and allow your meal to digest.

dignity
[dígnəti]
[R] 5898/86800

n. **위엄, 존엄**
[T] **되(게)근(엄)있디?(dignity)**
[유] solemnity, gravity
[예] I think everyone should be able to die with dignity.

✔ **dim**
[dim]
[R] 8169/86800

adj. v. **어둑한, 희미한, 어둑해지다**
[T] d(dark가) + im(임박): 어둑한
[유] dark, gray
[예] He sat in a dim corner of the waiting - room.

dimension
[diménʃən]
[R] 5049/86800

n. **치수, 크기, 차원**
[T] fourth **dimension**(4 차원)
[유] measure, size
[예] Please specify the dimensions(= the height, length and width) of the room.

✔ **diminish**
[dəmíniʃ]
[R] 11771/86800

v. **줄(이)다, 감소하다**
[T] **di(둘) + mini(작은) + sh:** 둘로 작게하다, 줄이다
[유] decrease, lessen, reduce [반] increse
[예] These memories will not be diminished by time.

✔ **dining**
[dáiniŋ]
[R] 4776/86800

n. **정찬**
[T] **다이닝(dining)**룸 - 저녁 잘 차려놓고 먹는 방
[예] They will be dining at seven o'clock.

✔ **dip**
[dip]
[R] 8831/86800

v. **담그다, 가라앉다**
[T] 손을 **딮(dip)게** - 깊게 **담그다**
[유] dunk, immerse
[예] Dip the fish in the batter, then drop it into the hot oil.

diplomacy
[diplóuməsi]
® 10434/86800

n. 외교(술)
❶ **뒤풀어멋있(diplomacy)게**: 외교는 뒤로 푸는거
[파] diplomat: 외교관 diplomatic: 외교의
[예] This is a situation that calls for tactful diplomacy.

✔ dipper
[dípər]
® 43533/86800

n. 국자
❶ **국자로 디퍼(dipper** - 깊은 곳까지 퍼서)
[예] This dipper is too hot to touch.

✔ direct
[dirékt, dai-]
® 836/86800

v. adj. **지시하다, 직접적인**
❶ direct는 직접 손으로 가리킨다는 말
⑨ point
[파] *direction*: 방향, 지시 *directly*: 직접
　　 director: 감독자 directory: 주소 성명록
[예] We need someone to direct traffic.

✔ disability
[dìsəbíləti]
® 5310/86800

n. 장애
❶ dis(부정어) + able(할 수 있는) + ity(명사형 어미)
[파] disabled: 장애가 있는
[예] The disabled man was unable to climb the stairs without help.

✔ disappear
[dìsəpíər]
® 5645/86800

v. **사라지다**
❶ **dis(부정어) + appear(앞이여): 앞에서 사라지다**
⑨ fade, vanish ⑪ appear
[파] disappearance: 사라짐
[예] The dinosaurs disappeared millions of years ago.

✔ disapproval
[dìsəprú:vəl]
® 11023/86800

n. 불허
❶ dis(부정어) + approval(앞으로 불러 인정): 불인정
⑨ disagreement, rejection
[파] disapprove 동의하지 않다
[예] Although they said nothing, she could sense their disapproval of her suggestion.

D

✔ disassemble
[dìsəsémbəl]
Ⓡ 순위외/86800

v. 해체하다
❶ dis(부정) + assemble(쎈불은 불을 모으다) 모으다의 반대이므로 해체하다
예 The repair man disassembled a watch.

✔ disaster
[dizǽstər]
Ⓡ 3322/86800

n. 재앙, 재해
❶ dis(부정의 뜻) + aster(별): 별이 부정적임, 재앙의 시작
⊕ catastrophe, tragedy
파 *disastrous*: 재난의 *disastrously*: 비참하게
예 It would be a disaster for me if I lost my job.

✔ discard
[diská:rd]
Ⓡ 17402/86800

v. 버리다
❶ dis(부정어) + card(카드): 카드를 버리다
⊕ abandon, throw away
예 Remove and discard the stems.

discern
[disə́:rn]
Ⓡ 16732/86800

v. 식별하다
❶ 대선(discern)나온 사람은 잘 **식별해라**
⊕ differentiate, discriminate, distinguish
예 I could just discern a figure in the darkness.

discharge
[distʃá:rdʒ]
Ⓡ 5246/86800

v. 짐을 내리다, 면제하다
❶ dis(부정어) + charge(부담지우다): 면제하다
⊕ excuse: 면제하다
예 I discharged a cargo ship.

✔ discipline
[dísəplin]
Ⓡ 1842/86800

n. v. 훈육, 규율, 훈련하다, 징벌하다
❶ 강의 실 뒤에서(disci) (문제) 풀(ple)고 (제자들)훈련시키다
⊕ pupil 파 disciple: 제자
예 She doesn't have enough discipline to make money.

disclose
[disklóuz]
Ⓡ 9205/86800

v. 드러내다, 폭로[적발]하다
❶ dis(부정어) + close(닫다): 드러내다
⊕ confess, reveal 파 disclosure: 폭로
예 The identity of the victim has not yet been disclosed.

discomfort
[diskʌmfərt]
® 9166/86800

n. 불편, 불쾌
❶ dis(부정어) + comfort(편안함): 불편함
㉔ uneasiness
㉚ You may feel a little discomfort for a few days after the operation.

discontent
[dìskəntént]
® 9700/86800

n. 불만
❶ dis(부정어) + content(만족, 내용): 불만
㉔ dissatisfaction
㉚ There was widespread discontent about the plan.

discord
[dískɔ:rd]
® 24216/86800

n. 불일치
❶ dis(부정어) + cord(마음): 마음이 같지 않음
㉔ disagreement
㉚ A note of discord has crept into relations between the two countries.

discourse
[dískɔ:rs]
® 3887/86800

n. v. 이야기, 이야기하다
❶ dis(둘이서) + course(커서): 둘이 커서 인생이야기
㉔ speak, lecture
㉚ A discourse on the nature of life after death.

discredit
[diskrédit]
® 19019/86800

n. 불신
❶ dis(부정어) + credit(신뢰): 믿지 못함
㉔ distrust, doubt
㉚ To her discredit, she never admitted her role in the scandal.

discreet
[diskrí:t]
® 10550/86800

adj. 사려 깊은, 신중한
❶ dis(둘이서) + creet(그리도) 신중한
㉔ careful, cautious
㉚ He was very discreet, only saying what was necessary.

discriminate
[diskrímənèit]
Ⓡ 12130/86800

v. **차별하다, 구별하다**
[T] dis (디스) + **criminate(크림이 났데):** 다른 크림보다 이 크림이 났다고 **차별하다**. 수학의 판별식 D
[유] differentiate, discern, distinguish
[파] discrimination: 차별
[예] She felt she had been discriminated against because of her age.

disdain
[disdéin]
Ⓡ 17439/86800

n. **경멸, 경멸하다**
[T] **뒤에서 대인(disdain** - 큰 사람)을 아랫사람들이 **경멸하다**
[유] contempt, scorn
[예] He regards the political process with disdain.

disease
[dizí:z]
Ⓡ 1152/86800

n. **질병**
[T] dis(부정어) + ease(편안함): 편치 않은 질병
[유] illness, sickness
[예] The first symptom of the disease is a very high temperature.

disgrace
[disgréis]
Ⓡ 10816/86800

n. **불명예, 치욕, 망신(거리)**
[T] dis(부정어) + grace(우아함, 은총): 불명예
[유] ignominy, shame [반] esteem, honor
[파] disgraceful: 수치스러운
[예] They were sent home in disgrace.

disguise
[disgáiz]
Ⓡ 8474/86800

n. **위장, 변장(하다)**
[T] **dis(뒤에서) + guise(가리지):** 위장하다
[예] He disguised himself by shaving his head and wearing a false beard.

disgust
[disgʌ́st]
Ⓡ 9407/86800

n. v. **싫증 혐오, 메스껍게 하다**
[T] 오늘도 **뒤**에서 서**서 갔었다.(disgust):** 운전기사가 **혐오**스러워서
[유] abhorrence, aversion, loathing
[파] disgusting: 메스꺼운
[예] She walked out in disgust.

✔ **dish**
[diʃ]
[R] 5020/86800

n. 접시, 요리, 음식
[T] **di(딜리셔스한 -** 맛있는) + sh(접시): 요리, 접시
[예] I washed the dishes instead of my wife.

disillusion
[dìsilú:ʒən]
[R] 27176/86800

n. 각성, 환멸
[T] dis(부정어) + illusion(환영): 환영 깨치기, 각성
[예] There is increasing disillusionment with the government.

disinterested
[disíntəristid]
[R] 21145/86800

adj. 사심 없는, 공평한
[T] dis(부정어) + interested(사심이 있는): 공평한
[유] impartial, unprejudiced: 공평한
[예] The judge's judgment was disinterested.

disloyal
[dislɔ́iəl]
[R] 29713/86800

adj. 불충한
[T] dis(부정어) + loyal(충실한): 불충실한
[유] traitorous, treacherous
[예] It would be disloyal to abandon them.

dismal
[dízməl]
[R] 12388/86800

adj. 음침한
[T] **음침한 뒤에서 뭘?(dismal)**
[유] gloomy
[예] What dismal weather!

✔ **dismay**
[disméi]
[R] 10338/86800

n. 당황
[T] **dismay(뒤에서** 팔을 **매어) 당황**
[유] confusion
[예] To my dismay, I did not get chosen for the job.

✔ **dismiss**
[dismís]
[R] 8019/86800

v. 해산하다, 해고하다, 퇴학시키다
[T] dis(부정어) + miss(그리워하다): 그리워하지 못하게 하다, 해산, 해고, 퇴학시키다
[파] dismissal: 해고
[예] The teacher dismissed the class early because she had a meeting.

disobedience
[dìsəbí:diəns]
[R] 18697/86800

n. **불순종**
[T] dis(부정어) + obedience(아빠다 - 아빠므로 순종). 불순종
[파] disobedient: 순종치 않는 disobey: 말 듣지 않다
[예] The dog was punished for its disobedience.

D

disorder
[disɔ́:rdər]
[R] 5023/86800

n. **무질서, 혼란**
[T] dis(부정어) + order(순서): 순서가 없음
[유] chaos, anarchy [반] cosmos
[예] The whole office was in a state of disorder.

dispense
[dispéns]
[R] 15685/86800

v. **분배하다, 나눠 주다, ~없이 지내다**(with와 **함께**)
[T] **dis(뒤에서) + pense(빼서)** 나누어주다
[유] share, deal
[예] The ATM only dispenses $20 bills.

disperse
[dispə́:rs]
[R] 17093/86800

v. **퍼뜨리다, 흩어지다**
[T] **dis(뒤에서) + perse(퍼서):** 퍼뜨리다
[유] scatter, spread
[예] Police dispersed the crowd that had gathered.

✔ **display**
[displéi]
[R] 1657/86800

v. **보이다, 전시하다**
[T] 백화점 **디스플레이(display)**는 그럴 듯하게 **보이게** 하기 위함
[유] show, exhibit
[예] Family photographs were displayed on the wall.

displease
[displí:z]
[R] 55101/86800

v. **불쾌하게 하다**
[T] dis(부정어) + please(기쁘게하다)
[유] annoy, disturb [반] please [파] displeasure: 불쾌
[예] I wouldn't want to do anything to displease him.

✔ **dispose**
[dispóuz]
[R] 10046/86800

v. **처리하다**
[T] dis(부정어) + pose(위치시키다): 위치시키지 않다, 없애버리다
[파] disposal: 처분 ***disposable***: 일회용품, 일회용의
disposed: ~하고픈 마음이 나는
[예] Paloma made sure to dispose of the rotting fruit.

disposition
[dìspəzíʃən]
[R] 9604/86800

n. 성질, 기질
[T] dis(부정어) + position(위치, 지위): 지위에서 벗어난 원래 기질
[유] nature, qualities
[예] She is of a nervous disposition.

✔ **dispute**
[dispjú:t]
[R] 2985/86800

n. 논쟁(하다)
[T] **dis(둘이서)** + (퍼)**붓데(pute):** 논쟁하다
[유] debate
[예] Can I my dispute my bill if it is inaccurate?

✔ **disregard**
[dìsrigá:rd]
[R] 11816/86800

v. 무시하다
[T] dis(부정어) + regard(생각하다): 무시하다
[유] neglect, ignore
[예] Please disregard what I said before.

✔ **dissent**
[disént]
[R] 10561/86800

v. 의견에 반대하다
[T] dis(부정) + sent(성 - 찬성): 찬성의 반대
[예] I dissented from the prevailing opinion about the matter.

dissolute
[dísəlù:t]
[R] 54817/86800

adj. 방탕한, 타락한
[T] **dis(둘이서)** + **solute(술로** 또): **방탕한**
[유] degenerate, dissolute
[예] He led a dissolute life, drinking and womanizing till his death.

dissolve
[dizálv]
[R] 12288/86800

v. 녹이다, 풀다
[T] **dissolve(되게잘게베)** (서) 녹이다, 풀다
[예] Dissolve two spoons of powder in warm water.

✔ **distinct**
[distíŋkt]
[R] 3011/86800

adj. 명백한, 명확한
[T] **뒤에서(dis) 튄(tinct)** - 튀다니 **명백한**
[유] clear, evident [반] vague
[파] distinction: 구별, 차이 *distinctive*: 독특한
distinctively: 특수하게 *distinguish*: 구별하다
distinguished: 탁월한
[예] There's a distinct smell of cigarettes in here.

✔ **distort**
[distɔ́:rt]
⊛ 16121/86800

v. 비틀다
❶ **트위스틀(distort)**잘 추네! - 잘 **비트**네
예 Arthritis distorted her wrist.

✔ **distract**
[distrǽkt]
⊛ 15734/86800

v. 정신을 딴 곳으로 돌리다
❶ dis(뒤에서) + tract(트랙터): 뒤에서 트랙터 소리로 정신을 딴 데로 돌리다
㊛ divert
㈜ distraction: 기분 전환
예 Don't distract her(from her studies).

distress
[distrés]
⊛ 5327/86800

n. v. 비탄, 고뇌, 조난, 괴롭히다
❶ **디(di)게 스트레스(stress)** 받으면 슬픔, **비탄**에 잠김
㊛ sorrow, grief
예 Many of the horses were showing signs of distress at the end of the race.

✔ **distribute**
[distríbju:t]
⊛ 9961/86800

v. 분배하다
❶ 나한테 **다섯 들(distri** - 병을 세는 단위 - 5리터 들이)이 **부었다(bute)** - 다섯 들이 **분배하다**
㊛ portion, share
㈜ *distribution*: 분배
예 The books will be distributed free to local schools.

district
[dístrikt]
⊛ 1304/86800

n. 지구, 지역, 구역
❶ Washington D.C의 D(=district)를 생각할 것
㊛ region, area
예 Where is the fashion district of New York?

distrust
[distrʌ́st]
⊛ 14522/86800

v. 믿지 않다
❶ dis(부정어) + trust(믿다): 불신하다
㊛ doubt, mistrust
예 She's always distrusted their promises.

disturb
[distə́:rb]
ℝ 9621/86800

v. 방해하다, 어지럽히다
❶ **뒤에서 떠들어봐(disturb) - 방해하다**
ⓐ annoy, bother, irritate
ⓟ *disturbance*: 방해
ⓔ I'm sorry to disturb you at such a late hour.

diverse
[divə́:rs, dai-, dáivə:rs]
ℝ 5821/86800

adj. 다양한, 다른
❶ **다양한 옷들 다 입었어(diverse)**
ⓐ different, various
ⓟ *diversity*: 상이(점), 다양성 *diversely*: 다양한
ⓔ New York is a very ethnically diverse city.

divert
[divə́:rt]
ℝ 12358/86800

v. 주의를 돌리다, 물길을 전환하다
❶ **앞만 보지 말고 뒤봐(divert)하면서 주의를 딴 데로 돌리다**
ⓐ distract
ⓔ The war has diverted attention (away) from the country's economic problems.

divide
[diváid]
ℝ 4718/86800

v. 나누다, 분리하다
❶ di(둘) + vide(나누다): 나누다
ⓐ separate, classify
ⓟ *division*: 분할, 분배
ⓔ After World War Two, Germany was divided into two separate countries.

divine
[diváin]
ℝ 5551/86800

adj. 신의, 신성한
❶ **사람은 앞만 보이지만 신은 뒤봐잉(divine) 뒤를 내다보는 신**
ⓐ holy, sacred
ⓔ They prayed for divine intervention.

divorce
[divɔ́:rs]
ℝ 4193/86800

n. 이혼(하다)
❶ di(둘)로 + vorce(보세): 하나가 아닌 둘 - 이혼하다
ⓔ The last I heard they were getting a divorce.

dizzy
[dízi]
® 13191/86800

adj. 어지러운, 현기증 나는
❶ 어지러워 디지(dizzy)겠다
⑨ giddy
[예] Complex math problems make me dizzy.

doctrine
[dáktrin]
® 4825/86800

n. 학설, 주의
❶ 닥터들이(doctrine) 주장하는 학설
⑨ principle, theory
[예] The government was founded on a doctrine of equality for all people.

✔ **document**
[dákjəmənt]
® 1925/86800

n. v. 문서(로 입증하다), 기록
❶ docu(독 구 - 글구를 읽음) + ment(명사형 어미)
여기서 독은 한문 읽을 독
⑨ record, register
[예] They are charged with using forged documents.

domain
[douméin]
® 4932/86800

n. 영토
❶ 인터넷 도메인(domain)생각하면 될 것
⑨ territory
[예] The forest is part of the king's domain.

✔ **domestic**
[douméstik]
® 1477/86800

adj. 국내의, 가정의, 길들여진
❶ 집에서 도마썼디?(domestic) - 가정에서 요리하려고 도마 썼지?
⑨ tame: 길들여진
[예] The couple enjoyed domestic happiness.

✔ **dominate**
[dámənèit]
® 7066/86800

v. 지배하다
❶ dom(지배) + ate(동사형어미) *condominium: 함께 지배하는 곳)
혹은 담(dom)을 만들어 담있는 곳까지 지배하다
⑨ control, govern
[예] One company has dominated the market for years.

151

✓ donate
[dóuneit, dounéit]
[R] 18225/86800

v. **기증하다**
[T] **돈냈데(donate)**
[유] contribute, endow
[파] ***donation***: 기부, 기부금 donor: 기증인
[예] An anonymous businesswoman donated one million dollars to the charity.

✓ donor
[dóunər]
[R] 9915/86800

n. **기증자**
[T] **돈너(donor)** - 돈을 넣어 **기증하다**
[예] He is one of the charity's major donors.

✓ doom
[du:m]
[R] 13061/86800

n. v. **나쁜 운명, ~의 운명을 정하다**
[T] 나쁜 **운명**이라도 어쩔 수 없이 **둠(doom)**
[유] fate, fortune [파] ***doomed***: 운명의, 불운의
[예] A sense of doom hung over the entire country.

✓ dormitory
[dɔ́:rmətɔ̀:ri]
[R] 22509/86800

n. **기숙사**
[T] **도움이(dormi)** 많이 되고 **똘이(tory)** - 똘똘해 해지는 곳
[예] There were fifty beds in the school dormitory.

✓ dorsal
[dɔ́:rsəl]
[R] 12734/86800

n. **등지느러미, 척추**
[T] **등살(dorsal)**
[예] I saw a shark's dorsal fin.

dose
[dous]
[R] 4967/86800

n. **복용량**
[T] 한 번 **복용** 시 **드세(dose)**요
[유] dosage
[예] Twenty or thirty of these pills would be a lethal dose.

✓ draft
[dræft]
[R] 3176/86800

n. v. **징집, 모집(하다), 초안을 잡다**
[T] ~할 사람 여기 **들러붙어(draft)** 하면서 **모집하다**
[유] conscription: 징집
[예] He avoided the draft because of a foot injury.

D

✔ **drag**
[dræg]
ⓡ 6180/86800

v. 끌다
❶ 컴퓨터의 **드랙(drag - 끌다)** 기능을 생각
ⓨ pull, draw
예 Pick the chair up instead of dragging it behind you!

✅ **drain**
[drein]
ⓡ 6468/86800

n. v. 배수(하다), 유출
❶ 더 레인(drain)온 것을 **빼내다** - 비가 온 것 빼
파 *drainage*: 배수
예 Drain the pasta thoroughly.

✔ **drastic**
[drǽstik]
ⓡ 9199/86800

adj. 철저한, 격렬한
❶ 들어서 틱(drastic) 알정도로 **철저한** 수업
ⓨ extreme ⓑ moderate 파 *drastically*: 격렬하게
예 Many employees have had to take drastic cuts in pay.

dread
[dred]
ⓡ 10225/86800

v. n. **두려워하다, 공포**
❶ 듣기만 **들어도(dread) 무섭다**
ⓨ fear, horror 파 dreadful: 무서운
예 He can't swim and dreads going in the water.

dreary
[dríəri]
ⓡ 16552/86800

adj. 쓸쓸한, 황량한
❶ 황량한 곳이 바로 들(판)이 어리(dreary)!: 쓸쓸한 들을 보고 하는 말
ⓨ bleak, dismal
예 His hometown is a dreary little town.

✅ **dribble**
[dríbəl]
ⓡ 33984/86800

v. 물방울이 뚝뚝 떨어지다, 공을 드리블하다
❶ 축구공을 **드리블(dribble)**하다
예 He dribbled wine on to the rug.

✔ **drift**
[drift]
ⓡ 5993/86800

n. v. 표류(하다), 떠돌다, 흐름, 경향
❶ 강아지가 **들에부터(drift)** 떠돌아다닌다
ⓨ float, rove
예 We saw a balloon drifting in the wind.

drought
[draut]
Ⓡ 9597/86800

n. 가뭄
❶ 가뭄에 땅이 벌어져 **들(이 완전) 아웃 (drought)**되어 **가뭄**
㉡ flood
㉔ This year (a) severe drought has ruined the crops.

drown
[draun]
Ⓡ 13470/86800

v. 익사하다
❶ 들어온(drawn) 물에 **익사**하다
㉔ He drowned in a boating accident.

drudgery
[drʌ́dʒəri]
Ⓡ 30847/86800

n. 고된 일
❶ 들(판)에 저리(drudgery) 고된 일
㉕ moil, toil
㉔ the drudgery of housework.

dual
[djú:əl]
Ⓡ 6415/86800

adj. 둘의
❶ du(둘) + al(형용사형어미)
㉕ double, paired, coupled
㉔ This room has a dual purpose, serving as both a study and a dining room.

due
[dju:]
Ⓡ 1522/86800

adj. 지불 기일이 된, 당연한
❶ 언제까지 해 **듀(due)!**
㉕ owing, unpaid 미납의 deserved: 당연한
㉔ The rent is due(=should be paid) at the end of the month.

dull
[dʌl]
Ⓡ 4611/86800

adj. 둔한, 무딘, 지루한
❶ 띨 띨(dull) 한 - 무디고 **둔한**
㉕ blunt, unsharpened ㉡ keen, sharp
㉔ She felt a dull ache at the back of her head.

dumb
[dʌm]
Ⓡ 8583/86800

adj. 말을 못하는, 벙어리의
❶ dumb(덤) 덤덤하여 **말 못하는**
㉕ mute, voiceless
㉔ He's been deaf and dumb since birth.

durable
[djúərəbəl]
[R] 13923/86800

adj. **오래 견디는, 튼튼한**
[T] **du(두**고두고) + **ra** (**오래**) + able(할 수 있는): 오래 견딜 수 있는
[유] enduring, lasting
[예] The machines have to be made of durable materials.

D

✓ **duration**
[djuəréiʃən]
[R] 4586/86800

n. **지속**
[T] **지속**되는 고통을 - 그만 **듀레이션(duration)**
[예] I suffered from a disease of long duration.

dusk
[dʌsk]
[R] 9861/86800

n. **어둑어둑함**
[T] **다(d)크**하고 어슥**어슥(usk)**한: 어둑어둑함
[유] nightfall, sunset, twilight [반] dawn
[예] As dusk fell, bats began to fly between the trees.

✓ **dust**
[dʌst]
[R] 3354/86800

n. **먼지**
[T] **먼지** 구덩이에 그냥 **뒀었다(dust)**
[예] I cleaned up a room thickly coated with dust.

✓ **dwell**
[dwel]
[R] 13606/86800

v. **살다, 거주하다**
[T] **들어 왈(dwell - 들어 와) 살자**
[유] live, dwell on
[파] dweller: 거주자 *dwelling*: 거주, 거주지
[예] She dwelt in remote parts of Asia for many years.

✓ **dynamic**
[dainǽmik]
[R] 4766/86800

adj. **역동적인**
[T] **힘 있는 다이나마이트(dynamic)**를 생각
[유] active, energetic [반] static
[예] We need a dynamic expansion of trade with other countries.

dynasty
[dáinəsti]
[R] 11664/86800

n. **왕조**
[T] **다 이내시디?(dynasty)**(왕조를 모신 건 바로 이 내시 지?)
[예] The Mogul dynasty ruled over India for centuries.

eager
[íːgər]
[R] 5529/86800

adj. **열망하는, 열심인**
[T] **이걸(eager)** 꼭 해야지 하며 **열심인**
[유] anxious, impatient, earnest, enthusiastic
[파] eagerness: 열심, 열망
[예] The teachers saw the children's eager faces.

✔ **earnest**
[ə́ːrnist]
[R] 9491/86800

adj. **열심인, 진지한**
[T] 남친이 **진지한** 목소리로 나 너 **원했었다(earnest)**
[유] eager
[파] ***earnestly***: 열심히, 진심으로
[예] He was a very earnest young man.

✔ **earthen**
[ə́ːrəən]
[R] 42084/86800

a. **흙으로 만든**
[T] earth(흙) + en(...한): 흙으로 만든
[예] I made an earthen jug.

✔ **earthquake**
[ə́ːrəkwèik]
[R] 11445/86800

n. **지진**
[T] earth(땅) + quake(깨): 땅을 깨는 것 - 지진
[예] In 1906 an earthquake destroyed much of San Francisco.

eccentric
[ikséntrik]
[R] 9835/86800

adj. **(행동 따위가) 별난**
[T] ec(바깥, ex의변형) + centr(중점) + ic(형용사형 어미): 바깥에만 중심을 둔 별난
[유] odd, peculiar, weird
[예] Sometimes she did eccentric behaviour.

✔ **ecology**
[iːkálədʒi]
[R] 10054/86800

n. **생태학, 생태계**
[T] eco(살아있는, 삶, 생) + logy(학문, 이론, 말)
[파] ***ecological***: 생태학의
ecologist: 생태학자
[예] She hopes to study ecology at college.

❖ economic
[èkənámik]
ⓡ 383/86800

adj. **경제의**
❶ eco(삶) + nomy(관리) + ic(형용사형 어미): 삶을 관리하는, 경제의
㈜ *economy*: 경제 *economics*: 경제학
economically: 경제적으로
㈖ The government's economic policies have led us into the worst recession for years.

economical
[èkənámikəl]
ⓡ 11282/86800

adj. **절약이 되는**
❶ 집 앞 가게 놔두고 큰 곳으로 가는 이유는?
이거(돈) 남으니까(economical)!!!!
㈜ frugal, thrifty ㈘ extravagant
㈖ There's increasing demand for cars which are more economical on fuel.

❖ ecosystem
[í:kousìstəm]
ⓡ 23214/86800

n. **생태계**
❶ eco(삶) + system(체계): 살아있는 것들의 체계, 생태계
㈖ Pollution can have disastrous effects on the delicately balanced ecosystem.

ecstasy
[ékstəsi]
ⓡ 9903/86800

n. **무아의 경지, 황홀**
❶ 마약 중 **엑스터시(ecstacy)**로 구속되는 사람이 많은 것은 **황홀한**가 보다
㈜ delirium, rapture
㈖ She threw her head back as if in ecstasy.

❖ edge
[edʒ]
ⓡ 1352/86800

n. **가장자리, 변두리**
❶ ABCD가 아니라 **변두리 E지(edge)**?
㈜ rim, border
㈖ They built the church on the edge of the village.

✔ edible
[édəbəl]
ⓡ 19537/86800

a. **식용의**
❶ eatable(먹을 수 있는)과 비슷함
㈖ I ate edible snails in france.

E

✔ edit
[édit]
[R] 11033/86800

v. **편집하다**
[T] 책이 어디가 **어딧(edit)지**? **편집**을 해야 함
[유] correct, reform
[파] edition: 판 *editor*: 편집자 editorial: 사설
[예] Janet edited books for a variety of publishers.

✔ effect
[ifékt]
[R] 388/86800

n. **효과, 영향, 결과**
[T] **이 빽 (effect)**이면 **효과**를 볼거야. 빽은 배경
[유] result, consequence: 결과
[파] *effective*: 효과적인 *effectively*: 효과적으로
effectiveness: 효과
[예] I think I'm suffering from the effects of too little sleep.

✔ efficiency
[ifíʃənsi]
[R] 2676/86800

n. **능률, 효력**
[T] **이삐색시(efficiecy - 예쁜색시)**있으면 인생에 **능률**이 오를거야
[파] efficient: 효율적인 *efficiently*: 능률적으로
[예] Our factory was operating at peak efficiency.

✔ elaborate
[ilǽbərit][ilǽbərèit]
[R] 5077/86800

adj. v. **정교한, 공들여 만들다**
[T] e(밖으로 늘리다) + labor(노동) + ate(형용사, 동사형 어미): 노동을 늘릴 만큼 정교한
[유] complicated, detailed
[예] They're making the most elaborate preparations for the wedding.

elastic
[ilǽstik]
[R] 10273/86800

adj. **탄력있는**
[T] e(밖으로) + last(지속시키다): 밖으로 당겨도 지속되는, 탄력있는
[유] flexible, pliable
[예] A lot of sportswear is made of very elastic material.

✔ elderly
[éldərli]
[R] 2045/86800

adj. **나이가 지긋한**
[T] **elder(앨**(자손들)**더** 가진 사람 - 연장자)
[유] old, aged [파] *elder*: 연장자 *eldest*: 최 연장의
[예] He happen to meet elderly relatives.

elect
[ilékt]
ⓡ 10720/86800

v. 선거[선출]하다
❶ 사회를 위해 **일해(elect)**하며 선출하다
ⓨ choose, vote 파 *election*: 선거, 선출
예 We elected him as our representative.

elegance
[éligəns]
ⓡ 11290/86800

n. 우아함
❶ 돌아가신 앙드레 김께서 하시던 그 **엘레강스(elegance) ~한** 분 - 우아한 분
ⓨ elegance, grace 파 *elegant*: 우아한
예 It was her natural elegance that struck me.

elegy
[élədʒi]
ⓡ 38433/86800

n. 애가, 비가(슬픈 노래)
❶ 슬픈 노래들으니 눈물 **일레지?(elegy)** - 눈물이 일지?
예 Gray's 'Elegy in a Country Churchyard' is a famous English poem.

element
[éləmənt]
ⓡ 1828/86800

n. 요소, 성분
❶ **성분**은 하나하나 **일일이(ele)** 따지는 것
ⓨ component, ingredient
파 *elementary*: 기본의, 초등의
예 List the elements which make up a perfect dinner party.

elevate
[éləvèit]
ⓡ 28166/86800

v. 올리다
❶ 엘리베이터 생각하면 이는 사람을 올리는 것
ⓨ raise, lift
파 *elevation*: 높이, 고도 *elevator*: 엘리베이터
예 I learned exercises that elevate the heart rate.

eliminate
[ilímənèit]
ⓡ 6590/86800

v. 제거하다, 탈락시키다
❶ 두 신랑감 중 **일 림이 낫데(eliminate)** - 이림이는 **탈락**
ⓨ abolish, exterminate
파 *elimination*: 배제, 제거
예 A move towards healthy eating could help eliminate heart disease.

eloquence

[éləkwəns]

® 26335/86800

n. 웅변

❶ 애(아기)로 큰(eloquence)사람으로서 **웅변**해 본 경험은 다들 있다

예 She was renowned for her eloquence and beauty.

emancipate

[imǽnsəpèit]

® 65926/86800

v. 해방하다

❶ e(밖으로) + man(사람을): 밖으로 사람을 꺼내다, 해방하다

㊀ free, liberate ㊂ enslave

예 He felt the only way to emancipate himself from his parents was to move away.

embark

[imbá:rk]

® 12747/86800

v. 배를 타다, 시작하다, 착수하다

❶ 임박(embark) 해서 **시작하다**, 혹은 em(~하게하다) + bark(배): 승선시키다

㊀ launch, start ㊂ disembark

예 We embarked at Liverpool for New York.

embody

[embádi]

® 17156/86800

v. 구체화하다

❶ em(~하게 하다) + body(몸): 몸으로 하게하다, 구체화하다, 영어 단어의 em, en 이 앞뒤에 들어가면 동사를 만든다, 뜻은 ~하게하다, 뒷 철자가 b,m,p일 경우에는 en으로 변한다

예 The legislature embodied a revenue provision in the new law.

✔ embrace

[imbréis]

® 7206/86800

v. 포옹하다, 포용하다

❶ 임 보래서(embrace) 포옹했다

㊀ hug, hold

예 She saw them embrace on the station platform.

✔ emerge

[imə́:rdʒ]

® 4207/86800

v. 나타나다

❶ 어떤 여자가 내가 너 **이모지**(emerge) 하며 **나타났다**

㊀ appear ㊂ submerge

c.f) *emergency*: 긴급

예 She emerged from the sea, blue with cold.

E

emigrate
[émǝgrèit]
®️ 23371/86800

v. 이민가다
❶ e(밖으로) + migrate(이동하다)
㊉ migrate
㊙ emigrant: 다른 나라로의 이주자 emigration: 이민
㋖ Thousands of Britons emigrate every year.

eminent
[émǝnǝnt]
®️ 11515/86800

adj. 저명한, 뛰어난
❶ e(밖으로) + minent(미는): 사람들이 자꾸 밖으로 미는 **유명한** 사람
㊉ famous, well - known
㋖ I met an eminent historian yesterday.

✿ emit
[imít]
®️ 20447/86800

v. 내뿜다
❶ e(밖으로) + mit(보내다)
㊙ *emission*: (빛, 열, 향기 따위의) 방사, 발산
㋖ The machine emits a high - pitched sound when you press the button.

✿ emotion
[imóuʃǝn]
®️ 5245/86800

n. 감정, 정서
❶ e(밖으로) + motion(움직임): 밖으로 나오는 정신의 움직임: 감정
㊉ feeling, sentiment
㊙ *emotional*: 감정[정서]의, 감정적인 *emotionally*: 감정적으로
㋖ Like a lot of men, he finds it hard to express his emotions.

emperor
[émpǝrǝr]
®️ 4096/86800

n. 황제
❶ em(엠~) + peror(봐라): 음 봐라 내가 **황제**니라
㋖ Caesar was an emperor of Rome.

✿ emphasis
[émfǝsis]
®️ 1870/86800

n. 강조
❶ 여배우가 돈을 많이 줘도 자기는 **안 벗었어(emphasis)** 하며 **강조**
㊙ *emphasize*: 강조하다
㋖ Schools here put great emphasis on written work and grammar.

empire
[émpaiər]
® 2701/86800

n. 제국
❶ 황제가 다스리는 **제국**은 커서 **안보이어(empire)**
㊀ kingdom
예 The emperor ruled the Holy Roman Empire.

✹ employ
[emplói]
® 4786/86800

v. 고용하다
❶ 에~(e) 몸(m)풀어(ploy)! - 스포츠에서도 몸을 푸는 것은 곧 감독
이 **쓰겠다**는 말
㊀ hire, engage
파 *employee*: 종업원 *employer*: 고용주 *employment*: 고용
예 How many people does your company employ?

✹ empty
[émpti]
® 1789/86800

adj. 빈
❶ **empty(**암티 - 수술한 것 때문에 그 부분이 **텅빈)**
㊀ vacant
예 I found an empty house near our village.

✹ enable
[enéibəl]
® 2114/86800

v. 가능하게 하다
❶ en(~하게 하다) + able(할 수 있는): 가능하게 하다
㊀ capacitate
예 Computerization should enable us to cut production
costs by half.

✔ enacted
[enǽktid]
® 11169/86800

a. 법령화 한
❶ en(하게하다) + acted(행동하는): 행동하게 하다
예 New York State has enacted a new tax law.

enchant
[entʃǽnt]
® 59712/86800

v. 매혹시키다
❶ en(인 - 사람) + Chant(찬 - 칭찬): 사람을 칭찬할 정도로 매혹시키다
㊀ bewitch, charm
예 The audience was clearly enchanted by her
performance.

enclose
[enklóuz]
ⓡ 12238/86800

v. 동봉하다, 둘러싸다
❶ en(~하게 하다) + close(닫은): 닫게 하다
예 Please enclose a curriculum vitae with your letter of application.

encounter
[enkáuntər]
ⓡ 4830/86800

v. 마주치다
❶ encounter(인 카운터 - 사람을 카운터서 마주치다
㊤ meet
예 On their way home they encountered a woman selling flowers.

encourage
[enkə́:ridʒ]
ⓡ 1983/86800

v. 격려하다, 장려하다
❶ en(~하게하다) + courage(용기): 용기를 갖게 하다
㊤ inspire, stimulate ㊥ discourage
파 *encouragement*: 격려, 장려
예 We were encouraged to learn foreign languages at school.

encyclopedia
[ensàikloupí:diə]
ⓡ 24304/86800

n. 백과사전
❶ encyclo(이것 저것 둘러서) + pedia(교육, 육아) 이것, 저것 가르쳐 줌
예 This is an encyclopedia of natural science.

endanger
[endéindʒər]
ⓡ 20873/86800

v. 위험에 빠뜨리다
❶ en(~하게 하다) + danger(위험): 위험하게 하다
㊤ imperil, jeopardize
예 He would never do anything to endanger the lives of his children.

endeavor
[endévər]
ⓡ 8993/86800

n. 노력(하다)
❶ endeavor(인제 봐): 인제두고봐 나도 노력할게
㊤ try, strive
예 In spite of our best endeavours, it has proven impossible to contact her.

endless
[éndlis]
[R] 5048/86800

adj. **끝없는**
[T] end(끝) + less(~이 없는)
[유] perpetual, continual
[파] *end*: 끝 *endlessly*: 끝없이, 계속적으로
[예] The possibilities are endless.

endow
[endáu]
[R] 30231/86800

v. **기부하다, 주다**
[T] **인도(endow)**적으로 **기부하다**
[유] donate
[예] The money will be used to endow the museum and research facility.

endure
[endjúər]
[R] 10839/86800

v. **견디다, 참다**
[T] **endure(견뎌)**
[유] bear, tolerate [파] endurable: 견딜 수 있는
[예] We had to endure a nine - hour delay at the airport.

enemy
[énəmi]
[R] 2870/86800

n. adj. **적, 적(국)의**
[T] **이놈이?(enemy)** 이런 말은 우호적이지 않은 사람(**적**)에게 쓰는 말
[유] opponent, rival
[예] He's made a few enemies in this company.

enforce
[enfɔ́:rs]
[R] 7053/86800

v. **강요하다, 시행하다**
[T] en(~하게하다) + force(힘): 힘을 쓰게 하다
[유] compel, force, pressure
[파] enforcement: 시행 *enforceable*: 시행할 수 있는
[예] The new teacher had failed to enforce any sort of discipline.

engage
[engéidʒ]
[R] 6326/86800

v. **종사시키다, 약혼시키다**
[T] 서로 **앵겨야지(engage - 붙어야) 약혼**하지
[유] employ, hire
[파] *engagement*: 약속, 약혼
[예] I have engaged a secretary to deal with all my paperwork.

✔ enhance
[enhǽns]
🅡 5545/86800

v. 강화하다, 올리다
🅣 en(~하게 하다) + hance(한 수): 한 수 올리다
🅢 strengthen, reinforce
🅔 You can enhance the flavor of the dish by using fresh herbs.

✔ enlarge
[enláːrdʒ]
🅡 17782/86800

v. 크게 하다, 넓히다
🅣 en(~하게 하다) + large(큰)
🅢 increase, expand 🅟 *enlargement*: 확장
🅔 They've enlarged the kitchen by building over part of the garden.

✔ enlighten
[enláitn]
🅡 27004/86800

v. 계몽하다, 설명해주다
🅣 en(~하게 하다) + light(빛) + en(~하게하다): 어둡고 무지한 곳에 빛을 비추다, 계몽하다
🅢 illuminate: 계몽하다
🅔 I don't understand this. Could you enlighten me?

enlist
[enlíst]
🅡 20116/86800

v. 병적에 편입하다
🅣 en(~하게 하다) + list(목록): 목록에 올리다, 병적리스트에 올리다
🅢 recruit
🅔 They both enlisted (in the navy) a year before the war broke out.

✔ enormous
[inɔ́ːrməs]
🅡 2403/86800

adj. 거대한, 막대한
🅣 e(밖으로) + norm(표준, 기준) + ous(형용사형 어미): 기준 밖으로 벗어난
🅢 huge, immense
🅔 He earns an enormous salary.

✔ enrich
[enrítʃ]
🅡 22501/86800

v. 풍부[부유]하게 하다
🅣 en(~하게 하다) + rich(풍요로운): 풍요롭게 하다
🅔 My life was greatly enriched by knowing her.

E

✔ enroll
[enróul]
ⓡ 순위외/86800

v. 등록하다
❶ en(인) + roll(명부): 사람을 명부에 올리다
⑨ register 파 *enrollment*: 등록, 입학
예 He is enrolled as a part - time student.

✔ ensure
[enʃúər]
ⓡ 993/86800

v. 보장하다
❶ en(~하게 하다) + sure(확실한): 확실하게 하다
⑨ confirm, guarantee
예 The airline is taking steps to ensure safety on its aircraft.

enterprise
[éntərpràiz]
ⓡ 2394/86800

n. 모험적 계획, 사업, 진취적 정신
❶ 엔터 프라이즈(모르는 분야에 enter: 들어가서 + prize로 생각하면 상을 받는 계획은 진취적인 정신)
파 enterprising: 진취적인
예 Don't forget this is a commercial enterprise - we're here to make money.

✔ enthusiasm
[enθú:ziæzəm]
ⓡ 3216/86800

n. 열광, 열정
❶ 앤 수지에 지음(enthusiasm) - 국가 발전을 생각해 이 건물은 수지에 지음. 수지 사람들 열광
⑨ excitement, passion 파 *enthusiastic*: 열광적인, 열중하는
예 After the accident he lost his enthusiasm for the sport.

entitle
[entáitl]
ⓡ 22805/86800

v. 자격을 주다
❶ en(~하게 하다) + title(자격): 자격을 주다
예 Being unemployed entitles you to free medical treatment.

✔ entrance
[éntrəns]
ⓡ 3087/86800

n. 입구, 입장
❶ enter(들어가다) + ance(명사형 어미)들어가는 곳, 입구
⑨ entry, access 파 *enter*: 들어가다
예 There are two entrances - one at the front and one round the back.

entreat
[entríːt]
ⓡ 77844/86800

v. **간청하다**
ⓣ entreat 안들이? 이거 들여와야 하는데 안들여?하며 **간청하다**
ⓢ beg, plead
예 I entreat you to help me.

entrust
[entrʌ́st]
ⓡ 35025/86800

v. **위임하다**
ⓣ en(~하게 하다) + trust(믿다): 믿고 맡기다
ⓢ assign, authorize
예 He didn't look like the sort of man you should entrust your luggage to.

✔ envious
[énviəs]
ⓡ 20649/86800

adj. **부러워하는, 시기하는**
ⓣ M, B였어(envious - 대통령을 **부러워하는**)
ⓢ jealous 파 *envy*: 부러워하다, 시기(하다)
예 I'm very envious of your new coat - it's lovely.

epldemic
[èpədémik]
ⓡ 10748/86800

adj. n. **유행히는, 전염(변)**
ⓣ epi(~사이) + dem(사람) + ic(일반적으로 형용사형 어미): 여러 사람들 사이에 돌아다니는, 혹은 요즘 유행하는 거 **이삐데(epidemic - 이쁘데)**
ⓢ widespread
예 Typhoid was epidemic.

epoch
[épək / íːpɔk]
ⓡ 21171/86800

n. **신기원, 신시대**
ⓣ 요즘은 e(이 - 이빨)가 **팍(pock)** 나오는 시대(electric, electronic, email, e - learning 등)
ⓢ period, era
예 The Civil War era was an epoch in 19th - century U.S. history.

equator
[ikwéitər]
ⓡ 19541/86800

n. **적도**
ⓣ 남반구 북반구를 접으면 **같아(equal)**지는 곳: equator 혹, **에쿠아도르** 생각하면 됨
예 Singapore lies on the Equator.

equip
[ikwíp]
® 17533/86800

v. 갖추다, 장비하다
❶ 애기 입(equip) 을 것 잘 갖추다
㊉ supply
㈜ *equipment*: 장비, 설비
㈀ It's going to cost $4 million to equip the hospital.

equivalent
[ikwívələnt]
® 2269/86800

adj. 동등한
❶ equal + value(같은 가치) + ent(형용사 형 어미): 동등한
㊉ equal, same
㈜ *equal*: 같은 *equality*: 같음
　　equally: 같게 *equation*: 같게 함
㈀ She's doing the equivalent job in the new company but for more money.

era
[íərə, érə]
® 3963/86800

n. 시대, 연대
❶ 우리가 어떻게 **일어(era)** 난 **시대**야?
㊉ period, epoch
㈀ The King's death marks the end of an era.

erect
[irékt]
® 9983/86800

v. adj. 똑바로 세우다, 똑바로 선
❶ e(~하게하다) + rect(바로서다): 세우다
㈀ She sat erect, listening for her name.

errand
[érənd]
® 23872/86800

n. 심부름
❶ 애란(errand) - 애들이란 **심부름**을 하게 되는 것
㊉ task
㈀ He was sent out on an urgent errand.

erupt
[irʌ́pt]
® 25397/86800

v. 분출하다
❶ eru(이루) + pt(피튀) - 이로 피 튀겨 **분출**하다
㊉ emit, vent
㈜ eruption: 분출
㈀ The volcano erupted with tremendous force.

essay
[ései]
Ⓡ 5097/86800

n. 수필
❶ es(바깥 - ex의 변형) + say(말하다): 밖에 대고 말하다: 세상에 말하는 이야기
예 For homework I want you to write an essay on endangered species.

essence
[ésəns]
Ⓡ 4614/86800

n. 본질
❶ 원래부터 **있었어(essence) - 본질**
⊕ nature, principle
파 *essential*: 본질적인 *essentiality*: 본질
예 Yet change is the very essence of life.

establish
[istǽbliʃ]
Ⓡ 1942/86800

v. 설립하다, 확립하다
❶ S대 불리(기 위해)서 설립하다
⊕ found, organize 파 establishment: 설립
예 These methods of working were established in the last century.

estate
[istéit]
Ⓡ 1881/86800

n. 재산
❶ 아버지 **재산 어서 떼야돼(estate) - 내 재산 줘**
⊕ property, belongings
예 She left her entire estate to her niece.

esteem
[istí:m]
Ⓡ 12772/86800

n. v. 존경, 존경하다
❶ S 팀(S대 - 서울대 들어간 팀)을 **존경**하다
⊕ respect, regard
예 There has been a drop in public esteem for teachers.

estimate
[éstəmit, -mèit][éstəmèit]
Ⓡ 3467/86800

n. v. 견적, 평가, 추정하다
❶ 내 친구는 **S대 메이트(estimate):** S대 친구, 여기서 S대는 어떤 대학인지 **추정**해야 함
⊕ guess presume 파 *estimation*: 의견, 판단
예 They estimate (that) the journey will take at least two weeks.

eternal
[itə́:rnəl]
® 7856/86800

adj. 영원한
❶ **영원히 안떠날(eternal)**
⊕ endless, everlasting 파 *eternally*: 영원히
예 Will you two never stop your eternal arguing!

ethical
[éθikəl]
® 6508/86800

adj. 윤리[도덕]의
❶ **사람들이 사는데 애쓸(ethi) 것(cal) - 윤리**
⊕ moral
파 *ethics*: 윤리, 윤리학 *ethically*: 도덕적으로
예 A medical procedure which most people believe to be ethical.

ethnic
[éθnik]
® 3838/86800

adj. 민족의
❶ **민족의 화합을 위해서 애쓰니(ethnic)?**
⊕ national, racial
예 A question on ethnic origin was included in the census.

evade
[ivéid]
® 16701/86800

v. 피하다
❶ **끓는 물 입에 대(evade)면 뜨거워 피하다**
⊕ avoid, elude
예 He can't evade doing military service forever.

evaluate
[ivǽljuèit]
® 6693/86800

v. 평가하다
❶ **e(밖으로) + value(가치) + ate(동사형어미): 밖으로 가치를 드러내는 것은 평가**
⊕ rate, appraise 파 *evaluation*: 평가
예 I evaluated a training program as effective.

eventual
[ivéntʃuəl]
® 6909/86800

adj. 궁극의
❶ **event(사건, 결국) + al(형용사형 어미): 최종사건까지 가는 - 결국의**
⊕ last, ultimate 파 *eventually*: 결국, 마침내
예 The Dukes were the eventual winners of the competition.

everlasting
[èvərlǽstiŋ]
® 21455/86800

adj. **영구한**
❶ ever(언제나) + lasting(지속적인)
⊕ eternal, infinite, perpetual, timeless
예 I wish someone would invent an everlasting light bulb.

E

✔ **evident**
[évidənt]
® 3528/86800

adj. **분명한**
❶ 애비단다(evident) - 분명한
⊕ clear, obvious
파 evidently: 분명하게 *evidence*: 증거
예 Her love for him was evident in all that she did.

evil
[íːvəl]
® 3274/86800

adj. n. **나쁜, 악**
❶ 사람은 항상 **사악**한 **입을(evil)**조심
⊕ bad, wicked
예 These people are just evil.

✔ **evolution**
[èvəlúːʃən]
® 3659/86800

n. **진화, 발전**
❶ 회사는 **이발로 선(evolution)** - 회사가 이발소부터 발전, 진화
⊕ development, growth 파 evolve: 진화하다
예 I studied the evolution of language at UB.

✔ **evolve**
[iválv]
® 11580/86800

v. **발전시키다**
❶ e(밖으로=ex) + volve(돌다), **이발 부(evolve)**를 헤어살롱으로 **발전시키다**
예 This idea was evolved from a casual remark.

✔ **exaggerate**
[igzǽdʒərèit]
® 17478/86800

v. **과장하다**
❶ 기분 좋을 때 **과장** 표현 중 **이거** 기분째져(exagger)하는 표현을 기억
⊕ magnify, overstate ⊛ understate
파 *exaggeration*: 과장
예 Don't exaggerate - it wasn't that expensive.

✓ **examine**
[igzǽmin]
[R] 2666/86800

v. **조(검)사하다**
[T] **이거 재밌(examine)**는지 **조사**하다
[유] test, inspect
[파] *exam*: 시험 *examination*: 시험, 검사
examiner: 시험관, 검사관
[예] You should have your eyes examined.

✓ **exceed**
[iksí:d]
[R] 6844/86800

v. **넘다, 능가하다**
[T] ex(밖으로) + ceed(가다 - 어원편 참조)
[유] excel, surpass
[파] excess: 초과, 과잉 excessive: 과도한, 지나친
[예] The final cost should not exceed $5000.

✓ **exception**
[iksépʃən]
[R] 3233/86800

n. **예외, 제외**
[T] ex(밖으로) + ception(받아들임): 다른 것은 안으로 받아들이고 이것만 밖으로 받아들임
[유] exclusion [반] inclusion
[파] *except*: ~을 제외하고 *exceptional*: 예외적인
[예] There are exceptions to every rule.

✓ **excessive**
[iksésiv]
[R] 4772/86800

a. **과도한**
[T] ex(밖으로) + cess(가다) + ive(형용사형 어미)
[예] Excessive sweating is the symptoms of influenza.

✓ **exclaim**
[ikskléim]
[R] 34989/86800

v. **외치다, 소리 지르다**
[T] **악써 크레임(exclaim** 자기 주장하느라) 자기 주장하느라 악 썼다는 말 - 소리치다
[유] shout, yell, cry [파] exclamation: 외침
[예] "You can't leave now!" she exclaimed.

✓ **exclude**
[iksklú:d]
[R] 5796/86800

v. **제외하다, 배척하다**
[T] ex(밖으로) + clude(닫다): 안으로 포함하지 않고 밖으로 빼고 닫다 - 제외하다
[유] eliminate, except
[파] *exclusion*: 제외 exclusive: 배타[독점]적인
[예] The price excludes local taxes.

excursion
[ikskə́:rʒən, -ʃən]
[R] 13129/86800

n. **소풍**
[T] ex(익사이티드로 생각) + cur(갈) + sion(명사형 어미): 신나서 감, 소풍
[유] jaunt, journey
[예] Next week we're going on an excursion.

✔ **execute**
[éksikjù:t]
[R] 12738/86800

v. **실시하다, 배우가 연기하다, 처형하다**
[T] exe(**엑 시 - 액션**실시하다)cue(**큐**하는 소리에 **연기하다**)
[유] perform: 실시하다, 배우가 연기하다
[파] ***execution***: 실행 ***executive***: 실행하는, 중역
[예] He was executed for murder.

exempt
[igzémpt]
[R] 9068/86800

v. adj. **면제하다, 면제된**
[T] **이그잼(exempt)부터 면제**(해주세요)
[유] excuse
[예] Small businesses have been exempted from the tax increase.

✔ **exert**
[igzə́:rt]
[R] 10461/86800

v. **노력하다**
[T] 잘못하면 **이거 져(exert** - 싸움에서 진다는 뜻)! **노력**해야 한다는 말
[파] ***exertion***: 노력
[예] I was too tired to exert myself.

✔ **exhaust**
[igzɔ́:st]
[R] 10638/86800

v. **다 써버리다**
[T] **이거 다썼다(exhaust)**
[유] use up, expend
[예] We seem to have exhausted this topic of conversation (= we have nothing new to say about it).

✔ **exhibition**
[èksəbíʃən]
[R] 1883/86800

n. **전시회**
[T] **이거 좀 보션(exhibition): 전시회** 좀 보라구
[유] show [파] ***exhibit***: 전시하다
[예] The photographs will be on exhibition until the end of the month.

✓ exit
[égzit, éksit]
[R] 6013/86800

n. v. **출구, 나가다**
[T] ex(밖으로) + it(가다 - circuit의 it도 '가다'의 뜻, circle이 원이므로 원으로 돌며 간다는 뜻)
[반] access, entrance
[예] Where is an emergency exit?

✓ exotic
[igzátik]
[R] 6480/86800

adj. **외국의, 이국풍의**
[T] 대개 외국에 처음 나가서 하는 말 **이거 좋다(exotic)**
[유] foreign
[예] She has many exotic flowers in her garden.

✓ expand
[ikspǽnd]
[R] 4721/86800

v. **넓히다, 확장[확대]하다**
[T] ex(밖으로) + pand(편다 - 늘어나다)
[유] enlarge, increase
[파] expansion 확장 *expanse*: 넓은 공간, 확장
[예] The air in the balloon expands when heated.

expedition
[èkspədíʃən]
[R] 6726/86800

n. **탐험 여행, 탐험대**
[T] ex(밖으로) + ped(발, 어린이, 교육) + tion(명사형 어미): 밖으로 발을 둠, 탐험
[유] exploration, trip
[예] The British expedition to Mount Everest is leaving next month.

✓ expel
[ikspél]
[R] 24327/86800

v. **내쫓다, 추방하다**
[T] **익수를 팰(expel)** - 익수를 패서 내 쫓다. 혹은 ex(밖으로) + pel(쫓다)
[유] eject, banish
[예] My brother was expelled from school for bad behaviour.

✓ expert
[ékspəːrt]
[R] 2357/86800

n. **전문가**
[T] **엑스 퍼뜩(expert) - X를 퍼뜩푸는거** 보면 **전문가**라는 뜻
[유] master, professional, specialist
[파] *expertise*: 전문지식
[예] My mother is an expert at dress - making.

expire
[ikspáiər]
® 18364/86800

v. 기한이 다 되다
❶ 익수 (학교에서) **파하여(expire)** 집에 돌아 올 **시간이 다 되다**
⊕ end, terminate
예 The contract between the two companies will expire at the end of the year.

explode
[iksplóud]
® 13591/86800

v. 폭발하다
❶ ex(밖으로) + plode(불었다): 밖으로 부풀면 커져서 폭발
⊕ blast, burst
파 *explosion*: 폭발 explosive: 폭발적인, 폭약
예 He was driving so fast that his car tire exploded.

exploit
[éksplɔit, iksplɔ́it]
® 6274/86800

n. v. 공훈, 착취하다, 개발하다
❶ 이 문제는 **익수가 풀어잇(exploit)**: 익수의 **공로**
⊕ deed, feat, accomplishment
예 He has never fully exploited his talents.

export
[ikspɔ́ːrt][ikspɔ́ːrt]
® 3441/86800

v. n. 수출하다, 수출(품)
❶ ex(밖으로) + port(항구): 항구 밖으로 수출품들 이 나감
⊕ market abroad, sell abroad ⊕ import
예 French cheeses are exported to many different countries.

expose
[ikspóuz]
® 10032/86800

v. 드러내다, 노출하다
❶ ex(밖으로) + pose(자세를 취함): 노출하다
⊕ uncover, show
파 exposition: 전시회 *exposure*: 노출
예 He damaged his leg so badly in the accident that the bone was exposed.

express
[iksprés]
® 2053/86800

v. n. 표현하다, 급행
❶ 안에 있는 것을 밖으로 눌러내다: 표현하다
⊕ represent
파 *expression*: 표현 *expressive*: 표현하는
예 Her eyes expressed deep sadness.

E

exquisite
[ikskwízit]
® 10707/86800

adj. 정교한, 우아한
ⓣ (수학의)엑스(가) (뭔지) 꿰듯(exquisite)정교한
ⓢ delicate, fine
예 Mr. Kim's singing voice is very exquisite.

extend
[iksténd]
® 3094/86800

v. 뻗다, 연장하다, 넓히다
ⓣ ex(밖으로) + tend(텐트 - 늘리다): 뻗다, 연장하다
ⓢ enlarge, broaden, expand
파 *extension*: 연장, 확장, 구내전화 extensive: 넓은
예 The Sahara Desert extends for miles.

extent
[ikstént]
® 1020/86800

n. 넓이, 크기, 정도, 범위
ⓣ 익수텐트(extent) - 익수가 쓴 텐트 의 크기
예 From the top of the Empire State Building, you can see the full extent of Manhattan (= the area it covers).

external
[ikstə́:rnəl]
® 2057/86800

adj. 외부의
ⓣ ex(바깥) + ternal(터널로 생각): 터널 외부의, - 외부의
ⓢ outside, exterior, outer ⓐ internal
예 He repaired the external walls of the house.

extinct
[ikstíŋkt]
® 12334/86800

adj. 멸종한
ⓣ 없어 딩(extinct) - 없어져 멸종한
ⓢ dead, vanished
파 *extinction*: 멸종, 소화 extinguish: 불을 끄다
예 There is concern that the giant panda will soon become extinct.

extra
[ékstrə]
® 1070/86800

adj. 여분의
ⓣ 엑스트라(extra)는 주인공 이외의 사람
ⓢ additional, surplus
예 Recently he's been working an extra two hours a day.

extract
[ikstrǽkt]
® 5412/86800

v. 뽑다
ⓣ 애써 트리(extract)를 뽑다
ⓢ pull ⓐ insert
例 The tooth was eventually extracted.

✓ extracurricular
[èkstrəkəríkjələr]
® 75040/86800

adj. 과외의
ⓣ extra(여분의) + curricular(교육과정의) 교과 이외의
例 Playing a sport for your school is considered an extracurricular activity.

✓ extraordinary
[ikstrɔ́:rdənèri]
® 3221/86800

adj. 대단한, 비범한
ⓣ extra(이외의) + ordinary(보통): 보통이 아닌
ⓢ uncommon, unique, unusual ⓐ common, ordinary
파 *extraordinarily*: 대단하게
例 He told the extraordinary story of his escape.

extravagant
[ikstrǽvəgənt]
® 11796/86800

adj. 사치스러운, 터무니없는
ⓣ 엑스트라가 버는거(extravagant)에 비해 **사치스러운**
ⓢ wasteful, prodigal
例 He rarely used taxis, which he regarded as extravagant.

✔ extreme
[ikstrí:m]
® 2686/86800

adj. n. 극단적인, 극단
ⓣ ex(밖으로) + treme((늘어)뜨림): 밖으로 늘어뜨리면 극단에 접하게 됨
ⓢ excessive, immoderate
파 *extremely*: 극단적으로, 매우
例 The people suffered from extreme poverty.

fable
[féibəl]
® 24402/86800

n. 우화, 이야기
ⓣ 펴 이불(fable) - 흥부 새끼들이 가난해서 한 이불 펴서 여러 명 덮은 **이야기** 생각할 것
ⓢ story, tale
例 My children read a fable about busy ants.

fabric
[fǽbrik]
ⓡ 4098/86800

n. **구조(물), 직물**
❶ **직물**을 보면 구멍이 뻥뻥 난 틈으로 바느질을 빼버림.. **빼버릭** (fabric -)
ⓢ textile
예 She bought dress fabric for her wedding.

✔ facility
[fəsíləti]
ⓡ 3955/86800

n. **시설, 설비**
❶ fac - 만들어 놓은 것 + ility - 만들어 논 시설
ⓢ equipment
예 DMZ has lots of military facilities.

✔ factor
[fǽktər]
ⓡ 1644/86800

n. **요인, 요소**
❶ factor(만들어 놓은 것) - fac, fic은 만든다는 뜻
ⓢ component, element
c.f) *factual*: 사실에 입각한 *fact*: 사실
예 Heavy snow was a contributing factor in the accident.

faculty
[fǽkəlti]
ⓡ 6029/86800

n. **능력, 교수단**
❶ **능력**이 있어야 남의 걸 **뺏것 디**(faculty)!
  혹은 학교가면 **교수님들 뵙것디**(faculty)!
ⓢ ability, capacity
예 She has a faculty for inspiring confidence in people.

fade
[feid]
ⓡ 11118/86800

v. **희미해지다, 바래다, 사라지다**
❶ 농구의 **fade away 슛**, 희곡의 **fade out**을 생각할 것. - 사라지다, **희미해지다**
ⓢ discolor: 바래다 disappear, vanish: 사라지다
예 My suntan is already fading.

✔ faint
[feint]
ⓡ 4896/86800

adj. n. **희미한, 어질어질한, 기절(하다)**
❶ 안개가 **배인**(faint) - 안개가 베여 **희미한**
ⓢ dim: 희미한 dizzy: 어질어질한 swoon: 기절(하다)
예 Did you heard a faint sound a while ago?

fair
[fεər]
® 1110/86800

adj. n. 공정한, 박람회
❶ 편파적 심판 빼어(fair)서 - 심판 빼고 **공정한**
㉦ impartial, unprejudiced ㉫ foul 파 *fairly*: 공평히
㉠ The trial was not fair.

faith
[feiθ]
® 1941/86800

n. 신뢰, 신앙
❶ 어렸을 때부터 신앙이 **배있어(faith)**
㉦ belief, trust
파 *faithful*: 충실한, 성실한 faithfully: 성실하게
㉠ She has no faith in modern medicine.

F

fallacy
[fǽləsi]
® 19830/86800

n. 잘못된 생각, 오류
❶ 중요한 것 빨라 쒸(fallacy)! - 핵심 뺀 **오류**
㉦ error, mistake
㉠ It is a common fallacy that women are worse drivers than men.

falter
[fɔ́:ltər]
® 28333/86800

v. 망설이다, 비틀거리다
❶ 話떨(말을 떨다 - **망설이다)**, 비틀(falter)거리다
㉠ My resolution should never falter.

fame
[feim]
® 6228/86800

n. 명성
❶ famous를 생각하면 쉽게 기억할 것
㉦ renown, reputation
㉠ She first rose to fame as a singer at the age of 16.

famine
[fǽmin]
® 9343/86800

n. 굶주림, 기아, 기근
❶ 범인(famine)은 가난하고 굶주린 사람
㉦ starvation, hunger
㉠ There were reports of refugees dying of famine.

fare
[fεər]
® 6940/86800

n. 승차 요금, 운임
❶ fare - f(fee피) a(내) re(레) - 피(**요금**)내레
㉦ price, fee
㉠ Train fares are going up again.

farewell
[fἐərwél]
Ⓡ 8923/86800

n. **작별, 작별 인사**
[T] **작별**하며 하는 인사 - 나중에 **뵈어욜(farewell)**
[유] goodbye, parting
[예] They said their farewells and headed home.

✔ **fascinate**
[fǽsənèit]
Ⓡ 38437/86800

v. **매혹하다**
[T] 내 정신을 **빴어네 잇(fascinate) - 매혹하다**
[유] charm, enchant
[예] Science has always fascinated me.

✔ **fast**
[fæst]
Ⓡ 1360/86800

n. adj. **단식, 고정된**
[T] Breakfast(단식을 깨트린게 아침 식사 - 사람은 음식이 부족해서 두끼만 먹었으므로 아침을 단식하다가 이를 깨트린 것이 아침 식사임)
[유] fasting: 단식 fixed: 고정된
[예] Hundreds of prisoners began a fast in protest about prison conditions.

✔ **fasten**
[fǽsn]
Ⓡ 23525/86800

v. **매다, 단단히 고정시키다**
[T] 못을 **빼선(fasten)**안되므로 **단단히 매다**
[유] tie, bind
[예] Make sure your seat belt is securely fastened.

fat
[fæt]
Ⓡ 2197/86800

adj. n. **살찐, 지방(이 많은)**
[T] 살 좀 **빼(fat) - 살찐**
[유] fatty
[예] I have horrible fat thighs.

✔ **fatal**
[féitl]
Ⓡ 5689/86800

adj. **치명적인, 운명적인**
[T] **뼈 이탈(fatal)** - 뼈가 이탈하면 **치명적인**
[유] deadly: 치명적인 fateful: 운명적인
[파] 인fate: 운명
[예] This illness is fatal in almost all cases.

fatigue
[fətíːg]
[R] 11199/86800

n. 피로
[T] 피곤해도 버티고(fatigue) 있어요
[유] tiredness, exhaustion
[예] She was suffering from fatigue and a stress - related illness.

✔ **faucet**
[fɔ́ːsit]
[R] 순위외/86800

n. 수도꼭지
[T] 뽀씻(faucet) - 수도꼭지 틀고 얼굴을 뽀얏게 씻음
[예] There is something wrong with the faucet of my house.

✔✔ **fault**
[fɔːlt]
[R] 2803/86800

n. 결점, 잘못
[T] 테니스 경기에서 서브를 잘 못 넣으면 심판이 하는 말은 폴트(fault) - 잘못
[유] defect: 결점 mistake: 잘못
[파] faultfinding: 흠잡기 faultless: 결점이 없는
[예] It's not my fault she didn't come!

✔✔ **favor**
[féivər]
[R] 34838/86800

n. 친절, 부탁, 호의
[T] 남이 나에게 호감 갖도록 옷을 빼입어(favor). 옷을 빼입는다는 말은 옷을 잘 입는다는 뜻
[유] good will, kindness
[파] *favorite*: 매우 좋아하는 *favorable*: 호의를 보이는 *favorably*: 호의적으로
[예] She's willing to help you but only as a favor to me.

✔ **fearful**
[fíərfəl]
[R] 8781/86800

adj. 무서운, 두려워하는
[T] 지옥에서 피워 불(fearful) - 무서운
[유] terrible, horrible [파] *fear*: 두려움
[예] He hesitated before ringing her, fearful of what she might say.

feat
[fiːt]
[R] 13298/86800

n. 공적
[T] 빛(feat)나는 공적
[유] achievement, accomplishment
[예] The Eiffel Tower is a remarkable feat of engineering.

feather
[féðər]
ⓡ 11137/86800

n. 깃털
❶ 깃털을 빼다(feather)
ⓢ plumage, plume
예 The birds of a feather flock together.

feature
[fíːtʃər]
ⓡ 1646/86800

n. v. 특징, 주연시키다
❶ 사람들에게 비쳐(feature)진 특징
ⓢ characteristic, peculiarity
예 Our latest model of phone has several new features.

federal
[fédərəl]
ⓡ 2596/86800

a. 동맹의, 연방의
❶ 패 들을(federal - 패거리 들을) 패거리는 동맹
예 FBI investigated the murder case.

fee
[fiː]
ⓡ 3251/86800

n. 요금, 수수료
❶ 비(fee): 복사 비, 식사비 등등
ⓢ price, fare
예 We couldn't pay the lawyer's fee.

feed
[fiːd]
ⓡ 3031/86800

v. 먹이다
❶ 배에다(feed) 음식을 먹이다
ⓢ feed on
예 The kids love feeding bread to the ducks.

fellow
[félou]
ⓡ 2241/86800

n. 동료, 친구
❶ 필로(fellow - feel로) 통하는 친구
ⓢ colleague, companion
예 He's a fellow of the American College of Surgeons.

female
[fíːmeil]
ⓡ 1274/86800

n. 여성(의), 암컷(의)
❶ 비(fe - 아닐 비) + male: 남성이 아님, 매일은 매 매일(male)은 매일 나가므로 남성
ⓢ womankind, womenfolk ㉠ feminine: 여성의
예 She was voted the best female vocalist.

ferry
[féri]
® 5869/86800

n. **나룻배**
❶ 페리(ferry)호를 타고 제주도를 간다
㉕ ferryboat
㉕ We're going across to France by/on the ferry.

fertile ✔
[fɔ́:rtl / -tail]
® 9993/86800

adj. **비옥한, 많이 낳는**
❶ 씨를 **퍼뜨릴(fertile)** - 씨 퍼뜨리게 **비옥한**
㉕ fruitful, productive
㉕ fertilize: 기름지게 하다 fertilizer: (화학) 비료
㉕ Many farmers are searching fertile soil.

fever
[fíːvər]
® 6738/86800

n. **열, 열병**
❶ 열이 많다 이브자리 **펴봐(fever)**
㉕ temperature
㉕ He's got a headache and a slight fever.

fiber ✔
[fáibər]
® 순위外/86800

n. **섬유질**
❶ **파이브(fiber)** 미니, 미에로 파이버(fiber)라는 음료수는 **섬유질**을 보강
㉕ It's important to get enough fiber in your diet.

fiction ✔
[fíkʃən]
® 4378/86800

n. **소설, 허구**
❶ fic(만들다) + tion(명사형 어미): 만든 것 - 허구
㉕ novel
㉕ They met a writer of children's fiction.

field ✔
[fíːld]
® 639/86800

n. **들판, 분야**
❶ 야구의 필드(들판에서 야구함)를 생각
㉕ plain
㉕ The cows were all standing in one corner of the field.

fierce ✔
[fiərs]
® 5116/86800

adj. **사나운, 맹렬한**
❶ 손을 물어서 나온게 **피여서(fierce) - 사나운**
㉕ savage, ferocious
㉕ Two men were shot during fierce fighting last weekend.

F

figurative
[fígjərətiv]
® 24112/86800

adj. 비유적인
❶ **비규**(비유 - **figu**) + tive(형용사형 어미)
㊀ allegorical, metaphorical
㉠ He found the figurative use of "allergy" to mean "a feeling of dislike".

figure
[fígjər]
® 547/86800

n. v. 숫자, 모양, 인물, 생각하다
❶ 빼고(figure) - **숫자**를 빼고
㉠ The vase is decorated with figures of birds and fish.

fin
[fin]
® 15311/86800

n. 지느러미
❶ 샥스(shark) + 핀(fin) - 상어 **지느러미** 요리
㉠ Have you ever tried shark's fin?

finance
[fínǽns]
® 1374/86800

n. 재정
❶ fi(fee로 생각) + nance(냈어): fee 내는 것은 돈이 나가는 것 - **재정**
㊊ *financial*: 재정의, 금융의
㉠ I took a course on public finance.

fit
[fit]
® 1254/86800

v. adj. (알)맞다, 맞추다, 알맞은, 건강한
❶ fitness 센터는 헬스센터
㊀ suit: 알맞다, set: 맞추다 ㊊ *fitness*: 건강함, 적당함
㉠ That jacket fits you perfectly.

fix
[fiks]
® 5447/86800

v. 수리하다, 고정시키다
❶ 삑사(fix) 리 난 것 **고정시키다**
삑사리 - 당구에서 의도한 곳 아닌 쪽으로 나가는 것
㊀ repair, mend ㊊ fixed: 고정된
㉠ They couldn't fix my old computer, so I bought a new one.

flame
[fleim]
® 6835/86800

n. v. 불꽃, 타오르다
❶ 불에 임(flame) - 불과 함께 하면 **타오른다**
㊀ blaze c.f) *flash*: 번쩍(이다), 문득 떠오르다
㉠ The flames grew larger as the fire spread.

flap
[flæp]
[R] 12283/86800

v. **날개를 퍼덕이다, 찰싹 때리다**
[T] 날개를 **펄랩(flap** - 펄럭)이다
[예] A bird flapped away.

flat
[flæt]
[R] 1205/86800

adj. **평평한, 타이어 바람 빠진**
[T] 어머니들 빨래해서 **풀에(flat)** 펴면 **평평한**
[유] plain, even
[예] An ice rink needs to be completely flat.

F

flatter
[flǽtər]
[R] 16901/86800

v. **아첨하다**
[T] 입술에 **부풀넣었다(flatter)**: 부풀어 이야기하다 - **아첨하다**
[유] adulate, compliment [파] ***flattery***: 아첨
[예] He flattered her with comments about her youthful appearance.

flavor
[fléivər]
[R] 5337/86800

n. **맛(을 내다)**
[T] 김치에 양념 **풀 어봐(flavor)** - **맛**을 낸다
[유] taste, savor
[예] Add a little salt to bring out the flavor of the herbs.

flaw
[flɔː]
[R] 17158/86800

n. **결점, 흠**
[T] **풀러(flaw)** 진 **결점** - 남의 결점이 들어남
[유] fault, defect
[예] This report is full of flaws.

flee
[fliː]
[R] 11900/86800

v. **도망치다**
[T] **뿌리(flee)**치고 **도망가다**
[유] escape
[예] In order to escape capture, he fled to the mountains.

flesh
[fleʃ]
[R] 3593/86800

n. **살, 육체**
[T] **불에 쉬(flesh)** 타는 **살** - 불에 쉽게 타는 살
[유] body
[예] Vegetarians don't eat animal flesh.

✔ **flexible**
[fléksəbəl]
[R] 3761/86800

adj. **구부리기 쉬운, 유연한**
[T] flex(구부리다) + ible(할 수 있는): 구부릴 수 있는
[유] elastic, pliable [반] inflexible
[예] She's been doing exercises to become stronger and more flexible.

✔ **flip**
[flip]
[R] 18330/86800

v. **손가락으로 튀기다, 찰싹 때리다, 페이지를 넘기다**
[T] 휴대폰기기 중 **플립(flip)**폰(손으로 툭)을 생각
[예] He flipped a coin.

✔ **float**
[flout]
[R] 7479/86800

v. **뜨다, 떠오르다**
[T] **풀로(물로) 뜨(flote)**다
[유] buoy [반] sink
[예] An empty bottle will float.

flock
[flɑk]
[R] 8523/86800

n. **떼**
[T] **풀로(flock)** 다니는 메뚜기 **떼**
[유] group, crowd
[예] Did you find a flock of sheep?

✔ **flood**
[flʌd]
[R] 5248/86800

n. v. **홍수, 범람하다**
[T] 물이 **플(흘)렀다(flood): **물이 **흘러 넘치다**
[유] deluge, inundation
[예] Our washing machine broke down yesterday and flooded the kitchen.

✔ **floppy**
[flápi]
[R] 11151/86800

a. **펄럭이는, 느슨한**(slack)
[T] 너플 너**플 높이(floppy) 펄럭이는** 태극기
[예] My dog has long and floppy ears.

flour
[flauər]
[R] 6863/86800

n. **밀가루**
[T] **밀가루**는 부 **풀러(flour)**오른다
[예] I bought a five - pound bag of flour in Tops.

flourish
[flə́:riʃ]
[R] 9212/86800

v. **번창[번영, 번성]하다**
[T] flou(흐르다) + rish(rich로 생각): 부자되게 흐르다 - **번영하다**
[유] succeed
[예] Watercolor painting began to flourish in Britain around 1750.

✔ **flow**
[flou]
[R] 1954/86800

v. n. **흐르다, 흐름**
[T] 물이 **흘러(flow)**간다
[유] stream, run c.f) fluency: 유창함 fluent: 유창한
[예] Many short rivers flow into the Pacific Ocean.

✔ **fluffy**
[flʌ́fi]
[R] 17702/86800

a. **보풀(솜털) 같은, 솜같이 가벼운, 시시한**
[T] **풀나비(fluffy)** - 풀위로 나는 **가벼운** 나비
[예] He has fluffy whiskers.

fluid
[flú:id]
[R] 4950/86800

adj. n. **유동성의, 유동체**
[T] 물이 **flu(흐르) + id(이다):** 흐르는 것이다 - 유동체
[유] liquid [반] solid
[예] If you have a fever you should drink plenty of fluid(s).

✔ **flush**
[flʌʃ]
[R] 9203/86800

v. **붉어지다, 물을 쏟아 씻다**
[T] 얼굴이 **붉어쉬(flush)다**
[유] blush: 붉어지다 rinse: 씻다
[예] She flushed with pleasure as she accepted the prize.

✔ **flutter**
[flʌ́tə:r]
[R] 19421/86800

v. **펄럭이다, 퍼덕거리다**
[T] 깃발이 **플러덕(flutter)**거리다 - 깃발이 **펄럭이는** 소리
[유] flap
[예] Brightly coloured flags were fluttering in the breeze.

✔ **foam**
[foum]
[R] 9172/86800

n. v. **거품, 거품이 일다**
[T] **거품(foam) 일다**
[유] froth, bubble
[예] Do you use shaving foam when you shave?

fold
[fould]
[R] 7271/86800

v. n. **접다, 접은 부분**
[T] 폴더(floder)라는 말 많이 들어봤을 것이다
공책을 잘 **접어** 놓은 것
[유] furl, collapse
[예] I folded the letter (in half) and put it in an envelope.

foliage
[fóuliidʒ]
[R] 8832/86800

n. adj. **잎, 잎이 무성한**
[T] **무성한 풀이지(foliage)**
[유] leafy: 잎이 무성한
[예] The dense foliage overhead almost blocked out the sun.

folk
[fouk]
[R] 4099/86800

n. **사람들, 민속**
[T] 민속촌을 영어로 folk village(민속마을)라고 함
또 미국인들은 Hi! folks 라고 인사함
[예] Ordinary folk can't afford cars like that.

follow
[fálou]
[R] 1069/86800

v. **동행하다**
[T] **빨(리) 오우(follow)**: 빨리 **같이 가자**고 하는 말
[유] come after, go behind
[파] *following*: 다음의, 다음에 말하는 것
[예] A dog followed us home.

folly
[fáli / fɔ́li]
[R] 7139/86800

n. **어리석음**
[T] folly(바보 - fool로)이해
[유] foolishness, stupidness
[예] She said that the idea was folly.

fond
[fand]
[R] 6361/86800

adj. **좋아하는**
[T] 아기는 **좋아하면 손을 빤다(fond)**
[유] like, favorite
[예] She was very fond of horses.

✔ foothill
[fúthìl]
Ⓡ 순위외/86800

n. 산기슭의 언덕(구릉)
❶ 발(foot) + 언덕(hill): 언덕의 발 부분
예 Foothill is a low hill at the bottom of a larger mountain.

✤ forage
[fɔ́:ridʒ]
Ⓡ 25304/86800

v. (식량) 찾아다니다, 약탈하다, 말, 소의 먹이
❶ 약탈은 남의 물건 함부로 뿌리지(forage)
예 I went foraging in the attic for old memory.

forbear
[fɔ:rbέə:r]
Ⓡ 58528/86800

v. 삼가다
❶ 사슴 뿔 베어(forbear) 가는 거 **삼가다**
⊕ restrain, refrain
예 We decided to forbear provoking him any further.

✤ forbid
[fə:rbíd]
Ⓡ 15490/86800

v. 금지하다
❶ 클럽에 홀비(forbid - 홀아비)는 **금지**하다
⊕ ban, prohibit
예 The law forbids the sale of cigarettes to people under the age of 16.

✤ force
[fɔ:rs]
Ⓡ 617/86800

n. v. 힘, 강요하다
❶ 팔써(force)서 **힘** 보여주다
⊕ compel, oblige: 강요하다 파 forceful: 강력한
예 She slapped his face with unexpected force.

✤ forecast
[fɔ́:rkæ̀st]
Ⓡ 5226/86800

n. 예상(하다), 일기 예보
❶ fore(미리) + cast(던지다): 미리(예보)를 던지다
⊕ predict, expect, anticipate
예 The weather forecast said it was going to rain later today.

forefather
[fɔ́:rfɑ̀:ðə:r]
Ⓡ 순위 外/86800

n. 선조
❶ fore(앞에) + father(아버지): 부친 전에 있는 조상
⊕ ancestor, progenitor, predecessor
예 Our forefathers bought this farm, and our family has worked it for three generations.

F

forehead
[fɔ́:rhéd]
® 5837/86800

n. 이마
❶ fore(앞) + head(머리): 머리 앞 쪽에 있는 이마
㉮ brow
㉙ She's got a high forehead.

foreign
[fɔ́(:)rin]
® 600/86800

adj. 외국의
❶ 한국 와서 다 **뽀린(훔친(forein))**외국인들
㉮ alien, oversea(s)
c.f) *foreigner*: 외국인
㉙ Spain was the first foreign country she had visited.

foremost
[fɔ́:rmòust]
® 9926/86800

adj. 최고의, 맨 처음
❶ fore(앞) + most(가장): 가장 앞, 최고의
㉮ at the very first, first of all: 맨 처음
㉙ She's one of the foremost experts on child psychology.

foresee
[fɔ́:rsí:]
® 16526/86800

v. 예견하다
❶ fore(미리) + see(보다): 미리보다, 예상하다
㉮ forecast, predict
㉕ foresight: 선견, 예지
㉙ I don't foresee any difficulties so long as we keep within budget.

foretell
[fɔ́:rtél]
® 50309/86800

v. 예언하다
❶ fore(미리) + tell(말하다)
㉮ prophesy, predict
㉙ He was a sixteenth - century prophet who foretold how the world would end.

forlorn
[fə:rlɔ́:rn]
® 19757/86800

adj. 고독한, 쓸쓸한
❶ **홀론(forlogn): 홀로 있는**, 고독한
㉮ desolate, lonely
㉙ She looked a forlorn figure standing at the bus stop.

❖ formal
[fɔ́:rməl]
ⓡ 1603/86800

adj. 정식의, 공식의, 형식적인
❶ form(폼) + al (형용사 어미)형태를 갖춘
ⓢ official, state c.f) *former*: 이전의, 전자(의)
파 formation: 형성 *format*: 형 *form*: 모양
예 You should follow formal procedures.

formula
[fɔ́:rmjələ]
ⓡ 3475/86800

n. 공식
❶ 공식은 정해진 **폼이라(formula)**는 게 있음
예 The product is made using a secret formula that the company refuses to reveal.

forsake
[fəːrséik]
ⓡ 35615/86800

v. 버리다
❶ **벌써(forsa) + 이것(ake) 버리니?**
ⓢ abandon, give up, desert
예 Do not forsake me!

fort
[fɔ:rt]
ⓡ 6790/86800

n. 요새
❶ 숨어서 **보다(fort)** 적의 동태를 보는 **요새**
ⓢ fortress
예 The remains of the Roman fort are well preserved.

fortitude
[fɔ́:rtətjùːd]
ⓡ 29385/86800

n. 인내, 용기
❶ **버티(forti) + 튜드(tude)**: 버티는 것은 **인내**
ⓢ endurance, patience: 인내
예 I thought she showed remarkable fortitude during that period.

✔ fossil
[fásl]
ⓡ 7647/86800

n. 화석(의)
❶ **퐈석(fossil)**하고 발음하면 화석과 유사함
예 A man found fossil insects by accident.

✔ foster
[fɔ́(:)stəːr]
ⓡ 4562/86800

v. 기르다, (성장을) 촉진하다
❶ **포스터(foster)** 붙이는 것은 어떤 일을 잘되게 홍보하기 위해
ⓢ bring up, nurse
예 Would you consider fostering (a child)?

F

foundation
[faundéiʃən]
ⓡ 2641/86800

n. 기초, 설립, 재단
❶ 어머니가 **파운데이션(foundation)**바르는 것은 일종의 **기초**화장임
⊕ establishment, institution: 설립
㈜ *found*: 설립하다 founder: 설립자
㈀ The foundation of a new state was established.

fountain
[fáuntin]
ⓡ 9208/86800

n. 분수, 샘
❶ **품(f)**어 나오는 **원천(ountain)** - 분수, 샘
⊕ spring: 샘
㈀ The crowd gathered around the fountain in the plaza.

fraction
[frǽkʃən]
ⓡ 5374/86800

n. 단편
❶ **뿌러 션(fraction)** - 부러뜨려 놓은 것(단편)
⊕ fragment, piece ㈜ fragment: 조각, 파편
㈀ Only a fraction of the city's population perished during the hurricane because of the government's improved warning system.

✔ fragile
[frǽdʒəl]
ⓡ 7742/86800

adj. 부서지기 쉬운, 연약한
❶ **뿌러질(fragile)** - 부서지기 쉬운
⊕ brittle, frail, delicate
㈀ Be careful with that vase - it's very fragile.

fragrance
[fréigrəns]
ⓡ 14732/86800

n. 향기
❶ fra(뿌려) + grance(grace로 이해 - 우아함): 향기
⊕ perfume, aroma
㈀ the delicate fragrance of roses.

✔ frame
[freim]
ⓡ 2886/86800

n. 구조
❶ 사람의 **구조**는 뼈레임(frame) - 뼈로 된 사람
⊕ structure, construction
c.f) *framework*: 틀, 구조, 뼈대
㈀ A bicycle frame is very simple.

✔ frank
[fræŋk]
® 2345/86800

adj. 솔직한
❶ 솔직한 말로 "너에게 맡겨도 **불안 커(frank)**"
ⓢ candid, direct 곱 *frankly*: 솔직히
예 To be perfectly frank with you, I don't think she's the woman for the job.

✔ freeze
[fri:z]
® 7483/86800

v. 얼다, 얼게 하다
❶ 눈이 **뿌리지(freeze)** - 눈이 뿌리면 길이 얼지
ⓢ congeal, ice
예 Water freezes to ice at a temperature of 0°C.

freight
[freit]
® 7240/86800

n. v. 운송, 화물을 싣다
❶ 화(f)물(r) 프라잇(freight - fly와 비슷 - 짐나르다)
ⓢ transport(ation), load
예 The ship carries both freight and passengers.

✔ frequency
[frí:kwənsi]
® 3358/86800

n. 자주 일어남, 주파수
❶ 불 잊게(freque) - 불이 **자주** 나니 잊게 해주오
곱 *frequent*: 빈번한 *frequently*: 종종
예 the increasing frequency of terrorist attacks.

friction
[fríkʃən]
® 11466/86800

n. 마찰
❶ 마찰이 생기면 불 일션(friction - 불이 일어남)
옛날인 들은 돌을 마찰시켜 불 일으킴
ⓢ rubbing
예 When you rub your hands together the friction produces heat.

✔ fright
[frait]
® 12434/86800

n. 놀람
❶ 불 나있(fright)어서 **놀람**
ⓢ fear, alarm
곱 *frighten*: 놀라게 하다
예 I lay in bed shaking with fright.

frivolous

[frívələs]

® 18701/86800

adj. 경솔한

❶ 비밀을 함부로 **불어버렸어(frivolous) - 경솔한**

⊕ careless, thoughtless

예 I think he sees her as a frivolous young woman.

frontier

[frʌntíə:r]

® 7703/86800

n. **국경(개척지와 미개척지의 중간), 미개척 영역**

❶ 앞으로 **튀어(frontier) -** 미개척지가 잘 나갈거야

혹은 front(다른 나라와 앞 대고 있는)지역

⊕ border, boundary

예 Nepal has frontiers with both India and China.

✔ frost

[frɔ:st]

® 7119/86800

n. **서리**

❶ 서리가 **뿌려 서(fros)**

예 There was a frost last night.

✔ frown

[fraun]

® 10912/86800

v. n. **눈살을 찌푸리다, 찌푸린 얼굴**

❶ 눈살을 찌**푸라운(frown)**

⊕ grimace

예 She frowned at me, clearly annoyed.

frugal

[frú:gəl]

® 32323/86800

adj. **소박한, 알뜰한**

❶ 오늘도 풀로 **갈(frugal - 농사짓기 위해)** 소박한 사람

⊕ thrifty, saving

예 She has a frugal lifestyle.

✔ fruitful

[frú:tfəl]

® 12219/86800

adj. **열매가 많이 열리는**

❶ friut(열매) + ful(full이 줄어든 것): 열매가 꽉 찬

⊕ fertile, productive

㴯 fruitless: 열매를 맺지 않는

fruit: 과일, 성과

예 I have a very fruitful tree that gives us plenty of apples every year.

frustrate
[frʌ́streit]
ⓡ 24356/86800

v. 좌절시키다
❶ 좌절해서 뿔 났었더랬어(frustrate)
ⓨ baffle 파 *frustration*: 조절, 욕구불만
예 It frustrates me that I'm not able to put any of my ideas into practice.

fuel
[fjúːəl]
ⓡ 2383/86800

n. 연료
❶ 불 피워(fuel) ! 아 **연료**가 있어야지?
ⓨ gasoline
예 Wood, coal, oil, petrol and gas are all different kinds of fuel.

fulfil(l)
[fulfíl]
ⓡ 6370/86800

v. 이행하다, 실현하다
❶ full(꽉 차게) + fill(채우다) 완전히 채우다, 실현하다
ⓨ perform, discharge
파 fulfillment: 이행, 수행, 완료
예 He has failed to fulfil his duties as a father.

function
[fʌ́ŋkʃən]
ⓡ 1187/86800

n. v. 기능, 함수, 역할을 하다
❶ 수학시간에 배운 f(x) - 함수 f가 function의 줄임
혹은 (연극배우가) **병신(fuction) 역할**을 잘 하다
ⓨ faculty 기능 파 *functional*: 기능의
예 The function of the veins is to carry blood to the heart.

fundamental
[fʌndəméntl]
ⓡ 2234/86800

n. adj. 기본, 기본적인
❶ 본다멘탈(fundamental) - 사람볼 때 가장 **기본**적인 멘탈(정신)을 본다
ⓨ basic, basis 파 *fundamentally*: 본질적으로
예 It's one of the fundamental differences between men and women.

funeral
[fjúːnərəl]
ⓡ 4068/86800

n. adj. 장례식, 장례의
❶ 비워 널(관)을(funeral) - 장례식을 준비하면서 죽은 사람 담을 관을 비워
예 The funeral will be held next Friday.

✔ **fur**
[fə::r]
[R] 6615/86800

n. **털, 모피**
[T] 모 피(f)털(ur)
[유] fell: 모피
[예] She stroked the rabbit's soft fur.

furious
[fjúəriəs]
[R] 5827/86800

adj. **격노한**
[T] **뿔이었어(furious) - 화가 나서** 뿔난 것 생각
[파] fury: 격분
[예] I was late and he was furious with me.

✔ **furnish**
[fə́:rniʃ]
[R] 18531/86800

v. **공급하다**
[T] **벌이 쉬(furnish)** 하면서 꿀을 **공급하다**
[유] provide, supply
[예] We'll furnish the food for the party.

✔ **furthermore**
[fə́:rðə:rmɔ̀:r]
[R] 3247/86800

adv. **게다가, 더욱이, 더**
[T] **빠다(further -** 버터) **더** 달라고 빠다모어**(more)**
[유] moreover, besides
[예] They're good and furthermore they're cheap.

fusion
[fjú:ʒən]
[R] 6292/86800

n. **용해, 연합**
[T] fuse(녹이다) + sion(명사형 어미): 녹임(용해)
[유] smelting: 용해
[예] The show is a fusion of news and entertainment.

✔ **fuss**
[fʌs]
[R] 7536/86800

n. **소란, 안달**
[T] 저스틴 비버를 **봤어(fuss)!**하면서 **소란**
[예] Justin put many girls into a fuss.

✔ **futile**
[fjú:tl, -tail]
[R] 13911/86800

adj. **쓸데없는, 무익한**
[T] **쓸데없는** 쓰레기는 **비워둘(futile)!**
[유] vain
[예] All my attempts to cheer her up proved futile.

✔ **fuzzy**
[fʌzi]
® 20587/86800

a. 솜털모양의, 분명하지 않은
❶ 솜털 같은 구름이 퍼지(fuzzy)다
예 I saw a plant with fuzzy leaves.

✔ **gain**
[gein]
® 1958/86800

v. 얻다, 획득하다
❶ 금메달 70개인(gain) - 금메달을 **획득**하다
㉮ get, obtain ㉯ lose
예 What do you hope to gain from the course?

gallant
[gǽlənt]
® 16919/86800

adj. 씩씩한, 여성에게 친절한
❶ 결혼(gallant)하려면 남자 **씩씩**하고 **친절**해야
㉮ valiant, brave
예 He offered her his seat in a gallant gesture.

✔ **gallery**
[gǽləri]
® 2347/86800

n. 미술관, 화랑
❶ 갤러리(gallery)는 화랑
예 She often visits a contemporary art gallery.

gamble
[gǽmbəl]
® 10811/86800

v. 도박하다
❶ 게임(gam)에 **불**(ble - 달러)걸어 도박하다
예 He gambles on the horses(= horse races).

✔ **game**
[geim]
® 656/86800

n. 게임, 사냥감
❶ 사냥 감(game)
㉮ bag, quarry
예 The king has game birds.

✔ **gap**
[gæp]
® 2848/86800

n. 틈, 차이
❶ 갑 갑(gap) 하면 **틈**을 두어야
㉮ crack, crevice: 틈
예 She has a small gap between her front teeth.

G

garage
[gərá:ʒ]
🅡 4220/86800

n. 차고
❶ 차고에 있는 것은 **카 라지(garage)**
예 Please put the car in the garage.

garbage
[gá:rbidʒ]
🅡 16202/86800

n. 쓰레기
❶ 쓰레기 갖다버리지(garbage)
㊎ trash, waste
예 The park was littered with garbage.

garment
[gá:rmənt]
🅡 9256/86800

n. 의류
❶ 갈 뭔(garment) - 갈아입을(의류)옷 뭔가?
㊎ clothing, clothes
예 The boy was busy putting on his garments.

gasp
[gæsp]
🅡 12922/86800

v. 헐떡거리다, 숨이 차다
❶ 개스 퍼(gasp) 져(가스가 퍼져) 숨 헐떡이다
㊎ pant
예 When she saw the money hidden in the box she gasped in surprise.

gather
[gǽðər]
🅡 5177/86800

v. 모으다, 모이다
❶ 옛날 계다(gather)하면 사람들이 모인다
㊎ collect
예 We gathered our things together and left quickly.

gaze
[geiz]
🅡 3800/86800

v. 응시하다
❶ 가제(gaze)눈으로 응시하다
㊎ stare, see
예 He spends hours gazing out of the window when he should be working.

gender
[dʒéndər]
🅡 4325/86800

n. 성(性)
❶ 트랜스 젠더(gender)라는 말 많이 들었을 것
㊎ sex
예 Does this test show the gender of the baby?

✔ **gene**
[ʤiːn]
® 3957/86800

n. 유전자
❶ gen(발생, 유전, 만듦): 뭔가 발생시키는 것: 유전자
e.g.) generator: 만들어내는 발전기
예 The illness is believed to be caused by a defective gene.

✔ **general**
[ʤénərəl]
® 251/86800

adj. n. 일반의, 보통의, 대장, 장군
❶ 쟤, 너를(general) 할 것 없이 **일반적인**, 혹은 **전하**(general)를 모시옵소서! **장군!!!**
ⓢ common, universal ⓐ special
ⓟ *generalize*: 일반화하다 generalization: 일반화
generally: 일반적으로
예 My general impression of the place was good.

✔ **generate**
[ʤénərèit]
® 4340/86800

v. 낳다, 발생하다
❶ gen(발생, 유전, 만듦) + ate(동사형, 형용사형)
ⓢ engender, produce c.f) *generation*: 세대, 발생
예 Her latest film has generated a lot of excitement.

✔ **generosity**
[ʤènərásəti]
® 9820/86800

n. 관대함, 너그러움
❶ 줘 늘였었지(generosity) - 뭘 늘 줬어? - **관대함**, 후함을 늘 줬었나 보군
ⓢ tolerance, liberality ⓟ *generous*: 관대한
예 Her friends take advantage of (= benefit unfairly from) her generosity.

✔ **genetics**
[ʤinétiks]
® 15479/86800

n. 유전학
❶ gen(발생) + ics(학문): 발생시키는 학문
ⓟ genetic: 유전학의 *geneticist*: 유전학자
genetically: 유전학적으로
예 I am getting a major in Genetics.

genial
[ʤíːniəl]
® 21988/86800

adj. 날씨가 온화한, 친절한
❶ 파도가 **잔잔해여**(genial) - 날씨가 **온화한**
ⓢ mild, pleasant
예 The headteacher is very genial/has a genial manner.

genius
[dʒíːniəs]
ⓡ 6595/86800

n. 천재
ⓣ 하늘이 **발생시킨(gen) + 이(i - 사람) + 였어(us): 천재**
ⓢ prodigy
ⓔ Einstein was a mathematical genius.

gentle
[dʒéntl]
ⓡ 3270/86800

adj. 온화한
ⓣ **gentleman(젠틀맨 - 신사)**을 생각하면 됨
ⓢ moderate ㉕ *gently*: 온화하게
ⓔ He's very gentle with his kids.

genuine
[dʒénjuin]
ⓡ 2915/86800

adj. 진짜의, 참된
ⓣ **genuine(진유인 - 진짜, 유 - 있는)** - 진짜 있는, 참된
ⓢ real, original ⓐ counterfeit ㉕ *genuinely*: 진짜로
ⓔ He wore a genuine leather jacket.

geography
[dʒiːágrəfi]
ⓡ 4983/86800

n. 지리학
ⓣ geo(땅) + graphy(씀): 땅에 대해 쓴 것은 지리
㉕ *geographical*: 지리학의, 지리적인
ⓔ The last course was studying the geography of the western United States.

geology
[dʒiːálədʒi]
ⓡ 8932/86800

n. 지질학
ⓣ geo(땅) + logy(학문, 이론, 말): 땅에 관한 학문은 지질학
ⓔ She became a geology teacher.

geometry
[dʒiːámətri]
ⓡ 11947/86800

n. 기하학
ⓣ geo(땅) + metry(측정, 우리가 몇 미터 할 때의 meter는 측정하다는 뜻): 땅을 측정하는 것은 기하학
ⓔ We have a geometry lesson in school.

germ
[dʒəːrm]
ⓡ 21975/86800

n. 세균, 싹
ⓣ **germ(점)** - 세균은 작은 점, 싹도 점처럼 작음
ⓢ bacteria, microbe
ⓔ Rats and flies spread germs.

❦ ghost
[goust]
📖 5670/86800

n. 유령
➊ 귀(gho)신다(st): 귀신이다
㊌ phantom, bog(e)y
㉠ Do you believe in ghosts?

✔ gill
[gil]
📖 8201/86800

n. 아가미
➊ 아가미 하면 물고기 숨 쉬는 길(gill) 떠올려
㉠ Gill is the organ through which fish and other water creatures breathe.

G

✔ glacier
[gléifər, gléisjər]
📖 18134/86800

n. 빙하
➊ 극에 서(glacier) 있는 것 - 빙하
㉠ Water from a melting glacier may be the source of a river.

✔ glance
[glæns, glɑ:ns]
📖 3524/86800

n. v. 힐끗 봄, 힐끗 보다
➊ 그래서?(grance)하면서 **힐끗 봄**
㊌ swift look, glimpse
㉠ She glanced around the room to see who was there.

✔ glare
[glɛər]
📖 10475/86800

v. n. 노려보다, 노려 봄
➊ 그래요?(glare) 하면서 **노려보다**
㊌ scowl ㉴ *glaringly*: 눈에 띄게
㉠ She gave me a fierce glare.

✔ glitter
[glítər]
📖 16155/86800

v. n. 반짝이다, 반짝거림
➊ gli(거리) + (불빛) tter(들) 이 **반짝이다**
㊌ shine, twinkle
㉠ Her diamond necklace glittered brilliantly under the spotlights.

❦ global
[glóubəl]
📖 2727/86800

adj. 전 세계의, 지구의
➊ globe(지구, 공) + al(형용사형 어미)
㊌ world ㉴ *globe*: 구(球), 지구(의), 전 세계의
㉠ Water shortage is a global problem.

gloomy
[glú:mi]
® 9253/86800

adj. 우울한, 어두운
❶ **구름이(gloomy)**끼어 있는 **우울한**
㊟ melancholy, dark
예 The cemetery is a gloomy place.

✔ glow
[glou]
® 7110/86800

v. 빨갛게 타다, 빛을 내다
❶ **곤로(glow** - 곤로와 발음 비슷, 참고로 곤로는 지금 가스레인지
가 나오기 전 70년, 80년 대의 소형 브루스타로 이해)에 불이
빨갛게 타다
㊟ radiate, beam: 빛을 내다
예 A nightlight glowed dimly in the corner of the
children's bedroom.

✔ glue
[glu:]
® 9005/86800

n. 풀, 아교
❶ **글루(glue** - 글 로) 쓴 편지 붙일 **풀**
㊟ paste
예 The hardware store offers several different glues.

✔ goodwill
[gúdwíl]
® 8145/86800

n. 호의, 친절
❶ good(좋은) + will(의지)
㊟ favor, kindness
예 She has goodwill toward all her coworkers.

gorgeous
[gɔ́:rdʒəs]
® 9767/86800

adj. 화려한
❶ **꼴 좋았어(gorgeous)**: 꼴이 **화려한**
㊟ dazzling, splendid
예 What a gorgeous dress!

gourd
[guərd]
® 60614/86800

n. 조롱박
❶ 박을 **고르다(gourd)**
예 I like the Spanish gourd.

✔ **govern**
[gʌ́vərn]

Ⓡ 10260/86800

v. **지배[통치]하다**
❶ govern(**거**느리고 **번**영시키다)
Ⓢ dominate, rule
Ⓟ *government*: 정부 *governmental*: 정부의
Ⓔ They accused the government of being unfit to govern.

✔ **grab**
[græb]

Ⓡ 7282/86800

v. **움켜잡다**
❶ 크랩(crab)을 그랩(grab)하다 - 게를 먹으러 움켜 잡다
Ⓔ A mugger grabbed my handbag.

✔ **gradual**
[græʤuəl]

Ⓡ 6783/86800

adj. **점진적인**
❶ **차차 그래 줘**(gradual, grade란 단어의 학년 올라가듯 점차적으로)
Ⓢ step-by-step
Ⓟ *gradually*: 점차
Ⓔ As you go further인south, you will notice a gradual change of climate.

✔ **grain**
[grein]

Ⓡ 4649/86800

n. **곡물, 낟알**
❶ gra(**갈**아 - 쟁기로 갈아) + in(**인** - 사람이) 먹고사는 것, 곡식
Ⓢ cereal, corn
Ⓔ Many birds eat grains of rice.

✔ **grammar**
[grǽmər]

Ⓡ 3737/86800

n. **문법**
❶ **그래 뭘**(grammar 문법) 알아야 영어를 읽지?
Ⓟ grammatical: 문법의
Ⓔ I took a German grammar course today.

✔ **grand**
[grænd]

Ⓡ 1804/86800

adj. **웅장한, 호화로운, 훌륭한**
❶ grand canyon(그랜드 캐년)생각해 봐요, 얼마나 웅장한지
Ⓢ magnificent, excellent
Ⓔ You've done a grand job.

grandstand
[grǽndstænd]
Ⓡ 24944/86800

n. 특별관람석
❶ grand(웅장한) + stand(연단): 특별관람석
[예] Grandstand is a set of seats arranged in rising rows from which people can easily watch events.

grant
[grænt]
Ⓡ 1390/86800

v. n. 승낙하다, 보조금
❶ 그런다(grant)고 승낙하다
⊛ subsidy: 보조금
[예] They gave her a grant to study abroad for one year.

grasp
[græsp]
Ⓡ 5193/86800

v. 움켜잡다, 파악하다
❶ 글에서 읍(grasp) 하고 의미를 파악하다
⊛ grab, seize
[예] Rosie suddenly grasped my hand.

grateful
[gréitfəl]
Ⓡ 3398/86800

adj. 고마워하는
❶ 그래 또 베풀(grateful)어 주셔서 감사하는
⊛ thankful ⊜ ungrateful 파 *gratitude*: 감사
[예] I'm so grateful (to you) for all that you've done.

gravely
[greivli]
Ⓡ 14857/86800

adv. 엄하게, 중대하게, 진지하게
❶ 그래봐라(gravely)!하며 엄하게 경고함
⊛ strictly, rigidly 파 *grave*: 무덤, 엄한
[예] He walked gravely back home from school with his failing report card.

gravity
[grǽvəti]
Ⓡ 6211/86800

n. 중력
❶ grave(무거운) + ity(명사형 어미): 무거운 힘 - 중력, 무거운 힘이니까 그래 벗자(gravity)
[예] I learned the laws of gravity in middle school.

graze
[greiz]
Ⓡ 21976/86800

v. (가축이) 풀을 뜯어먹다
❶ gra(ss)(풀을) + ze(째)먹다 - 풀을 째서(뜯어서 먹다)
⊛ feed, pasture
[예] The cows were grazing.

✔ **greed**
[gri:d]
® 11400/86800

n. 탐욕
❶ 그리도(greed) 큰 **욕심**
⊕ avarice, rapacity
예 I don't know why I'm eating more - it's not hunger, it's just greed!

✔ **greet**
[gri:t]
® 10304/86800

v. 인사하다
❶ 연말에 백화점에 크게 붙인 글 Season's **Grettings** - 연말에 하는 **인사**를 생각할 것
예 I greeted her by saying Hello.

grief
[gri:f]
® 5537/86800

n. 큰 슬픔
❶ 그리(슬)퍼(grief)
⊕ distress, sorrow 파 grieve: 슬퍼하다
예 Her grief at her son's death was terrible.

grln
[grin]
® 6230/86800

v. 이를 드러내고 웃다
❶ 껄껄(gr) 인(in - 이는) 드러내고 웃다
예 I assumed things had gone well for him as he had a big grin on his face.

✔ **grip**
[grip]
® 4466/86800

n. v. 잡음, 꽉 쥐다, 이해하다
❶ 글 입(grip - 글의 앞)을 꽉 잡아야 전체를 이해하게 된다, 혹은 골프의 글립 생각
⊕ grasp, clutch
예 The baby gripped my finger with her tiny hand.

gross
[grous]
® 3652/86800

adj. 총계의
❶ GNP는 gross national product을 줄인 말(국민 총생산)로 gross는 총 합이라는 뜻 임
⊕ total
예 She earns $30,000 a year gross.

ground [graund]
[R] 603/86800

n. 이유, 근거
[T] 그라운드(ground)는 운동장인데 선수들이 운동하는 기초와 근거가 됨
[유] reason, cause [파] *groundless*: 근거없는
[예] Do you have any ground for suspecting them?

grudge [grʌʤ]
[R] 20352/86800

v. 주기 아까워하다
[T] 주기 아까우니까 그러지(grudge)?
[유] begrudge
[예] She grudged every hour she spent helping him.

grumble [grʌ́mbəl]
[R] 24484/86800

v. 불평하다
[T] 그럼 불(grumble) 평해도 돼요?
[유] complain
[예] "You never hang your coat up," she grumbled.

guarantee [gæ̀rəntíː]
[R] 3150/86800

v. n. 보증하다, 보증
[T] 미국에서는 제품에 대해 lifetime guarantee(평생 보증)광고를 종종 볼 수 있어요. 개런티는 보증하는 것
[유] warrant, assure [파] *guaranteed*: 안전한
[예] The video recorder comes with a two - year guarantee.

guilty [gílti]
[R] 2384/86800

adj. 유죄의, 죄의식을 느끼는
[T] 길에서 튀(guilty) 면 뭔가 죄 있는 것 같은
[유] convicted [반] innocent [파] *guilt*: 죄
[예] I feel so guilty about forgetting her birthday.

gust [gʌst]
[R] 23958/86800

n. 돌풍
[T] 돌풍이 거세다(gust)
[예] There was a violent gust in Buffalo.

gym [ʤim]
[R] 13206/86800

n. 체육관, 체조, 체육
[T] 운동하면 몸에서 김 나지용(gymnasium)
[예] I go to the gym twice a week.

habitat
[hǽbətæt]
ⓡ 7231/86800

n. 서식지, 거주지
❶ 애비 택(habitat - 애비가 사는 宅(집)): 거주지
⊕ home
예 With so many areas of woodland being cut down, a lot of wildlife is losing its natural habitat.

half-hearted
[hǽf-háːrtid]
ⓡ 순위외/86800

a. 마음이 내키지 않는
❶ half(절반) + heart(마음) = 마음이 절반만 있는
예 I don't like her half - hearted attempt to work.

halfway
[hǽfwéi]
ⓡ 6524/86800

adj. 중간쯤까지, 중간쯤의
❶ half(중간) + way(길)
⊕ midway, intermediate
예 She started feeling sick halfway through dinner.

halt
[hɔːlt]
ⓡ 4692/86800

v. n. 멈추다, 정지
❶ 헐떡(halt)이다 가 숨이 멈추다
⊕ stop, cease
예 "Halt!" called the guard. "You can't go any further without a permit."

handicapped
[hǽndikæ̀pt]
ⓡ 5176/86800

adj. 장애가 있는
❶ 핸드 깝깝(handicapped) - (손이) 불편한, 장애가 있는
⊕ disabled 파 *handicap*: 신체장애
예 He has been handicapped since his motorcycle accident.

handle
[hǽndl]
ⓡ 2601/86800

v. n. 다루다, 손잡이
❶ handle은 손(hand)에서 나온 것인데 손으로 다루다, 우리가 아는 핸들은 자동차의 운전대로 알지만 이것은 잘못된 영어로 미국에서 자동차의 운전대는 steering wheel이라고 한다
⊕ treat, manage
예 He repaired a door handle.
　 I thought he handled the situation very well.

H

hang
[hæŋ]
ℝ 2951/86800

v. 매달다, 걸다, 교수형에 처하다
🔵 5 행(hang)시를 지어 집에 **걸다**, 혹은 교수형(hang)에 처하다
㉦ suspend
㈜ A heavy gold necklace hung around her neck.

hangar
[hǽŋɚr]
ℝ 18593/86800

n. 헛간, 격납고
🔵 휑할(hangar)헛간
㈜ Hangar is usually enclosed area for housing and repairing aircraft.

harbor
[háːrbɚr]
ℝ 33556/86800

n. 항구
🔵 ha - 河(물 하), bor(볼 - 볼 수 있는): 물 볼 수 있는 항구
㉦ port
㈜ Our hotel room overlooked a pretty little fishing harbour.

hardly
[háːrdli]
ℝ 1162/86800

adv. 거의 ~않다
🔵 hardly(아들이 - 아이들이)공부를 **거의 ~않다**
㉦ scarcely
㈜ I could hardly hear her at the back.

hardship
[háːrdʃip]
ℝ 9151/86800

n. 고난
🔵 hard(힘든) + ship(정신), 혹은 **하드는 쉽**(hard ship)게 먹을 수 없음
㉦ suffering, distress
㈜ She had economic hardship three years ago.

hardworking
[háːrdwɚ̀ːrkiŋ]
ℝ 31289/86800

adj. 근면한
🔵 hard(열심히) + working(일하는): 열심히 일하는, 근면한
㉦ diligent, industrious
㈜ John is very hardworking.

hardy
[háːrdi]
ℝ 6890/86800

adj. 튼튼한, 고통에 견디는
🔵 나 튼튼 hardy(하디)?
㉦ strong, sturdy
㈜ A few hardy souls continue to swim in the sea even in the middle of winter.

✓ harm
[hɑ:rm]
® 3190/86800

n. v. 손해, 손상, 해치다
❶ harm(암) - 암은 큰 **손상**
㉦ damage, injury
㈎ *harmful*: 해로운 *harmless*: 무해한
㉙ Missing a meal once in a while never did anyone any harm.

✓ harness
[hɑ́:rnis]
® 11035/86800

n. 말에게 채우는 도구
❶ h는(horse) ar은(accessories)말 악세서리
㉙ The farmer has a set of harness.

✓ harsh
[hɑ:rʃ]
® 5212/86800

adj. 거친, 귀에 거슬리는, 가혹한
❶ 이것 좀 **하쉬**(harsh)죠? **거친** 음조로
㉦ rough, rude ㉧ smooth ㈎ *harshness*: 거침
㉙ She has faced some extremely harsh criticism.

✓ harvest
[hɑ́:rvist]
® 6531/86800

v. n. 수확하다, 수확
❶ 요즘 농촌에는 harve(할비 - 할아버지) + vest(벗었다): 할아버지들이 곡식을 베서 **수확하다**
㉦ harvest, reap
㉙ We had a good harvest this year.

haughty
[hɔ́:ti]
® 27424/86800

adj. 거만한
❶ 부 호티(haughty - 부자 티) 내면서 **거만한**
㉦ arrogant, disdainful
㉙ She has a rather haughty manner.

✓ haul
[hɔ́:l]
® 9880/86800

v. 운반하다, 끌어당기다
❶ haul(홀 - 구멍)로 **끌어당기다**
㉦ carry, transport
㉙ They hauled the boat out of the water.

H

haunt
[hɔ:nt]
ⓡ 13839/86800

v. 자주 방문하다, 유령이 출몰하다
ⓣ haunt(혼 들이)자주 방문하다
ⓨ frequent
예 Some people believe that the ghost of an old sea captain haunts the beach.

✔ haven
[héivən]
ⓡ 9410/86800

n. 항구, 안식처
ⓣ haven(하(한문 河로 생각) 이본: 물을 본) 항구, 또 발음과 철자가 heaven과 비슷하므로 천국 (haven)은 안식처라고 기억
ⓨ port, harbor
예 The garden was a haven from the noise and bustle of the city.

hazard
[hǽzərd]
ⓡ 7788/86800

n. 위험, 우연
ⓣ 해(피해) 줬다(hazard): 남에게 해를 주는 것은 위험
ⓨ danger, peril
예 The busy traffic entrance was a hazard to pedestrians.

headmaster
[hédmǽstər]
ⓡ 6333/86800

n. 교장
ⓣ head(우두머리) + master(선생): 우두머리 선생은 교장
ⓨ principal
예 George was appointed the headmaster of Liverpool College, a school which took over 800 pupils.

✔ headquarters
[hédkwɔ̀:rtərz]
ⓡ 3389/86800

n. 본부
ⓣ Head(머리) + quarter(집): 본부
예 NY Police headquarter is located in Albany.

✔ heal
[hi:l]
ⓡ 10983/86800

v. 고치다, 치료하다
ⓣ 발 아픈 힐(heal - heel 과 철자는 다르지만) 고치다
ⓨ cure, remedy
예 The wounds were gradually healing (up).

✔ **heap**
[hi:p]
[R] 8309/86800

n. **쌓아올린 것(더미), 쌓아올리다**
[T] 비가 와서 물이 **heap(힙)**까지 **쌓이다**
[유] pile
[예] The bodies lay in heaps in the war.

hearty
[há:rti]
[R] 17433/86800

adj. **마음으로부터의, 기운찬**
[T] heart(마음) + y: 마음을 다한
[유] sincere, wholehearted
[예] I gave you a hearty welcome.

heathen
[hî:ðən]
[R] 26481/86800

n. **이교도, 이방인, 불신앙자**
[T] 동양에서는 백인은 얼굴 **히던(heathen) 이방인**
[유] unbeliever [반] believer
[예] I met a missionary sent to distant lands to convert the heathens.

heed
[hi:d]
[R] 15471/86800

v. n. **주의하다, 주의**
[T] 페인트 칠 해놓은 거 **희다(heed). 조심해라**
[유] attention, regard
[예] She failed to heed the warnings.

heir
[ɛər]
[R] 7150/86800

n. **상속인**
[T] 너는 돈이나 **헤어(heir - 돈 세어)**: 돈 **상속**받으니 돈이나 헤어(세어)
[유] inheritor, successor [반] benefactor
[예] Despite having a large family, they still had no son and heir.

✔ **helpless**
[hélplis]
[R] 8013/86800

adj. **무력한**
[T] help(도움) + less(~없는): 도움이 없는(무력한)
[유] powerless, impotent [반] capable
[파] ***help***: 돕다 ***helpful***: 도움이 되는, 유용한
[예] I am helpless in these days.

hemisphere
[hémisfiər]
Ⓡ 7537/86800

n. 반구
Ⓣ hemi(절반) + sphere(공, 지구): 지구의 절반 반구, 철자에 hemi, semi가 나오면 절반
예 Some bears live in the northern hemisphere.

✔ **hence**
[hens]
Ⓡ 2118/86800

conj. 그러므로
Ⓣ 한국말로 **해서(hense) - 그래서**
유 therefore, for this reason
예 The cell phone is best quality and hence satisfactory.

heredity
[hirédəti]
Ⓡ 26914/86800

n. 유전, 세습
Ⓣ **허리 좋디(heredity)? 유전**이야
파 hereditary: 부모에게 물려받은
예 Diet and exercise can influence a person's weight, but heredity is also a factor.

heretic
[hérətik]
Ⓡ 37087/86800

n. 이단자, 이교도
Ⓣ **here(에러** 난) + tic(이론, 학문): 잘못된 이론, 이단
유 heathen
예 The church regards them as heretics.

✔ **heritage**
[héritidʒ]
Ⓡ 4361/86800

n. 유산
Ⓣ 아버지에게 물려받은 **허리띠 지(heritage)**
유 inheritance, legacy
예 These monuments are a vital part of the cultural heritage of South America.

hermit
[hə́:rmit]
Ⓡ 26323/86800

n. 수행자, 은둔자
Ⓣ **허름한 밑(hermit)**에서 숨어 수행하는 **은둔자**
유 recluse
예 For many years he lived as a hermit at a cabin in the woods.

✔ hesitate
[hézətèit]
ⓡ 10334/86800

v. 망설이다, 주저하다
❶ 공부 방해 되는데 휴대폰 **해지 돼야 돼**(hesitate)? 말아야 돼? **망설이다**
ⓨ waver
㊅ *hesitancy*: 망설임 *hesitatingly*: 주저하면서
㉝ "Do you love me?" she asked. He hesitated and then said, "I'm not sure".

hexagon
[héksəgàn]
ⓡ 38140/86800

n. 6각형
❶ hexa(6) + gon(각 형): 6각 형
㉝ A hexagon has one more side than a pentagon.

✔ hide
[haid]
ⓡ 3620/86800

v. n. 숨기다, 짐승의 가죽
❶ 이건 **아이다**(아니다 - hide)하면서 숨기다
ⓨ conceal, cover
㉝ She used to hide her diary under her pillow.

hideous
[hídiəs]
ⓡ 12203/86800

adj. 무서운
❶ hi(아이) + deous(데어서): 아이가 불에 데어서, **무서운**
ⓨ horrible, terrible
㉝ The hideous mask will give us all nightmares.

✔ hierarchy
[háiərà:rki]
ⓡ 4925/86800

n. 계급제도
❶ high(높은) + archy(계급제도, 군주)
㉝ This system has hierarchy.

highly
[háili]
ⓡ 1114/86800

adv. 매우, 고도로, 비싸게
❶ highly developed society(고도로 발전된 사회)
ⓨ exceedingly, very
㊅ *high*: 높은
㉝ He got a highly paid job.

H

hinder
[híndər]
® 15982/86800

v. 방해하다
❶ 흰(띠) 둘(hinder)러 방해하다: 대개 데모하는 사람들이 머리에 흰 띠를 두르고 영업을 방해하며 자기들 주장을 편다
㊦ inhibit, restrain
㊌ hindrance: 방해
㊚ High winds have hindered fire fighters in their efforts to put out the blaze.

hire
[haiər]
® 4844/86800

v. 고용하다
❶ 여기서 일 하여(hire)!하며 고용하다
㊦ employ, engage
㊚ I was hired by the first company I applied to.

historic
[histɔ́(:)rik]
® 3860/86800

adj. 역사상 유명한
❶ 히스토리 익히(ic) 알고 있는 역사상 유명한
㊦ well - known
㊌ history: 역사 historian: 역사가 historical: 역사상
㊚ The court made a historic decision last week.

hitch
[hitʃ]
® 21655/86800

v. 말 따위를 매다
❶ H(horse) + itch(잇지) - 말을 잇는다
㊦ tie, fasten
㊚ He hitched the horse to a post.

hobby
[hábi]
® 9922/86800

n. 취미
❶ 취미 활동하는데 들어가는 회비(hobby)
㊦ taste, interest
㊚ Ben's hobby is restoring vintage motorcycles.

hollow
[hálou]
® 6634/86800

n. adj. 빈 공간, 속이 빈, 목소리가 힘없는
❶ 홀로(hollow)여서 밥을 안 먹어 속이 빈
㊦ empty, vacant
㊚ Hollow means an unfilled space.

holy
[hóuli]
[R] 3164/86800

adj. **신성한, 성스러운**
[T] 신에게 **홀리는(holy)** - 성스러운
[유] sacred, divine
[예] Jesus christ is a holy person.

homage
[hάmidʒ]
[R] 12141/86800

n. **존경, 충성맹세**
[T] 아버지가 엄마 앞에서 내가 가장 중요하게 여기는 곳은 **홈이지(homage)**하면서 **충성 맹세**하다
[유] respect, esteem
[예] On this occasion we pay homage to him for his achievement.

✓ **homesick**
[hóumsìk]
[R] 23670/86800

adj. **향수의**
[T] home(집) + sick(아픈): 집이 그리워서 아픈 ,향수
[유] nostalgic
[예] As I read my mother's letter, I began to feel more and more homesick.

✓ **hop**
[hαp]
[R] 10982/86800

v. **깡충 깡충 뛰다**
[T] **호프(hop)**마시고 즐거워 **뛰다**
[예] I hopped on a moving train.

✓ **horizon**
[həráizən]
[R] 5735/86800

n. **지평선, 수평선**
[T] **호라이**(해라이 - 해가) **진(horizon) 수평선**
[유] skyline [파] horizontal: 수평의
[예] The moon rose slowly above the horizon.

horn
[hɔ:rn]
[R] 6970/86800

n. **경적, 뿔, (뿔)나팔**
[T] 한국에는 **호른(horn)**으로 알려진 나팔, 그리고 자동차 경적은 크락션(회사이름)이 아니라 honk라고 한다
[유] whistle
[예] Yong blew honked his horn.

horrible
[hɔ́ːrəbəl]
Ⓡ 4901/86800

adj. 무서운, 끔찍한
❶ 울어불(horrible) - 울어버릴 정도로 **무서운**
Ⓢ terrible, fearful
囲 *horrify*: 소름끼치게 하다 *horrific*: 무서운
　　horror: 공포
예 He's got a horrible cold.

hospitality
[hɑ̀spitǽləti]
Ⓡ 7583/86800

n. 환대
❶ hos(집 house)에서 나온 말로 원래 병원이 아니라 집 처럼 편
　안 곳이라는 뜻. 집처럼 편안하게 해주므로 환대
Ⓢ hearty welcome, warm reception
예 The local people showed me great hospitality.

host
[houst]
Ⓡ 3062/86800

n. v. 주인, 개최하다
❶ 하우스샀다(host) - 하우스 샀으면 **주인**
囲 hostess: 여주인
예 We thanked our hosts for the lovely evening.

hostile
[hástil]
Ⓡ 4969/86800

adj. 적의 있는, 적대하는
❶ 호스틀(hostile - 집주인을) 적대하는
Ⓢ antagonistic, unfriendly
囲 *hostility*: 적의
예 I'm not hostile to the idea of change as such.

household
[hauśhòuld]
Ⓡ 2537/86800

n. a. 가족, 가족의
❶ Household(집 올 다 - 가족 모두 다)
예 She is running household effectively.

huge
[hjuːdʒ]
Ⓡ 1313/86800

adj. 거대한, 막대한
❶ 손으로 헤지(huge - 헤아리지)못할 정도로 거대한
Ⓢ gigantic, titanic
예 They live in a huge house.

✤ humanity
[hju:mǽnəti]
® 6130/86800

n. **인류, 인간성**
❶ human(인간) + ity(성질을 나타내는 명사형 어미)
㉵ man, mankind
㉷ *human*: 인간 *humanitarian*: 인도주의자
㉠ The massacre was a crime against humanity.

✓ humble
[hʌ́mbəl]
® 8190/86800

adj. **겸손한, 검소한, 초라한**
❶ 함불(humble) - 아무거나 함부로 입는 **검소한**
㉵ modest, unassuming
㉷ humbly: 겸손하게 humility: 겸손
㉠ He's very humble about his success.

humid
[hjú:mid]
® 19201/86800

adj. **습기 찬**
❶ 이집은 **습기차는** 게 **흠이다(humid)**
㉵ damp, moist
㉠ New York is very hot and humid in the summer.

humiliate
[hju:mílièit]
® 26727/86800

v. **창피를 주다, 모욕하다**
❶ 흠 일리(흠이 일다 - humili) + ate(동사, 형용사형 어미)남의 흠
을 일게 하면서 **창피를 주다**
㉵ insult, shame
㉠ How could you humiliate me by questioning my
judgment in front of everyone like that?

✤ hurt
[hə:rt]
® 2203/86800

v. **상처 내다, 고통을 주다, 아프다**
❶ **상처**가 나서 **헐(hurt)**었다
㉵ injure, hurt, wound
㉠ My head hurts.

✓ hydrogen
[háidrədʒən]
® 6226/86800

n. **수소**
❶ hydro(수소) + gen(발생)
㉠ Hydrogen is the first element on the periodic table of
element.

hygiene
[háidʒi:n]
® 8381/86800

n. 위생
❶ 깨끗 해진(hygiene) 위생
㊀ sanitation
예 Dental hygiene is very important to children.

hypocrisy
[hipάkrəsi]
® 14068/86800

n. 위선
❶ hypo(아래, hyper는 위) + crisy(다스림): **입아? 그렇지?(hypocrisy)** 하면서 입으로만 그렇게 말함(위선)
예 Hypocrisy is an often used tool for political ambition.

hypothesis
[haipάθəsis]
® 4959/86800

n. 가설
❶ hypo(아래) + thesis(논문, 정립): 정립되지 않은 이론 - 가설
㊀ assumption, theory
예 Several hypotheses for global warming have been suggested.

iceberg
[άisbə:rg]
® 18129/86800

n. 빙산
❶ ice(얼음) + berg(빙산): 말 대로 얼음 산
예 There was a huge iceberg blocking the path of our boat.

✔ identity
[aidéntəti]
® 2508/86800

n. 정체(성), 신원, 동일함
❶ Id 확인 한다는 말 많이 들었을 것이다. 바로 **identity**의 앞 두 글자를 말하는 것이다
파 *identify*: 확인하다, 동일시하다 *identical*: 똑같은
identifiable: 동일함을 증명할 수 있는
identification: 신원확인,
예 In prison people often suffer from a loss of identity.

idiot
[ídiət]
® 9547/86800

n. 천치, 바보
❶ idiot(이리 왔)을 이디엇이라고 발음하는 **바보**
㊀ fool, stupid
예 Don't be such an idiot!

✔ **idle**
[áidl]
[R] 9121/86800

adj. v. **한가한, 게으름 피우다**
[T] **아이들(idle)은** 공부해라 해도 **게으름 피우는**
[유] lazy, neglect: 게으름 피우다
c.f) *idler*: 게으름뱅이
[예] He's a very able student, he's just bone idle.

ignoble
[ignóubəl]
[R] 42724/86800

adj. **천한, 비열한**
[T] ig(부정어) + noble(귀족의): 귀족이 아닌, 천한
[유] low, mean [반] noble
[예] Such an ignoble act is completely unworthy of a military officer.

✔ **ignorance**
[ígnərəns]
[R] 6500/86800

n. **무지, 무식**
[T] **ig - 이거 + norance - 몰랐어?** 공부 안하고 놀아서
[유] illiteracy [파] *ignorant*: 무지한
[예] Public ignorance about the disease is still a cause for concern.

✔ **ignore**
[ignɔ́:r]
[R] 3673/86800

v. **무시하다**
[T] 애걸하자 **이거 놓아(ignore)!** 하면서 **무시하다**
[유] disregard, neglect
[예] I smiled at her but she just ignored me.

illegal
[illí:gəl]
[R] 3699/86800

adj. **불법의**
[T] il(부정어) + legal(합법적인) 합법적인의 반대, 불법의, 내가(legal) 하니까 합법
[유] unlawful [반] legal
[예] Prostitution is illegal in some countries.

illiterate
[ilítərit]
[R] 18323/86800

adj. **문맹의**
[T] il(부정어) + liter(글자를 아는 - letter로 이해): 글자를 모르는
[유] ignorance
[예] A surprising percentage of the population are illiterate.

illogical
[iládʒikəl]
[R] 18421/86800

adj. 비논리적인
[T] il(부정어) + logic(논리): 논리의 반대, 비논리적인
[유] unreasonable [반] reasonable
[예] It is illogical to think that things will change on their own.

illuminate
[ilú:mənèit]
[R] 18469/86800

v. 밝게 하다, 설명하다, 계몽하다
[T] 이 룸(room)이 - illumi (빛을)내야 돼(nate)
[유] brighten, lighten
[예] The streets were illuminated with strings of coloured lights.

illusion
[ilú:ʒən]
[R] 7543/86800

n. 환상, 환영
[T] 꿈(환상)이 이루젼(illusion - 이뤄져)
[유] fantasy, dream
[예] The magician's illusion was so convincing that everyone was fooled.

✔ **illustrate**
[íləstrèit]
[R] 5136/86800

v. (실례나 도해로) 설명하다
[T] 일레씩(illus - 하나의 예) + 들었다(trate)
[유] explain, demonstrate
[파] illustration: 삽화, 실례
[예] The exhibition will illustrate how life evolved from water.

✔ **imaginary**
[imǽdʒənèri]
[R] 8646/86800

adj. 상상의
[T] imagi(이미지 - 상상) + ary(형용사형 어미): 상상의
[유] fanciful, fantastic
[파] *imagination*: 상상(력) *imagine*: 상상하다
imagination: 상상(력) *imaginative*: 상상의
[예] The story is set in an imaginary world.

✔ **imbricate**
[ímbrikit]
[R] 순위외/86000

a. v. (지붕, 비늘모양이) 겹친, 겹치다
[T] 지붕을 겹치러 인부들이 갔데(imbricate)
[예] Imbricate is lying lapped over each other in regular order.

✔ imitate
[ímitèit]
Ⓡ 17218/86800

v. 모방하다
❶ imi(이미지) + 멧데(tate): 이미지를뜨다 - 모방하다
㉠ copy 패 *imitation*: 모방
예 He's very good at imitating his father's voice.

✔ immature
[ímətjúər]
Ⓡ 12605/86800

adj. 미숙한
❶ 입 맞추(immature - 키스) 기에는 아직 **미숙한**
예 She's rather immature for her age, don't you think?

✔ immediate
[imí:diit]
Ⓡ 1684/86800

adj. 즉석의
❶ im(부정어) + med(중간) + ate(형용사, 동사형어미)
㉠ instant, quick 패 *immediately*: 즉시
예 We must make an immediate response.

immemorial
[ìmimɔ́:riəl]
Ⓡ 32088/86800

adj. 태고의
❶ im(부정어) + memorial(기억의): 기억 못할 정도의 오랜, 태고의
㉠ ancient, primeval
예 Stories passed down from time immemorial.

immense
[iméns]
Ⓡ 5565/86800

adj. 거대한, 막대한
❶ 크기가 **이만했어(immense): 거대한**
㉠ enormous, vast 패 immensely: 막대하게
예 They spent an immense amount of time getting the engine into perfect condition.

✔ immigrant
[ímigrənt]
Ⓡ 13980/86800

n. 이주자
❶ im(안으로) + migrate(이주하다) + ant(사람): 안으로 이주해온 사람
㉠ emigrant 패 immigrate: 이민 오다 immigration: 이민
예 Illegal immigrants are sent back across the border if they are caught.

imminent
[ímənənt]
Ⓡ 8133/86800

adj. 절박한
❶ 이미 넌(imminent) 앞으로 **절박한**
㉠ impending
예 A strike is imminent.

immortal
[imɔ́:rtl]
® 16730/86800

adj. 죽지 않는
❶ im(부정어) + mortal(살지 못할(mortal)): 죽지 않는
㊦ undying, eternal ㊻ immortality: 불사, 불멸
㊁ immortal God.

immune
[imjú:n]
® 7164/86800

adj. 면역의
❶ 세균이 들어와도 (상처가) **아문(immune): 면역된**
㊁ He seems to be immune to colds - he just never gets them.

❤ impact
[ímpækt]
® 1382/86800

n. 영향, 충돌, 충격
❶ 임 패(impact - 님을 패): 충돌, 영향
㊦ influence, effect
㊁ The bullet explodes on impact.

✔ impair
[impéər]
® 23498/86800

v. 해치다, 손상하다
❶ 강도가 **님을패어(impair) 다치게 하다**
㊁ Smoking impaired his health.

impartial
[impá:rʃəl]
® 15130/86800

adj. 공평한
❶ im(부정어) + part(부분) + ial(형용사형 어미): 부분적이지 않고 공정한
㊦ just, fair ㊻ partial
㊁ A trial must be fair and impartial.

✔ impatience
[impéiʃəns]
® 11939/86800

n. 성급함, 조바심
❶ im(부정어) + patience(인내, 참을성): 참을성 없음
㊻ *impatient*: 참지 못하는 *impatiently*: 참을 수 없는
㊁ I was impatient to get the movie tickets.

impending
[impéndiŋ]
® 12237/86800

adj. 절박한
❶ im(님) + pending(뺀딩)─님에서 뺀다! 곧 헤어질 위기의, 절박한
㊦ imminent
㊁ The disaster seems to be impending.

222

imperative
[impérətiv]
[R] 10143/86800

adj. **명령적인, 강제적인**
[T] **im(임) + pera(빼라)** + tive(형용사형 어미) - 임에서 빼라. 서로 헤어져라. 명령적인
[유] pressing
[예] "Eat your spinach!" is an imperative sentence.

✔ **imperfect**
[impə́:rfikt]
[R] 14051/86800

adj. **불완전한**
[T] im(부정어) + perfect(완전한): 불완전한
[유] incomplete
[예] We're living in an imperfect world.

imperialism
[impíəriəlìzəm]
[R] 12256/86800

n. **제국주의**
[T] im(**님** 한 분이) + perial(정치를 **펴리어**) + ism 님 한 분이 다스리는 제국주의
[파] imperial: 제국의, 황제의
[예] The age of imperialism was gone.

✔ **impersonal**
[impə́:rsənəl]
[R] 11788/86800

adj. **비인격적인**
[T] im(부정어) + personal(인간적인, 개인적인) - 비인격적인
[예] She has a very cold and impersonal manner.

implement
[ímpləmənt]
[R] 5180/86800

n. **기구, 도구**
[T] **약이 imple(안풀** 리면) + 저어줄 **ment(뭔)**도구가 있어야 함
[유] tool, instrument
[예] He used agricultural implements in his garden.

implore
[implɔ́:r]
[R] 54822/86800

v. **애원하다, 탄원하다**
[T] **im(님) + plore(풀어)**: 임 풀어달라고 애원하다
[유] beg, plead
[예] She implored her parents not to send her away to school.

imply
[implái]
® 5391/86800

v. 함축하다, 암시하다
❶ im(안에) + ply(접다 - 어원편 참조): 안에 담고있다, 함축하다
㊌ suggest암시하다 囲 *implication*: 함축, 암시
예 Are you implying (that) I'm fat?

import
[impɔ́:rt]
® 5643/86800

n. v. 수입, 수입하다
❶ im(안) + port(항구): 항구 안으로 들어오는 것은 수입
㊉ export
예 We import a large number of cars from Japan.

impose
[impóuz]
® 4483/86800

v. 강요하다
❶ im(임) + pose(포주)가 나쁜 행위를 강요하다: 임포주가 불법 행위를 강요
㊌ force, compel
예 I don't want them to impose their religious beliefs on my children.

impoverish
[impávəriʃ]
® 63119/86800

v. 가난하게 하다
❶ im(부정어) + pover(밥을): 밥이 없다, 가난하게 하다
예 The new law is likely to further impoverish single parents.

impress
[imprés]
® 9766/86800

v. 인상을 주다
❶ im(안에) + press(압박을 주다): 인상은 정신으로 (안에서) 느끼는 것
囲 *impression*: 인상, 감명
impressive: 인상적인, 감동적인
impressively: 감동적으로
예 He tried to impress me with his extensive knowledge of wine.

imprint
[imprínt]
® 18546/86800

n. v. 자국, 누르다, 찍다
❶ Im(안에) + print(도장 새기다)
예 The police investigated the imprint in the mud.

✔ **imprison**
[imprízən]
® 38098/86800

v. **투옥하다, 감금하다**
❶ im(안) + prison(감옥): 감옥 안에 넣다, 수감하다
㊂ incarcerate, jail ㊏ imprisonment: 투옥
㊐ He was imprisoned in 1965 for attempted murder.

improbable
[imprábəbəl]
® 13296/86800

adj. **있을 법 하지 않은**
❶ im(부정어) + probable(확률이 있는) 확률이 없는
c.f) probability(풀어봐 맞을): 확률
㊐ It's highly improbable that Norris will agree.

improper
[imprápər]
® 13342/86800

adj. **부적당한**
❶ im(부정어) + proper(적당한): 적당하지 않은
㊂ inappropriate, unsuitable ㊎ proper
㊐ Is it considered improper to wear such a short skirt to a formal occasion?

✔ **improve**
[imprú:v]
® 1667/86800

v. **개선하다, 향상하다**
❶ **improve(임 부러버)**임씨 부러워, 부럽다는 말은 임씨가 뭔가 발전이 있었다는 말
㊂ better, reform
㊏ *improvement*: 개선, 향상
㊐ He did a lot to improve conditions for factory workers.

✔ **imprudent**
[imprú:dənt]
® 41246/86800

a. **경솔한, 무모한**
❶ 외롭다고 **입부르던(imprudent) 무모한** 재수생
㊐ It is very imprudent to study without a good teacher.

impudent
[impjədənt]
® 41688/86800

adj. **뻔뻔스러운, 건방진**
❶ im(임 - 임금) + pudent(담배 피우던) - 임금 앞에서 담배 피우던 **건방진**
㊂ shameless, unabashed
㊐ The teacher scolded an impudent child.

✔ impulse
[ímpʌls]
ⓡ 8702/86800

n. 충동
ⓣ im(안에서) + pulse(맥박): 안에서 하고자하는 맥박이 뜀, 충동
ⓤ urge ⓟ *impulsive*: 충동적인
ⓔ He bought her flowers on a sudden impulse.

✔ impure
[impjúər]
ⓡ 34654/86800

a. 불결한
ⓣ Im(부정) + pure(순수한)
ⓔ Impure water contaminated the river.

inability
[ìnəbíləti]
ⓡ 6603/86800

n. 무능
ⓣ in(부정어) + ability(능력): 무능력, 부정어로 in ,im,il, ir을 쓰는 기준은 뒷 소리의 영향에 따른다, 양순음, b,m,p는 서로 어울리므로 뒷 철자가 b,m,p면 앞의 부정에는 im이 된다, 뒷 철자가, r이면 ir, l이면 il, 나머지는 거의 in이다
ⓤ incompetency
ⓔ Inability to use a computer is a serious disadvantage when you are applying for jobs.

✔ inaccurate
[inǽkjərit]
ⓡ 11899/86800

adj. 부정확한
ⓣ in(부정어) + accurate(정확한 - 앞에서 배운 단어): 부정확한
ⓤ imprecise, incorrect ⓦ precise, accurate
ⓟ *inaccurately*: 부정확하게
ⓔ Their estimate of the cost of the project was extremely inaccurate.

✔ inactive
[inǽktiv]
ⓡ 15096/86800

adj. 활동적이지 않는
ⓣ in(부정어) + active(활동적인): 활동적이지 않은
ⓤ static ⓦ active
ⓔ It's bad for your health to be physically inactive.

inadequate
[inǽdikwit]
ⓡ 3849/86800

adj. 부적당한, 불충분한
ⓣ in(부정어) + adequate(적당한): 부적당한
ⓤ deficient, insufficient
ⓔ This work is woefully(=extremely) inadequate - you'll have to do it again.

inappropriate
[ìnəpróupriit]
® 6053/86800

adj. **부적당한**
❶ in(부정어) + appropriate(적당하면 **앞으로 뿌려 잇**): 부적당한
㋐ insufficient, inadequate
㋐ His casual behaviour was wholly inappropriate for such a formal occasion.

✔ inaudible
[inɔ́:dəbəl]
® 30131/86800

a. **알아들을 수 없는**
❶ in(부정) + aud(듣다) + ible(할 수 있는)
㋐ He spoke so quietly that he was almost inaudible.

inborn
[ìnbɔ́:rn]
® 36545/86800

adj. **타고난, 선천적인**
❶ in(안에서) + born(타고난): 선천적인
㋐ innate, native
㋐ She seems to have an inborn talent for physics.

incapable
[inkéipəbəl]
® 7926/86800

adj. **할 수 없는**
❶ in(부정어) + capable(할 수 있는): 할 수 없는
㋐ unable ㋑ able
㋐ I think she's incapable of love.

✔ incentive
[inséntiv]
® 5905/86800

adj. n. **자극적인, 장려하는, 유인**
❶ in(안에) + cent(돈 단위,센트) + tive(일반적으로 형용사형 어미): 안에 돈 주면서 장려하는
㋐ The rising cost of electricity provides a strong incentive to conserve energy.

incessant
[insésənt]
® 23112/86800

adj. **끊임없는**
❶ incessant(인사성) - 어른보면 **끊임없는** 인사성
㋐ continue
㋐ Incessant complaints are not necessary.

✔ incidental
[insədéntl]
® 13598/86800

adj. **부수적으로 일어나는**
❶ incidental (인사하면?) 인사는 사람을 만나면 **부수적으로 일어남**
㋑ *incident*: 사건
㋐ Try not to be distracted by incidental details.

inclination
[ìnklənéiʃən]
ⓡ 11064/86800

n. 마음의 기울기, 경향
❶ in(인 - 사람) + cli(기울이) + tion(명사형 어미) 사람 마음이 기울어 - 기울기, 경향
㊌ disposition, leaning: 경향
㊊ incline: (마음이) 기울다, 경향이 있다
  inclined: ~할 마음이 내키는
㊐ My own inclination would be to look for another job.

✔ include
[inklú:d]
ⓡ 643/86800

v. 포함하다
❶ in(안) + clude(닫다): 안에 넣고 닫다 - 포함하다
㊌ contain ㊋ exclude ㊊ inclusion: 포함
㊐ The bill includes tax and service.

incomparable
[inkάmpərəbəl]
ⓡ 28971/86800

adj. 견줄 데 없는, 비교할 데 없는
❶ in(부정어) + compare(비교하다) + able(할 수 있는): 비교할 수 없는
㊌ inimitable, matchless
㊐ The company had incomparable skill.

incompetence
[inkάmpətəns]
ⓡ 136621/86800

n. 무능력
❶ in(부정어) + competence(능력): 무능력
㊌ inefficiency, incapacity ㊊ incompetent: 무능한
㊐ Because of his incompetence, we won't make our deadline.

✔ incomplete
[ìnkəmplí:t]
ⓡ 8949/86800

adj. 불완전한
❶ in(부정어) + complete(완전한): 불완전한
㊌ deficient, unfinished ㊋ complete
㊐ The building is still incomplete.

inconsistent
[ìnkənsístənt]
ⓡ 9564/86800

adj. 일치하지 않는
❶ in(부정어) + consistent(일치하는): 일치하지 않는
㊌ incompatible ㊋ consistent
㊐ These findings are inconsistent with those of previous studies.

✔ inconvenience
[inkənví:njəns]
® 12395/86800

n. 불편
❶ in(부정어) + convenience(편안함): 편하지 않음
㉵ discomfort ㉙ inconvenient: 불편한, 형편이 나쁜
㉵ We had the inconvenience of being unable to use the kitchen for several weeks.

✔ incorporate
[inkɔ́:rpərèit]
® 6617/86800

v. 회사로 만들다, 단체조직으로 만들다
❶ in(안) + corporate(회사): 회사 안에 넣다
㉵ A company became incorporated with B.

✔ incorrect
[inkərékt]
® 9047/86800

adj. 부정확한
❶ in(부정어) + correct(올바름): 부정확한
㉵ inaccurate ㉙ *incorrectly*: 부정확하게
㉵ Dr. Kim's diagnosis was incorrect.

✔ increase
[inkrí:s,´--]
® 571/86800

n. v. 증가, 증가하다
❶ increase(잉크리쉬 쓰는 사람이): 증가하다
㉵ increment ㉙ *increasingly*: 점점
㉵ Incidents of armed robbery have increased over the last few years.

✔ incredible
[inkrédəbəl]
® 6111/86800

adj. 믿어지지 않는, 엄청난
❶ in(부정어) + cred(믿음) + ible(형용사형 어미): 믿을 수 없는. cred는 크레디트 카드를 생각
㉵ amazing, awesome
㉙ *incredibly*: 믿을 수 없을 만큼
㉵ I heard an incredible story from her.

incurable
[inkjúərəbəl]
® 25151/86800

adj. 고칠 수 없는, 불치의
❶ in(부정) + curable(치료할 수 있는): 치료할 없는
㉵ hopeless, irrecoverable
㉵ I cured an incurable disease.

indebted
[indétid]
[R] 17957/86800

adj. **빚을 지고 있는, 은혜를 입고 있는**
[T] in(안에) + debted(빚을 지고 있는): 빚을 진
[예] We're deeply indebted to you for your help.

indecisive
[ìndisáisiv]
[R] 29739/86800

adj. **결단성이 없는**
[T] in(부정어) + decisive(결정적인): 결정을 못하는
[유] irresolute
[예] He is widely thought to be an indecisive leader.

✔ **indeed**
[indíːd]
[R] 508/86800

adv. **정말, 참으로**
[T] in(안에) + deed(행동): 속에서 행동하는 - 정말로
[유] truly, really
[예] We live in strange times indeed.

indefinite
[indéfənit]
[R] 14686/86800

adj. **불명확한, 일정하지 않은**
[T] in(부정어) + define(한정하다 - fin은 끝내다는 뜻 finish를 생각해보라): 끝낼 수 없는, 불명확한
[유] ambiguous, undetermined [반] definite
[예] The project has been postponed for an indefinite period.

✔ **independence**
[ìndipéndəns]
[R] 2266/86800

n. **독립**
[T] in(부정어) + depend(~에 매달리다) + ence(명사형 어미): ~에 매달리지 않음: 독립
[유] self - help [반] dependence
[파] ***independent***: 독립한 ***independently***: 독립하여
[예] Mexico gained its independence from Spain in 1821.

✔ **index**
[índeks]
[R] 2175/86800

n. **지표, 집게손가락, 색인**
[T] in(사람) + dex(댁 수): 사람 댁(집) 수 - 지표를 세려면 집게 손가락으로 일일이 가리켜야 함
[예] Try looking up 'heart disease' in the index.

indicate
[índikèit]
® 2435/86800

v. 가리키다, 지적하다
❶ 몇 사람이 **이리갔데(indicate)** - 이쪽으로 갔다고 손가락으로 **가리키다**
㈜ point out, point at 파 indication: 지적
예 Please indicate which free gift you would like to receive.

indifferent
[indífərənt]
® 9855/86800

adj. 무관심한
❶ indifferent(**안디 뻔한** - 뻔 한 것 아는데): 뻔히 아는 것은 **무관심**할 수 밖에
㈜ unconcerned, careless 파 *indifference*: 무관심
예 He found it very hard teaching a class full of indifferent teenagers.

indigestion
[indidʒéstʃən]
® 24591/86800

n. 소화불량
❶ in(부정어) + digest(소화하다) + tion(명사형 어미): 소화 안 됨
예 Do you suffer from indigestion after you have eaten?

indignation
[ìndignéiʃən]
® 12539/86800

n. 분개
❶ indignation(**안다고 나선** - 안다고 나서더니 모른다고 오리발내서) - **분개**
㈜ resentment
예 The decision to close the factory has aroused the indignation of the townspeople.

indirectly
[indirékli]
® 6862/86800

adv. 간접적으로
❶ in(부정어) + direct(직접적인) + ly(부사형 어미): 직접적이지 않게
반 direct
예 He answered very indirectly.

indispensable
[ìndispénsəbəl]
® 11965/86800

adj. 절대 필요한
❶ in(부정어) + dispens(뒤서 뺄 수) + able(할 수 있는): 뒤에서 뺄 수 없는: 필요한
㈜ necessary
예 This book is an indispensable resource for researchers.

231

individual
[ìndəvídʒuəl]
® 497/86800

n. adj. 개인(의), 개개의
- ❶ in(부정어) + divide(둘로 나누는) + al(형용사형 어미): 둘로 나눌 수 없는 개별의
- ㊂ personal, private: 개인의
- 㴪 *individualism*: 개인주의 *individualist*: 개인주의자
  individualistic: 개인주의자의 *individuality*: 개성
- 㨆 We try to treat our students as individuals.

✔ indivisible
[ìndivízəbəl]
® 32663/86800

a. 나눌 수 없는
- ❶ in(부정) + divisible(나눌 수 있는)
- 㨆 Is it true that obesity and diabetes are indivisible?

indolent
[índələnt]
® 42140/86800

adj. 나태한
- ❶ indolent(인도란 - 따뜻한 지역의 나라이기에) 대개는 움직이기 싫어해서 **나태한**
- ㊂ idle, lazy
- 㨆 She is indolent and irresponsible.

✔ indoor
[índɔ̀:r]
® 7654/86800

adj. 실내의
- ❶ in(안에) + door(문): 문안의, 실내의
- ㊀ outdoor
- 㨆 She likes indoor sports.

✔ indubitable
[indjú:bətəbəl]
® 63815/86800

a. 의심여지가 없는
- ❶ in(부정어) + dubitable(둘로 보여서 의심스러운)
- ㊂ unquestionable
- 㨆 My success is dubitable fact.

✔ induce
[indjú:s]
® 9598/86800

v. 꾀다, 유도하다
- ❶ in(안으로) + duc(끌다 - 어원편 참조): 안으로 끌어들이다, 유인하다
- ㊂ tempt, allure
- 㴪 induct: 끌어들이다 induction: 끌어들임(유도)
- 㨆 The advertisement is meant to induce people to eat more fruit.

inductive
[indʌ́ktiv]
ⓡ 27393/86800

adj. 귀납적인
❶ 안으로(in) 끌어들여(ductive) 어떤 결론을 맺는 - 귀납적인
ⓥ deductive
예 I came to this conclusion using inductive reasoning.

indulge
[indʌ́ldʒ]
ⓡ 11351/86800

v. 욕망이나 정열 따위를 충족하다
❶ in(인 - 사람이) + dulge(달지 - 어떤 일에 달콤함을 느껴) **욕망을 충족하다**
ⓨ gratify, satisfy
예 The museum is an excellent place to let children indulge their curiosity about dinosaurs.

✎ industrial
[indʌ́striəl]
ⓡ 856/86800

adj. 산업의
❶ in(인 - 사람) + dustry(다 섯더리) + al(형용사형 어미): 국가가 일어선 것은 **산업의** 효과
㉠ *industrialization*: 산업화 *industrialize*: 산업화하다
industry: 산업, 근면
예 There are thousands of industrial uses for plastic.

industrious
[indʌ́striəs]
ⓡ 24256/86800

adj. 근면한
❶ industrious(인 다 섯더랬어) - 사람이 다 섰던 것(일어난 것)은 **근면한** 때문
ⓨ diligent, hard working
예 She's extremely competent and industrious.

ineffective
[ìniféktiv]
ⓡ 9330/86800

adj. 효과 없는
❶ in(부정어) + effective(효과): 효과 없는
ⓨ ineffectual, inefficient
예 The treatment was ineffective against the disease.

✔ inefficient
[ìnifíʃənt]
ⓡ 10271/86800

adj. 효율적이지 않은
❶ in(부정어) + efficient(효율적인): 비효율적인
ⓨ ineffective, ineffectual
예 Existing methods of production are expensive and inefficient.

inequality
[ìnikwálǝti]
® 8262/86800

n. 같지 않음, 불평등
❶ in(부정어) + equal(수학시간에 배운 이꼬르 - 같음) + ity(명사형 어미): **같지 않음**
예 The law has done little to prevent racial discrimination and inequality.

inevitable
[inévitǝbǝl]
® 3381/86800

adj. 피할 수 없는
❶ in(부정어) + evitable(피할 수 있는): 피할 수 없는
㊂ inescapable, unavoidable
파 inevitably: 필연적으로
예 The accident was the inevitable result of carelessness.

inexperienced
[inikspíǝriǝnst]
® 11291/86800

adj. 경험이 없는
❶ in(부정어) + experienced(경험 있는): 경험 없는
㊂ raw, unpracticed, untrained
예 They are young inexperienced parents and need support.

infamous
[ínfǝmǝs]
® 14794/86800

adj. 불명예스런, 악명 높은
❶ in(부정어) + famous(유명한): 악명 높은
㊂ notorious: 악명 높은 ㊉ honorable
예 He committed an infamous crime.

✤ infant
[ínfǝnt]
® 4867/86800

n. 유아
❶ infant(앙팡 - T.V에 나온 선전 기억하시나요?): 유아
㊂ baby 파 infancy: 유년 시대, 초기
예 He showed us a picture of his infant daughter.

✔ infect
[infékt]
® 27793/86800

v. 전염시키다
❶ in(안에) + fec(만들다 - fic, fec) - 안에 만들어 놓다, 다른 사람 안에도 만들어 전염
㊂ contaminate
파 infection: 전염, 감염
예 All the tomato plants are infected with a virus.

infer
[infə́:r]
[R] 15003/86800

v. 추론하다
[T] **infer(안 풀어** - 발음을 천천히 해 보삼.) 안 풀어져서 추론(대충 맞추는 것)하다
[유] assume, presume [파] inference: 추론
[예] I inferred from her expression that she wanted to leave.

inferior
[infiəriər]
[R] 7852/86800

adj. 열등한
[T] **inferior(인 피리어**(피래미여)! 사람이 피라미여! - **열등한** 사람
[유] lower [반] superior [파] inferiority: 열등
[예] These products are inferior to those we bought last year.

✔ **infinite**
[ínfənit]
[R] 7385/86800

adj. 무한한
[T] in(부정어) + fin(끝) + ite(형용사형 어미): 끝이 없는
[유] endless, limitless [반] limited [파] *infinity*: 무한대
[예] The universe is theoretically infinite.

✔ **inflation**
[infléiʃən]
[R] 2244/86800

n. 통화팽창으로 인한 물가폭등
[T] in(안에서) + fla(부풀어오르다) + tion(명사형): 팽창
[반] deflation
[예] The government has been unable to control inflation.

inflexible
[infléksəbəl]
[R] 17588/86800

adj. 구부러지지 않는
[T] in(부정어) + **flex**(구**부러지**다) + ible(할 수 있는): 구부러지지 않는, 불굴의, 융통성 없는
[유] firm, rigid
[예] Shoes made of inflexible plastic hurt my feet.

inflict
[inflíkt]
[R] 14508/86800

v. 고통을 주다, 상처주다
[T] **in(인** - 사람) + **flict**(아**프릭**): 사람이 아프면 고통을 준 것
[예] These insects are capable of inflicting a painful sting.

I

influence
[ínfluːəns]
ⓡ 970/86800

n. v. 영향, 영향을 미치다
ⓣ in(안에) + flu(흘러) + ence(명사형): 안에 흘러 들어감, 영향
ⓢ effect, impact
ⓟ *influential*: 영향을 미치는 influenza: 유행성 감기
ⓔ At the time she was under the influence of her father.

inform
[infɔ́ːrm]
ⓡ 5312/86800

v. 알리다
ⓣ in(인 - 사람) + form(봄): 사람이 봄. 사람이 보는 것은 정보
ⓢ notify, report ⓟ *information*: 정보
ⓔ I informed my boss that I was going to be away next week.

informal
[infɔ́ːrməl]
ⓡ 3756/86800

adj. 비공식의, 비공식적인
ⓣ in(부정어) + form(형식) + al(형용사형 어미): 형식이 없는, 비공식적인
ⓢ unofficial
ⓔ 'Hi' is an informal way of greeting people.

infrasound
[ínfrəsàund]
ⓡ 68711/86800

n. 초저주파로 들을 수 없는 음
ⓣ infra(아래) + sound(소리) - 초저주파
ⓢ ultrasound
ⓔ We'll use infrasound to monitor our treatment.

ingenious
[indʒíːnjəs]
ⓡ 12027/86800

adj. 독창적인, 정교한
ⓣ ingenious(인재 너였어) - 인재가 발명한 **독창적인**
ⓢ creative, originative
ⓔ My ingenious solution will be helpful.

ingratitude
[ingrǽtətjùːd]
ⓡ 39672/86800

n. 은혜(감사)를 모름
ⓣ in(부정어) + gratitude(감사): 감사를 모름
ⓢ ungratefulness
ⓔ His ingratitude has hurt and angered his family.

ingredient
[ingríːdiənt]
® 10232/86800

n. 성분, 원료
❶ ingredient(인 그리 되언 - 사람은 그렇게 만들어졌음
   - 사람이 만들어진 **성분**)
㊀ component, element
㉠ The list of ingredients included 250g of almonds.

✔ inhabit
[inhǽbit]
® 17184/86800

v. 거주하다, 서식하다
❶ in(안에) + habit(애비 - 혹은 어원편 참조하면 살다의 뜻): 안에
   애비가 살다, **거주하다**
㊀ dwell, live   ㉣ *inhabitant*: 거주자
㉠ These remote islands are inhabited only by birds.

I

inherent
[inhíərənt]
® 5861/86800

adj. 타고난, 고유의
❶ in(안에) + herent(붙어있는): 원래 안에 붙어있는, 타고난
㊀ inborn, innate
㉠ He has an inherent sense of fair play.

inherit
[inhérit]
® 13468/86800

v. 물려받다, 상속하다
❶ inherit(인 혈이 - 사람 피가)사람 피는 물려받는다 부모로부터
㊀ take over, succeed to
㉣ inheritance: 상속재산
㉠ All her children will inherit equally.

initial
[iníʃəl]
® 1558/86800

adj. n. 처음의, 초기의, 머리글자
❶ initial(일 - 1 이셜)2가 아니고 1 이셜 - **처음의**
㊀ first, early
㉣ initiate: 시작하다 initiative: 주도권
㉠ My initial surprise was soon replaced by delight.

✤ injury
[índʒəri]
® 2196/86800

n. 부상
❶ injury(인 죽으리) - 사람 죽을 정도이므로 **부상**
㊀ wound
㉣ injure: 다치게 하다 injurious: 해로운
㉠ I am suffering from a back injury.

injustice
[indʒʌ́stis]
[R] 9799/86800

n. **부정**
[T] in(부정어) + justice(정의): 부정
[유] unfairness, iniquity
[예] The law is part of an effort to correct an old injustice.

inn
[in]
[R] 5221/86800

n. **여관, 호텔**
[T] 홀리데이 인(Holiday Inn) 생각해보면 Inn은 숙박하는 곳
[예] We stayed at a cozy little inn in the country.

✓✓ **inner**
[ínər]
[R] 2250/86800

adj. **안의, 내적인**
[T] **in - 안에 ner(넣어)** - 안의
[유] inside [반] outer
[예] She led the guests to an inner room.

✓✓ **innocent**
[ínəsnt]
[R] 3573/86800

adj. **무죄의, 순진한**
[T] **innocent(흰 옷은):** 흰 옷은 결백, **순수의** 상징으로 결백한, 죄 없는
[유] guiltless
[예] He firmly believes that she is innocent of the crime.

✓ **innovate**
[ínouvèit]
[R] 31805/86800

v. **혁신하다**
[T] in(안을) + nova(새로운 - new와 같은 뜻, 어원편 참조) + ate(동사형어미) - 안을 새롭게 하다
[파] ***innovation***: 혁신
[예] The fashion industry is always desperate to innovate.

innumerable
[injú:mərəbəl]
[R] 15008/86800

adj. **무수한**
[T] in(부정어) + number(수) + able(~할 수 있는): 셀 수 없는
[유] many
[예] The project has been delayed by innumerable problems.

input
[ínpùt]
[R] 2838/86800

n. **투입**
[T] input(안에 놓다): 안에 놓다를 한자로 **투입**
[예] The data is ready for input into a computer.

✔ **inquiry**
[ínkwáiəri]
ⓡ 2829/86800

n. 문의
❶ **인 콜이(enquiry)** - 사람이 전화 한 것은 **문의**하기 위해
囮 *inquire*: 묻다
예 No one ever made an inquiry about the lost shipment.

✔ **insect**
[ínsekt]
ⓡ 8546/86800

n. 곤충, 벌레
❶ **이쌔(insect)**끼! 하며 나를 **벌레**같이 보다
㊌ bug
예 Ants, beetles, butterflies and flies are insects.

✔ **insecure**
[ìnsikjúər]
ⓡ 14392/86800

adj. 불안전한
❶ in(부정어) + secure(안전한): 불완전한
㊌ unstable
예 He still feels insecure about his ability to do the job.

insensitive
[ìnsénsətiv]
ⓡ 14906/86800

adj. 감각이 둔한
❶ in(부정어) + sensitive(감각적인 - 우리가 많이 듣는 sense에서 나온 말): 감각이 없는
㊋ sensitive
예 His feet seem to be insensitive to pain.

insert
[insə́:rt]
ⓡ 8801/86800

v. 끼워 넣다
❶ in(안에) + sert(서): 안에 서 있으라고 끼워 넣다
㊋ extract
예 Insert the key into the lock.

✔ **insight**
[ínsàit]
ⓡ 5539/86800

n. 통찰력
❶ in(안을) + sight(봄): 안을 보는 것은 통찰력
㊌ penetration, vision
예 He is a leader of great insight.

I

insignificance
[ìnsigníf ikəns]
[R] 25401/86800

n. **대수롭지 않음**
[T] in(부정어) + significance(중요성 - 앞 철자 보면 sign - 싸인이 들어가지 않음): 중요하지 않음
[유] unimportance, trivialness
[파] ***insignificant***: 무의미한, 하찮은
[예] I love the pride whose measure is its own eminence and not the insignificance of someone else.

insincere
[ìnsinsíər]
[R] 35604/86800

adj. **불성실한**
[T] in(부정어) + sincere(신실해): 신실하지 못한
[반] sincere
[예] She gave me an insincere apology.

insist
[insíst]
[R] 4984/86800

v. **주장하다**
[T] 내가 손을 씻었는데 **안 씻었다(insist)**고 엄마가 **주장하다**
[유] maintain, persist
[파] insistency: 주장 ***insistent***: 강요하는
[예] She insisted on seeing her lawyer.

insolent
[ínsələnt]
[R] 30001/86800

adj. **오만한**
[T] **insolent(인살 안** - 인사를 안 하는) - **오만한**
[유] arrogant, impudent
[예] The child is an insolent young man.

inspect
[inspékt]
[R] 9423/86800

v. **점검하다**
[T] in(안을) + spect(보다): 안을 보는 것은 조사, 점검하기 위해
[유] examine, investigate [파] inspection: 조사
[예] After the crash both drivers got out and inspected their cars for damage.

inspiration
[ìnspəréiʃən]
[R] 5711/86800

n. **영감, 고취**
[T] in(안에) + spirit(정신) + tion(명사형 어미): 안에 정신을 넣어줌, 고취, 영감
[유] instillation, inculcation: 고취
[파] ***inspire***: 고무[격려]하다, 불어넣다
[예] His paintings take their inspiration from nature.

instability
[ìnstəbíləti]
ⓡ 10220/86800

n. 불안정
❶ in(부정어) + st(stand - 서다를 줄인 말) + ability(능력): 설 수 있는 능력이 없음 - 불안정
㊌ insecurity
㊐ The instability of the euro continues.

✔ install
[instɔ́:l]
ⓡ 8414/86800

v. 설치하다
❶ in(안에) + stall(사달 - 사다리): 안에 사다리를 설치하다
㊌ establish, locate ㉣ *installation*: 설치
c.f) *installer*: 설치자, 임명자
㊐ The plumber is coming tomorrow to install the new washing machine.

✔ instead
[instéd]
ⓡ 1392/86800

adv. 그 대신에
❶ instead(인수 대): 인수 대신에
㊐ You can go instead of me, if you want.

✔ instinct
[ínstiŋkt]
ⓡ 6561/86800

n. 본능, 직관
❶ in(안에) + stinct(섰당 - 섰다): 사람 안에 있는 본능이 섰다
㊌ intuition직관 ㉣ *instinctive*: 본능적인
㊐ It is instinct that tells the birds when to begin their migration.

✔ institute
[ínstətjù:t]
ⓡ 1907/86800

v. n. 설립하다, 협회
❶ (협회는) institute(인사동 됐다) - 협회는 인사동에 설립했다
㊌ establish ㉣ *institution*: 단체, 기관
㊐ the Massachusetts Institute of Technology.

✔ instruct
[instrʌ́kt]
ⓡ 13777/86800

v. 가르치다, 지시하다
❶ instruct(인수 들었다) - 인수가 수업을 들었다는 말은 누가 가르쳤다는 말
㊌ teach
㉣ *instruction*: 가르침, 지시 instructive: 교훈적인
instructor: 교사, 지도자
㊐ The police have been instructed to patrol the building and surrounding area.

instrument
[ínstrəmənt]
ℝ 3503/86800

n. 도구, 악기
❶ 인수 들어 뭔(instrument)? 악기가 연주하는 음악을 인수가 듣나?
ⓤ tool, implement
예 Which instrument do you play?

insufficient
[ìnsəfíʃənt]
ℝ 5768/86800

adj. 불충분한
❶ in(부정어) + sufficient(충분한): 충분하지 않은
ⓤ incomplete
예 One day is insufficient time.

insulate
[ínsəlèit]
ℝ 27917/86800

v. 격리하다, 방음하다, 단열하다
❶ Insulate(인술했데): 전염병 환자들을 인술해서 격리시켜 놨음
예 We can insulate a house against heat loss.

insult
[ínsʌlt][´]
ℝ 9464/86800

n. v. 모욕, 모욕하다
❶ 인 석(insult) - 이 녀석 하며 모욕하다
ⓤ contempt, affront
예 She felt they had insulted her by repeatedly ignoring her questions.

insurance
[inʃúərəns]
ℝ 1452/86800

n. 보험(금)
❶ in(인 - 사람이) + sure(확실해지는) + ance(명사형)
어려운 일에 대비 확실히 하는 것 - 보험
ㅍ insure: 보험에 들다 *insurer*: 보험회사, 보험업자
예 Life insurance is needed.

intact
[intǽkt]
ℝ 6104/86800

adj. 본래대로의, 손상되지 않은
❶ intact(안 대) - 손을 안대, 본래대로의
ⓤ untouched
예 It's difficult to emerge from such a scandal with your reputation still intact.

intake
[íntèik]
ℝ 6404/86800

n. 흡입구, 입구, 섭취
❶ In(안으로) + take(받아들이다) - 입구, 섭취
예 You need an adequate intake of vitamin.

integrate
[íntəgrèit]
® 8516/86800

v. 통합하다
❶ 수학 시간에 배운 인테그럴, 기호(적분기호 ∫ - 통합하다)생각해 보라
㉤ unify 㲳 integration: 통합
㉢ The car's design successfully integrates art and technology.

✔ **integrity**
[intégrəti]
® 5343/86800

n. 성실, 완전
❶ integrity(인태 그렇지) - 인태라는 이름을 가진 애가 그렇지, **성실하지**
㉤ sincerity
㲳 *integral*: 완전한
㉢ The earthquake may have damaged the building's structural integrity.

✔ **intelligent**
[intéliədʒənt]
® 4482/86800

adj. 총명한, 지성적인
❶ 인테리(intelli)라는 말을 많이 듣기 때문에 이 단어는 쉽게 암기 할 수 있다
㉤ wise, clever
㲳 *intellect*: 지적 능력 *intelligence*: 지능
intellectual: 지적인
㉢ I am a highly intelligent young man.

❖ **intend**
[inténd]
® 4194/86800

v. ~할 작정이다
❶ 나 잠시 후에 **닌텐도(intend)할 작정이다**
㉢ I intended to go France next year.

❖ **intensity**
[inténsəti]
® 5013/86800

n. 강렬함
❶ in(인 - 사람) + tensity(떼썼지): 사람이 떼 쓸 때의 강렬함을 생각해 볼 것
㲳 *intensive*: 집중적인 *intensify*: 강렬하게 하다
intense: 강렬한
㉢ The explosion was of such intensity that it was heard five miles away.

intention
[inténʃən]
ⓡ 2145/86800

n. 의도
ⓣ 인텐션(intention - <u>**인(이사람) 때문이션 - 고의)**</u>
ⓢ intent, purpose
ⓟ intend: 의도하다 *intent*: 의도 *intently*: 열심히
ⓔ He has good intentions, but his suggestions aren't really helpful.

inter
[intɔ́:r][intər]
ⓡ 167775/86800

v. prep. 매장하다, ~사이에
ⓣ <u>인 터(inter - 인(사람)을 터)에 묻다, 인터내셔널(international - 국가 사이의)를 생각해 보시면 암기에 도움이 될 거예요</u>
ⓢ bury
ⓔ Many of the soldiers were interred in unmarked graves.

interaction
[intərǽkʃən]
ⓡ 3829/86800

n. 상호작용
ⓣ inter(서로 간의, 사이 - 어원편 참조) + action(행동) - 상호 작용
ⓢ reciprocal action ⓟ *interact*: 상호작용하다
ⓔ Language games are usually intended to encourage student interaction.

intercourse
[íntərkɔ̀:rs]
ⓡ 7533/8680

n. 교제, 성적인 교류
ⓣ inter(서로간의, 사이) + course(진전, 경로, 강의): 서로간의 교제
ⓢ association, friendship
ⓔ Our delightful intercourse had come to a sudden end.

interfere
[ìntərfíər]
ⓡ 6793/86800

v. 방해하다, 간섭하다
ⓣ inter(서로, 사이) + fere(피워) - 서로 **방해** 작전을 **펴(fere)**
ⓢ butt in, intervene ⓟ *interference*: 방해
ⓔ It's their problem and I'm not going to interfere.

intermediate
[ìntərmí:diət]
ⓡ 5736/86800

adj. 중간의
ⓣ inter(~사이) + mediate(중간의): 중간의
ⓢ middle, midway, halfway
ⓔ There are three levels of difficulty in this game: low, intermediate and high.

intermission
[ìntərmíʃən]
ⓡ 48746/86800

n. 막간, 휴게 시간
ⓣ inter(~사이) + mission(임무, 보냄): 시간을 보내는 사이 - 막간
ⓢ break, interval
ⓔ We'll return after a brief intermission.

internal
[intə́:rnl]
ⓡ 1526/86800

adj. 내부의
ⓣ internal(인 터널 - 터널 안): 내부의
ⓢ inside, inner ⓐ external
ⓔ He sustained injuries to his arms, legs and several internal organs.

international
[ìntərnǽʃənəl]
ⓡ 415/86800

adj. 국제적인
ⓣ inter(~사이) + national(국가의): 국가 간의
ⓢ global, worldwide ⓟ *internationally*: 국제적으로
ⓔ She has achieved international fame.

interpret
[intə́:rprit]
ⓡ 5803/86800

v. 해석하다, 통역하다
ⓣ inter(사이에서) + pret(풀이): 사이에서 말 풀이하다 - 해석하다
ⓢ translate
ⓟ *interpretation*: 통역 interpreter: 통역관
ⓔ A jury should not interpret the silence of a defendant as a sign of guilt.

interrupt
[ìntərʌ́pt]
ⓡ 11483/86800

v. 방해하다
ⓣ inter(~사이) + rupt(깨다 - 어원편 참조): 사이를 깨다: 방해하다
ⓢ interfere, intrude
ⓟ *interruption*: 중단
ⓔ I wish you'd stop interrupting.

intersection
[ìntərsékʃən]
ⓡ 18314/86800

n. 교차로
ⓣ inter(서로) + section(나눔): 차가 교차로에서 나뉨
ⓢ cross
ⓔ The accident occurred at a busy intersection.

I

interval
[íntərvəl]
® 5669/86800

n. 간격, 틈
❶ 투수가 공 던질 때 **인터벌(interval)**이 길다는 말은 간격이 길다는 말
㊦ gap, distance
㈀ The sun shone for brief intervals throughout the day.

intervene
[íntərvíːn]
® 7093/86800

v. 개입하다, 끼이다
❶ inter(~사이에) + vene(vent - 가다): ~가운데로 가는 것은 방해하다
㊦ interrupt
㈀ We will leave on time unless some crisis intervenes.

intimate
[íntəmit]
® 6354/86800

adj. 친밀한
❶ inti(인치 - 아주 가까운) + mate(친구) - 친밀한
㊦ familiar, close
㈀ We both have intimate relationships.

✔ intolerable
[intálərəbəl]
® 11212/86800

adj. 참을 수 없는
❶ in(부정어) + **tolerable(딸 낳불 - 참을 수 있는):** 참을 수 없는, 요즘은 딸 낳으면 더 좋음
㊦ unbearable, unendurable
㈀ The situation has become intolerable.

intonation
[íntənéiʃən]
® 12441/86800

n. 억양
❶ **intonation(인 또 내이소** - 단어에 경상도 **억양**이 들어있는 듯하다)
㊦ modulation
㈀ The end of a sentence that is not a question is usually marked by falling intonation.

intoxicate
[intáksikèit]
® 28522/86800

v. 취하게 하다
❶ in(안에) + **toxic(독**이) + ate(동사, 형용사형 어미): 안에 독이 있어 취하게 하다, 미국에서 음주 운전을 driving while intoxicated, 줄여서 DWI(취중(酔中) 운전)라고 한다
㈀ The little bit of beer I drank was not enough to intoxicate me.

246

intricate
[íntrəkit]
Ⓡ 10865/86800

adj. 뒤얽힌
❶ <u>인들얽혔데(intricate - 사람들이 얽혔데)</u>: 뒤얽힌
⊕ complex, complicated
예 The watch mechanism is extremely intricate and very difficult to repair.

introduce
[íntrədjú:s]
Ⓡ 2819/86800

v. 소개하다, 도입하다
❶ <u>intro(안으로) + duce(이끌다)</u>: 도입하다
파 *introduction*: 도입 introductory: 소개의
예 I'd like to introduce my younger son, Mark.

introspect
[íntrəspékt]
Ⓡ 순위외/86800

v. 자기 반성하다
❶ <u>Intro(안) + spect(보다)</u>: 자기 안을 보며 반성하다
예 His defeat in the world championship made him introspect his preparation.

intrude
[intrú:d]
Ⓡ 22695/86800

v. 침입하다, 끼어들다
❶ **intrude(인 들어오다** - 사람이 들어오다)
⊕ encroach, invade
파 intrusion: 침입
예 The plane intruded into their airspace.

intrust(=entrust)
[intrʌ́st]
Ⓡ 35025/86800

v. 위탁하다
❶ <u>in(인 - 사람을) + trust(믿고)</u>: 사람을 믿고 맡기다, 위탁하다
⊕ authorize, consign
예 We entrusted our financial adviser with the investment of all of our savings.

invade
[invéid]
Ⓡ 16459/86800

v. 침략하다
❶ **invade(인 베이다** - 사람 칼로 베서 침략하다): **침략하다**
파 invader: 침략자 *invasion*: 침입, 침략
예 The troops invaded at dawn.

invalid
[ínvəlid]
® 8378/86800

adj. 병약한, 논거가 박약한
❶ in(인 - 사람) + valid(약 따위를 **발리다**): 약 발리는 사람은 **병약한**, 혹은 in(부정어) + valid(타당한): (논거 따위가) 타당하지 않은
㉠ ailing, ill
㈎ My driving licence is invalid in America.

✔ invaluable
[invǽljuəbəl]
® 8110/86800

adj. 매우 귀중한
❶ in(부정어) + valuable(가치 있는): 가치로 **벨로 불**(벨로부를 수 있는 사람은 귀한, 따질 수 없게 중요한, 매우 귀중한
주의: valueless가 가치 없는 이라는 뜻이므로 invaluable(매우 귀중한)과 혼동하지 말 것
㉠ priceless, valuable ㉡ worthless
㈎ The new job will provide you with invaluable experience.

invert
[invə́:rt]
® 35009/86800

v. ~을 거꾸로 하다, 뒤집다
❶ in(인 - 사람) + vert(발): 사람이 발부터 나오면(머리부터 나와야) 거꾸로 된 것
㉠ reverse, switch
㈎ The lens inverts the image.

✇ invest
[invést]
® 5111/86800

v. 투자하다
❶ invest(인 베스트) - 사람이 최고다, 사람에게 투자하자
㉠ finance, fund ㈕ *investment*: 투자
㈎ The institute will invest 5 million in the project.

investigate
[invéstəgèit]
® 3788/86800

v. 조사하다
❶ in(인 - 사람이) + vestig(봤었다구) + ate(동사, 형용 어미): 사람이 봤었다면 이미 조사한 것
㉠ examine, research
㈎ The police are still investigating the murder.

✔ invisible
[invízəbəl]
® 6023/86800

adj. 눈에 보이지 않는
❶ in(부정어) + vi(보다 - 영어의 vi, spi, spe는 보다는 뜻) + ible (~할 수 있는): 볼 수 없는
㉠ unseen
㈎ The aircraft is designed to be invisible to radar.

✔️ involve
[invÁlv]
® 2406/86800

v. 말아 넣다, 관계하다, 포함하다
❶ in(인 - 사람이) + volve(**밟아**): 사람이 밟아 말아넣다, 혹은 사람이 밟았으므로 관련되다
㊌ contain, include: 포함하다
㉠ involvement: 연루
㉡ I prefer teaching methods that actively involve students in learning.

✔ iron
[áiərn]
® 2134/86800

n. 철, 다리미
❶ 아이롱(iron) 다리미라는 말 부모님들이 많이 쓰시는데 들어 보신 적이 있나요?
혹은 암기를 위해 **아 !이런(iron) 철** 없는 자식이라고 외워보세요
㊌ steel
㉡ Iron rusts easily.

✔ ironic
[airánic]
® 8777/86800

adj. 사실과 반대되는 말을 쓰는, 반어적인, 비꼬는
❶ 사람들이 "아이러니(irony)하다"라는 말을 쓰는 것을 종종 듣는데 뭔가 현실과 맞지 않을 경우에 쓰는 말로 풍자적인 경우에 쓰는 말이다
㊌ cynical, sarcastic: 비꼬는
㉡ She has an ironic sense of humor.

irrational
[iræʃənəl]
® 11101/86800

adj. 불합리한
❶ ir(부정어) + rational(이성, 합리적인): 불합리한
㊌ illogical ㊉ rational
㉡ His parents were worried by his increasingly irrational behaviour.

✔ irregular
[irégjələr]
® 8651/86800

adj. 불규칙한
❶ ir(부정어) + regular(규칙적인): 규칙적이지 않은
㊌ erratic, random
㊉ regular
㉠ *irregularity*: 불규칙(성)
㉡ The stone has an irregular shape.

I

irrelevant
[iréləvənt]
ⓡ 5718/86800

adj. 적절하지 않은
ⓣ ir(부정어) + relevant(적절한): 부적절한
ⓝ relevant
ⓔ His comment is completely irrelevant.

irresistible
[ìrizístəbəl]
ⓡ 11254/86800

adj. 저항할 수 없는
ⓣ ir(부정어) + resist(다시 서다 - 반항하다) + ible(~할 수 있는): 저항할 수 없는
ⓨ overpowering
ⓟ *irresistibly*: 저항할 수 없게
ⓔ The force of the waves was irresistible.

irresponsible
[ìrispʌ́nsəbl]
ⓡ 12364/86800

adj. 책임이 없는
ⓣ ir(부정어) + responsible(책임지는): 책임이 없는
ⓝ *responsible* - 니서 빤스빌 - 남의 빤스빌렸음, *책임*져야 함
ⓔ She made irresponsible comments that helped cause the riot.

irrigation
[ìrəgéiʃən]
ⓡ 16203/86800

n. 물을 댐
ⓣ 물을 대었으니 물을 일어 가이소(irrigation)
ⓔ Buffalo city established an irrigation ditch.

irritate
[írətèit]
ⓡ 25216/86800

v. 짜증나게 하다, 화나게 하다
ⓣ irri(이리) + tate(태웠데 - 속을 태웠데): 속 태우며 짜증나게 하다
ⓨ enrage, exasperate
ⓟ *irritable*: 성미가 급한 *irritation*: 성나게 함
ⓔ After a while her behaviour really began to irritate me.

isle
[ail]
ⓡ 5673/86800

n. 작은 섬
ⓣ ile(아일) + 섬(중간에 묵음이라 빠진 s) - 아이 섬: 작은 섬
ⓨ island, isle, islet
ⓔ Explore the more remote Caribbean isles.

✔ **isolate**
[áisəlèt]
[R] 12625/86800

v. **격리시키다, 고립시키다**
[T] i(아이) + so(서) + late(늦게까지): 아이가 늦게까지 서있게 고립시키다
[유] separate, segregate
[파] *isolation*: 고립
[예] He was isolated from all the other prisoners.

✔ **issue**
[íʃu:]
[R] 589/86800

n. v. **논점, 발행, 발행하다**
[T] **논쟁거리 있슈(issue)**? 그리고 잉(i)수(s)증 **발행 있슈(issue)**?
[유] point
[예] Environmental issues wll be discussed today.

✔ **itch**
[itʃ]
[R] 26137/86800

n. **가려움**
[T] **i(이)**가 나를 **쳐(tch)**가려운 - 이가 물어 **가려운**
[예] My right leg itches.

✔ **item**
[áitəm]
[R] 2621/86800

n. **품목, 기사**
[T] 이 가게에 이 **물품 있뎀(item)**?
[유] story, article: 기사
[예] The restaurant has a long menu of about 50 items.

✔ **jagged**
[dʒǽgid]
[R] 15310/86800

a. **톱니같이 지그재그한**
[T] 지그 재그(jag)한
[예] The country has a jagged coast.

jail
[dʒeil]
[R] 6051/86800

n. **감옥, 교도소**
[T] 교도소가 죄지은 사람에게는 **제일(jail)**좋은 곳
[유] prison
[예] They spent ten years in jail for fraud.

✔ **jam**
[dʒæm]
[R] 6850/86800

n. v. **혼잡, 쑤셔넣다**
[T] traffic **jam**(교통 혼잡), 잼을 병속에 **쑤셔넣다**
[유] congestion
[예] I was late because of traffic jam.

J

jar
[dʒɑːr]
® 9402/86800

n. 단지, 항아리
❶ 신주 단지 잘(jar)모셔
㊀ pot, crock
例 a jam jar.

jaw
[dʒɔː]
® 6669/86800

n. 턱
❶ 턱 부러 져(jaw)
例 My broken jaw needs operation.

jealousy
[dʒéləsi]
® 8945/86800

n. 질투
❶ 저 녀석이 젤로(가장) 씨(jealousy) 질투 나
㊀ envy 派 jealous: 질투하는
例 He was driven crazy with jealousy.

join
[dʒɔin]
® 1384/86800

v. ~에 합류하다
❶ join(주인): ~에 합류하면 자기도 주인이 됨
㊀ associate, combine
例 He insisted that I join them for lunch.

journalist
[dʒɚ́ːrnəlist]
® 5531/86800

n. 기자, 언론인
❶ jounal(저 늘) 질문만 하는 기자
㊀ reporter, columnist 派 journal: 신문, 잡지
例 She became a freelance political journalist.

journey
[dʒɚ́ːrni]
® 2088/86800

n. 여행
❶ 여행하니까 좋으니(journey)?
㊀ travel, trip
例 I love going on long journeys.

joyful
[dʒɔ́ifəl]
® 18477/86800

adj. 기쁜
❶ joy(조이 - 좋으이) + ful(완전): 완전 좋은, 기쁜
㊀ delightful, happy 派 joy: 기쁨 joyous: 즐거운
例 Christmas is such a joyful time of year.

✪ judge
[dʒʌdʒ]
® 1509/86800

v. 판단하다, 재판하다, 재판관
❶ judge(졌지)? 졌지? 하고 묻는 것은 판단을 요함
ᴨ *judgement*: 판단, 관결
예 You should not judge people by their appearance.

✪ junk
[dʒʌŋk]
® 9807/86800

n. 쓰레기(의), 고물
❶ junk(정크 - 중고와 발음 비슷): 중고 고물
㉮ trash, waste
예 We ought to clear out this cupboard - it's full of junk.

✪ justify
[dʒʌ́stəfài]
® 4213/86800

v. 정당화하다
❶ just(정당한) + ify(만들다 - 어원편 참조): 정당화하다, just - 이 물건어디서 났냐?고 묻자 주웠다(just)고 정당한 이유를 밝혔다
㉮ vindicate
ᴨ *justice*: 정의 justification 정당화 *just*: 올바른, 정당한
예 I can't really justify taking another day off work.

juvenile
[dʒúːvənəl, -nàil]
® 8745/86800

adj. 젊은, 나이 어린
❶ juvenile(주번할 아일): 대개 주번 할 아이는 나이어린, **젊은** 학생이다
㉮ young, youthful
예 She criticized his juvenile behavior at the party.

✔ keen
[kiːn]
® 2620/86800

a. 날카로운, 예민한
❶ 신경이 **날카로워** 쌍 심지 **킨(keen)**
㉮ Sharp, sensitive
예 A keen edge cut my finger.

✪ kettle
[kétl]
® 7507/86800

n. 주전자, 솥
❶ 끼워 **틀(kettle)** 주전자나 솥을 만들려면 주물 틀에 끼운다
㉮ pot: 솥
예 Stick the kettle on and we'll have a nice cup of tea.

K

kindergarten
[kíndərgà:rtn]
® 29940/86800

n. 유치원
❶ kindle(낀다) + garten((학교) 가던) - 유아기와 학교 가는 사이에 끼는 시기는 유치원
㉠ preschool, nursery school
㉠ Her daughter has just started kindergarten.

kindle
[kíndl]
® 53073/86800

v. 불을 붙이다
❶ 불을 킨들(kindle)밝아지나?
㉠ fire, light
㉠ Please kindle a fire in the barbecue.

kite
[kait]
® 8913/86800

n. 연, 솔개
❶ 날리면 멀리 가있(kite)는 연
㉠ I will participate in kite - flying.

kneel
[ni:l]
® 23280/86800

v. 무릎 꿇다, 굴복하다
❶ knee(무릎) + l(을): 무릎을 꿇다: 격투기 보면 니(knee)킥이라는 말, 이걸 생각해도 돼요
㉠ bend, yield, surrender 㸱 knee: 무릎
㉠ She knelt (down) beside the child.

labor
[léibər]
® 21851/86800

n. v. 노동, 노동하다
❶ la(나) 일 봐(bor): 나 일 본다 - 노동하다
㉠ work, toil c.f) laborer: 노동자
㉠ He rested from his labors.

laboratory
[lǽbərətɔ̀:ri]
® 3434/86800

n. 실험실
❶ 에디슨이 하는 말: 실험하게 나 좀 laboratory(내 버려둬라)
㉠ Laboratory tests suggest that the new drug may be used to treat cancer.

lack
[læk]
® 1014/86800

n. v. 결핍, 부족, 결핍하다, 부족하다
❶ (금) 액(lack)부족
㉠ want, shortage
㉠ Her only problem is lack of confidence.

254

lad
[læd]
ⓡ 4368/86800

n. 젊은이, 소년
❶ l(린)a(아)d(들) - 어린 아들, 소년
㈜ youth
㉯ lass: 소녀
㉲ He's a nice lad.

✔ **ladder**
[lǽdə:r]
ⓡ 5835/86800

n. 사다리
❶ 사다리를 타고 오 **르다(ladder - 발음이 래더지만)** - 계속 발음해 보면 오르다와 비슷
㉲ She was up a ladder, cleaning the window.

---

lade
[leid]
ⓡ 70807/86800

v. 싣다, 적재하다
❶ 레이다(lade - radar지만)탑재하다
탑재한다는 말은 싣고 있다는 뜻
㈜ load
㉲ The trucks were heavily laden with produce for the market.

---

lag
[læg]
ⓡ 14682/86800

v. n. 뒤떨어지다, 지체, 지연
❶ 돈 냇(lag)! 월세 **밀린** 사람보고
㈜ be behind: 뒤떨어지다 delay: 지체
㉲ Sales are lagging at the moment.

✔ **lament**
[ləmént]
ⓡ 21500/86800

v. 한탄하다, 슬퍼하다
❶ 왜 **나만(lament)**신세가 이래? 하며 **한탄하다**
㈜ deplore, mourn
㉲ The poem opens by lamenting (over) the death of a young man.

✔ **land**
[lænd]
ⓡ 441/86800

v. 상륙하다, 착륙하다
❶ **내린다(land)**는 곧 **착륙**한다는 말
㈜ settle, disembark
㉲ We should land in Madrid at 7am.

L

landscape [lǽndskèip]
[R] 2935/86800

n. **풍경**
[T] land(땅) + scape(광경): 땅을 보는 광경, 풍경
[유] scenery
[예] The cathedral dominates the landscape for miles around.

languish [lǽŋgwiʃ]
[R] 51245/86800

v. **원기가 없어지다, 시들다**
[T] 힘을 **남기셔(languish)**야 합니다. **시들해**지는 사람을 보고
[예] He has been languishing in jail for the past twenty years.

lapse [læps]
[R] 13937/86800

n. **쇠퇴, 시간의 경과, 잘못**
[T] 그는 **쇠퇴**하고 있는 흑인 **랩**(음악)**써(lapse)**
[예] The bribe shows a lapse of justice.

lately [léitli]
[R] 7848/86800

adv. **최근에**
[T] **내 이틀(lately)** 전에 즉 **최근에**
[유] recently, of late
[예] I haven't been feeling so well lately.

latitude [lǽtətjù:d]
[R] 17581/86800

n. **위도**
[T] lateral(측면)의 lati + tude(성질, 상태의 명사어미) 위도
[반] longitude
[예] Madrid and New York City are on nearly the same latitude.

latter [lǽtə:r]
[R] 1330/86800

adj. **후자(의), 나중의**
[T] **놔 둬(latter** - 발음이 놔둬와 비슷) 그건 **나중에** 할께
[유] the other [반] former
[예] In the latter stages of the fight he began to tire.

launch [lɔ:ntʃ]
[R] 3055/86800

v. **진수시키다, 착수하다**
[T] **눈치(launch** - 발음이 눈치와 비슷)작전에 **착수하다.** 게임이나 사업 론칭한다는 말 많이 함
[유] begin
[예] The scheme was launched a year ago.

✔ launderer
[lɔ́:ndərər]
Ⓡ 순위외/86800

n. 세탁업자
❶ 빨래는 **넌더리(laundry)**나! + 사람(er)
예 The launder didn't launder well.

laundry
[lɔ́:ndri]
Ⓡ 10692/86800

n. 세탁소, 세탁물
❶ 빨래라면 **런더리(laundry)**난다
⊕ washing: 세탁물
예 I've got to do(= wash) my laundry.

✔ lawsuit
[lɔ́:sùːt]
Ⓡ 27190/86800

n. 소송
❶ **law(법)** + **suit(소)**: 법으로 하는 **소송**
⊕ case
예 I gained a lawsuit.

✰ lay
[lei]
Ⓡ 1005/86800

v. 놓다, 눕히다, (알을) 낳다
❶ 놓 **래이(lay)** - 놓다
⊕ put, place: 놓다
예 She laid the baby on the bed.

layer
[léiə:r]
Ⓡ 3591/86800

n. 층
❶ 머리에 겹겹이 **층**을 내어(layer)
⊕ stratum
예 There was a thin layer of oil on the surface of the water.

✰ leaf
[li:f]
Ⓡ 5217/86800

n. 잎사귀
❶ **잎(leaf** - 발음 하면 닢)
ⓟ leaflet: 작은 잎, (광고용) 전단
예 He was sweeping up leaves in his garden.

✔ leak
[li:k]
Ⓡ 10598/86800

v. 새어 나오다
❶ **이크(leak)**가스가 새 네!!
⊕ vent, escape
예 Oil leaked out of the car.

L

lean
[li:n]
ⓡ 6073/86800

v. adj. 기대다, 마른, 살코기의
ⓣ 여린(lean)그대가 내게 **기대다**
ⓐ recline: 기대다
예 Lean your head back a bit.

leap
[li:p]
ⓡ 6868/86800

v. 뛰어오르다, 도약하다
ⓣ 기 립(leap)하며 **뛰어오르다**
ⓐ jump, spring
예 The cat suddenly leaped into the air.

lease
[li:s]
ⓡ 3988/86800

n. v. 임대차 계약, 임대차하다
ⓣ 방 있어(lease)? 임대차하다
예 They took out a five - year lease on the house.

leather
[léðə:r]
ⓡ 3568/86800

n. 가죽
ⓣ 가죽이 너덜(leather) 너덜
ⓐ skin
예 This jacket was made from real leather.

lecture
[léktʃə:r]
ⓡ 4508/86800

n. v. 강의, 강의하다
ⓣ le(lesson) + cture(가쳐): 레슨을 가르쳐 - 강의하다
ⓐ discourse, speech 파 lecturer: 강사
예 Who's giving the lecture this afternoon?

legacy
[légəsi]
ⓡ 6804/86800

n. 유산
ⓣ 부모님 **유산 내것이(legacy)**다
ⓐ inheritance, bequest
예 An elderly cousin had left her a small legacy.

legal
[lígəl]
ⓡ 750/86800

adj. 합법적인, 법률의
ⓣ legal(리 걸 - 이게 **걸**리는 건지) **법률의** 판단
ⓐ lawful 반 illegal
예 What you did was not legal.

legend
[lédʒənd]
[R] 6089/86800

n. **전설**
[T] **legend(오래 전해온) 전설**
[유] tradition, folk tale
[파] ***legendary***: 전설적인
[예] This match will go into tennis legend (= it will always be remembered).

legislation
[lèdʒisléiʃən]
[R] 1469/86800

n. **입법(법률제정)**
[T] **리(이) 짓을 내이션(legislation)** - 이 짓을 밖으로 내도 되는지 아닌지는 법률제정에 따라
[유] lawmaking
c.f) legitimate: 합법적인, 정당한
[예] More legislation is needed on this matter.

lengthen
[léŋkθən]
[R] 27300/86800

v. **늘이다**
[T] length(길이) + en(~하게 하다): 길게 하다
[유] stretch, extend [반] shorten [파] ***length***: 길이
[예] I'll have to lengthen this skirt.

leopard
[lépə:rd]
[R] 17918/86800

n. **표범**
[T] **leo(라이온) + pard(파트):** 라이온과 파트로 비슷
[예] Can the leopard change the spot?

leper
[lépə:r]
[R] 34393/86800

n. **나병 환자, 문둥이**
[T] **내 버(leper)** 려둔 **문둥이**들
[유] leprous patient
[예] Mother Teresa had opened homes for lepers, people with AIDS, and unwed mothers.

lessen
[lésn]
[R] 17152/86800

v. **적어지다, 적게 하다**
[T] less(덜) + en(~하게 하다): 적게 하다
[유] decrease, diminish [파] ***less***: 더 적은
[예] A healthy diet can lessen the risk of heart disease.

L

lever
[lévə:r]
Ⓡ 9440/86800

n. 지레
❶ 지 레 봐(lever)
⊕ handspike
예 I made this with simpe devices, like pullies and levers.

liable
[láiəbəl]
Ⓡ 3949/86800

adj. ~하기 쉬운
❶ 면접가면 나이야 볼(liable) - 나이보기 쉬운
⊕ apt, likely 파 liability: 책임, 경향이 있음
예 He's liable to make a fuss if you wake him.

liaison
[líːəzɑ̀n]
Ⓡ 6988/86800

n. 연락, 접촉
❶ 그 사람과는 연락이 잘 이어진(liaison)
⊕ contact, connection
예 Administrators need to establish a close liaison with employees.

liberal
[líbərəl]
Ⓡ 1839/86800

n. 자유주의의
❶ 니 버럴(liberal) - 너가 벌어 너가 쓰는 것은 자유
파 liberate: 해방하다 liberation: 해방 liberty: 자유
예 She is a liberal Democrat who married a conservative Republican.

license
[láisəns]
Ⓡ 14588/86800

n. v. 면허, 면허증, 면허를 내주다
❶ 나이 쓴(license) 면허증: 면허증은 주민등록증 대신, 나이도 써 있음
⊕ permission
예 Several companies have been licensed to sell these products.

lick
[lik]
Ⓡ 13768/86800

v. 핥다
❶ 강아지가 니 코(lick) 핥다
⊕ lap
예 He licked the chocolate off his fingers.

❤ lie
[lai]
® 1953/86800

v. n. **눕다, ~에 있다, 거짓말, 거짓말하다**
❶ lie가 거짓말이라는 뜻은 아실 것이고, **에라이(lie)**하며 눕다 ~ **리에(lie - 어디에 (있다))**로 기억
㉱ falsehood, untruth: 거짓말
㈀ A pen lay on the desk.

❤ lift
[lift]
® 2332/86800

v. n. **들어 올리다, 차에 태워주기, 승강기**
❶ 스키장 가면 **리프트(lift)**타는데 그 거 생각
㉱ raise
㈀ Could you help me lift this table, please?

✔ ligament
[lígəmənt]
® 29403/86800

n. **인대, 띠(유대)**
❶ **인대** 늘어져 다 **리가 먼(ligament)** - 다리못쓰는
㈀ Ligament is tissue in the body that connect bones together, limiting movements in joints.

likely
[láikli]
® 389/86800

adj. **할 것 같은, 있을 법한**
❶ 신발이 **나이키라(likely) 좋아할 것 같은**
㉱ apt, liable
㈀ Do remind me because I'm likely to forget.

❤ likewise
[láikwàiz]
® 6261/86800

adv. **마찬가지로**
❶ like(~와 같은) + wise(현명한, 방식)
㉱ alike, similarly
㈀ The owner of the restaurant is likewise the owner of the deli next door.

✔ limestone
[láimstòun]
® 8149/86800

n. **석회암**
❶ lime(회는 먼지 **나임**) + **stone**(돌): 석회암
㈀ This building is made up of limestone.

✔ **limit**
[límit]
[R] 2055/86800

n. v. **제한, 제한하다**
[T] **이 미터(limit)로 제한**하다
[유] restriction, restraint
[파] ***limitation***: 한계, 제한 ***limitless***: 무한의
[예] We set a time limit of thirty minutes for the test.

✔ **line**
[lain]
[R] 408/86800

n. **직업, 선**
[T] line은 직(직업)선이고
[파] ***linear***: 직선의
[예] Sign your name on the dotted line.
"What line of work are you in?" "I'm a teacher."

linger
[líŋgər]
[R] 16850/86800

v. **오래 머무르다**
[T] 병원에서 **링거(linger)** 맞느라 **오래 머무르다**
[유] stay out
[예] The smell from the fire still lingered days later.

✔ **link**
[liŋk]
[R] 1940/86800

v. n. **연결하다, 고리**
[T] 인터넷 용어로 링크(link) 걸어 놓는다는 말 많이 들어봤을 것이다
[유] ring, loop: 고리
[예] The third link of the silver chain needs to be reordered.

liquid
[líkwid]
[R] 3651/86800

n. adj. **액체, 액체의, 유동하는**
[T] **니끼다(liquid)** - 니끼하면 기름이 흐르는 것 같은 **유동의,** 액체의
[유] fluid
[예] Mercury is a liquid at room temperature.

✔ **literacy**
[lítərəsi]
[R] 7333/86800

n. **읽고 쓸 줄 앎**
[T] **레터(liter** - letter) **알았지(racy)?:** 글자를 읽고 쓸 줄 알았어
[반] illiteracy
[파] literate: 글을 읽고 쓸 줄 아는(사람) literal: 글자 그대로의
[예] Far more resources are needed to improve adult literacy.

literary
[lítərèri]
ⓡ 2887/86800

adj. 문학의
❶ liter(letter로 보자) + ary(형용사형 어미): 글자의, 문학의
㉮ bookish 파 *literature*: 문학
㉠ Mystery fiction is only one of many literary forms.

litter
[lítər]
ⓡ 8827/86800

v. n. 어지럽히다, 쓰레기
❶ 래다(litter) 버린 쓰레기: 내다 버린 쓰레기
㉮ disarrange, scatter
㉠ About 2% of fast - food packaging ends up as litter.

livelihood
[láivlihùd]
ⓡ 15976/86800

n. 생계, 살림
❶ lively(활발한, 생기 있는) + hood(신분, 처지, 상태): 살고 있는 상태 - 생계
㉮ living
㉠ That farm is his livelihood.

liver
[lívər]
ⓡ 4958/86800

n. 간
❶ liver(해석해 보면 살게 해주는 것 - 인간의 장기중 숭요한 두 가지는 심장(heart)과 간이므로 liver는 간)
㉠ This is a virus which infects the liver.

livestock
[láivstak]
ⓡ 7851/86800

n. 가축
❶ live(살아있는) + stock(소 다 - 발음이 비슷): 소는 가축
㉠ There is a market where livestock are bought and sold.

loan
[loun]
ⓡ 2594/86800

n. v. 대출, 빌려주다
❶ 논(loan)을 담보잡고 대출
㉮ lending ㉠ He got a car loan.

local
[lóukəl]
ⓡ 181/86800

adj. 장소의, 지방의
❶ 어느 장소로 갈(local)건지 요?
㉮ provincial, regional: 지방의
파 *locate*: 위치를 알아내다 *location*: 위치, 야외촬영
locational: 장소의
㉠ Our children all go to the local school.

lock
[lɑk]
® 3554/86800

v. n. 잠그다, 가두다, 자물쇠
❶ 자물쇠 **로(lo) 꽉(ck)** 잠그다
㊤ fasten
예 I heard someone turn a key in the lock.

locomotive
[lòukəmóutiv]
® 8550/86800

n. 기관차
❶ loco(이동 이라는 뜻의 결합사 - 놓고) + motive(움직이는 것 - 여기서는 mobile의 뜻) 놓고 달려라 기관차!
예 Locomotives are far more efficient than trailer trucks.

lodge
[lɑdʒ]
® 5314/86800

n. v. 여관, 숙박하다
❶ 라 지(lodge - 나 자) - 나 잔다고,. - 숙박하다
㊤ hotel, inn
예 The refugees needed to be lodged and fed.

lofty
[lɔ́:fti]
® 15422/86800

adj. 높은, 숭고한
❶ 높디(lofty)? 높은
㊤ high, tall
예 He set lofty goals for himself as a teacher.

log
[lɔ(:)g]
® 6063/86800

n. 통나무, 수학의 로그
❶ 라(L)무가 오그(OG)리고 있는 - 통나무
예 I slept like a log.

logic
[lάdʒik]
® 3882/86800

n. 논리, 논리학
❶ log(말이나 사고를 나타내는 말) + ic(학문 명칭): 사고에 관한 학문 - 논리학 혹은 아직(logic)은 덜 논리적인으로 암기
㈎ logical: 논리의 논리적인 logos: 이성
예 There's some logic to what he says.

logograph
[lɔ́:gəgræf]
® 순위외/86800

n. 생략부호($ - 달러)
❶ 로고(logo)로 + graph(쓴 것): 상징으로 쓴 것
예 $ is logographic writing.

❖ lonely
[lóunli]
Ⓡ 4755/86800

adj. 외로운
➊ 왜 날 혼자 놓으니?(lonely) - **외로운**
㊌ alone, solitary
㊒ lonesome: 쓸쓸한 *loneliness*: 외로움
㊁ He was lonely without his wife and children.

❖ long
[lɔ:ŋ]
Ⓡ 164/86800

adv. v. **오랫동안, 간절히 바라다**
➊ long이 오랫동안이라는 뜻은 다 아실 것이고 동사로 오래동안 (long)부모님이 사시길 간절히 바라다
㊌ long for, desire
㊒ *longing*: 갈망
㊁ I've been waiting a long time.
I'm longing for news of him.

✔ longevity
[lɑndʒévəti]
Ⓡ 20701/86800

n. **장수, 수명**
➊ long(긴) + evity(아비지): 아버지 수명이 김
㊁ My family has enjoyed longevity.

✔ loose
[lu:s]
Ⓡ 3111/86800

adj. **헐거운, 풀린**
➊ 허리띠를 풀러 **놔서(loose)헐거운**
㊌ unfastened, untied
㊔ fast
㊒ *loosen*: 풀다
㊁ There were some loose wires hanging out of the wall.

lord
[lɔ:rd]
Ⓡ 587/86800

n. **주인**
➊ **주인**은 일 안하고 **놀다(lord)**
㊌ monarch, ruler
㊁ He became a lord upon the death of his father.

✔ lore
[lɔ:r]
Ⓡ 22491/86800

n. **지식, 전승, 가르침**
➊ 차전놀이(lore)는 전승
㊁ The minister accentuated a lore of Christ.

Ⓛ

lot
[lɑt]
Ⓡ 519/86800

n. 제비뽑기(복권), 땅, 운명
Ⓣ 로또(lotto), lottery(복권)이라는 단어가 전부 lot에서 나온 말이며, parking lot(주차장 - 이 때 lot은 땅이라는 뜻)도 많이 주변에서 들을 수 있는 말이다
㊐ fortune, luck: 운명
㉠ We drew lots to decide who would go.
They're planning to build a house on a vacant lot on 35th Street.

lotus
[lóutəs]
Ⓡ 7827/86800

n. 연 꽃, 영국의 스포츠카
Ⓣ 물위에 연꽃으로 떴어(lotus)
㉠ Lotus is imaginary plant from Greek myth.

lower
[lóuər]
Ⓡ 801/86800

v. adj. 낮추다, 보다 낮은
Ⓣ low(낮은)에서 나온 말 이라고 생각하면 쉽게 기억할 수 있다. 비교급의 경우에(보다 낮은) low(낮은) + er(비교급 er)이 붙어 만들어졌다
㊐ drop, reduce
㊀ heighten
㉠ Interest rates have been lowered again.

loyalty
[lɔ́iəlti]
Ⓡ 4960/86800

n. 충의, 충성
Ⓣ 로열티(loyalty)잘 내는 미국프랜차이즈 들은 본사에 충성스러운
㊐ fidelity, devotion 파 loyal: 충성스러운, 충실한
㉠ His loyalty was never in question.

lunar
[lú:nər]
Ⓡ 17123/86800

adj. 달의
Ⓣ 토끼가 달에 노나(lular)? - 달의
㉠ The lunar cycle is about 29.5 days.

lung
[lʌŋ]
Ⓡ 7441/86800

n. 폐
Ⓣ 낭(lung)패(폐): 낭패라는 말로 기억해보자
㉠ He filled his lungs with the clean and fresh air.

lure
[luər]
ⓡ 13567/86800

v. 유혹하다
❶ **누워(lure)**하며 유혹하다
ⓢ allure, attract
예 She was lured into the job by the offer of a high salary.

lurk
[lə:rk]
ⓡ 26489/86800

v. 잠복하다, 살며시 가다
❶ 럴 꼭(lurk)잡을 거야: 너를 꼭 잡을 거야 - **잠복하다**
ⓢ slink, sneak
예 Someone was lurking in the shadows.

✔ luxurious
[lʌgzúəriəs]
ⓡ 11233/86800

adj. 사치스러운, 호화로운
❶ 럭(억)주어리었어(luxurious - 억 주어리었어): 돈을 억을 준다구?
호화스러운, **사치스러운**
ⓢ extravagant, lavish
파 *luxury*: 사치, 사치품 *luxuriant*: 번성한, 화려한
예 They have a very luxurious house.

M

✔ machinery
[məʃí:nəri]
ⓡ 3710/86800

n. 기계류
❶ machine(기계) + ery(영어 단어에, y, ry, ery 등이 붙으면 여러
개를 모아놓았다는 뜻이다. poetry - 시집, dictionary - 사전,
factory - 공장)
ⓢ machines 파 *machine*: 기계
예 His hand was injured when he got it caught in the
machinery.

✔ magazine
[mǽgəzín]
ⓡ 2157/86800

n. 잡지
❶ 판 매가 준(magazine) 잡지
ⓢ journal, periodical
예 She has written articles for several women's magazines.

✔ magnificent
[mægnífəsənt]
ⓡ 4251/86800

adj. 웅장한, 멋진
❶ magn(큰 - 어원편 참조, 예로 메가 들어간 상호가 상당히 많은
데 다 크다는 뜻이다) + fic(만든) + ent(형용사형 어미): 크게 만드
는, 웅장한
ⓢ grand, superb c.f) *magnify*: 확대하다 *magnitude*: 큼, 크기
예 He gave a magnificent performance.

main
[mein]
® 353/86800

adj. **주요한**
❶ 우리 돈 벌이는 너에게 **메인(main)**: 네가 그 만큼 **주요한**
㊌ principal, chief 팬 *mainly*: 주로
예 The main thing is not to worry.

maintain
[meintéin]
® 1877/86800

v. **지속하다, 주장하다**
❶ main(주요한 부분이) + tain(떼인): 주요 부분이 떼인 상태에서도
지속하다
㊌ keep up 팬 maintenance: 유지, 보수
예 We have standards to maintain.

majestic
[mədʒéstik]
® 15743/86800

adj. **위엄 있는**
❶ **위엄 있는** 체육 선생님께 **맞았었지(majestic)**
㊌ dignified, stately 팬 majesty: 존엄
예 The majestic Montana scenery will leave you breathless.

major
[méidʒəːr]
® 295/86800

adj. n. **주요한, 전공**
❶ 미국 야구 **메이져(major)**리그 생각하면 쉽게 기억할 수 있고
대학에서 what is your major? 하면 전공을 물어보는 것이다
㊌ special study: 전공 팬 *majority*: 대다수, 과반수
예 Sugar is a major cause of tooth decay.

male
[meil]
® 915/86800

n. adj. **남성, 남성의, 수컷, 수컷의**
❶ 매일(male)일하러 가는 게 **남성**
㊌ masculine: 남성의 ㊁ female
예 It is very much a male - dominated industry.

malice
[mǽlis]
® 14723/86800

n. **악의, 원한**
❶ mal(나쁜 - 어원편 참조) + ice(있어): 나쁜거 있어 - 원한, 혹은 그
남자 악의를 품고 있어서 내가 **말렸어(malice)**
㊌ ill will
예 I bear him no malice(= do not want to harm or
upset him).

✔ malnutrition
[mæ̀lnju:tríʃən]
ⓡ 19894/86800

n. 영양실조
❶ mal(나쁜) + nutrition(영양 - 음식을 넣 드리션): 영양실조
㊌ unbalanced nutrition
㈁ Many of the refugees are suffering from severe malnutrition.

mammal
[mǽməl]
ⓡ 16075/86800

n. 포유동물
❶ 엄마보고 **젖** 달라고 **맘마(mammal)**한다
㈁ Humans, dogs, elephants and dolphins are all mammals.

✔ manage
[mǽnidʒ]
ⓡ 2457/86800

v. 이럭저럭 ~해내다, 경영하다
❶ mana, manu등은 **손** 이라는 뜻(manacle - 수갑) + age(동사형 어미): 경영한다는 것은 손으로 지시하는 것이므로
㉪ *management*: 경영, 관리 *manageable*: 다루기 쉬운 *manager*: 경영자
㈁ His job involved managing large investment funds.

✔ mandatory
[mǽndətɔ̀:ri]
ⓡ 7204/86800

a. 강제의
❶ **(강제로)몸다털이(mandatory)** - 경찰이 몸 털어
㊌ obligatory
㈁ Class participation is mandatory.

manifest
[mǽnəfèst]
ⓡ 9305/86800

adj. v. 명백한, 명백히 하다
❶ **manifest(많이 봤었다)** - 많이 본 것은 그 만큼 **분명한** 것
㊌ evident, obvious
㈁ Their religious beliefs are manifested in every aspect of their lives.

✔ manipulate
[mənípjəlèit]
ⓡ 10645/86800

v. 조종하다, 잘 다루다
❶ mani(손) + pul + ate(형용사 형, 동사형 어미): 손으로 다루다
㊌ control
㉪ *manipulation*: 교묘한 조작 *manipulation*: 교묘히 다루기
㈁ Throughout her career she has very successfully manipulated the media.

M

mankind
[mæ̀nkáind]
ⓡ 7981/86800

n. 인류
❶ man(인간) + kind(류): 인류
ⓢ human beings, humanity
예 Mankind has always been obsessed by power.

man-made
[mæn-meid]
ⓡ 48357/86800

adj. 인조의
❶ man(사람) + made(만든): 사람이 만든, 인조의
ⓢ artificial
예 It's a man - made lake.

manned
[mænd]
ⓡ 15771/86800

a. (승무원, 사람이) 탄
❶ man(사람): 사람이 있는
예 What is the first manned spacecraft?

manner
[mǽnə:r]
ⓡ 1692/86800

n. 방법, 예의범절
❶ manner 좋아야 한다는 말 많이 들어봐서 쉽게 알 것이고 in this manner가 이런 방식으로라는 뜻이다. 방식이라는 뜻 있다는 것도 알아 두자
ⓢ way, method
예 He was elected in the normal manner.

mansion
[mǽnʃən]
ⓡ 9194/86800

n. 대저택
❶ 한국 사람들은 공동주택을 상당히 선호하지만 대개 미국인 들은 **맨션(masion)**에서 살고 싶어한다. 맨손(mansion)으로 시작해서 장만한 **대저택**
예 The street is lined with enormous mansions where the rich and famous live.

manual
[mǽnjuəl]
ⓡ 3744/86800

adj. n. 손의, 안내 책자
❶ manu(손) + al(형용사 어미): 손으로 하는, 손으로 쓴 안내 책자도 매뉴얼이다 고 알아두자
ⓢ leaflet, pamphlet: 안내 책자 ⓟ manually: 손으로
예 The computer comes with a 600 - page instruction manual.

manufacture
[mænjəfǽktʃə:r]
[R] 4878/86800

n. v. **제조, 제조업, 제조하다**
[T] manu(손) + fac(만들다) + ture(명사형 어미): 손으로 만듦(제조업)
[유] making, production
[파] ***manufacturer***: 제조자
[예] He works for a company that manufactures car parts.

manuscript
[mǽnjəskrìpt]
[R] 8111/86800

n. **(손으로 쓴) 원고**
[T] manu(손) + script(쓰다): 손으로 쓴 것(원고)
[유] copy, contribution
[예] He sent the 400 - page manuscript to his publisher.

mar
[mɑ:r]
[R] 12685/86800

v. **손상시키다**
[T] **망(mar)**가 뜨리다
[유] damage
[예] Sadly, the text is marred by careless errors.

margin
[mɑ́:rdʒin]
[R] 5453/86800

n **가장자리, 매매 차익**
[T] 가장자리는 후 **미진(margin)**으로 기억하고 일상에서 장사하는 분들이 **마진(margin -** 매매차익)이 안 남는다는 말 많이 듣는다
[유] edge, border
[예] If I have any comments to make, I'll write them in the margin.

marine
[məríːn]
[R] 4106/86800

adj. **바다의**
[T] **바다에서** 잡아 **말린(marine)** 물고기들, submarine(잠수함, sub는 아래라는 뜻)
[예] The oil slick seriously threatens marine life around the islands.

mars
[mɑ:rz]
[R] 9840/86800

n. **화성**
[T] 물이 다 **말랐어(Mars) - 화성**의 화는 불
[예] Mars is the planet fourth in order from the Sun.

martial
[má:rʃəl]
ⓡ 11221/86800

a. 군사의, 전쟁의
❶ 전쟁으로 맞설(martial)
예 Soldiers shoud have martial spirit.

marvel
[má:rvəl]
ⓡ 19238/86800

v. n. 놀라다, 경탄
❶ 놀라지 마 벌(marvel)써
㊀ admiration, wonder: 경탄
파 marvelous: 놀라운, 훌륭한
예 We paused to marvel at the view.

masculine
[mǽskjəlin]
ⓡ 8986/86800

adj. 남성의, 남자다운
❶ 택시 운전사 들은 마수걸인(masculine) 남성을 (첫 손님으로) 선호한다
㊀ male ㊤ feminine
예 I like a man to be masculine, but not too masculine.

mass
[mæs]
ⓡ 1403/86800

adj. n. 대량의, 덩어리
❶ mass(많 수 - 발음이 비슷): 대량의
㊀ lump덩어리 파 *massive*: 부피가 큰, 대량의
예 The sauce was now a sticky mass at the bottom of the pan.

master
[mǽstə:r]
ⓡ 1565/86800

n. v. 능숙한 사람(거장), 숙달하다
❶ master(마스터): 나 영어 다 마스터했다 - 숙달했다
㊀ maestro: 거장
예 He was a master of disguise.

masterpiece
[mǽstə:rpì:s]
ⓡ 12929/86800

n. 걸작
❶ master(거장) + piece(조각, 단편, 작품): 거장의 작품
㊀ masterwork, great work
예 'The Last Supper' is widely regarded as Leonardo da Vinci's masterpiece.

match
[mætʃ]
[R] 1063/86800

n. v. **시합, 성냥, 어울리다**
[T] 타이틀 **매치(match** - 시합), 남녀 둘이 매치(match - 잘 어울린다)가 잘 된다
[유] befit, suit: 어울리다
[예] Liverpool have a match with (= against) Blackburn next week.

material
[mətíəriəl]
[R] 725/86800

n. adj. **재료, 자료, 물질, 물질의**
[T] **맛 튀어리어(material):** 맛이 튈려면 좋은 **재료**를 써야 함
[유] substance, stuff [파] *materialism*: 유물론
[예] Crude oil is used as the raw (= basic) material for making plastics.

mathematics
[mæθəmǽtiks]
[R] 4363/86800

n. **수학**
[T] **맞춰 맞췄어(mathematics):** 수학 문제풀면서 하는 말 - 맞춰 맞췄어
[파] *math*: 수학 *mathematical*: 수학의 *mathematician*: 수학자
[예] My mathematics is not very good.

mature
[mətjúə:r]
[R] 4445/86800

adj. v. **익은, 성숙한, 성숙하다**
[T] **성숙**해야 입 **맞추어(mature)**
[유] ripe [파] *maturity*: 성숙
[예] He's very mature for his age.

maxim
[mǽksim]
[R] 8204/86800

n. **격언(교훈의 말)**
[T] **교훈의 말** 들을 걸.. 후회가 **막심(maxim)**
[유] proverb, saying
[예] It's a common maxim that "a watched pot never boils," but that's not literally true.

maximum
[mǽksəməm]
[R] 2006/86800

adj. **최대한, 최대한의**
[T] 수학 시간에 배우는 최대값 max는 maximum이다. 최소값 min은 minimum
[반] minimum
[예] The bomb was designed to cause the maximum amount of damage.

M

meadow
[médou]
Ⓡ 9315/86800

n. 목초지, 초원
Ⓣ 소가 주인보고 하는 말: 풀 많은 곳에 **매둬**(meadow)
㊂ grassland, prairie
㉠ There was a path through the meadow to the village.

meager
[míːgər]
Ⓡ 75946/86800

adj. 야윈, 빈약한
Ⓣ 밥도 못 **미겨**(meager) - 밥도 못 먹어 **야윈**
㊂ poor, thin, scanty
㉠ The prisoners existed on a meagre diet.

✤ mean
[miːn]
Ⓡ 192/86800

v. n. adj. 의미하다, 수단, 비열한
Ⓣ 내가 말하는 **의 민**(mean) - 의미는
㊂ way, method: 수단
㉣ *meaning*: 의미 *meaningful*: 의미있는, 의미심장한
    meaningfully: 의미심장하게
㉠ What does this word mean?

✔ meantime
[míːntàim]
Ⓡ 5511/86800

n. 그 동안
Ⓣ meantime - 미인과 타임을 보낸 **그 동안**
㊂ *meanwhile*
㉠ Your computer won't be arriving till Thursday. In the meantime, you can use Jude's.

✤ measure
[méʒər]
Ⓡ 1597/86800

v. n. 재다, 조치, 척도
Ⓣ 키를 재려면 나를 바르게 **매줘**(measure - 붙잡아 줘), 공부안하는 아들에게 아빠의 **조치**는 **매줘**(measure - 매 때려줘)
㊂ gauge ㉣ measurement: 측정
㉠ This machine measures your heart rate.

✔ mechanic
[məkǽnik]
Ⓡ 15409/86800

n. 기계공, 수리공
Ⓣ **말켜놔**(mechanic) - 고장나면 **수리공** 한테
㉣ *mechanical*: 기계의, 기계적인 mechanism: 기계(장치), 기구
㉠ I depend upon my mechanic to keep my car running properly.

274

✔ **mediate**
[míːdièit]
Ⓡ 18304/86800

v. **조정하다**
❶ med(중간) + ate(동사형어미): 중간에서 조정하다
㉠ Negotiators are trying to mediate this matter.

✔ **medical**
[médikəl]
Ⓡ 1095/86800

adj. **의학의**
❶ 매디 칼(medical - 칼을 매어두는 것은 수술하려고)
㉨ *medicine*: 약, 의학 *medically*: 의학적으로
㉠ Her recovery was a medical miracle.

medieval
[mìːdíːvəl]
Ⓡ 3648/86800

adj. **중세의, 낡은**
❶ interval (시간 간격)이라는 단어에서 끝 부분 - val 이 시간 간격이라고 가정하면 medie(중간이라는 뜻 - 영어 단어에 med, mid 는 중간, 예를 들면 middle school, meddle - 간섭하다, 등이 있다) + val(시간 간격): 중간 시간의, 중세의
㉨ old fashioned, outdated: 낡은
㉠ They're using a computer system that seems positively medieval by today's standards.

✔ **meditate**
[médətèit]
Ⓡ 35474/86800

v. **명상하다**
❶ 머리 아파 **명상**하더니 **머리 트였다**(meditate)
㉨ *meditation*: 묵상
㉠ Sophie meditates for 20 minutes every day.

mediterranean
[mèdətəréiniən]
Ⓡ 5955/86800

n. adj. **지중해, 지중해의**
❶ med(중간) + terra(땅): 중간 땅의 - 지중해의
㉠ The Eastern end of the Mediterranean is a moderately friendly place.

✔ **medium**
[míːdiəm]
Ⓡ 2845/86800

n. adj. **매개물, 매체, 중간의**
❶ 잘 아는 단어 media(매스 미디어 할 때)의 단수형으로 med가 중간이므로 중간의
㉨ middle, midway: 중간의
㉠ These T - shirts are available in three sizes: small, medium, and large.

meet
[mi:t]
ⓡ 696/86800

v. 충족시키다, 대처하다, 마중하다
❶ meet가 만나다(encounter)의 뜻이라는 것은 다 알지만, 충족시키다(충족시키는 것도 그 부족함과 만나야 한다), 대처하다(대처도 어려움과 만나야 하고), 마중하다(마중도 가서 만나야 한다) 등의 뜻이 있다는 걸 알아두어야 한다
⊕ cope with: 대처하다
예 We haven't yet been able to find a house that meets our needs/requirements.

melancholy
[mélənkàli]
ⓡ 12858/86800

n. adj. 우울, 우울한
❶ 기분이 맨날 꼬리(melancholy)가 붙어(꼬리가 붙으면 찝찝하므로) 우울하다
⊕ gloom, depression
예 She was in a melancholy mood.

melt
[melt]
ⓡ 9413/86800

v. 녹다
❶ 묽다(melt)
예 Snow melted because of nice weather.

membership
[mémbərʃip]
ⓡ 1945/86800

n. 회원자격
❶ member(회원) + ship(단어 뒤에 붙어 신분, 상태, 자격을 나타냄): 회원 자격
파 member: 회원
예 Annual membership is $200.

memorable
[mémərəbəl]
ⓡ 7893/86800

adj. 기억할 만한
❶ memory(기억) + able(~할 수 있는) 기억할 수 있는
⊕ impressive, unforgettable
파 memorial: 기념관, 기념물 memorize: 기억하다, 암기하다 memory: 기억
예 She gave a memorable performance.

menace
[ménəs]
ⓡ 11042/86800

n. v. 위협, 위협하다,
❶ 범인이 여기 사람 매났어(menace)하며 위협하다
⊕ threaten, intimidate
예 Drunk drivers are a menace to everyone.

mend
[mend]
[R] 14403/86800

v. **고치다, 개선하다**
[T] 대통령 선거 때 후보가 경제 성장의 짐을 내가 **맨다(mend) - 나아지게 하다**
[유] repair, fix
[예] Could you mend this hole in my shirt?

mental
[méntl]
[R] 1771/86800

adj. **정신의**
[T] **mental(맨틀** - 사람이 갖고 있는 틀): 정신의
[유] spiritual [반] physical [파] *mentally*: 정신적으로
[예] His physical and mental health had got worse.

mention
[ménʃən]
[R] 2168/86800

n. v. **언급, 언급하다**
[T] **맨 이션(mention) ! -** 난 남자라고 범인이 **언급하다**
[유] refer to, make reference to
[예] Did she mention me in her letter?

merchandise
[mə́:rtʃəndàiz]
[R] 17411/86800

n. **상품**
[T] (백화점가면) **물, 천,**(등 상품이) **다 있어(merchandise)**
[유] commodity, product [파] merchant: 상인
[예] Shoppers complained about poor quality merchandise and high prices.

mercy
[mə́:rsi]
[R] 6601/86800

n. **자비, 고마운 일**
[T] 내 죄를 **勿示(mercy** - 물시: 한문으로 보지 않는다는 말)하시는 하나님의 **자비**
[유] compassion, pity
[파] merciless: 무자비한 *merciful*: 자비로운 *mercifully*: 자비롭게
[예] The prisoners pleaded for mercy.

merely
[míərli]
[R] 1359/86800

adv. **단지, 오직**
[T] 낚시해 봐야 **단지** 몇 **미어리(merely** - 마리라고 생각)
[유] only, solely [파] *mere*: 단순한
[예] I wasn't complaining, I merely said that I was tired.

M

✔ merge
[məːrdʒ]
® 10872/86800

v. 합병하다, 융합되다
❶ 신문지를 **합치려고 돌돌 말지(merge)** - 종이 똘똘 마는 것 생각
ⓤ combine, unify
예 They decided to merge the two companies into one.

✔ merit
[mérit]
® 6331/86800

n. 장점, 가치, 공로
❶ **몇 잇(merit** - 몇 가지 잇 점)
ⓤ worth, advantage 예 Her ideas have merit.

✔ merriment
[mérimənt]
® 36164/86800

n. 웃고 즐김
❶ merry(명랑한) + ment(명사형 어미)
예 My house is filled with merriment.

✔ mess
[mes]
® 3938/86800

n. v. 혼란, 엉망, 엉망으로 만들다
❶ **엉망이면 매스(mess - 칼)를 대야함**
ⓤ confusion, disorder
예 Go and clear up that mess in the kitchen.

✤ metal
[métl]
® 2185/86800

n. 금속
❶ **메달(metal - medal과 발음 비슷)은 금속(금, 은, 동) 만들어짐**
예 Metal, paper and glass can be recycled.

✤ method
[méθəd]
® 1126/86800

n. 방법
❶ 스파르타 교육방법은 **매 쏟아(method)** - 스파르타는 매를 많이 이용하는 교육**방법**
ⓤ way, manner
예 Travelling by train is still one of the safest methods of transport.

✤ metropolitan
[mètrəpálitən]
® 4909/86800

adj. 대도시의
❶ metro(지하철, 도시권) + politan(빨리 탄) 지하철 빨리 탄 - 지하철 타는 곳은 대 도시
파 metropolis: 중심지 *metro*: 도시권 행정(부)의
예 He was drawn to the metropolitan glamour and excitement of Paris.

might
[mait]
ⓡ 143/86800

n. 힘
❶ 마이(migh - 내가) 트(t) - 내가 튼튼해지는 **힘**
㊌ energy, power ㊊ mighty: 힘센, 강력한
㊐ She struggled with all her might to get free.

migrate
[máigreit]
ⓡ 14892/86800

v. 이주하다
❶ migrate(이주하다 - 층간 소음 **마이그래** - 많이 그래서) 이주하다
㊌ emigrate, immigrate
㊐ These animals migrate annually in search of food.

military
[mílitəri]
ⓡ 878/86800

adj. n. **군대의, 군대**
❶ 적을 **밀어뜨리(military)**는 것은 군대가 함
㊌ army, troops
㊐ He has had a long military career.

miller
[mílər]
ⓡ 3995/86800

n. **방앗간 주인, 미국제 맥주**
❶ **(방앗간 주인**이) 인절미 좀 **밀어(miller)**
㊐ Miller is the one that operates a mill.

mimic
[mímik]
ⓡ 17455/86800

v. n. **흉내 내다, 모방자**
❶ mime(마임 - 동작 묘사), 판토마임 기억할 것
㊌ imitate
㊐ I can mimic several actors.

miner
[máinər]
ⓡ 13721/86800

n. **광부**
❶ mi를 발음 미로 생각하면 mi(밑에) + ner(넣은것) 파내는 사람 - 밑에 넣은 것 파내는 사람은 **광부**
㊌ pitman, digger ㊊ *mine*: 채굴하다
㊐ Two injured miners were brought out of the mine earlier.

mingle
[míŋgəl]
ⓡ 27450/86800

v. **혼합하다**
❶ 음식을 **밍글(mingle)** 때 양념을 잘 **섞어야**
㊌ mix
㊐ The two flavors mingle well.

M

miniature
[mínɪətʃər]
ⓡ 7752/86800

n. 축소형
❶ mini(작은) + ture(명사형 어미): 작은 것
예 I bought some miniature furniture for my niece's dolls' house.

minimum
[mínəməm]
ⓡ 2025/86800

n. adj. 최소, 최소의
❶ minimum(mini - 작은, 최소의)
반 maximum
예 We need a minimum of ten people to play this game.

✔ **minister**
[mínɪstər]
ⓡ 368/86800

n. 목사, 장관
❶ minister(머니 싫다 - 목사님은 청렴해야), minister(民(백성) 이섰다 - 잘하는 장관으로 인해)
유 clergyman, pastor
파 ministry: 부(部)
예 Our minister gives an interesting sermon every week.

✔ **minor**
[máɪnər]
ⓡ 2038/86800

adj. n. 보다 작은, 소수의, 미성년자
❶ minor(작은, 덜 중요한 - 미국야구 마이너 리그 생각해 볼 것)
유 smaller, lesser
파 *minority*: 소수, 소수파
예 She suffered only minor injuries.

✔ **minute**
[mínɪt][maɪnjúːt]
ⓡ 1140/86800

n. adj. 분, 상세한, 사소한
❶ minute(분)으로 따져보면 상당히 상세한
유 trivial, trifling: 사소한
예 The equipment is able to detect the minutest errors.

miracle
[mírəkəl]
ⓡ 6740/86800

n. 기적
❶ 미라 클(miracle) - 죽어있는 미라가 커진다고? - 기적이네
파 miraculous: 기적의
예 I can't promise a miracle cure, but I think we can improve things.

✔ mischief
[místʃif]
® 12662/86800

n. 해악, 악 영향
❶ mis(결혼 안 한 miss로 가정) + chief(우두머리): 결혼 안한 미스가 우두머리가 되자 **악 영향**이 우려된다고 나이 많은 사원들이 주장
⊕ harm, evil
예 It's hard to keep him out of mischief.

miser
[máizər]
® 42611/86800

n. 구두쇠
❶ 내가 왜 **마이죠(miser)**?: 남 한테 왜 월급마이죠?하는 사장 **구두쇠**
⊕ pinchpenny, cheapskate
예 The old miser would not give any money to the poor children.

✔ misery
[mízəri]
® 6012/86800

n. 불행, 비참
❶ 내가 **머저리(misery)**된 것은 **불행**한 일
⊕ unhappiness
파 *miserable*: 비참한 *miserably*: 불쌍하게
예 Ten years of marriage to him have made her life a misery.

✔ mislead
[mislí:d]
® 21322/86800

v. 잘못 이끌다
❶ mis(잘못, 부정어) + lead(이 끌다): 잘 못 이끌다
⊕ misdirect, misguide
예 The early results misled us into thinking we would win the election easily.

✔ miss
[mis]
® 781/86800

v. 놓치다, 그리워하다
❶ 코 밀서(miss)놓치다
⊕ lose, fail
예 I missed the beginning of the film.

✔ mission
[míʃən]
® 3469/86800

n. 사절단, 임무, 전도
❶ mis(보내다) + sion(명사형 어미): (어떤 임무를 띠고 보내짐 - 선교단, 사절단)
⊕ duty, task임무 파 missionary: 선교사, 전도의
예 Your mission is to isolate the enemy by destroying all the bridges across the river.

M

281

mist
[mist]
® 6507/86800

n. 안개
❶ **안개** 때문에 희 **미했었다(mist)**
㊙ fog
㊀ The early - morning mist soon lifted/cleared.

mixture
[míkstʃəːr]
® 2959/86800

n. 혼합
❶ mix(혼합) + ture(명사형 어미): 혼합
㊙ mixing, admixture 파 *mix*: 섞다
㊀ Their latest CD is a mixture of new and old songs.

mob
[mɑb]
® 9177/86800

n. 군중, 폭도
❶ mob(움직이다 - mov, mob는 움직인다는 뜻): 군중과 폭도는 움직이는 사람들
㊙ crowd, multitude
㊀ Fifty people were killed in three days of mob violence.

mock
[mɑk]
® 9160/86800

v. 비웃다
❶ **막(mock)**대하며 **비웃다**
㊙ sneer, scoff
㊀ She made fun of him by mocking his limp.

mode
[moud]
® 3401/86800

n. 형식, 방법
❶ Uni - sex mode(남녀를 안 가리고 옷을 입는 방식): mode는 형식, 방법
㊙ method, manner: 방법
㊀ Railways are the most important mode of transport for the economy.

moderate
[mɑ́dərèit]
® 5361/86800

adj. 알맞은, 절제하는, 중용의
❶ mod, mid, med(중간의) + ate(형용사, 동사형 어미): 적당한, 중간의
㊙ proper, adequate 파 *moderation*: 완화
파 moderation: 알맞음, 중용, 절제
㊀ He's a moderate drinker.

modest
[mádist]
ⓡ 3866/86800

adj. **겸손한, 조심성 있는**
❶ 친구 집에 갔더니 **마더 있었다(modest)** 그래서 조심하는, **겸손한**
㊤ unassuming ㉠ *modesty*: 겸손
㉠ He's very modest about his achievements.

modification
[màdəfikéiʃən]
ⓡ 6864/86800

n. **변경**
❶ mod(맞) + fic(만들다) + tion(명사형 어미): 맞게 만듦, 변경
㊤ amendment, change ㉠ *modify*: 수정하다
㉠ The program can be used on all computers without modification.

moisture
[mɔ́istʃər]
ⓡ 8845/86800

n. **습기, 수분**
❶ 물(습기) **있었죠(moisture)**
㊤ damp(ness), humidity
㉠ These plants need a rich soil which retains moisture.

mold
[mould]
ⓡ 24685/86800

n. v. **틀, 형성하다**
❶ 뻥 뚫린 틀에 **몰다(mold)**
㊤ cast, matrix
㉠ Are those molds dry yet?

mole
[moul]
ⓡ 10376/86800

n. **두더지, 물질의 양을 나타내는 단위**
❶ 화학에 나오는 **몰(mole), 두더지 몰**
㉠ My mother was as blind as a mole.

momentary
[móuuməntəri]
ⓡ 14959/86800

adj. **순간적인**
❶ moment(순간) + ary(형용사형 어미): 순간의
㊤ temporary, transitory ㉠ *moment*: 순간
㉠ He experienced a momentary loss of consciousness.

monarch
[mánərk]
ⓡ 8493/86800

n. **군주**
❶ mono(하나) + arch(우두머리): 하나 있는 우두머리, 왕
㊤ sovereign, ruler
㉠ The ruling monarch of Britain at that time was Queen Elizabeth I.

M

monetary
[mánətèri]
® 3325/86800

adj. 돈의
❶ money(돈) + ary(형용사형 어미)
㊍ pecuniary 파 *money*: 돈
예 The monetary unit of the UK is the pound.

monitor
[mánitər]
® 3992/86800

n. v. 감시자, 감독하다
❶ mon(감시하다 - 어원편 참조), 혹은
모니터(monitor) 한다는 말 많이 들어봤을 거예요
모니터는 감시하고 감독한다 는 말 입니다
㊍ supervise: 감독하다
예 United Nations monitors were not allowed to enter the area.

monk
[mʌŋk]
® 9695/86800

n. 수도사, 수도승
❶ 도를 오래 닦으면 하면 멍(monk)해 짐
㊍ monastic
예 Monks are devoted to the service of the church.

monologue
[mánəlɔ̀:g]
® 22356/86800

n. 독백, 독백극
❶ mono(하나 - 어원편 참조) + logue(말) 혼자하는 말, 독백
㊍ soliloquy 파 *monopoly*: 독점
예 The play begins with the main character's monologue.

monotonous
[mənátənəs]
® 18494/86800

adj. 단조로운
❶ mono(하나) + tone(톤 - 어조) + ous(형용사 형 어미): 어조가 하나인, 단조로운
㊍ dull, humdrum
파 monotony: 단조로움
예 The music became monotonous after a while.

monster
[mánstər]
® 5991/86800

n. 괴물
❶ 얼굴이 괴물처럼 monster(몬 쓰다 - 못 쓰겠다)
예 Inflation has become an economic monster.

monument
[mánjəmənt]
® 8875/86800

n. 기념비, 기념물
❶ **기념비**를 세웠더니 **몬 잊뉴만**(monument - 못 잊는구먼)
㊌ memorial 팬 monumental: 기념비적인
예 In the square stands a monument to all the people killed in the war.

mood
[mu:d]
® 2948/86800

n. 기분, 분위기
❶ "남자가 무드(mood - 분위기)가 있어야지"하는 말 생각하면 쉽게 기억할 수 있어요
㊌ feeling sentiment
예 She's in a bad mood.

mop
[map]
® 16374/86800

n. v. 긴 자루 달린 걸레, 청소하다
❶ mop(맙 - 마루 앞): 마루 앞 걸레
예 I mop floor every morning.

moral
[mɔ́(:)rər]
® 1897/86800

adj. n. 도덕의, 교훈
❶ 도덕은 삶의 예절을 **모를**(moral)사람들을 가르치는 교훈
㊌ instructive, edifying
팬 *morally*: 도덕상으로 *morality*: 도덕(성)
예 It's her moral obligation to tell the police what she knows.

moreover
[mɔːróuvə:r]
® 2340/86800

adv. 게다가, 더욱이
❶ more(더) + over(이상): 더욱 더
㊌ in addition, besides
예 The whole report is badly written. Moreover, it's inaccurate.

mortal
[mɔ́:rtl]
® 11456/86800

adj. 죽을 운명의
❶ 사람들은 반드시 **죽음**은 mortal(맡아)놨다
㊌ deadly ㊋ immortal 팬 mortality: 사망
예 For all men are mortal.

M

✔ **motivate**
[móutəvèit]
[R] 17764/86800

v. **동기를 주다**
[T] motive(동기 - mo는 움직이게 한다는 뜻) + ate(동사형, 형용사형 어미) - 동기를 주다
[유] prompt, actuate
[파] ***motivation***: 동기 부여 motive: 동기
[예] Like many people, he's motivated by greed.

✔ **mount**
[maunt]
[R] 4789/86800

v. **오르다, 위치가 높아지다**
[T] mountain을 생각하면 **오르는** 것이므로
[예] My mother mounted the stairs slowly.

mourn
[mɔ:rn]
[R] 24991/86800

v. **슬퍼하다, 애도하다**
[T] **mourn - 모(두) 운:** 모두 울고 슬퍼하다
[유] lament sorrow
[예] She was still mourning for her brother.

moving
[mú:viŋ]
[R] 1044/86800

adj. **감동시키는**
[T] move(움직이는) + ing: 감동하는 것은 마음을 움직이는 것
[유] touching
[예] I find some of Brahms's music deeply moving.

✔ **mud**
[mʌd]
[R] 4442/86800

n. **진흙**
[T] 피부 좋아지라고 **머드(mud)** 팩 한다고 하는 말 많이 들어보셨죠? 진흙으로 팩을 한다는 뜻
[파] ***muddy***: 진흙의
[예] The vehicles got bogged down in the heavy mud.

✔ **multiple**
[mʌ́ltəpəl]
[R] 3667/86800

adj. **다수의, 다양한**
[T] multi(많다는 뜻) + ple(접는다는 뜻 - ply와 같은 뜻 - 어원편 참조): 여러 번 접은, 다수의, 다양한
[유] a lot of, numerous
[파] ***multiply***: 곱하다 multitude: 다수 ***multi***: 많은
[예] We made multiple copies of the report.

mumble
[mʌ́mbəl]
ⓡ 35158/86800

v. 중얼거리다
❶ m(monk - 수도사가) + umble(염불) - 스님이 염불을 **중얼거리다**
⊕ murmur
例 She mumbled something about being too busy.

mummy
[mʌ́mi]
ⓡ 3553/86800

n. 미라
❶ **몸이**(mummy)썩지 않는 **미라**
例 The ancient Egyptians used the mummification process to create a mummy.

murder
[mə́ːrdəːr]
ⓡ 1729/86800

n. v. 살인, 살인하다
❶ 범인은 사람 죽이고 **묻어**(murder)
⊕ manslaughter, homicide 파 murderer: 살인자
例 There were three murders in the town last year.

muscle
[mʌ́səl]
ⓡ 4700/86800

n. 근육
❶ **근육**이 있어야 남성다운 muscle(멋을)내지
⊕ sinew(s)
例 These exercises build muscle and increase stamina.

muse
[mjuːz]
ⓡ 20854/86800

v. n. 명상하다, 심사숙고하다, 시, 음악, 학예를 주관하는 신
❶ 뮤즈(muse - 음악과 시)를 들으며 명상하다
⊕ meditate, ponder
例 I began to muse about/on the possibility of starting my own business.

mutual
[mjúːtʃuəl]
ⓡ 3939/86800

adj. 서로의, 공동의
❶ 부부에게 **서로 잘 맞춰**(mutual) 살아
⊕ each other's, one another's
例 Both countries are acting to their mutual advantage.

myriad
[míriəd]
ⓡ 15542/86800

adj. 무수한
❶ **무수한** 여친을 **미리 얻으**(myriad) 면 좋겠다
⊕ countless, innumerable
例 The old system's problems were myriad.

M

myth
[miθ]
[R] 5346/86800

n. 신화
[T] 단군 **신화**를 **믿씁(myth)**니까?
[유] legendary
[파] ***mythical***: 신화의
[예] Most societies have their own creation myths.

naked
[néikid]
[R] 4228/86800

adj. 발가벗은
[T] **발가벗은** 상태로 **내 있기도(naked)** 민망한
[유] undressed, bare
[예] The children were half naked.

namely
[néimli]
[R] 4047/86800

adv. 즉
[T] name(이름) + ly(부사형 어미): 다른 이름을 대보면 - 달리 말하면
[유] in other words, that is (to say)
[예] There's always one person stuck with cleaning up the mess, namely me.

nap
[næp]
[R] 19988/86800

n. v. 낮잠, 잠깐 졸다
[T] **나른(na) + 푸(p):** 나른하면 푸푸 하는 거 낮잠
[유] siesta
[예] Grandpa usually has/takes a nap after lunch.

narrate
[næréit,ˊ--]
[R] 71458/86800

v. 이야기하다
[T] **나레이(narrate)**! - 나라고 **이야기 하다**. TV에 나래이션(narration)이라는 단어 자주 나온다
[유] tell
[예] Documentaries are often narrated by well - known actors.

narrow
[nǽrou]
[R] 2032/86800

adj. 좁은
[T] **좁은** 학교 **내로**(안으로 - narrow)다니다
[유] cramped
[반] wide, broad
[예] The little village has very narrow streets.

✔ nationality
[nὰʃənǽləti]
Ⓡ 8964/86800

n. **국적, 국민성**
❶ nation(국가) + ity(추상적인 뜻을 나타내는 명사형 어미)
⊕ citizenship
파 *nation*: 국가 *national*: 국민의, 국가의
예 What nationality are you?

naughty
[nɔ́:ti]
Ⓡ 9176/86800

adj. **장난꾸러기인**
❶ 조금도 손에서 뭘 **놓치**(naughty)않는 **장난꾸러기**
⊕ mischievous
예 She gave him a naughty smile.

✔ navigate
[nǽvəgèit]
Ⓡ 24934/86800

v. **항해하다**
❶ navi(항해하다 - 길을 찾아가다) + ate(동사, 형용사형 어미) 차에 있는 내비(navigation)가 항해하다는 뜻
파 navigation: 항해, 항공 *navigator*: 항해자
예 Sailors have special equipment to help them navigate.

✔ nearby
[níərbái]
Ⓡ 2747/86800

adj. adv. **가까운, 가까이**
❶ near(가까운) + by(옆): 가까운 옆, 가까운
⊕ almost, about: 가까이
예 I noticed a policeman standing nearby.

✔ nearly
[níərli]
Ⓡ 873/86800

adv. **거의**
❶ 니 허리(nearly) **거의** 40인치 되겠다
⊕ almost
예 She's nearly as tall as her father now.

✔ necessarily
[nèsəsérəli]
Ⓡ 1810/86800

adv. **반드시, 필연적으로**
❶ (입원한 아들) 빚이라도 **반드시 내서살리리**(nacessarily)
⊕ inevitably
파 *necessary*: 필요한 *necessitate*: 필요로 하다
  necessity: 필요
예 That's not necessarily true.

negative
[négətiv]
® 2132/86800

adj. 부정적인, 소극적인
❶ 내가 티비(negative) 나오는 것에 모두 **부정적인** - 내가 TV나오면 꺼버린대나???
⊕ pessimistic, skeptical ⊛ affirmative, positive
㉠ We received a negative answer to our request.

neglect
[niglékt]
® 6251/86800

v. 소홀히 하다, 무시하다
❶ 너 그래(neglect) 봐라 하며 **무시하다**
⊕ ignore, disregard: 무시하다 ㉣ *negligence*: 태만
㉠ I'm afraid I've rather neglected my studies this week.

negotiate
[nigóuʃièit]
® 5899/86800

v. 협상하다
❶ 니 고시 했데(negotiate)! 내가 스카웃 할게 - **협상하자**
㉠ I'm negotiating for a new contract.

nervous
[nə́:rvəs]
® 3114/86800

adj. 초조한, 신경의, 신경질적인
❶ 길가다 깡패를 만나 쳐다보면 왜 쳐다보냐면서 **날 봤어?(nervous) 왜 쳐다봐? 하며 신경질 내죠**
⊕ high - strung: 신경질적인
㉣ *nerve*: 신경 *nervousness*: 신경성, 신경과민
㉠ I was too nervous to speak.

net
[net]
® 1536/86800

n. 그물, 정량(순)
❶ 인터 넷(net)의 net은 그물, GNP의 N은 net(순) - net income은 순 수입
⊕ dose: 정량
㉠ Dolphins often get tangled in the nets that are used to catch tuna fish.

neurochemical
[njùəroukémikəl]
® 순위외/86800

a. 신경화학의
❶ neuro(신경) + chemical(화학의)
㉠ The term "neurochemical" is chemical processes and phenomena related to the nervous system.

neutral
[njú:trəl]
® 5095/86800

adj. 중립의, 중성의
❶ 내가 이걸 **누 주럴**(neutral)?: 내가 이걸 누구를 주겠니? 난 **중립을 지킬 거야**
파 *neutrality*: 중립
예 The peace conference would have to be held in a neutral country.

nevertheless
[nèvə:rðəlés]
® 1424/86800

adv. 그럼에도 불구하고
❶ 남들보다 기부할 옷 없음**에도 네벌 더 냈어**(nevertheless)
유 for all
예 It was a predictable, but nevertheless funny, story.

niche
[nitʃ]
® 12324/86800

n. v. 장식을 위한 파놓은 벽면, 적소, 안치하다
❶ 나는 인재를 적재, **적소**에 **넣 취**(niche)
예 I finally found my niche as a teacher.

niece
[niːs]
® 11654/86800

n. 조카딸, 여자 조카
❶ n(**누나**) + iece(**여았어**): 누나 여 아이는 내게 **조카딸**
파 nephew: 조카
예 If he's my uncle, then I'm his niece.

nigger
[nígə:r]
® 20210/86800

n. (경멸적) 깜둥이
❶ 얼굴이 너무 **닉어**(nigger)**까만**
예 I worked like a nigger for a month.

nightmare
[náitmɛ̀ə:r]
® 5499/86800

n. 악몽
❶ 밤(night)매어(mare) - 밤에 매이는 것은 **악몽**
유 bad dream
예 I shouldn't have watched that movie - it'll give me nightmares.

noble
[nóubəl]
® 5017/86800

adj. n. 고귀한, 귀족
❶ **귀족**이라고 **노벌** (noble) - 돈을 벌지 않음
유 high, exalted 반 ignoble 파 nobility 고결함
예 His followers believe they are fighting for a noble cause.

N

nod
[nɑd]
[R] 8388/86800

v. n. **끄덕이다, 끄덕임**
[T] 니가 용이니? **나다(nod)**하고 **끄덕이다**
[예] Many people in the audience nodded in agreement.

nominate
[nάmənèit]
[R] 16944/86800

v. **지명하다, 임명하다**
[T] nom(name에서 나온 말) + ate(동사, 형용사형 어미): 이름을 부르다, 지명하다
아카데미 상 나미내이션 되었다고 흔히 들을 수 있는 말이다
[유] appoint, designate
[예] Would you like to nominate anyone for/as director?

✔ **nonsense**
[nάnsens]
[R] 5021/86800

n. **무의미, 허튼 말**
[T] non(부정어) + sense(의미): 무의미
[유] meaninglessness, insignificance
[예] This report is nonsense and nothing but a waste of paper.

✔ **norm**
[nɔ:rm]
[R] 7055/86800

n. **표준**
[T] **norm(놈)** - 놈은 표준 욕
[유] standard, level
[파] *normal*: 정상의, 표준의 *normally*: 정상적으로
[예] Smaller families have become the norm.

✔ **notation**
[noutéiʃən]
[R] 11121/86800

n. **특수표기법**
[T] **특수표기법**은 **노트에 있어(notation)**
[예] I can read musical notation.

✔ **note**
[nout]
[R] 958/86800

n. v. **메모 각서, 주석, 지폐, 주목하다**
[T] 우리가지고 다니는 **노트(note)**는 적고 주목하기 위한 것
[유] memo, memorandum
[파] notable: 주목할 만한 noted: 유명한
notice: 주목, 통지, 주목하다, 알아차리다
noticeable: 눈에 띄는 notify: 알리다, 신고하다
[예] He left a note to say he would be home late.

✔ notice
[nóutis]
⑧ 1109/86800

n. v. 통지, 주목, 알아차리다
❶ **노트(에)써(notice)놔서 금방 알아차리다**
㈀ Please give me enough notice to prepare for your arrival.

✔ notion
[nóuʃən]
⑧ 2706/86800

n. 생각, 개념
❶ 좀 **생각** 좀 하고 노션(notion) - 생각하고 놀아
㈎ general idea, concept: 개념
㈀ I have only a vague notion of what she does for a living.

notorious
[noutɔ́:riəs]
⑧ 7629/86800

adj. 소문난, 악명이 높은
❶ 나 털이었어(notorious): 나 은행털이었어, 은행털이로 **악명 높은**
㈎ infamous
㈀ The company is notorious for paying its bills late.

✔ nourish
[nə́:riʃ]
⑧ 30687/86800

v. 영양분을 주다
❶ **양분을 넣으리 쉬(nourish)**
㈍ nourishment: 영양
㈀ This cream is supposed to help nourish your skin.

✔ novel
[návəl]
⑧ 2428/86800

adj. n. 새로운, 신기한, 소설
❶ 나 볼(novel) 새로운 소설 - 내가 볼 소설
㈎ strange: 신기한
㈍ novelty: 신기함 *novelist*: 소설가
㈀ His latest novel is selling really well.

✔ nowadays
[náuədèiz]
⑧ 5045/86800

n. adv. 오늘날, 요즈음
❶ now(지금) + days(날들): 지금 날 들은 요즘
㈎ at present, these days
㈀ Who remembers those films nowadays?

nuclear
[njú;kliə:r]
® 1268/86800

adj. 핵(무기)의, 원자력의
❶ 국제 사회의 累(누를 끼치다의 **누**) 끼리여(nuclear) - 국제에 누 끼쳐 꺼리는 핵무기
㊐ atomic: 원자력의
㈎ North Korea has a nuclear capability.

nuisance
[njú:səns]
® 7091/86800

n. 귀찮음, 방해, 불쾌
❶ 귀찮아서 **누었었어**(nuisance)
㊐ disturbance, obstruction방해
㈎ I've forgotten my umbrella what a nuisance!

numerous
[njú:mərəs]
® 2995/86800

adj. 수많은
❶ num(number - 수) + **merous(멀었어)**: 수를 세려면 아직 멀었어 - 수 많은
㊐ many, myriad
㈎ We have discussed these plans on numerous occasions.

nursery
[nə́:rsəri]
® 4689/86800

n. 탁아소, 종묘원
❶ nurse(간호사 - 돌봐주는 사람) + ry(모아둔 곳): 돌봐주는 사람 모아둔 곳 - 탁아소
㊐ daycare center
㈎ We get our flowers from a local nursery.

nurture
[nə́:rtʃə:r]
® 22097/86800

n. 양육(하다), 자양물
❶ 아기가 울면서 **영양분 넣줘 (nurture)!**
㊐ bringing: up, foster
㊏ *nutrition*: 영양 *nutritious*: 영양의 *nutritional*: 영양의
㈎ She wants to stay at home and nurture her children.

oath
[ouə]
® 10705/86800

n. 맹세, 서약, 선서
❶ 나는 글 로써(oath) 맹세합니다
㊐ pledge, vow
㈎ Medieval knights took an oath of allegiance/loyalty to their lord.

✔ obey
[oubéi]
⑧ 8693/86800

v. **따르다, 복종하다**
❶ 앞에서도 나왔지만 **아버이(obey)말 복종해야**
㉑ comply, submit
㈎ *obedience*: 복종, 순종 obedient: 복종하는
㈊ The soldiers refused to obey orders.

✔ object
[ábdʒikt][əbdʒékt]
⑧ 1629/86800

n. v. **물건, 대상, 목적, 반대하다**
❶ **아부 직(object)** 직장(아부를 많이 해야 하는 직장)을 부모가 **반대하다**
㉑ purpose, aim: 목적
㈎ *objection*: 반대, 이의
   objective: 목적, 객관적인
   objectively: 객관적으로
㈊ Look, there's a strange object in the sky!

✔ obligatory
[əblígətɔ̀:ri]
⑧ 14873/86800

adj. **의무적인**
❶ **아버리(obli - 아버지)가 똘이(tory - 아들 이름)키우는 것은 의무적인 일**
㉑ mandatory
㈎ oblige: 의무를 지우다
   obligation: 의무, 은혜
   obligate: ～에게 의무를 지우다
㈊ The medical examination before you start work is obligatory.

oblivion
[əblíviən]
⑧ 17120/86800

n. **망각**
❶ **5불이 비어(oblivion) - 어디 갔지?5불이(망각)**
㉑ forgetfulness
㈊ These toys will be around for a year or two, then fade into oblivion.

obscure
[əbskjúər]
⑧ 6236/86800

adj. v. **어두운, 애매한, 흐리게 하다**
❶ **애매한 건 없었구여(obscure)**
㉑ ambiguous, vague: 애매한
㈊ The origins of the language are obscure.

O

observance
[əbzə́:rvəns]
[R] 18659/86800

n. 준수
[T] **5부 젤 반 수(observance): 차량 5부제를** 반드시 **준수**
[유] compliance, conformity
[예] Religious observances such as fasting can be hard to follow.

✔ **observation**
[àbzərvéiʃən]
[R] 3267/86800

n. 관찰
[T] **없죠? 보이소(observation) 관찰** 잘 했어야죠
[유] survey
[파] observatory 관측소, 천문대 ***observe***: 관찰하다, 준수하다 ***observer***: 관찰자
[예] The police are keeping the suspect under observation.

✔ **obstacle**
[ábstəkəl]
[R] 9554/86800

n. 장애물
[T] **아빠(ob)는 스타클**(랩트)(stacle)가 아들의 공부 **장애물**이라 생각
[유] barrier, hurdle
[예] The biggest obstacle in our way was a tree trunk in the road.

obstinate
[ábstənit]
[R] 24398/86800

adj. 완고한, 고집 센
[T] **옵! 쎄다 니(너)(obstinate)** 고집이
[유] stubborn, obdurate
[예] Her refusal was obstinate.

✔✔ **obtain**
[əbtéin]
[R] 2207/86800

v. 얻다, 획득하다
[T] **얻데 인(obtain) - attain**도 마찬가지로 암기: **얻다**
[유] get, receive [파] ***obtainable***: 얻을 수 있는
[예] Sugar is obtained by crushing and processing sugar cane.

✔✔ **obvious**
[ábviəs]
[R] 1214/86800

adj. 명백한, 분명한
[T] 앞에서 나온 아빠시리즈 기억아세요? 친자 확인 해보니 **분명한 아비였어(obvious)**
[유] evident, clear [파] ***obviously***: 명백히
[예] It's obvious (that) she doesn't like him.

occasion
[əkéiʒən]
® 1934/86800

n. 경우(번), 때, 행사
❶ 그 때가 언제 예요? 어(저)께 이전(occasion)
   그 행사를 내가 **어케 잊언?(occasion)**
   - 그 행사를 내가 어떻게 잊어?
㊌ time, moment
㊂ *occasional*: 가끔의 *occasionally*: 가끔
㊐ We met on several occasions to discuss the issue.

occupation
[àkjəpéiʃən]
® 3929/86800

n. 직업, 점령
❶ **직업을 얻고파션(occupation)** - 직업을 얻고 싶어서
㊌ job, career
㊂ *occupied*: 종사하는 *occupy*: 점령하다, 종사하다
㊐ In the space marked 'occupation' she wrote 'police officer'.

occur
[əkə́:r]
® 1824/86800

v. 발생하다, 떠오르다
❶ 사건이 **어케(occur)발생했나요?**
㊌ arise, happen
㊂ *occurrence*: 발생, 사건
㊐ An accident involving over ten vehicles has occurred in the east - bound lane.

octopus
[áktəpəs]
® 21702/86800

n. 문어
❶ octo(숫자로 8 - 어원 편 참조 - 문어다리는 8):
㊐ The marine biologist was looking forward to studying the octopus.

odd
[ɑd]
® 2255/86800

adj. 이상한, 여분의, 홀수의
❶ **odd(홋):** 발음이 홋이라고 나서 **홀수의,** 앗(odd)? 그러면 뭔가 이상한 일에 대한 감탄이므로 이상한, odd number(홀수), even number은 짝수
㊌ peculiar, strange
㊐ Her father was an odd man.

odor
[óudər]
Ⓡ 9178/86800

n. 냄새, 향기
❶ 고기 집에서 **옷을(odor) 냄새로** 베게하다
Ⓨ smell, scent
예 The cheese has a strong odor.

✔ offense
[əféns]
Ⓡ 2660/86800

n. 위반, 공격
❶ **옷 뺏어(offense)!** 하며 공격, 옷 뺏는 건 **위반**
Ⓨ violation, infringement
Ⓑ defense
파 *offend*: 화나게 하다, 위반하다
　offensive: 무례한, 불쾌한, 공격의
예 Driving without a licence is an offence.

✔ offer
[ɔ́(:)fər]
Ⓡ 614/86800

n. v. 제공, 제공하다
❶ **앞에(offer) 제공하다**
Ⓨ present, furnish
예 Can I offer you (= Would you like) a drink?

✔ official
[əfíʃəl]
Ⓡ 1043/86800

n. adj. 공무원, 공식적인
❶ office가 사무실이라는 뜻 말고 공직이라는 뜻이 있어요, 그래서 공직의, 공식적인, 공직의 일을 하는 사람이라는 뜻이 official에 있습니다
Ⓨ formal: 공식적인
Ⓑ officious
파 *office*: 임무, 공직 *officer*: 장교, 공무원
예 He visited China in his official capacity as America's trade representative.

✔ offspring
[ɔ́:fspriŋ]
Ⓡ 7311/86800

n. 자손, 소산(결과물)
❶ **예뻐서 뿌린(offspring) 자손**
Ⓨ descendant, posterity
예 In the case of the guinea pig, the number of offspring varies between two and five.

omen
[óumən]
® 22431/86800

n. 징조, 전조
❶ 으메(omen)라고 소리지르면 안 좋은 **징조**
㉠ sign, indication
㉢ Many people believe that a broken mirror is an omen of bad luck.

✔ **omit**
[oumít]
® 19209/86800

v. 생략하다
❶ 5밑(omit)은 **생략하다**
㉠ delete, exclude ㉣ omission: 생략
㉢ She was omitted from the list of contributors to the report.

✔ **ongoing**
[ángòuiŋ]
® 9155/86800

a. 진행 중인
❶ on(부사로 계속하여) + going(가고 있는): 계속 중인
㉢ My teaching is ongoing.

✔ **onlooker**
[ánlùkər]
® 33043/86800

n. 구경꾼
❶ on(위에서) + looker(보고 있는 사람)
㉢ Curious onlookers watched the Royal wedding.

O

❖ **operation**
[àpəréiʃən]
® 1016/86800

n. 운영, 운전, 작용, 수술
❶ 옷 팔아서(operation) 회사 운영하고 수술하면 **아퍼라 ! 션 (opperation)**
㉠ management, administration
㉣ *operate*: 작용하다, 수술하다
㉢ Less profitable business operations will have difficulty in finding financial support.

❖ **opinion**
[əpínjən]
® 1369/86800

n. 의견
❶ 내 **의견**은 이런데 **오빠는(opinion)**?
㉠ view, idea
㉢ What's your opinion on the matter?

✔ **opponent**
[əpóunənt]
[R] 5466/86800

n. adj. **상대, 반대자, 반대하는**
[T] 경기 중 **상대**방의 **옷보는(opponent)**
[유] rival, antagonist
[파] oppose: 반대하다, 대항하다
opposite: 정반대의, 정반대에 있는 것
[예] She is a formidable opponent in the race for senator.

✔ **opportunity**
[àpərtjú:nəti]
[R] 995/86800

n. **기회**
[T] **아빠 돈있지(opportunity)?** 돈 탈 **기회**
[유] chance, occasion
[예] Everyone will have an opportunity to comment.

✔ **opposite**
[ápəzit]
[R] 1699/86800

a. **맞은편의, 반대의**
[T] **맞은편**에 **오빠집(opposite)**
[예] My house is located in the opposite side.

oppress
[əprés]
[R] 43617/86800

v. **압박하다**
[T] ob(노출, 충돌, 저항의 뜻 여기서는 뒤에 철자 p가 와서 op의 형태) + press(누르다): 압박하다
[유] repress, suppress [파] oppression: 압박
[예] For years now, the people have been oppressed by a ruthless dictator.

✔ **optimal**
[áptəməl]
[R] 8678/86800

a. **최적의**
[T] 승용차 **옵티마를(optimal)** 생각 - 차가 **최적인**
[예] Under optimal condition, I'll take final exam.

✔ **optimistic**
[àptəmístik]
[R] 6133/86800

adj. **낙천적인**
[T] **앞 터(opti) + 미쓰다(mist)** + ic(형용사형): 결혼 안한 미쓰가 앞날이 터 있다고 생각하면 **낙천적인**
[유] sanguine [반] pessimistic
[예] She is optimistic about her chances of winning a gold medal.

option
[ápʃən]
[R] 1880/86800

n. **선택권**
[T] 넌 **선택권**이 **없션(option)**
[유] choice, selection
[예] The best option would be to cancel the trip altogether.

oracle
[ɔ́(:)rəkəl]
[R] 8927/86800

n. **성스러운(신의) 메시지**
[T] 오라(ora) + cl(크라이스트) + e(에게): 예수 믿으라는 **성스러운 메세지**
[예] The wise oracle predicted that I would win the Olympics.

oral
[ɔ́:rəl]
[R] 3835/86800

adj. **입의, 구술의, 구두의**
[T] **혀럴(oral)** - 입으로 하는
[유] verbal: 구두의 [파] orator: 웅변가 *orally*: 구두로
[예] As part of her oral examination, she had to recite the names of all the presidents.

orbit
[ɔ́:rbit]
[R] 8954/86800

n. v. **궤도, 궤도를 그리다**
[T] **원으로(or)** + **빛(bit)** - 빛이 **궤도**를 그리다
[예] The satellite is now in a stable orbit.

ordain
[ɔ:rdéin]
[R] 41703/86800

v. **명령하다, (신이) 운명지우다**
[T] **오 대원(ordain)** 앞을 맡으라고 (장군이) 명령하다. (장군이) **운명지우다**
[유] command, order
[예] The process was ordained by law.

order
[ɔ́:rdər]
[R] 427/86800

n. v. **순서, 명령, 명령하다, 주문하다**
[T] 순서대로 **오다(order)**, 오다(order - 음식점에서는 주문)
[유] sequence, procedure
[예] The children lined up in order of age.

ordinary
[ɔ́:rdənèri]
[R] 1478/86800

adj. **보통의, 평범한**
[T] **보통** 경력으로 이력서 **어디내리(ordinary)**?
[유] common, usual [파] *ordinarily*: 보통
[예] They wanted more stories about ordinary people and fewer stories about the rich and famous.

O

✔ organ
[ɔ́:rgən]
® 5784/86800

n. **오르간**, (생물의) 기관
❶ 파이프 **오르간**.. 쉬운 단어 오관(organ) - 다섯 가지 감각 기관
㉮ harmonium
㉠ *organic*: 유기체의, 기관의, 유기적인 *organism*: 유기체
㉖ The organ that pumps blood is the heart.

✔ organize
[ɔ́:rgənàiz]
® 8048/86800

v. **조직하다**
❶ 얽어 나줘(organize - 조직은 옷을 짜듯이 실을 얽어 나가는 것) - **조직하다**
㉮ arrange, array ㉠ *organization*: 조직(화)
㉖ They organized a meeting between the teachers and students.

✔ oriental
[ɔ́:riéntl]
® 8997/8680

adj. n. **동양의, 동양인**
❶ 우리엔 틀(oriental)이 동양인 이야 - 우리 애는 **동양인**의 틀을 가지고 있어
㉡ occidental, Western
㉠ orientation: 방향 결정, 안내 *orient*: 동양
㉖ She has an oriental character.

✔ origin
[ɔ́:rədʒin]
® 3252/86800

n. **기원, 발단**
❶ 월드컵에서 **우리 진(origin)**발단은 - 우리가 진 발단?
㉠ *original*: 원래의, 독창적인 *originality*: 독창성
  originate: 비롯되다
㉖ Her ethnic origins are French.

ornament
[ɔ́:rnəmənt]
® 16603/86800

n. v. **장식, 장식하다**
❶ 오너(orna - 주인으로 이해) 방 만(ment) 장식하면 됨
㉮ adorn, embellish: 장식하다
㉖ She wore a hair ornament.

✔ osteoporosis
[àstioupəróusis]
® 29577/86800

n. **골다공증**
❶ 골다공증 어서 때워 뼈를 써서(osteoporosis)
㉖ Osteoporosis is serious disease to older women.

otherwise
[ʌ́ðərwàiz]
® 1170/86800

adv. (만약) **그렇지 않으면, 의견이 다르게**
❶ 아들 와야지(otherwise) 그렇지 않으면 당신 도와줄 사람 없어
㉺ if not
㉞ I'd better write it down, otherwise I'll forget it.

outcast
[áutkæ̀st]
® 26239/86800

a. n. 내 **쫓긴, 버림받은, 추방당한 사람**
❶ out(밖으로) + cast(던지다)
㉞ This town was settled by outcasts.

outcome
[áutkʌ̀m]
® 2671/86800

n. **결과, 성과**
❶ out(밖으로) + come(나온 거): 밖으로 나온 결과, 성과
㉺ result, consequence
㉞ It's too early to predict the outcome of the meeting.

outdo
[àutdú:]
® 42881/86800

v. **~보다 뛰어나다**
❶ out이 ~보다의 뜻이 있음 e.g.)outrun(~보다 빨리 달리다): out
(~보다) + do(하다): ~보다 잘하다
여기서는 ~보다(out) + 하다(do): ~보다 잘하다
㉺ surpass, excel
㉞ He always tries to outdo everybody else in the class.

outdoor
[áutdɔ̀:r]
® 6820/86800

adj. **집 밖의**
❶ out(밖) + door(문): 문 밖의, 집 밖의
㉺ open - air, outside ㉝ indoor
㉞ Sara's not really the outdoor type.

outgoing
[áutgòuiŋ]
® 9843/86800

adj. **사교적인, 나가는**
❶ out(밖으로) + going(나가는): 사교적인
㉺ sociable
㉞ She has an outgoing personality.

outing
[áutiŋ]
® 10886/86800

n. **소풍**
❶ outing(밖으로 나가기)
㉞ His family took a weekend outing.

O

outlet
[áutlet]
[R] 10238/86800

n. **배출구, 판매 대리점**
[T] out(밖으로) + let(새게하다): 배출구, 그 밖에 아울렛(판매점)은 많이 들어보셨을 듯
[유] vent
[예] Writing poetry was his only form of emotional outlet.

outline
[áutlàin]
[R] 4518/86800

n. v. **개요, 윤곽을 그리다**
[T] out(밖으로) + line(선을 긋다): 윤곽을 그리다
[유] summary, synopsis
[예] The pictures were drawn in outline and then filled in with color.

outlive
[àutlív]
[R] 44997/86800

v. **~보다도 오래 살다**
[T] out(~보다) + live(살다): ~보다 오래 살다
[유] outlast, outwear
[예] No mother wants to outlive her children.

outlook
[áutlùk]
[R] 6323/86800

n. **전망, 예측**
[T] out(밖을) + look(보다): 예측
[유] prospect
[예] Despite our differences in outlook, we got along together very well.

output
[áutpùt]
[R] 1707/86800

n. **생산, 출력**
[T] out(밖으로) + put(놓다): 생산, 출력
[유] production
[예] Last year British manufacturing output fell by 14%.

outskirts
[áutskə:rts]
[R] 9881/86800

n. **변두리**
[T] out(바깥) + skirts(가장자리): 바깥 외곽
[유] suburb
[예] The factory is on the outskirts of New Delhi.

✔ outstanding
[àutstǽndiŋ]
ⓡ 3175/86800

adj. **눈에 띄는, 뛰어난**
❶ out(밖에) + standing(서있는): 남은 안에 있는데 자기만 밖에서 있으므로 눈에 띄는
㊂ conspicuous, perceptible, remarkable
㈜ It's an area of outstanding natural beauty.

✔ oval
[óuvəl]
ⓡ 9568/86800

adj. **타원형의**
❶ O(둥그런 오가)val(별): 영어의 O자가 벌 받으면 찌그러져서 **타원형**이 됨
㊂ egg - shaped, oviform
㈜ Her eyes were large ovals.

✔ overall
[óuvərɔ̀:l]
ⓡ 1323/86800

adj. adv. **전체의, 전체적으로**
❶ over(걸쳐) + all(전체): 전체에 걸쳐, 전체적으로
㊂ entire, general
㈜ The overall situation is good, despite a few minor problems.

✔ overbearing
[òuvərbéəriŋ]
ⓡ 29244/86800

a. **고자세의, 거만한**
❶ 수학못하냐? **오빠(한테) 배워랑(overbearing)** 수학 잘한다고 **고자세의**
㊂ domineering, dictatorial
㈜ She has a pompous and overbearing father.

✔ overcome
[òuvərkʌ́m]
ⓡ 3438/86800

v. **극복하다**
❶ 이 추위를 **극복**하기 위해서는 **오바(over) 컴!(come)** - 오바가 있어야 추위 **극복하다**
㊂ defeat, subdue, vanquish
㈜ Eventually she managed to overcome her shyness in class.

✔ overestimate
[òuvəréstəmèit]
ⓡ 30537/86800

v. **과대평가하다**
❶ over(~ 위에) + estimate(평가하다): 과대평가 하다
㊂ overrate, overvalue ㊤ underestimate
㈜ They were forced to the conclusion that they had overestimated his abilities.

overhead
[óuvərhéd]
® 6079/86800

adv. adj. 머리 위에, 머리 위의
❶ over(~위에) + head(머리): 머리 위에
예 This room needs overhead lighting.

✔ overhear
[òuvərhíər]
® 39664/86800

v. 우연히 엿듣다
❶ over(~위로) + hear(듣다): 내 귀 위로 듣다, 우연히 듣다
예 I overheard a very funny conversation on the bus this morning.

✎ overlook
[òuvərlúk]
® 13596/86800

v. 간과하다
❶ over(~위로) + look(보다): 위로 보면 아래가 안보일 수 밖에 그러므로 간과하다
예 The detective overlooked an important clue.

✔ overnight
[óuvərnàit]
® 4385/86800

adj. adv. 밤을 새는, 하룻밤사이에
❶ over(넘어서) + night(밤): 밤을 넘어서
예 He stayed overnight and went home the next day.
The novel made her famous overnight.

✔ overpopulation
[òuvərpápjuléiʃən]
® 48701/86800

n. 인구 과잉
❶ over(넘어서) + population(인구 - 밥푸래이션 - 사람이므로 밥 달라고): 넘어선 인구
⊕ surplus population
예 He is studying the problem of deer overpopulation.

✔ overseas
[óuvərsì:(z)]
® 2591/86800

adj. adv. 해외의, 해외로
❶ over(넘어서) + sea(바다): 바다 넘어서, 해외로
⊕ foreign: 해외의 abroad: 해외로
예 The troops were sent overseas.

✔ overtake
[òuvərtéik]
® 18127/86800

v. ~을 따라 잡다, 덮치다
❶ over(위에서) + take(잡다): 대개 뒤에서 따라 잡을 때 위에서 잡는다
예 We managed to overtake and board the train.

overthrow
[òuvərəróu][óuvərəròu]
ⓡ 10855/86800

v. n. 뒤집어엎다, 타도하다, 타도
❶ over(위로) + throw(던지다): 타도하다
㉮ overturn, strike down
㉠ The heavy winds overthrew numerous telephone poles and trees.

overturn
[óuvərtə̀:rn]
ⓡ 19917/86800

v. n. 뒤집어엎다, 전복
❶ over(위로) + turn(회전시키다): 뒤집어엎다
㉮ overthrow, subversion, upset
㉠ The burglars had overturned all the furniture in the house.

✤ overweight
[òuvərwéit]
ⓡ 13033/86800

adj. 중량 초과의
❶ over(넘어서) + weight(몸무게): 몸무게 초과의
㉮ obese, chubby
㉠ He used to be very overweight.

✔ overwhelm
[òuvərhwélm]
ⓡ 22374/86800

v. 압도하다
❶ over(오바 - 넘어서) + whelm(윔): 암기대회에서 암기(윔)를 오버하게 함, 완전 압도하다
㉮ overpower, suppress ㉵ *overwhelming*: 압도적인
㉠ Roman troops were overwhelmed by barbarians.

overwork
[òuvərwə̀:rk]
ⓡ 37079/86800

v. n. 과로시키다, 과로
❶ over(넘어서) + work(일하다): 일을 너무하다
㉮ overexertion, excessive labor ㉯ underwork
㉠ Don't overwork yourself on that new job.

✤ owe
[ou]
ⓡ 6041/86800

v. 빚지고 있다, 은혜를 입다
❶ 오(owe)!놀라운 주님의 은혜, 은혜는 돌려말하면 빚을 지는 것이므로 **은혜를 입다**
㉠ He says he doesn't owe anybody.

307

own
[oun]
® 127/86800

adj. v. **자기 자신의, 소유하다**
❶ 오너(owner - 소유자)라는 말 생각
㊦ have, possess 파 *owner*: 소유자
예 They own several homes.

oxygen
[áksidʒən]
® 4471/86800

n. **산소**
❶ oxy(산소) + gen(생성물)혹은 산소가 없으면 **악 쓰죠(oxygen)**
예 Freedom is the oxygen without which science cannot breathe.

ozone
[óuzoun]
® 5975/86800

n. **오존**
❶ 오존층의 **오존(ozone)**
예 Scientists are concerned about ozone depletion.

pace
[peis]
® 3017/86800

n. **속도, 걸음**
❶ 페이스(pace - 속도) 를 잘 조절하라는 말 많이 들었을 거예요
㊦ speed, rate
예 When she thought she heard someone following her, she quickened her pace.

pack
[pæk]
® 2835/86800

n. **꾸러미, 담배 한 갑, 짐을 싸다**
❶ 담배 한 **팩 (pack)** - 한 **꾸러미**
예 Give me a pack of cigarettes.

paddle
[pædl]
® 15804/86800

v: **노를 젓다, 라켓으로 치다, 매를 때리다**
❶ 파돌(paddle)헤치며 **노를 젓다**
예 Indiana Jones paddled long canoes.

pain
[pein]
® 1402/86800

n. **고통, 수고**
❶ 발이 폐인(pain) - 발이 패여서 **고통**
㊦ agony, anguish, suffering
파 painful: 아픈
예 She was in constant pain.

palazzo
[pəlɑ́ːtsou]
ⓡ 13986/86800

n. 이태리 관공서, 궁전, 대 저택
❶ 이 비싼 집 좀 팔아줘(palazzo)
⊕ Palace
㉮ Palazzo is a large building as a museum or as a place of residence in Italy.

pale
[peil]
ⓡ 2762/86800

adj. 핼쑥한, 창백한, 색 따위가 엷은
❶ 몸이 거의 뼈일(pale)정도로 핼쑥한
⊕ ashen, pallid
㉮ She has a naturally pale complexion and dark hair.

palm
[pɑːm]
ⓡ 5937/86800

n. 손바닥, 야자
❶ 손바닥 한 뼘(palm)
㉮ This tiny device fits into the palm of your hand.

panel
[pǽnl]
ⓡ 2674/86800

n. 칸막이, 널빤지, 구획, 공개토론자
❶ 판넬(panel) 혹은 패널이라고 들어보셨을 것임
㉮ One of the ceiling panels needs to be replaced.

pang
[pæŋ]
ⓡ 20551/86800

n. 고통, 고민
❶ 총을 팽(pang)맞고 고통스러워하다
⊕ pain, agony, suffering
㉮ We hadn't eaten since yesterday and the hunger pangs were getting harder to ignore.

panic
[pǽnik]
ⓡ 4205/86800

n. 공포, 공황
❶ 나를 두들겨 패니(panic) 공포스러워
⊕ fear, terror
㉮ Jennifer was in a panic about her exam.

pant
[pænt]
ⓡ 40769/86800

v. 헐떡이다
❶ 숨을 헐떡이며 땅을 판다(pant)
⊕ gasp, puff
㉮ Matteo arrived at the top of the hill, panting and covered in sweat.

papyrus
[pəpáiərəs]
® 38145/86800

n. 고대 이집트의 제지 원료
❶ 페이퍼(종이)로서(papyrus)
예 Papyrus is from ancient Egypt.

paradise
[pǽrədàis]
® 6952/86800

n. 천국, 낙원
❶ 낙원 상가에 가면 악기 팔아 다 있어(paradise)
⊕ heaven, Eden
예 His idea of paradise is to spend the day lying on the beach.

paradox
[pǽrədàks]
® 9280/86800

n. 역설, 이치에 맞지 않은 말
❶ para(반대의 뜻) + dox(의견): 예상과 반대
예 I think the paradox of poverty in the midst of plenty.

paragraph
[pǽrəgræf]
® 3523/86800

n. 단락
❶ para(퍼라) + graph(쓴 거): 쓴거 펴라, 펴라는 것 보니 짧은 글이 아니고 긴 문장(단락)인 것 같음
예 The two introductory paragraphs were written by the editor.

parallel
[pǽrəlèl]
® 2832/86800

adj. n. v. 평행의, 평행선, 평행시키다
❶ 쭉 펴라 (para + ll(라인)el(을): 쭉 펴라 라인(선)을 - 평행의
예 These two sentences are parallel in structure.

paralyz(s)e
[pǽrəlàiz]
® 41854/86800

v. 마비시키다
❶ 팔아(para) + 이제(lyze) 말 좀 들어라 - 마비된 팔아! 이제 말 좀 들어라
⊕ numb 파 paralysis: 마비
예 The drug paralyses the nerves so that there is no feeling or movement in the legs.

parcel
[pá:rsəl]
® 8770/86800

n. 꾸러미, 소포
❶ 엄마가 팔을(parcel) 꾸러미에 싸서 보내셨어
⊕ package, packet: 소포
예 The parcel was wrapped in plain brown paper.

parliament
[pá:rləmənt]
Ⓡ 1049/86800

n. (영국) 국회
❶ **국회**로 가려면(국회의원 되려면) **팔아 모은(parliament)** 거 다 써야
⊕ assembly, congress
예 She was elected to Parliament in 1997.

❤ part
[pɑ:rt]
Ⓡ 168/86800

n. v. **부분, 역할, 나누다**
❶ part - 콩 **팔(part)**은 신체의 부분
⊕ partition, portion: 부분 role, function: 역할
파 partial: 부분적인, 불공평한
예 The entire book is good, but the best part is the ending.

partake
[pɑ:rtéik]
Ⓡ 34583/86800

v. **참가하다, 몫을 받다**
❶ par(부분 - part가 줄은 말) + take(받다) - 부분적으로 받다, 함께 하다, 몫을 받다
⊕ join in, participate, share
예 Would you care to partake of a little wine with us?

✔ participation
[pɑ:rtìsəpéiʃən]
Ⓡ 3425/86800

n. **참가**
❶ part(부분) + cipa(싶어) + tion(명사형 어미): 부분이 되고 싶어함 - 참가
⊕ joining, entry
파 *participate*: 참가하다 participant: 참가자
예 The grade is made up of two exams and participation.

❤ particle
[pá:rtikl]
Ⓡ 9133/86800

n. **작은 조각, 극소량**
❶ part(부분) + cle(작다는 뜻을 나타내는 접미사 - let, - ette도 작다는 뜻을 나타냄): 작은 부분
e.g.) wristlet: 토시, 팔목 끈 cigarette ⊕ piece, bit
예 There is not a particle of evidence to support their claim.

P

particular
[pərtíkjələr]
® 410/86800

adj. 특별한
❶ 특별한 파티골라(particular)
⊕ special, unique 파 *particularly*: 특히
예 The computer program will be of particular interest to teachers.

party
[pá:rti]
® 206/86800

n. 당파, 일행, 파티
❶ part(부분) + y(모아 놓은 것): 어떤 뜻을 같이 하는 부분들의 모임, 당 - 민주당, 공화당의 당파
⊕ faction
예 The senator is loyal to his party.

passage
[pǽsidʒ]
® 2495/86800

n. 통행, 글 한 구절,
❶ 나 passage(패스 지? - 버스 통과지?)
⊕ passing, transit
예 The bathroom's on the right at the end of the passage.

passenger
[pǽsəndʒər]
® 4331/86800

n. 승객
❶ 버스인줄(passenger) 알고 탄 사람(승객)
예 There were two passengers in the car in addition to the driver.

passerby
[pǽsərbai]
® 순위 外/86800

n. 통행인
❶ pass(통과) + by(옆): 옆을 통과하는 통행인
예 The gunmen opened fire, killing a policeman and a passer - by.

passion
[pǽʃən]
® 3854/86800

n. 열정, 정열
❶ 열심히 영어를 팠션(passion) - 열심히 했어
⊕ ardor, fervor 파 *passionate*: 정열적인
예 Her performance is full of passion and originality.

passive
[pǽsiv]
® 5472/86800

adj. **소극적인, 수동적인**
❶ passive(패스 봐 - 축구 선수가 패스하는 것만 봐) - 소극적인
㊊ inactive ㊗ active
㋩ He's very passive in the relationship.

paste
[peist]
® 11986/86800

n. **풀, 반죽**
❶ pepper paste(고추장), bean paste(된장)를 기억하고(풀처럼 된 걸 paste) 암기해보세요
㊊ dough: 반죽
㋩ Sujebee needs flour-and-water paste.

pastime
[pǽstàim]
® 18475/86800

n. **오락, 기분 전환**
❶ past(보내다) + time(시간): 보내는 시간, 오락시간
㊊ amusement(s), recreation
㋩ Baseball has been a national pastime for years.

pasture
[pǽstʃər]
® 9992/86800

n. **목장, 목초지**
❶ **목장**에서 우유 **빼서 줘(pasture)**
㊊ ranch, meadow
㋩ The horses were grazing in the pasture.

pat
[pæt]
® 4076/86800

v. **가볍게 두드리다**
❶ **살 살 패(pat) - 가볍게 두드리다**
㊊ tap
㋩ I bent down to pat the little puppy.

patch
[pætʃ]
® 4888/86800

n. **옷 깁는 헝겊조각**
❶ **배추(patch) 잎 같은 헝겊조각**
㋩ I bought a patch over the eye.

patent
[pǽtənt, péit-]
® 7050/86800

n. **특허**
❶ 물건의 **패턴도(patent)** 흉내내면 안 되는 **특허**
㋩ They were sued for patent infringement.

P

path
[pæθ]
ⓡ 1651/86800

n. 작은 길
ⓣ path(패스 - pass로 생각해서 통과하려면 길이 있어야): 길
ⓢ course, route
예 The fire destroyed everything in its path.

pathetic
[pəθétik]
ⓡ 8956/86800

adj. 측은한
ⓣ pathy(마음, 감정, 병, 요법등을 나타내는 말 - 어원편 참조) + ic
(형용사형 어미) - 마음 쓰는
ⓢ sad, piteous, pitiful
예 The blind, old dog was a pathetic sight.

patient
[péiʃənt]
ⓡ 1251/86800

adj. n. 환자
ⓣ 다리가 삐어션(patient) 환자
ⓢ enduring, forbearing
파 patience: 인내 patiently: 참을성 있게
예 The teacher treated her students in a patient and understanding way.

patriot
[péitriət]
ⓡ 20422/86800

n. 애국자
ⓣ 3.1 운동 때 태극기 퍼트리었(patriot)던 애국지사
파 patriotism: 애국심
예 He was a great patriot who devoted his life to serving his country.

patron
[péitrən]
ⓡ 8355/86800

n. 후원자
ⓣ 좋은 후원자 덕분에 내 꿈이 피었더런(patron)
ⓢ supporter, sponsor
예 Mr. Hwang is a well - known patron of several charities.

pause
[pɔːz]
ⓡ 4402/86800

n. v. 잠시 멈춤. 잠시 멈추다
ⓣ 선생님이 수업을 하다 보자(pause)하시면서 잠시 멈추다
ⓢ stop
예 After a long, awkward pause someone asked a question.

pavement
[péivmənt]
ⓡ 5714/86800

n. 포장 도로, 차도
❶ 펴봐 면(pavement) 지 안 나게 - 도로 **포장**하는 이유는 아스팔트를 **펴봐(서) 면**지 안 나게 하려고
⊕ paved road ⊕ dirt road
펜 *pave*: 포장하다
예 He broke up the pavement.

paw
[pɔ:]
ⓡ 19701/86800

n. 발톱 있는 동물의 발
❶ 파(pa)톱있는 동물의 **바우(paw** - 발음) - **발톱**있는 동물의 발
예 The dog injured his paw.

payment
[péimənt]
ⓡ 1892/86800

n. 지불
❶ pay(뻬이 - 뼈빠지게 **일 한 것**) + ment(명사형 어미): 페이 먼 (payment) 저 **지불** 해 주세요
⊕ paying 펜 *pay*: 지불하다
예 Payment is due on the first of every month.

pear
[pɛər]
ⓡ 18250/86800

n. 서양 배
❶ 나는 **배여(pear)!** - 그래 배구나
예 I'd like to eat a pear as dessert.

peasant
[pézənt]
ⓡ 4980/86800

n. 농부, 시골 사람
❶ pea(피 - 완두 콩) + sant(준): 콩(pea)준(sant) **농부**
⊕ farmer
예 Most of the produce sold in the market is grown by peasant farmers.

peculiar
[pikjú:ljər]
ⓡ 5496/86800

adj. 독특한
❶ **독특한** 사람을 보면 우린 이렇게 말 하죠: **별꼴이여(peculiar)**
⊕ distinctive, unique 펜 peculiarity: 특색, 버릇
예 She has the most peculiar ideas.

pedestrian
[pədéstriən]
Ⓡ 11128/86800

n. 보행자
❶ ped(발이라는 뜻 - 에를 들면 pedal) + ian(사람): 발을 이용해 다니는 사람: 보행자
예 The death rate for pedestrians hit by cars is unacceptably high.

peel
[pi:l]
Ⓡ 8522/86800

n. v. 과일껍질, 과일 껍질을 벗기다
❶ p(퍼) + eel(일): 과일 벗기(p)길(eel)과 발음이 비슷
⊕ skin
예 Peel, core and chop the apples.

peer
[piər]
Ⓡ 7829/86800

n. v. 동료, 자세히 들여다보다
❶ 동료들끼리 이야기꽃을 피워(peer)
⊕ colleague, companion, associate
예 He was respected and admired by his peers.

penalty
[pénəlti]
Ⓡ 3461/86800

n. 형벌
❶ 축구에서 페널티(penalty) 킥은 벌로 주는 거예요
⊕ punishment 파 *penalize*: 벌을 주다
예 The company was given a severe penalty for the violation.

pendulum
[péndʒələm]
Ⓡ 18338/86800

n. 흔들거리는 추(진자)
❶ pend(매달리다) + 주렁주렁(dulum - 흔들려서)
예 The pendulum swings back and forth.

penetrate
[pénətrèit]
Ⓡ 10593/86800

v. 꿰뚫다, 간파하다
❶ 펜이 뚫었다(penetrate) - 펜이 종이를 뚫었다
⊕ pierce, cut [run] through
예 These bullets can penetrate armor.

peninsula
[pinínsələ]
Ⓡ 9796/86800

n. 반도
❶ peni(반이) + su(섬) + la(이라): 반도
e.g) Korean peninsula: 한 반도
예 They built their house on a narrow peninsula.

✔ penniless
[pénilis]
® 23437/86800

adj. **무일푼의**
❶ penny(푼돈) + less(~이 없는) - 펜이 없어(less)
  돈이 없어서 펜도 없어
⊕ broke, destitute
㉔ She was unemployed and penniless.

✔ penny
[péni]
® 4414/86800

n. **미국 1센트 동전, 작은 돈**
❶ 나는 **작은 돈**이라 빼니?(penny)
㉔ penny - wise and pound - foolish.

pension
[pénʃən]
® 2256/86800

n. **연금**
❶ pen(매달다 - 어원편 참조) + sion(명사형 어미)
  연금에 생활이 매달림
⊕ annuity
㉔ They find it hard to live on their state pension.

pensive
[pénsiv]
® 38208/86800

adj **깊은 생각에 잠겨 있는**
❶ 펜(pen) + sive(씹어): 펜을 씹어 가면서 **깊은 생각에 잠긴**
⊕ meditative, thoughtful
㉔ She became withdrawn and pensive, hardly speaking
  to anyone.

pentagon
[péntəgən]
® 15503/86800

n. **5각형, Pentagon - 미국 국방부**
❶ penta(5 - 어원편 참조,e,g,)펜티움 컴퓨터) + gon(각형): 5각 형
㉔ The general attended a meeting at the Pentagon.

✔ perceive
[pərsíːv]
® 7613/86800

v. **지각하다, 알아차리다**
❶ 벌써봐(perceive)서 **알아차리다**
⊕ notice, recognize
㉕ *perception*: 지각 *perceptual*: 지각 있는
㉔ I thought I perceived a problem, but I wasn't sure.

perform
[pərfɔ́:rm]
Ⓡ 3053/86800

v. 실행하다, 공연하다
❶ 발품(perform)팔아가며 **실행하다**
ⓢ effect, execute
ⓟ *performance*: 수행, 공연 *performer*: 행위자
ⓔ Computers can perform a variety of tasks.

perfume
[pɔ́:rfju:m]
Ⓡ 10569/86800

n. 향기, 향수
❶ 퍼 피움(perfume) - **향기**가 퍼지게 **피움**
ⓢ fragrance, aroma, scent
ⓔ What perfume are you wearing?

peril
[pérəl]
Ⓡ 15700/86800

n. 위험
❶ 피를(peril) 흘릴 수 있을 정도로 **위험**한
ⓢ danger, risk
ⓟ perilous: 위험한
ⓔ I never felt that my life was in peril.

period
[píəriəd]
Ⓡ 367/86800

n. 기간, 마침표
❶ 꽃이 피어리(period)는 - 꽃이 피는 건 봄 **기간**
ⓢ term ⓟ periodical: 정기의
ⓔ The study will be carried out over a six - month period.

perish
[périʃ]
Ⓡ 21691/86800

v. 죽다, 멸망하다
❶ 너네 까불면 **패리 씨~**(perish) - 까불면 **죽는다**는 말
ⓢ die, pass away
ⓔ He believes that Europe must create closer ties or it will perish.

permanent
[pɔ́:rmənənt]
Ⓡ 2228/86800

adj. 영구적인, 불변의
❶ 엄마의 **퍼머는**(permanent) **영구적인** 것(변하지 않으라고 하는 것)
ⓢ constant, lasting, eternal
ⓟ permanently: 영구히
ⓔ She made a permanent home in this country.

✔ **permission**
[pəːrmíʃən]
® 3000/86800

n. 허가, 허락
❶ per(완전히, 매우의 뜻 - 어원편 참조) + mission(보냄 - 어원편 참조): 완전히 보내 줌
⊕ allowance, authorization, consent
㈜ *permit*: 허락하다, 허가증
㈜ You will need permission from the council to extend your garage.

perpetual
[pərpétʃuəl]
® 11185/86800

adj. 영원한, 끊임없는
❶ 영원한 별 빛도(perpetual)
⊕ incessant, continual
㈜ They lived in perpetual fear of being discovered and arrested.

perplex
[pərpléks]
® 66146/86800

v. 당황하게 하다
❶ 서해 바다에 놀러갔는데 친구가 **뻘 뿌려서(perplex)당황했다**
⊕ confuse, embarrass
㈜ perplexed: 당황한
㈜ Questions about the meaning of life have always perplexed humankind.

persecute
[páːrsikjùːt]
® 52408/86800

v. 학대하다, 박해하다
❶ 발씻구(persecute) 오라고 부인이 **학대하다**
⊕ abuse
㈜ They were persecuted for their beliefs.

persevere
[pàːrsəvíər]
® 30736/86800

v. 인내하다
❶ 가게주인이 점원보고 하는 말 - 좀 **참지** 내가 없다고 **벌써 비워(persevere)가게를?**
⊕ be patient(with), endure, bear
㈜ perseverance: 인내
㈜ The education director is persevering in his attempt to obtain additional funding for the school.

✔ **persist**
[pə:rsíst]
[R] 10716/86800

v. **고집하다**
[T] 냄새나는 데 **발 씻었다(persist)**고 **고집하다**
[유] insist, maintain
[파] persistent: 고집하는 *persistence*: 고집
[예] If the pain persists, consult a doctor.

✔ **personality**
[pə̀:rsənǽləti]
[R] 3256/86800

n. **성격, 인격, 개성**
[T] personal(인간적인, 개인적인) + ity(명사형 어미); 사람됨, 인격, 개성
[유] character
[예] She has a very warm personality.

✔ **personnel**
[pə̀:rsənél]
[R] 2916/86800

n. adj. **직원, 인사부, 인사의**
[T] **벌 써 낼(personnel) 직원** 인사이동이 있네요
[유] staff, employee
[예] For more information about the job, please contact the personnel manager.

✔ **perspective**
[pə:rspéktiv]
[R] 3125/86800

n. **전망, 시각**
[T] per(완전히, 매우) + spect(보다): 통틀어 봄; 시각, 전망
[유] point of view, viewpoint: 시각
[예] He writes from a Marxist perspective.

✔ **persuade**
[pə:rswéid]
[R] 3741/86800

v. **설득하다**
[T] 범인에게 자수하고 **벌 싸다(persuade** - 벌 받는 것이 싸다)고 **설득하다**
[유] induce, urge [반] dissuade
[파] persuasion: 설득 *persuasive*: 설득력이 있는
[예] It's no use trying to persuade him (that) you're innocent.

pertinent
[pə́:rtənənt]
[R] 13157/86800

adj. **타당한, 적절한**
[T] 전 과목 A 맞았는데 **파티는(pertinent) 적절한**
[유] appropriate, proper [반] impertinent
[예] Chapter One is pertinent to the post - war period.

pessimist
[pèsəmíst]
® 45378/86800

n. 비관론자
❶ 패시(pessi - 사람 이름으로 가정) + mist(못 쓰다)
펩시가 못 쓰다고 말하는 **비관론자들**
⑫ optimist ⑪ pessimistic: 비관적인, 염세적인
㉿ Don't be such a pessimist!

✔ pest
[pest]
® 11543/86800

n. 해충, 골칫거리
❶ **해충**이 물어 **피섰다(pest)**
㉿ I was often a pest in my house.

✔ pesticide
[péstəsàid]
® 15754/86800

n. 해충제
❶ pest(해충) + cide(죽이다): 해충제
㉿ The pesticides that farmers spray on their crops kill pests.

✔ pet
[pet]
® 5540/86800

n. v. 애완동물, 귀여워하다
❶ pe(삐 - 뽀삐강아지 이름)t(cat의 마지막 글자)
강아지, 고양이등 **애완동물**
⊕ love, make a pet of: 귀여워하다
㉿ They have several pets - a dog, two rabbits.

petition
[pitíʃən]
® 5846/86800

n. v. 기원, 탄원, 청원하다
❶ 잘 버티션(petition)! - 잘 버티라고 **기원**
⊕ entreaty, supplication
㉿ I signed a petition against the proposed closure of the local hospital today.

petty
[péti]
® 8127/86800

adj. 사소한, 마음 좁은
❶ 잊어버려.... **좁은** 마음 폈지(petty)?
⊕ trivial, trifling
㉿ Prisoners complain that they are subjected to too many petty rules and restrictions.

P

phantom
[fǽntəm]
Ⓡ 16723/86800

n. 유령
🅣 팬텀(phantom) 오브 오페라 - 오페라의 **유령**
Ⓢ ghost, bog(e)y
예 The book is about the phantoms that are said to haunt the nation's cemeteries.

phase
[feiz]
Ⓡ 2165/86800

n. 면, 단계, 국면
🅣 phase는 face와 비슷, face가 얼굴의 겉면이므로 이것은 얼굴의 겉면이 아니라 모든 일의 면, 국면, 단계로 기억해 봅시다
Ⓢ stage, step: 단계
예 We're entering a new phase in international relations.

✔ phenomenon
[finámənan]
Ⓡ 4013/86800

n. 현상
🅣 피납니다(phenomenon) - 피나는 것은 일어나는 현상
Ⓢ appearance
예 Gravity is a natural phenomenon.

✔ philosopher
[filásəfər]
Ⓡ 10084/86800

n. 철학자
🅣 phil(좋아하다 - 어원편 참조) + sophy(지혜) + er(사람, 사물): 지혜를 좋아하는 사람, 철학자
叫 *philosophy*: 철학
예 Plato was a Greek philosopher.

phobia
[fóubiə]
Ⓡ 28437/86800

n. 공포 증세
🅣 전쟁 **공포**로 잘 때 **포 비어**(phobia) - 포병이 포를 베고 잠
Ⓢ morbid fear
예 I've got a phobia about worms.

✔ phosphorescence
[fàsfərésəns]
Ⓡ 61329/86800

n. 발광성, 푸른 빛
🅣 phosphorous(새벽 별) + ence(명사형어미): Photo는 빛 임을 떠올릴 것
예 Phosphorescence is giving off light after radiation has hit it.

phrase
[freiz]
[R] 3106/86800

n. 어구
[T] 모르는 **어구를 풀어야지(phrase)**
[예] Answer the questions in complete sentences, not phrases.

physical
[fízikəl]
[R] 1065/86800

adj. **신체의, 물질적인, 물리적인**
[T] **physic(뼈지)** + al(형용사형 어미): 뼈는 신체의 일부분이므로 신체의
[유] material, objective: 물질적인
[파] ***physically***: 물리적으로
c.f) ***physics***: 물리학 ***physicist***: 물리학자
[예] I'm not a very physical sort of person(= I don't enjoy physical activities).

physician
[fizíʃən]
[R] 11007/86800

n. **내과 의사**
[T] 외과의사는 칼로 수술하며 **썰젼(surgeon)**. 하지만 내과의사는 칼 안주니까 **삐졌션(physician)**. 삐진 내과의사
[예] You should always consult a physician if you develop a high fever.

pierce
[piərs]
[R] 19407/86800

v. **꿰뚫다, 관통하다**
[T] 귀 **뚫는 것을 피어 싱(piercing)**
[유] penetrate, perforate
[예] I couldn't wear these earrings because my ears aren't pierced.

piety
[páiəti]
[R] 17645/86800

n. **경건, 신앙심**
[T] 장로교회는 **경건 파였지(piety)**
[유] devotion, reverence
[예] He was admired for his extreme piety.

pile
[pail]
[R] 4558/86800

n. v. **더미, 쌓아올리다**
[T] 일 중독자는 **파 일(pile - 일을 자꾸 파)**을 그래서 일이 산**더미**지
[유] heap, stack [예] I've got piles things to do today.

pill
[pil]
ⓡ 10108/86800

n. 알약
❶ Pill(퍼 알): 펴 알약
㉠ tablet, tabloid
㉝ My mother takes three or four pills a day.

pillow
[pílou]
ⓡ 8874/86800

n. 베개
❶ 베개 빌라우(pillow)?
㉠ headrest
㉝ Do you prefer a feather pillow or a foam pillow?

✔ **pine**
[pain]
ⓡ 6904/86800

n. 솔나무, 간절히 사모하다
❶ 산에 가면 널린 폭풍에 파인(pine) 소나무
㉝ I lost my way in a pine forest.

✔ **pioneer**
[pàiəníər]
ⓡ 9529/86800

n. 개척자
❶ 없었던 분야를 파 온 이여(pioneer) 그대는 개척자이십니다
㉠ colonist, settler
㉝ The pioneers went west across North America, cutting down forests.

✔ **pitch**
[pitʃ]
ⓡ 3319/86800

v. n. 던지다, 음의 높이
❶ 야구의 피쳐(pitcher)를 생각하면 쉽게 기억할 수 있는 단어, pitch(음 높이가 높다)는 말도 들어보셨을 거예요
㉠ fling, hurl
㉝ He pitched for the Mets last year.

✔ **pity**
[píti]
ⓡ 4262/86800

n. 불쌍히 여김, 유감스러운 일
❶ 사람이 비리 비리(pity)해서 불쌍히 여김
㉠ compassion, sympathy
㉝ The girl stood gazing in/with pity at the old lion in the cage.

plague
[pleig]
[R] 10344/86800

n. v. **전염병, 괴롭히다**
[T] 병이 뭐야? p(pest - 흑사병, 전염병) + lague(라구): 페스트 라구 !!!! 전염병이라구
[유] epidemic
[예] The country was hit by a plague of natural disasters that year.

✔ **plain**
[plein]
[R] 2421/86800

adj. n. **평범한, 평야**
[T] **풀이 있(plain)는 평범한** 평야
[유] average, ordinary
[예] She wore a plain black dress.

✔ **planet**
[plǽnət]
[R] 4645/86800

n. **행성**
[T] **별이니?(planet)**
[유] globe, primary
[예] Might there be intelligent life on other planets?

✔ **plant**
[plænt]
[R] 1263/86800

n. v. **식물, 공장, 심다**
[T] **풀은다(plant)**식물이고 심은 것. power plant에서 plant는 발전소라는 뜻
[유] factory, mill: 공장, sow: 심다
[예] I planted corn this year.

✔ **plate**
[pleit]
[R] 2455/86800

n. v. **접시, 도금하다**
[T] **접시**에 물감을 **뿌렸다(plate)**
[예] We need paper plates more for our party.

plausible
[plɔ́:zəbəl]
[R] 8158/86800

adj. **그럴듯한**
[T] 선생님이 수학 문제를 **풀어줘바(plausible):** 아주 **그럴 듯해**
[유] specious, very likely
[예] It is a plausible explanation for the demise of the prehistoric species.

playwright
[´-ràit]
ⓡ 18310/86800

n. 극작가
❶ play(극) + wright(제작자): 극작가
㊌ dramatist, writer
㖊 The playwright wrote several plays in the last year.

plaza
[plá:zə]
ⓡ 21527/86800

n. 광장
❶ 서울광장 건너편 **프라자(plaza-)** 호텔을 생각
㖊 We are supposed to meet plaza hotel.

plead
[pli:d]
ⓡ 13284/86800

v. 간청하다, 항변하다, 변호하다
❶ 제발 풀러달(plead)라고 **간청하다**
㊌ beg, implore ㊊ plea: 구실, 탄원
㖊 "Give us more time," they pleaded.

pleasant
[pléznt]
ⓡ 3427/86800

adj. 즐거운, 유쾌한
❶ 즐거운 잔치에 **Pleasant(불러준)** - 즐거운 일에 pleasant(불러준)
㊌ delightful, joyful
㖊 It was pleasant to sit down after standing for hours.

pledge
[pledʒ]
ⓡ 9389/86800

n. v. 맹세, 약속, 맹세하다
❶ 교실에 휴지를 **버리지(pledge)**않겠다고 **맹세**하다
㊌ oath, vow
㖊 I give you this ring as a pledge of my everlasting love for you.

plentiful
[pléntifəl]
ⓡ 12628/86800

adj. 풍부한
❶ 풀엔 티(plenty)가 많음 - 풀에는 티가 많이 섞여 있음 + ful(full 이 줄은 말 - 가득 찬)
㊌ abundant, rich ㊊ *plenty*: 많음
㖊 Strawberries are plentiful in the summer.

plethora
[pléθərə]
ⓡ 19558/86800

n. 과다
❶ 너무 많아 버렸어라우(plethora)!
㖊 There's a plethora of books about the English.

plot
[plɑt]
ⓡ 4137/86800

n. 음모, 줄거리
❶ 불러(plot) 모아 꾸민 **계략**
ⓢ conspiracy, intrigue
예 The plots of his books are basically all the same.

plow(US), plough(UK)
[plau]
ⓡ 11335/86800

n. v. 쟁기, 쟁기질하다
❶ 흙을 쟁기로 갈고 **푸라우(plow)!**
ⓢ cultivate, farm
예 These fields have been under the plough for centuries.

plump
[plʌmp]
ⓡ 10316/86800

adj. 부푼, 부드럽고 풍만한
❶ 몸무게 **불음(plump) - 부푼**, 포동포동한
ⓢ chubby, fleshy
예 He's got rather plump since I last saw him.

✔ **poison**
[pɔ́izən]
ⓡ 7191/86800

n. v. 독, 독살하다
❶ 이미 퍼진(poison) 독
ⓢ toxicant
예 Poverty is a poison to society.

✔ **polarity**
[poulǽrəti]
ⓡ 25603/86800

n. 양극성, 대립(정반대)
❶ polar(극의), North pole - 북극
예 This movie is based on the polarity of the two main characters.

✔ **policy**
[pɑ́ləsi]
ⓡ 339/86800

n. 정책, 방침
❶ politics(아래 참고)에서 나온 말, 정치하는 사람들이 하는 것은 정책
예 What is your party's policy on immigration?

polish
[pɑ́liʃ]
ⓡ 4218/86800

v. n. 닦다, 윤내다, 광택(제)
❶ 구두닦이가 팔로 쉭(polish) 닦다
ⓢ rub up, burnish, shine
예 Polish your shoes regularly to protect the leather.

polite
[pəláit]
ⓡ 6369/86800

adj. 공손한, 예의바른
❶ 선생님! 하고 **공손**하게 **불렀데(polite)**
ⓢ courteous, respectful 패 *politeness*: 공손
예 I'm afraid I wasn't very polite to her.

politics
[pálitìks]
ⓡ 1388/86800

n. 정치, 정치학
❶ 말로 하지 않고 **발로뛰었어(politics)** 는 정치
ⓢ government, administration
패 *political*: 정치의 *politically*: 정치적으로 politician: 정치가
예 He is planning to retire from politics next year.

pollen
[pálən]
ⓡ 14619/86800

n. 꽃가루
❶ 봄 되면 **펄렁(pollen)**날리는 꽃가루
예 Bees pollinate the plants by carrying the pollen from one flower to another.

pollute
[pəlú:t]
ⓡ 27427/86800

v. 오염시키다
❶ **발로다(pollute) 오염시키다**
ⓢ contaminate, stain 패 *pollution*: 오염, 공해
예 We won't invest in any company that pollutes the environment.

pomp
[pɑmp]
ⓡ 26092/86800

n. 화려함, 멋진 풍경
❶ 뉴욕의 **밤(pomp)**은 화려해
ⓢ splendor, pageantry
예 Despite all the pomp of his position, he has only limited powers.

ponder
[pándər]
ⓡ 20543/86800

v. ~을 깊이 생각하다
❶ 난 생각하면 깊이 **판다(ponder)**
ⓢ deliberate, weigh
예 She sat back for a minute to ponder her next move in the game.

popular
[pápjələr]
ⓡ 956/86800

adj. 대중적인, 인기 있는
❶ 노래 뭐할까? 팝불러(popular)! 대중적인 노래 불러
ⓢ current, prevalent
ⓟ *popularity*: 인기, 대중성
예 She's the most popular teacher in school.

population
[pùpjəléiʃən]
ⓡ 744/86800

n. 인구, 주민
❶ 밥 풀레이션(population - 밥을 풀레 어디에? 사람 입에(인구 - 사람 입을 한자로 하면)
ⓢ residents, dwellers: 주민
ⓟ populate: 거주시키다
예 What is the population of Buffalo?

porch
[pɔːrtʃ]
ⓡ 10655/86800

n. 현관, 건물의 출입구
❶ 현관에서 보초(porch) 서!
예 My house has a large front porch.

portable
[pɔ́ːrtəbəl]
ⓡ 7304/86800

adj. 휴대용의
❶ porter(짐꾼, 문지기) + able(~할 수 있는 이라는 뜻의 형용사형 어미): 휴대용의, 포터라는 말은 히말라야 포터들(짐꾼들)에서 쉽게 알 수 있음
예 Portable devices such as MP3 players are becoming increasingly popular.

portion
[pɔ́ːrʃən]
ⓡ 6613/86800

n. 부분, 몫
❶ 뿌셔(portion) - 뿌시 면 부서져서 한 부분이 나옴
ⓢ part, section
예 I accept my portion of the blame.

portrait
[pɔ́ːrtrit]
ⓡ 4792/86800

n. 초상화
❶ 볼드레잇(portrait) - 볼 들어 초상화 그리느라 볼 들으라고!!!!
ⓟ *portray*: 그리다
예 She's commissioned an artist to paint her portrait.

P

✔ pose
[pouz]
® 6640/86800

n. v. 자세, 자세를 취하다, 제기하다
❶ 포즈(pose)취하다, pose는 놓다는 뜻 - 어원편
㊌ posture, position 파 *position*: 위치, 상태, 태도
예 We all posed for our photographs in front of the Lincoln Memorial.

✔ positive
[pázətiv]
® 1220/86800

adj. 긍정적인, 적극적인
❶ 빠져티비(positive) - TV에 적극적인, **긍정적인**
㊌ affirmative, constructive
예 The book had a positive influence on me.

✔ possess
[pəzés]
® 5203/86800

v. 소유하다
❶ 퍼줬어(possess) - 퍼 주면 받아야지! **소유하다**
㊌ hold, own 파 *possession*: 소유 *possessions*: 재산
예 I don't possess a single DVD (= I don't have even one DVD).

✔ possible
[pásəbəl]
® 254/86800

adj. 가능한
❶ 봤어 불(possible)? - 불 봤는지 **가능성**을 물음
㊌ likely, probable 파 *possibility*: 가능성
예 Is it possible to buy tickets in advance?

posterity
[pastérəti]
® 20875/86800

n. 자손, 소산
❶ post(뒤) + terity(딸이지): 딸 뒤에 - 자손
㊌ offspring, progeny
예 Every attempt is being made to ensure that these works of art are preserved for posterity.

postpone
[poustpóun]
® 14175/86800

v. 미루다, 연기하다
❶ post(뒤 - 어원편 참조) + pone(놓다 - 어원편 참조): 뒤에 놓다, 연기하다
㊌ put off, delay, hold off, defer
예 They decided to postpone their holiday until next year.

postscript
[póustskrìpt]
[R] 12675/86800

n. **추신**
[T] post(뒤에) + script(쓰다): 뒤에 쓰다, 추신
[유] P.S=post script
[예] There was the usual romantic postscript at the end of his letter - PS I love you.

✔ **pot**
[pɑt]
[R] 4150/86800

n. **단지, 항아리, 냄비**
[T] 커피 **포트(pot** - 주전자, 냄비)
[유] jar, crock
[예] Fill a large pot with salted water.

potent
[póutənt]
[R] 8442/86800

adj. **강력한, 세력있는**
[T] **포 튼(potent)** - 적군에게 쏘려고 포를 튼 **강력한**
[유] mighty, powerful [반] impotent
[예] The Berlin Wall was a potent symbol of the Cold War.

✔ **potential**
[pouténʃəl]
[R] 902/86800

adj. n. **잠재적인, 잠재력**
[T] 장기 둘 때 **포뗐어(potential)** - 차, 포 다 떼면 이길 **잠재력**이 약하다는 이야기
[파] *potentialities*: 가능력
[예] A number of potential buyers have expressed interest in the company.

✔ **pound**
[paund]
[R] 1490/86800

n. v. **무게와 화폐 단위, 두드리다**
[T] **파온다(pound):** 두드리며 땅을 **파온다**
[유] bang: 두드리다
[예] They stole jewellery valued at £50 000 (= 50 000 pounds).
He pounded his fist on the table.

✔ **pour**
[pɔ:r]
[R] 6019/86800

v. **따르다, (퍼)붓다, 쏟다**
[T] 물을 **푸어(pour)** 붓다 - 퍼붓다
[예] I spilled the juice while I was pouring it.

poverty
[pávərti]
® 3092/86800

n. 가난, 빈곤
❶ 밥 없지(poverty)? 가난 한가 보네
㋐ indigence, penury
㋐ Two million people in the city live in abject (= very great) poverty.

powerful
[páuərfəl]
® 1431/86800

adj. 강력한
❶ power(힘) + ful(full을 줄인 말 - 꽉찬): 힘이 꽉 찬, 힘이 있는
㋐ mighty, strong ㋧ power: 힘
㋐ The President is more powerful than the Prime Minister.

practice
[prǽktis]
® 565/86800

n. 연습, 실행
❶ 음식 연습하다 불에뎄어(practice)
㋐ training, drill, exercise
㋧ practical: 실제적인, 실용적인
practicable: 실행할 수 있는 practically: 실제적으로
㋐ I can't see how your plan is going to work in practice.

prairie
[préəri]
® 26946/86800

n. 대초원
❶ 풀에 리(prairie) - 풀이 리(理) - 풀이 리(행정구역)까지 이어짐 - 대초원
㋐ grassland, plains
㋐ Millions of buffalo once roamed the prairies.

praise
[preiz]
® 4978/86800

n. v. 칭찬, 칭찬하다
❶ 우승한 선수들에게 꽃가루 뿌리 제(praise) - 칭찬하다
㋐ applause, admiration
㋐ He should be praised for his honesty.

pray
[prei]
® 5358/86800

v. 기도하다
❶ 선수들이 play(프레이)하기 전에 눈물 pray(눈물뿌리)기도 한다.
- 이기게 해달라고)
㋐ She knelt and prayed silently.

preach
[priːtʃ]
® 15453/86800

v. 설교하다
❶ p(pastor - 목사)가 + reach(도달하다, 전달하다): 목사가 전달하는 것은 설교
⊕ sermonize, moralize
예 The minister preached the gospel in our church on Sunday.

precaution
[prikɔ́ːʃən]
® 15246/86800

n. 조심
❶ pre(미리) + causion(꼬션): 전자상가가면 싸게 해준다고 미리 꼬션, 조심해야
⊕ vigilance, guard
예 They failed to take the necessary precautions to avoid infection.

precede
[prisíːd]
® 18706/86800

v. ~에 앞서다
❶ pre(미리) + cede(가다 - 어원편 참조): 미리 가다, 앞서다
⊕ antecede, antedate 퐈 precedent: 전례
예 Riots preceded the civil war.

✔ **precious**
[préʃəs]
® 4664/86800

adj. 귀중한, 값비싼
❶ 사람 구하기 위해 **소중한 목숨을 버리셨어(precious)**
⊕ valuable, inestimable
예 You're so precious to me.

✔ **precipitation**
[prisìpətéiʃən]
® 18442/86800

n. 강수량, 낙하
❶ 비가 **뿌리시피(precipi)**
예 The annual precipitation totals 1400 inches in Buffalo.

✔ **precise**
[prisáis]
® 3271/86800

adj. 정확한
❶ pre(미리) + cise(싸이즈로 생각): 미리 싸이즈를 재서 정확한
⊕ exact, correct
퐈 *precision*: 정확
예 He caught me at the precise moment that I fainted.

P

predecessor
[prédisèsər]
[R] 7550/86800

n. **전임자, 선배, 조상**
[T] pre(미리) + cess(가다 - 어원편 참조) + or(사람): 미리 간 사람이므로 조상
[유] elder, senior: 선배 [반] successor: 후임자
[예] My predecessor worked in this job for twelve years.

✔ **predict**
[pridíkt]
[R] 5712/86800

v. **예언하다**
[T] pre(미리) + dic(말하다 - 어원편 참조): 미리 말하다, dictionary - 말 모아놓은 것이므로 사전
[유] prophesy, foretell
[파] prediction: 예언, 예보 *predictor*: 예언자
[예] It's still not possible to accurately predict the occurrence of earthquakes.

predominant
[pridámənənt]
[R] 12590/86800

adj. **뛰어난, 우세한**
[T] pre(미리) + dominant(지배한): 미리 지배한, 우세한, dom은 지배하다의 뜻
[유] dominant
[예] Dancers have a predominant role in this performance.

preface
[préfis]
[R] 11660/86800

n. **머리말**
[T] pre(미리) + face(얼굴, 면): 책의 앞면, 머리말
[유] foreword, introduction, prologue
[예] In his preface, the author says that he took eight years to write the book.

✔ **prefer**
[prifə́:r]
[R] 2662/86800

v. **더 좋아하다, 선호하다**
[T] pre(미리) + fer(나르다): 미리 나르다, 좋아하는 것을 빼앗길까봐 미리 나르다
[파] *preferable*: 더 마음에 드는 *preference*: 선호
[예] Do you prefer hot or cold weather?

✔ **prefix**
[prí:fiks]
[R] 28856/86800

n. **접두사**
[T] **pre(앞, 미리) + fix(붙이다)**: 앞에 붙이는 것이므로 접두사
[예] Morpheme has prefix or suffix.

prejudice
[prédʒudis]
ⓡ 5850/86800

n. 편견
❶ pre(미리) + judice(주뒤써 - 주둥이 써): 알아보지도 않고 미리 생각해 놓음 - **편견**
⊛ bias ㉙ prejudiced: 편견을 가진
㉖ He has a prejudice against fast - food restaurants.

preliminary
[prilímənèri]
ⓡ 4698/86800

adj. 예비의
❶ pre(미리) + liminary(임하느라): 미리 임하려고 준비하는 예비의
⊛ reserve, spare
㉖ The team was eliminated in the preliminary round of the tournament.

premature
[prìːmətjúər]
ⓡ 8082/86800

adj. **조숙한**
❶ pre(미리) + mature(성숙한) - **조숙한** 입 **맞추어(mature)** - 입 맞추는 사람은 성숙하므로
㉖ Too much exposure to the sun can cause the premature aging of skin.

preoccupy
[priːákjəpai]
ⓡ 55497/86800

v. 마음을 빼앗다, 먼저 차지하다
❶ pre(미리) + occupy(차지하다): 미리 차지하다
㉙ *preoccupied*: 선취된
㉖ The question of life after death has preoccupied many philosophers.

P

prepare
[pripéər]
ⓡ 3166/86800

v. 준비하다
❶ pre(미리) + pare(펴): 미리 펴 놓고 공부 준비하다
⊛ ready ㉙ *preparation*: 준비
㉖ Have you prepared for your interview?

prescribe
[priskráib]
ⓡ 16197/86800

v. 규정하다, 처방하다
❶ pre(미리) + scribe(쓰다): 미리 써놓고 나중에 약사에게 가져가다 - **처방하다**
⊛ ordain ㉙ prescription: 규정, 처방
㉖ The drug is often prescribed for ulcers.

present
[prézənt]
ⓡ 412/86800

adj. n. v. 현재, 현재의, 선물, 출석한, 제공하다
❶ 그대가 **풀어준(present)** 선물, 현재형이 뭔지 **풀어준(present)** 선생님
⊕ gift, souvenir: 선물
평 presence: 출석, 존재 *presentation*: 발표, 제출
c.f) presently: 곧
예 They gave me theatre tickets as a present. I am very busy at the present moment.

preservation
[prèzərvéiʃən]
ⓡ 6581/86800

n. 보존
❶ pre(미리) + servation(절 봐선): 미리 절을 보고 (불공드릴 곳 잘) **보존**하다
⊕ conservation, storage 평 *preserve*: 보존하다
예 The cathedral is in a poor state of preservation.

press
[pres]
ⓡ 749/86800

v. n. 누르다, 누름, 인쇄기, 출판물
❶ 대장장이가 **불에서(press)** 쇠를 누르다
⊕ push 평 *pressure*: 압력, 압박하다
예 Press the button to start the machine.

prestige
[prestíːdʒ]
ⓡ 7102/86800

n. adj. 위신, 명성, 명성이 있는
❶ pre(미리) + stige(서태지): 미리 초대가수 서태지가 와서 **위신**이 슨
⊕ dignity, honor
예 The company has gained international prestige.

presume
[prizúːm]
ⓡ 10617/86800

v. 상상하다, 생각하다
❶ pre(미리) + sume(좀): 그 때 닥쳐서 하지 말고 미리 좀 **생각해라**
⊕ suppose, assume
예 I presume (that) they're not coming, since they haven't replied to the invitation.

pretend
[priténd]
ⓡ 5956/86800

v. ~인 체하다
❶ 지갑을 가져 왔어야 돈을 **뿌릴텐데(pretend)** 하면서 돈 **있는 체 하다**
⊕ assume, feign
예 She's not really hurt - she's only pretending.

✔ prevail
[privéil]
ⓡ 11818/86800

v. 우세하다, 널리 보급되다
❶ pre(미리) + vail(보일): 특정 광고판이 미리(pre) **보일(vail)** 정도로 **우세하다**
㊦ predominate
㊌ *prevalent*: 유행하는 *prevalence*: 유행
㊊ This attitude still prevails among the middle classes.

✔ prevent
[privént]
ⓡ 1516/86800

v. 막다, 예방하다
❶ pre(미리) + vent(빈터): 데모하지 못하게 미리 **빈터(prevent)**를 **막다**
㊌ *prevention*: 예방 *preventive*: 예방의
㊊ His disability prevents him (from) driving.

✔ previous
[príːviəs]
ⓡ 808/86800 .

adj. 이전의
❶ pre(미리) + vi(보다) + ous(형용사형 어미) - 앞 선 것을 보는, 이전의
㊦ earlier, former ㊌ *previously*: 이전에
㊊ He has two daughters from a previous marriage.

✔ prey
[prei]
ⓡ 5012/86800

n. v. 먹이, 잡아먹다
❶ 고기를 잡으려면 **먹이를 뿌려이(prey)**
㊦ food, feed
㊊ A hawk hovered in the air before swooping on its prey.

✔ priceless
[práislis]
ⓡ 18755/86800

adj. 값을 매길 수 없이 귀중한
❶ price(가격) + less(~이 없는), **주의 !** 값이 싸다는 말이 아니라 가격을 매길 수 없을 정도로 중요한 이라는 뜻이에요
㊦ invaluable, precious ㊌ price: 가격
㊊ A priceless collection of vases was destroyed.

✔ priest
[priːst]
ⓡ 4112/86800

n. 성직자, 목사
❶ **목사**로서 세상 욕심을 **버렸었다(priest)**
㊦ minister, clergyman
㊊ Many in the Anglican Church are still opposed to women priests.

P

✔ **primary**
[práimeri]
[R] 1081/86800

adj. **주요한, 초기의, 초등의**
[T] **보라이(pri) 머리(mary)** - 보라! 이 머리, 머리는 주요하고 사람의 신체 중 가장 초기의
[유] main, principal
[파] prime: 제일의, 주요한 *primarily*: 첫째로
[예] The Red Cross's primary concern is to preserve and protect human life.

✔ **primitive**
[prímətiv]
[R] 4566/86800

adj. **원시의, 원시적인**
[T] **풀이 (몇)미터 보(primitive)**다 더 난 **원시의**
[유] primeval [파] primitiveness: 원시성
[예] Primitive races colonized these islands 2000 years ago.

✔ **principal**
[prínsəpəl]
[R] 2075/86800

adj. n. **주요한, 교장**
[T] **프린스**(왕자) - **뻘(principal)**; 왕자는 **중요한** 그리고 학교의 왕자는 **교장**. principal은 철자의 A가 들어가므로 주요한, 그리고 학교의 서열 A 이신 교장선생님으로 기억
[유] main, primary
[예] That was my principal reason for moving.

✔ **principle**
[prínsəpəl]
[R] 1258/86800

n. **원리, 원칙**
[T] **뿌린씨(가) 풀(principle)**이 나려면 **원리 원칙**에 잘 따라야 함
마지막 발음이 [l]로 끝나므로 한글로 하면 ㄹ로 끝났다고 생각하고 원리(리의 ㄹ)라고 기억할 것
[예] The organization works on the principle that all members have the same rights.

✔ **prior**
[práiər]
[R] 4944/86800

adj. **이전의, 우선하는**
[T] **이전 것**(우선했던 것)은 **버려야(prior)**
[유] previous, past [반] posterior [파] *priority*: 우선
[예] The course required no prior knowledge of Spanish.

✔ **prison**
[prízn]
[R] 1604/86800

n. **감옥**
[T] 날 **풀어존 !!!(prison)** - 날 풀어줘 ! **감옥**에서
[유] jail [파] prisoner: 죄수
[예] She was sent to prison for six months.

❖ private
[práivit]

ℝ 554/86800

adj. **사적인, 사유의**

❶ **벌어** 이 빚(private - 개인적인 빚) 갚을 거야

� individual, personal

㊓ *privacy*: 사생활

㊵ She has a small office which is used for private discussions.

privilege
[prívəlidʒ]

ℝ 5024/86800

n. **특권**

❶ **특권**을 얻어야 돈이 **빨리벌리지**(priviledge)

� special right, prerogative

㊵ Healthcare should be a right, not a privilege.

❖ prize
[praiz]

ℝ 3030/86800

n. v. **상품, 소중히 하다**

❶ 그랜져를 **프라이즈**(prize - **상품**)로 줄테니 소중히 간직해라

� goods, commodities

㊵ The prize money for literary competitions can be as high as $40 000.

✔ pro
[prou]

ℝ 7701/86800

a. **직업적인, 찬성하여**

❶ Pro는 직업, pro vs con(찬성 대 반대)

㊵ There are pros and cons about the matter.

❖ probability
[prὰbəbíləti]

ℝ 5171/86800

n. **가망성**

❶ **불어봐** (해서) 불었지(probability) - 음주 운전 측정 불면 내가 음주 **가망성** 있을까봐

� chance, possibility ㊓ *probable*: 있을 법한 *probably*: 아마

㊵ What is the probability of winning?

✔ probe
[proub]

ℝ 6172/86800

n. v. **정밀 조사, 탐사하다**

❶ 비밀을 풀어보(probe)려고 **정밀 조사**하다

� investigation, examination

㊵ The interviewer probed deep into her private life.

P

proceed
[prousí:d]
ⓡ 4095/86800

v. 나아가다, 처리하다
❶ pro(앞으로) + ceed(가다): 나아가다
⊕ advance
㈜ *procedure*: 절차, 진행 *process*: 과정, 진행
　procession: 행렬
㈜ Preparations for the festival are now proceeding smoothly.

proclaim
[proukléim]
ⓡ 18742/86800

v. 선언하다
❶ 팬들이 프로(pro) + claim(요구하다) 그래서 프로 전향을 **선언하다**
⊕ announce, declare ㈜ proclamation: 선언, 포고
㈜ All the countries have proclaimed their loyalty to the alliance.

prodigal
[prádigəl]
ⓡ 28351/86800

adj. 낭비하는, 방탕한
❶ pro(프로) + digal(뒤갈 - 뒷골목 갈 - 왠지 뒷 골목하면 안 좋은 인상): 프로가 돼 돈을 많이 벌면 술집 가서 방탕한
⊕ extravagant, wasteful
㈜ There have been rumours that he has been prodigal with company funds.

produce
[prədjú:s]
ⓡ 858/86800

v. 생산하다
❶ pro(앞으로) + duc(이끌어 내다): 물건을 내다
⊕ make, manufacture
㈜ *product*: 생산품 *productive*: 결실 많은
　productivity: 생산성 *production*: 생산
㈜ France produces a great deal of wine for export.

profess
[prəfés]
ⓡ 28544/86800

v. 공언하다
❶ pro(앞에서) + fess(말하다, 자백하다): 여러 사람 앞에서 말하다 - 공언하다
⊕ declare
㈜ *profession*: 직업, 전문직 *professional*: 전문 직업인
　professor: 교수
㈜ She professes not to be interested in money.

✔ **proficient**
[prəfíʃənt]
Ⓡ 25514/86800

adj. 숙달한
Ⓣ pro(프로) + fic(만들다) + ent(형용사형 어미) 프로처럼 만들어내는 숙달한
㊌ masterful, skillful
c.f) *profit*: 이익, 이익이 되다 *profitable*: 이익이 되는
㉑ She's proficient in two languages.

✔ **profound**
[prəfáund]
Ⓡ 5519/86800

adj. 깊은, 심오한
Ⓣ pro(앞으로) + **found(파 온):** 앞으로 계속 파면 깊은 곳까지 파게 됨
㊌ deep ㊧ superficial 파 *profoundly*: 심오하게
㉑ His mother's death when he was aged six had a very profound effect on him.

✤ **progress**
[prágrəs]
Ⓡ 1255/86800

n. v. 진보, 나아가다
Ⓣ pro(앞으로) + gress(가다 - 어원편 참조): 나아가다
㊌ advance, improvement
파 *progressive*: 진보적인, 전진하는 *progressively*: 진보적으로
㉑ Technological progress has been so rapid over the last few years.

✔ **prohibit**
[prouhíbit]
Ⓡ 18504/86800

v. 금지하다
Ⓣ prohi(프로에) + bit(빚): 프로에게 빚지는 것을 **금지하다**
㊌ ban, forbid 파 prohibition: 금지
㉑ Parking is strictly prohibited between these gates.

✤ **project**
[prədʒékt]
Ⓡ 641/86800

n. v. 계획, 설계, 연구 계획, 계획하다, 설계하다
Ⓣ pro(앞으로) + ject(싸놓은 것): 계획, 설계
㊌ plan, scheme
㉑ My next project is decorating the kitchen.

prolong
[proulɔ́:ŋ]
Ⓡ 17980/86800

v. 연장하다
Ⓣ pro(앞으로) + long(길게 하다): 늘리다
㊌ extend, lengthen
㉑ She chewed each delicious mouthful as slowly as she could, prolonging the pleasure.

P

prominent
[prámənənt]
ⓡ 3853/86800

adj. 탁월한, 두드러진
❶ 내 제품이 **탁월하다니 보람있는(prominent)**
ⓢ outstanding, exceptional
예 The government should be playing a more prominent role in promoting human rights.

promise
[prámis]
ⓡ 2525/86800

n. v. 약속, 약속하다, 전망
❶ pro(앞으로) + mis(보내다): 약속은 앞으로 보내서 지키는 것
ⓢ pledge, vow 퐈 promising: 유망한, 장래성 있는
예 The government have promised that they'll reduce taxes.

promote
[prəmóut]
ⓡ 3034/86800

v. 승진시키다, 촉진하다
❶ pro(앞으로) + mot(보내다): 직장에서 나를 앞으로 보내는 것은 승진하는 것
ⓢ elevate, upgrade ⓑ demote
퐈 *promotion*: 승진, 촉진
예 Advertising companies are always having to think up new ways to promote products.

prompt
[prʌmpt]
ⓡ 8036/86800

adj. 신속한, 즉석의
❶ 머리에 **뽈남(prompt) 신속한** 조치 필요
ⓢ immediate, instant
예 The bishop's speech has prompted an angry response from both political parties.

prone
[proun]
ⓡ 8179/86800

adj. ~하기 쉬운
❶ **프론(prone) - 프로는** 돈 벌기 **쉬운**
ⓢ apt, liable
예 He was prone to depressions even as a teenager.

pronounce
[prənáuns]
ⓡ 15769/86800

v. 발음하다
❶ 발음이 어떻게 나와? 발음은 입에서 공기 **불어나왔어(pronounce)**
ⓢ vocalize
퐈 pronouncement: 선언 *pronunciation*: 발음
예 How do you pronounce your surname?

✔ proof
[pru:f]
Ⓡ 3435/86800

n. adj. **증명, 증거, ~을 견디는**
❶ 눈을 **부릅(proof)**뜨고 나를 보면 화났다는 **증거**
c.f) waterproof: 물을 견디는 - 방수의
㊞ evidence
㊟ prove: 증명하다
㉘ Do they have any proof that it was Hampson who stole the goods?

propaganda
[pràpəgǽndə]
Ⓡ 6431/86800

n. **선전**
❶ 불어 강좌에 곧 **불어파(프랑스 사람)간다(propaganda)**고 **선전**
㊞ publicity, propagandism
㉘ He was accused of spreading propaganda.

✔ proper
[prápər]
Ⓡ 1589/86800

adj. **적절한**
❶ 불어 강좌에는 **불어파(proper)가 적절한**
㊞ appropriate, fit
㊟ *properly*: 똑바로, 적당하게
propriety: 적당
㉘ If you're going to walk those sort of distances you need proper walking boots.

✔ property
[prápərti]
Ⓡ 783/86800

n. **재산, 소유물, 특성**
❶ 이웃위해 내 **재산** 모두 **풀어팔지(property)**
㊞ possessions, fortune
㉘ The club does not accept responsibility for loss of or damage to club members' personal property.

prophecy
[práfəsi]
Ⓡ 15000/86800

n. **예언**
❶ **프로(pro)**가면 **빚지(phecy)**다고 점장이 **예언** - 프로 가면 빚질 거라고 예언
㊞ prediction
㉘ These doom and gloom prophecies are doing little to help the economy.

proportion
[prəpɔ́ːrʃən]
ⓡ 1622/86800

n. 비율
❶ pro(앞) + portion(몫): 앞에 있는 몫 - 비율
⑨ ratio, rate
예 The report shows that poor families spend a larger proportion of their income on food.

✔ proposal
[prəpóuzəl]
ⓡ 2385/86800

n. 제안, 신청, 청혼
❶ 프로 포즈(propose)에서 나온 말
⑨ proposition, suggestion 패 *propose*: 제안하다, 청혼하다
예 Congress has rejected the latest economic proposal put forward by the president.

proposition
[prɑ̀pəzíʃən]
ⓡ 5585/86800

n. 명제, 제의
❶ pro(앞에) + position(위치): 앞에 놓여있는 당면 명제
⑨ thesis, statement
예 They were debating the proposition that 'All people are created equal'.
I've put my proposition to the company director for his consideration.

✔ propriety
[prəpráiəti]
ⓡ 20700/86800

n. 적당함, 예의 바름
❶ 프로(pro)는 돈을 벌어(pri)야 적당함
예 I debated the propriety of the punishment that I was given.

✔ prose
[prouz]
ⓡ 7623/86800

n. 산문
❶ 풀어써(prose): 산문은 이야기 서술(풀어쓴) 한 것
예 I've always preferred reading prose to poetry.

prosecution
[prɑ̀səkjúːʃən]
ⓡ 4148/86800

n. 실행, 기소
❶ 범인이 죄를 불어서 구속(prosecution)기소
⑨ execution, performance
예 A number of the cases have resulted in successful prosecution.

prospect
[práspek]
® 3015/86800

n. 전망
❶ pro(앞을) + spect(봄): 전망
㊦ view, outlook 팬 prospective: 기대되는
예 Is there any prospect of the weather improving?

prosper
[práspər]
® 17360/86800

v. 번영하다
❶ 벌었어 펴(prosper) - 돈 벌었어 인생 펴
㊦ flourish, thrive
팬 prosperity: 번영 prosperous: 번영하는
예 A lot of microchip manufacturing companies prospered at that time.

protect
[prətékt]
® 1978/86800

v. 보호하다, 지키다
❶ 나보고 프로? **프로 택도(protect)** 없다 하며 아마튜어를 **지키다**
㊦ defend, guard
팬 *protection*: 보호 *protective*: 보호하는
예 He heard protests from the crowd.

protest
[prətést]
® 2737/86800

n. v. 항의, 항의하다
❶ 술도 안마셨는데 음주 **불어테스트(protest)** 하길래 **항의하다**
㊦ protestation, remonstrance
예 A big crowd of demonstrators were protesting against cuts in health spending.

provide
[prəváid]
® 411/86800

v. 공급하다
❶ 어린이는 재미있는 **프로바야돼(provide)**하며 TV 프로를 **공급하다**
㊦ supply, give
팬 provided: 만약 ~라면 providence: 신의 뜻
providing: 만약 ~라면 provision: 공급
예 All meals are provided throughout the course.

provoke
[prəvóuk]
® 10085/86800

v. 화나게 하다, 도발하다
❶ **부러 볶아(provoke** - 일부러 나를 달달 볶아) **화나게 하다**
㊦ enrage, anger
예 His remarks provoked both tears and laughter.

prudent
[prú:dənt]
® 11409/86800

adj. 신중한, 분별 있는

❶ 경찰을 **부르던(prudent)** 말든 **신중한** 행동해라

⊕ careful, cautious

예 The firm was commended for its financial prudence.

✔ psychological
[sàikəládʒikəl]
® 3375/86800

adj. 심리적인

❶ psycho(정신, 심리) + logy(학문, 이론, 말) + ic:

파 *psychologist*: 심리학자 psychology: 심리학 *psycho*: 정신

예 We are concerned with the physical and psychological
well - being of our employees.

✸ public
[pʌ́blik]
® 220/86800

adj. n. 공공의, 대중

❶ **대중**을 **배불리(public)**는 정부

⊕ common

c.f) *publication*: 출판 *publicity*: 평판
publish: 출판하다, 발표하다 *publisher*: 출판업자

예 We need to increase public awareness of the disease.

✔ pulse
[pʌls]
® 6817/86800

n. 맥박

❶ **팔써(pulse) 맥박**을 잼

⊕ pulsation

예 Exercise increases your pulse rate.

✔ punctual
[pʌ́ŋktʃuəl]
® 35012/86800

adj. 시간을 지키는

❶ **빵 주어(punctual) 시간을 잘 지키는** 학생

파 *punctually*: 시간을 어김없이

예 His letter was completely without punctuation.

✸ punish
[pʌ́niʃ]
® 11634/86800

v. 벌하다

❶ 이게 자네 **벌이시(punish)** - 사투리 같은데 번역하면 이게 자네
벌이야

⊕ penalize, discipline 파 punishment: 형벌

예 He punished the class by giving them extra work.

✔ pupil
[pjúːpəl]
Ⓡ 3845/86800

n. 학생, 눈동자
❶ 퍼필(pupil - 퍼 분필) - **학생**이 공부를 배우려면 그리고 **눈동자**도 펴
⊕ student
예 The school has over 400 pupils.

✔ purchase
[pə́ːrtʃəs]
Ⓡ 2263/86800

v. 구입하다
❶ 얼마주고 **샀어**? 팔 줬어(purchase) - 8만원 주고
⊕ buy
예 Tickets must be purchased two weeks in advance.

✔ pure
[pjuər]
Ⓡ 2879/86800

adj. 순수한, 깨끗한, 결백한
❶ 내가 바람 **피워(pure)**? - 나는 **결백하다는** 이야기지
⊕ clean, innocent 파 *purely*: 순수하게
예 The mountain air was wonderfully pure.

✔ purpose
[pə́ːrpəs]
Ⓡ 1096/86800

n. 목적, 의도
❶ pur(pro(앞이) 변형) + pose(포즈)=propose하는 것이 목적
⊕ aim, object
예 She had the operation entirely for cosmetic purposes.

✔ pursue
[pərsúː]
Ⓡ 4391/86800

v. 쫓다, 추구하다
❶ pur(pro) + suit(수): 프로에서 수(최고 성적을) 추구하다
⊕ chase, run after 파 *pursuit*: 추구
예 The car was pursued by helicopters.

puzzle
[pʌ́zl]
Ⓡ 10112/86800

n. v. 당황, 수수께끼, 당황하게 하다
❶ 퍼질(puzzle) 정도로 **당황한**, 퍼즐이 수수께끼라는 것은 아실 듯
⊕ riddle, mystery 파 puzzled: 당황한
예 Scientists have been trying to solve this puzzle for years.

✔ quack
[kwæk]
Ⓡ 21850/86800

n. 돌팔이, 꽥꽥 우는 소리
❶ 돌팔이 의사가 돌 맞고 내는 소리 **꽥(quack)**
예 He is notorious quacks of the day.

P

quadrangle
[kwádræ̀ŋgəl]
[R] 40482/86800

n. 4각형
[T] quadra(4) + angle(각형, 영어의 gon도 각형): 4각형
[유] quadrilateral
[예] Since the weather was sunny, the convocation was held outside in the college's quadrangle.

quaint
[kweint]
[R] 17809/86800

adj. 이상한, 진기한
[T] 뭔가가 **꼬인(quaint) 이상한** 상황
[유] queer, strange
[예] The fishing village was very quaint.

✔ **qualification**
[kwɑ̀ləfikéiʃən]
[R] 5988/86800

n. 자격, 증명서
[T] **골라픽케이션(qualification)** - 아무나 **자격**을 주는 게 아니라 골라서 준다
[유] requirement, eligibility [파] ***qualify***: 자격을 주다
[예] You'll never get a good job if you don't have any qualifications.

✔ **quality**
[kwáləti]
[R] 596/86800

n. 질
[T] 신발이 **꼴**(멋)**났지**(quality) - 신 발 **질**이 좋아서
[반] quantity
[예] Their products are of very high quality.

quantity
[kwántəti]
[R] 3775/86800

n. 양
[T] **양**이 너무 많아 먹다 **관뒀지(quantity)**
[유] amount, volume [반] quality
[예] We consumed vast quantities of food and drink that night.

✔ **quarrel**
[kwɔ́:rəl]
[R] 10248/86800

n. v. 싸움, 싸우다
[T] 콰를(**quarrel - 화를**) 돋워서 **싸웠어**
[유] dispute, brawl
[예] They had a bitter quarrel about some money three years ago and they haven't spoken to each other since.

❖ quarter
[kwɔ́:rtər]
ⓡ 1386/86800

n. 4분의1, 15분, 군대 막사
❶ 쿼터는 4분의 1이라는 뜻으로 많이 들어보셨을 듯, head quarter 는 사령부
⊕ fourth
例 My house is situated a mile and three - quarters from here.

queer
[kwiər]
ⓡ 14417/86800

adj. 기묘한
❶ 이 한자가 **기묘하다**는 **기여(queer)** - 기상한 춈
⊕ odd, strange
例 I had a queer feeling that something bad was about to happen.

❖ questionnaire
[kwèstʃənéər]
ⓡ 6302/86800

n. 설문지
❶ question(질문) + naire(내어): 질문내어 설문지
例 Visitors to UB should fill in a questionnaire.

❖ quit
[kwit]
ⓡ 7546/86800

v. 그만두다, 끊다
❶ 나는 곧(quit)그만 둘거야
⊕ cease, stop
例 I'm going to quit smoking.

quiver
[kwívər]
ⓡ 23249/86800

v. 떨리다
❶ 휴대폰 켜봐(quiver) - 진동하고 있어
⊕ tremble, vibrate
例 Lennie's bottom lip quivered and tears started in his eyes.

✔ quote
[kwout]
ⓡ 5354/86800

v. 인용하다
❶ 글을 꿔 왔다(quote): 글을 다른데서 가져오는 것은 **인용**
⊕ cite 파 *quotation*: 인용
例 Can I quote you on that?

Q

radical
[rǽdikəl]
® 2481/86800

adj. 근본적인, 극단적인
- ❶ rad(뿌리 - 예를 들면 radish는 무, eradicate는 뿌리를 밖(e)으로 들어내다 이므로 근절하다는 뜻) + ical(형용사형 어미)
- ⊕ extreme: 극단적인
- 예 He was known as a radical politician.

rage
[reidʒ]
® 5880/86800

n. v. 격노, 몹시 화내다
- ❶ 화나니까 화를 내지(rage)
- ⊕ fury, violent anger
- 예 I was frightened because I had never seen him in such a rage before.

rainfall
[réinfɔ:l]
® 12829/86800

n. 강우, 강수량
- ❶ rain(비) + fall(떨어짐): 강우
- ⊕ precipitation: 강수량
- 예 Heavy rainfall ruined the match.

rainforest
[reinfɔ(:)rist]
® 12037/86800

n. 열대 다우림
- ❶ rain(우) + forest(림)
- 예 Rainforest is a forest in a tropical area which receives a lot of rain.

raise
[reiz]
® 1660/86800

v. n. 들어 올리다, 기르다, 모으다, 임금인상
- ❶ (돈 좀) 내 이제(raise) - 모으다, 힘 좀 내 이제(raise) - 들어 올리게 Would you give me a raise? - 임금 올려주세요
- ⊕ lift
- 예 He raised the window and leaned out.

rally
[rǽli]
® 5071/86800

v. n. 다시 모으다, 집결, 집회
- ❶ 내일이(rally) 집결하는 날이야
- ⊕ assembly, congregation
- 예 5000 people held an anti - nuclear rally.

✔ **ramp**
[ræmp]
ⓡ 12254/86800

n. 경사로
❶ 경사로라 위험표시로 **램프(ramp)**를 깜빡
ⓢ sloping surface
예 I pushed my mother's wheelchair up the ramp.

✔ **ranch**
[ræntʃ]
ⓡ 24736/86800

n. v. 목장, 목장에서 일하다
❶ 소가 **목장** 주변의 풀들을 보고 **왠 초(ranch)?**
예 She went to work on a ranch.

random
[rǽndəm]
ⓡ 4548/86800

adj. 임의의
❶ 아무 **라돔(random)** - 아무라도 **임의대로**
ⓢ optional
예 We asked a random sample/selection of people what they thought.

✔ **range**
[reindʒ]
ⓡ 458/86800

n. v. 범위, 산맥, 걸쳐 있다
❶ 내 **인제(range)**에서 살아(인제는 사는 **범위** 그리고 강원도라 산맥이 걸쳐 있음)
ⓢ scope, sphere
예 There is a wide range of opinions on this issue.

✔ **rank**
[ræŋk]
ⓡ 3899/86800

n. v. 계급, 순위, 순위를 기록하다
❶ 랭킹(ranking - 순위)이라는 단어를 알면 쉽게 기억하실 듯
ⓢ class, grade
예 Having a large income is one of the advantages of rank(= high position).

✔ **rapid**
[rǽpid]
ⓡ 2729/86800

adj. 빠른
❶ 재빨리 내빼도(rapid)! - **재빨리 도망가줘**
ⓢ fast, swift
파 *rapidly*: 빨리, 급속히
예 The 1990s were a period of rapid change/growth.

R

rapport
[ræpɔ́ːr]
ⓡ 15605/86800

n. 친밀한 관계, 접촉
❶ 그녀는 래뻤다(rapport) - 예쁘다니 **친한관계**)
ⓢ : relation, connection
예 I try to establish close rapport with my student.

rapture
[ræptʃəːr]
ⓡ 28587/86800

n. 큰 기쁨
❶ 크게 기뻐 넙죽(rapture)절하는 신랑
ⓢ ecstasy, bliss
예 He listened to the music with an expression of pure rapture on his face.

rare
[reəːr]
ⓡ 2176/86800

adj. 드문, 고기를 살짝 구운
❶ 시간 좀 내어(rear)! 라고 말하면 시간 내기 **드물다**는 말, 고기 먹을 때 rare하면 고기피 내어 라는 말로 살짝만 익히라는 말이 됨
ⓢ infrequent, uncommon 파 *rarely*: 좀처럼 ~않다
예 The museum is full of rare and precious treasures.

rate
[reit]
ⓡ 500/86800

n. 비율, 속도, 요금
❶ 식사 **요금 냈데(rate)** 8: 2비율로 냈데(rate) 그래서 열 받아서 자동차 속도 냈데(rate)
ⓢ ratio, percentage
예 The taxi was going at a tremendous rate.

rational
[ræʃənl]
ⓡ 3817/86800

adj. 이성적인, 합리적인
❶ 저 번에 내가 돈 냈으니 이 번에는 그쪽에서 **내이소(ration)** - **그래야 합리적인**
ⓢ reasonable, sensible
예 He was too upset to be rational.

ravage
[rævidʒ]
ⓡ 58323/86800

n. v. 파괴, 황폐, 황폐해지다
❶ 발라드가 살면 **황폐**해지는 것은 **랩이지(ravage)**
ⓢ destruction, demolition
예 The area has been ravaged by war.

✔ **raw**
[rɔ:]
[R] 3670/86800

adj. **날것의, 가공하지 않은**
[T] 그대 **로(raw)–날 것의**, 가공하지 않은
[유] fresh, uncooked
[예] I bought raw fish yesterday.

✔ **ray**
[rei]
[R] 4116/86800

n. **광선**
[T] **빛**을 **내이(ray) 혹은** X - ray 생각하면 됨
[유] light
[예] Light rays bend as they pass from air to water.

✔ **razor**
[réizə:r]
[R] 12297/86800

n. v. **면도칼, 면도하다**
[T] **레이져(razor)**로 **면도**하다
[유] Shave
[예] He is as sharp as a razor.

✔ **react**
[ri.ǽkt]
[R] 5977/86800

v. **반응하다**
[T] re(다시) + act(행동하다): 상대방의 행동에 다시 행동하다(반응하다)
[유] respond
[파] *reaction*: 반응, 반작용 *reactive*: 반동의
[예] She slapped him and called him names, but he didn't react.

✔ **readily**
[rédəli]
[R] 3353/86800

adv. **쉽사리, 기꺼이**
[T] ready(준비 된) + ly(부사형, 형용사형 어미): 준비되어 있으므로 쉽사리
[유] easily, with ease
[파] *ready*: 준비가 된
[예] He readily agreed to help.

✔ **realm**
[relm]
[R] 6831/86800

n. **왕국, 영역**
[T] 동물의 왕국을 보면 **내음(realm - 냄새)**으로 **영역**을 표시
[유] field, sphere: 영역
[예] Her interests are in the realm of practical politics.

R

✔ reap
[ri:p]
®16582/86800

v. 수확하다
❶ 립(입)(reap)으로 먹을 것을 **수확하다**
c.f) leap: 뛰다 립(한자로 설 립), 서서 뛰므로
㊛ gather, harvest
㈄ He reaped large profits from his investments.

✔ rear
[riə:r]
®3395/86800

n. v. 뒤, 기르다
❶ 리어(rear) 카를 생각해보면 짐 싣는데 가 **뒤**에 있다
아기를 달 래어(rear)**기르다**
㊛ behind, back
㈄ The horse had injured one of its rear legs.

✔ reasonable
[rí:zənəbəl]
®1659/86800

adj. 합리적인
❶ reason(이유) + able(~할 수 있는): 이유가 될 수 있는, 합리적인
㊛ rational, sensible
㈜ *reason*: 이유 *reasonably*: 합리적으로
㈄ If you tell him what happened, I'm sure he'll
understand - he's a reasonable man.

✔ reassemble
[rì:əsémbəl]
®44417/86800

v. 다시 모으다
❶ re(다시) + assemble(모으다)
㈄ After school, the alumni reassembled.

rebel
[rébəl]
®6571/86800

n. adj. v. 반역자, 반역의, 반역하다
❶ 반역자는 립을(rebel - 입을)찢는다
㊛ traitor, insurgent
㈄ The rebels took over the capital and set up a new
government.

rebuke
[ribjú:k]
®21236/86800

v. n. 비난하다, 비난
❶ 신발회사 리복에서 짝가 rebuke(리북)을 **비난하다**
㊛ blame, reproach
㈄ I was rebuked by my manager for being late.

recall
[rikɔ́:l]
[R] 3040/86800

v. n. **회상하다, 제품회수**
[T] re(다시) + call(부르다): 기억 속에 있는 것을 다시 부르다
[유] remember
[예] He recalled (that) he had sent the letter over a month ago.

recede
[risí:d]
[R] 31857/86800

v. **물러가다**
[T] re(다시, 뒤로) + cede(가다 - 어원편) - 물러가다
[유] retreat, withdraw
[예] The painful memories gradually receded in her mind.

receipt
[risí:t]
[R] 6406/86800

n. **영수증**
[T] re(다시, 뒤로) + ceipt(받다): 다시 받는 것 혹은 뒤에 받는 것은 영수증
[파] *receive*: 받다 *reception*: 받아들이기
receiver: 수령인 *receptive*: 잘 받아들이는
[예] Make sure you are given a receipt for everything you buy.

recent
[rí:sənt]
[R] 615/86800

adj. **최근의**
[T] 몇일 **래 쓴(recent)** - 몇 일 내에 쓴 돈 - **최근의**
[유] latest [파] *recently*: 최근
[예] Is that a recent photo?

recess
[rí:ses]
[R] 18208/86800

n. **휴식, 휴교**
[T] re(뒤로) + cess(가다) - 학교안가고 뒤로?
[예] My mom will come to school during the noon recess.

rechargeable
[ri:tʃɑ́:rrdʒəbəl]
[R] 41898/86800

n. **재충전 할 수 있는**
[T] re(다시) + charge(충전하다) + able(할 수 있는)
[예] This is a rechargeable battery.

recipe
[résəpì:]
[R] 6242/86800

n. **요리법**
[T] **이 숍이(recipe)** - 이 스프 **요리법**은 요?
[예] Do you know a good recipe for wholemeal bread?

R

recite
[risáit]
ⓡ 23675/86800

v. 읊다, 암송하다
❶ 이 싸이트(recite) 주소는 **외워라**
폐 recital: 독주회
예 She proudly recited the Oath of Allegiance.

reckless
[réklis]
ⓡ 10436/86800

adj. 무모한
❶ 래 그랬어?(reckless) - 왜 그랬어? **무모한** 행동임을 암시
⑨ rash
예 He was found guilty of reckless driving.

reckon
[rékən]
ⓡ 4146/86800

v. 계산하다
❶ 내 껀(reckon) 내가 **계산할게**
⑨ calculate, count
예 How much do you reckon (that) it's going to cost?

recognize
[rékəgnàiz]
ⓡ 4140/86800

v. 알아보다, 인정하다
❶ 내꺼고 나 이제(recognize)알아 - 내 꺼고!(내 것인지 **알아보면서**)
폐 *recognition*: 알아보기
예 I hadn't seen her for 20 years, but I recognized her immediately.

recollect
[rèkəlékt]
ⓡ 26381/86800

v. 회상하다
❶ re(다시, 뒤로) + collect(모으다): 기억을 다시 모으다, 회상하다
⑨ recall, remember 폐 recollection: 회상, 기억
예 Can you recollect his name?

recommend
[rèkəménd]
ⓡ 4642/86800

v. 추천하다
❶ 수술하려는 사람보고 내 꾸멘데(recommand)서 하세요 하며 **추천하다**
폐 recommendation: 추천
예 A friend recommended this restaurant.

reconcile
[rékənsàil]
ⓡ 11225/86800

v. 화해시키다, 조정하다
❶ 이건싸(울)일(reconcile)이 아니야 하며 **화해시키다**
⑨ conciliate, propitiate 폐 *reconciliation*: 화해
예 It can be difficult to reconcile your ideals with reality.

✔ recover
[rikʌ́və:r]
® 4259/86800

v. 되찾다, 회복하다
❶ re(다시) + cover(감싸다): 보호하다, 파괴된 것을 다시 감싸면 회복하다
㈜ regain, restore
㈜ *recovery*: 회복
㈜ She had a heart attack but is recovering well.

✔ recreate
[rékrièit]
® 18577/86800

v. 기분 전환시키다
❶ re(다시) + create(만들어내다): 기분 따위를 다시 만들다
㈜ amuse, entertain
㈜ recreation: 기분 전환, 오락 *recreational*: 기분전환의
㈜ An old summer resort where families have been recreating for over a century.

✔ recruit
[rikrú:t]
® 7312/86800

v. 새로 모집하다
❶ 우리 회사를 위해 **구를(recruit - 회사에서 굴리므로)사원 모집하다**
㈜ *recruitment*: 신병(신규)모집
㈜ Public schools are recruiting new teachers.

✔ rectangular
[rektǽŋgjələ:r]
® 10487/86800

a. 직각의
❶ rect(바로 선) + angle(각)=직각
㈜ I saw a rectangular pyramid in Egypt.

✔ recur
[rikə́:r]
® 19791/86800

v. 다시 발생하다, 순환하다
❶ **니코(recur) 병이 재발하다**
㈜ occur, circulate
㈜ If the pain recurs, you need to operate.

✔ recycle
[ri:sáikəl]
® 21390/86800

v. 재활용하다
❶ re(다시) + cycle(순환시키다): 재활용하다
㈜ reutilize, reclaim
㈜ The Japanese recycle more than half their waste paper.

R

✔ reduce
[ridjú:s]

® 1444/86800

v. 줄이다, 감소시키다
- ❶ re(뒤로, 다시) + duce(이끌다): 뒤로 이끌어내면 자꾸 빼므로 감소시키다
- ㊎ diminish, lessen 파 *reduction*: 감소
- 예 My weight reduces when I stop eating sugar.

✔ reed
[ri:d]

® 7339/86800

n. 갈대
- ❶ 갈대로 지붕을 잇다(reed)
- 예 I saw the reeds along the edge of a pond.

✔ refer
[rifə́:r]

® 2611/86800

v. 언급하다, 참조하다
- ❶ 리플(refer) 달아 뭐라 언급하다 또, 니풀(refer) 수학참고서 reference book(참고서)
- ㊎ mention, allude 파 *reference*: 참조, 언급
- 예 Most of the patients we see here were referred by other doctors.

✔ refine
[rifáin]

® 21574/86800

v. 세련되게 하다, 정제하다
- ❶ re(다시, 뒤로) + fine(좋게 하다): 다시 좋게 만들다
- 파 refined: 세련된 refinement: 세련
- 예 Engineers spent many months refining the software.

✔ reflect
[riflékt]

® 2600/86800

v. 반사하다, 반영하다, 반성하다
- ❶ 니뿔냈(reflect)던 것 반성(반영, 반사)해라
- ㊎ reverberate
- 파 *reflection*: 반사, 심사숙고
- 예 He saw himself reflected in the shop window.

reform
[ri;fɔ́:rm]

® 1747/86800

v. 개혁하다, 개혁
- ❶ re(다시) + form(형태를 갖추다), 니 폼 바꿔!
- ㊎ innovate, improve
- 파 reformer: 개혁가
- 예 Who will reform Britain's unfair electoral system?

refrain
[rifréin]
[R] 13451/86800

v. n. **삼가하다, 후렴**
[T] **나쁘래 인(refrain)** - 사람에게 나쁘데.. 삼가다
[유] abstain, forbear
[예] The sign on the wall said "Please refrain from smoking."

✔ **refresh**
[rifréʃ]
[R] 24679/86800

v. **상쾌하게 하다**
[T] re(다시) + fresh(신선한): 다시 신선하게 하다
[유] exhilarate
[예] She can refresh his recollection with a piece of green cheese, if that will help.

refuge
[réfju:dʒ]
[R] 7145/86800

n. **피난, 피난처**
[T] **내 피하지(refuge)** - 내가 피할 곳**(피난처)**
[유] shelter [파] refugee: 난민, 난민의
[예] The climbers slept in a mountain refuge.

refund
[rí:fʌnd][rifʌ́nd]
[R] 14341/86800

n. v. **환불, 환불하다**
[T] re(다시) + fund(돈): 돈을 다시 돌려주다
[유] drawback
[예] Can I get a refund on this?

✔ **refusal**
[rifjú:zəl]
[R] 4529/86800

n. **거절**
[T] **리 !피우잘(refusal)** - 나보고 담배 피우자 하길래 **거절하다**
[유] rejection [파] ***refuse***: 거절하다
[예] My request for more money was met with a flat refusal.

✔ **regard**
[rigá:rd]
[R] 2448/86800

v. **여기다, 간주하다**
[T] **려기다(regard):** 여기다
[유] treat, take, see, view, deem, look upon
[파] regarding: ~에 관하여 ***regardless***: 관계없는
[예] Her parents always regarded her as the cleverest of their children.

R

✔ **region**
[rí:dʒən]
[R] 1035/86800

n. **지역, 특정부위**
[T] **리지연(region)** - 이 **지역**
[유] zone, district [파] ***regional***: 지역적인
[예] The bird returns to this region every year.

✔ **register**
[rédʒəstə:r]
[R] 3070/86800

v. n. **등록하다, 기록부**
[T] **니 재수다(register)**하자 재수생학원에 **등록**
[유] enroll [파] ***registration***: 기입, 등록
[예] I registered the car in my name.

✔ **regret**
[rigrét]
[R] 5006/86800

n. v. **후회, 후회하다, 유감, 유감으로 생각하다**
[T] **니 그랬(regret)**던 것을 **후회**하는 구나
[유] repentance, remorse
[파] ***regretful***: 유감으로 생각하는 ***regretfully***: 유감으로
[예] I left school at 16, but I've had a great life and I have no regrets.

✔ **regulate**
[régjəlèit]
[R] 9592/86800

v. **규정하다, 조절하다**
[T] 교통이 **내 굴러(regular)** - 내 차가 굴러다니게 신호등을 **조절하다**로 기억
[파] regulation: 규제
[예] You can regulate the temperature in the house by adjusting the thermostat.

reign
[rein]
[R] 4536/86800

n. v. **통치, 군림, 통치하다**
[T] 가수 **레인(reign** - rain으로 생각)이 한 동안 가요계를 통치하고 **군림**. 다음의 rein과 비교하여 철자 g가 더 있으므로 g가 발음이 ㄱ이므로 가수로 생각할 것
[유] rule, government
[예] Queen Victoria reigned over Britain from 1837 to 1901.

rein
[rein]
[R] 16289/86800

n. **고삐**
[T] **말(r)에있(ein)** 는 **고삐**
[예] You pull on both reins to stop or slow a horse, but only the left rein to turn left.

✔ reinforce
[rì:infɔ́:rs]
⑧ 7592/86800

v. 강화하다
❶ rein(고삐) + force(힘을주다) - 고삐에 힘을 주다 - 강화하다
⊕ strengthen, intensify
例 The pockets on my jeans are reinforced with double stitching.

✔ reinstall
[riinstɔ́:l]
⑧ 순위외/86800

v. 다시 설치하다
❶ re(다시) + install(설치하다): install(**인수돌** (상)차리다, 설치하다) 다시 설치하다
例 I reinstalled the Internet game program.

✔ reject
[ridʒékt]
⑧ 5222/86800

v. 거절하다, 거부하다
❶ re(다시) + ject(쏘다): 거절하다
⊕ refuse, decline 派 rejection: 거절
例 The committee rejected my proposal.

✔ rejoice
[ridʒɔ́is]
⑧ 21245/86800

v. 기뻐하다
❶ re(다시, 뒤로) + joice(기쁨 - joy와 비슷): 기뻐하다
⊕ delight
例 Everyone rejoiced at the news of his safe return.

✔ relative
[rélətiv]
⑧ 2086/86800

n. adj. 친척, 상대적인
❶ rela(내 너) + tive(티비): 나와 너 친척끼리 TV 출연
⊕ kinfolk(s)
派 *relate*: 관계시키다 *relation*: 관련 *relationship*: 관계
relatively: 비교적 *relevant*: 관련된, 적절한
relativism: 상대주의 *relativeness*: 상대적임
例 All her close relatives came to the wedding.

✔ relax
[rilǽks]
⑧ 4688/86800

v. 긴장 풀다, 편히 쉬다
❶ 놀랐어?(relax) - 긴장 풀어
⊕ relieve, rest 派 *relaxation*: 긴장을 풂
例 After work she relaxed with a cup of tea and the newspaper.

R

relay
[ríːlei]
® 12936/86800

n. 교대
🎯 달리기 할 때 **릴레이**(relay)생각하면 될 듯
㊀ alternation, rotation
📝 I was told the news first and then I relayed it to the others.

✔ release
[rilíːs]
® 1547/86800

v. n. 풀어 주다, 해방, 방출
🎯 **닐 놨어**(release): 너를 **풀어놨어**. 풀어주다
㊀ disengage, free
📝 He was released from prison after serving two years of a five - year sentence.

✔ relevance
[réləvəns]
® 4887/86800

n. 관련, 적당함
🎯 relative와 관련
📝 This matter has no relevance to my effort.

✔ reliable
[riláiəbəl]
® 3943/86800

adj. 믿을 수 있는
🎯 **니**(re)**라이**(li(e))**야 不**(able) - 너는 거짓말 안하는, 믿을 수 있는
㊀ credible, believable
📖 *reliance*: 신뢰 *rely*: 의지하다, 믿다 *reliant*: 믿는
📝 Is your watch reliable?

relic
[rélik]
® 19936/86800

n. 유물, 유골
🎯 **오 래 릭**(relic) - 오래 있었던 **유물**
㊀ remains, hangover
📝 The archeological team found some relics from the Stone Age.

✔ relief
[rilíːf]
® 1544/86800

n. 완화, 구원
🎯 **내일 립**(relief) - 죽게 된 사람이 내일 리브(live)? 내일이면 병세가 **완화**
㊀ mitigation, alleviation
📖 *relieve*: 완화시키다, 구제하다
📝 After the exam, I felt an incredible sense of relief.

❤ religion
[rilídʒən]
Ⓡ 2295/86800

n. 종교
Ⓣ 하나님! 복을 내려줘!(religion) - 종교
㈜ *religious*: 종교의, 종교적인
㈖ There are many religions, such as Buddhism, Christianity, Hinduism, Islam, and Judaism.

relish
[réliʃ]
Ⓡ 11527/86800

n. 맛, 흥미
Ⓣ 맛을 내리쉬(relish)
㈜ taste, flavor, savor
㈖ The relish of wine.
She plays the role with great relish.

✔ reluctant
[rilʌ́ktənt]
Ⓡ 4247/86800

adj. 마음 내키지 않는
Ⓣ 복권금액으로 **일억 탄**(reluctant) - 복권 금액으로 적어서(로또는 20억인데) 마음이 **내키지 않는**
㈜ unwilling
㈖ I was having such a good time I was reluctant to leave.

❤ remain
[riméin]
Ⓡ 1136/86800

v. n. 남아 있다, 나머지, 유적
Ⓣ 남아 있(remain) - 남아있는
㈜ remainder: 나머지
㈖ The doctor ordered him to remain in bed for a few days.

❤ remark
[rimáːrk]
Ⓡ 5446/86800

n. v. 소견, 주목, 주목하다
Ⓣ 니 말(remark) - 너의 소견
㈜ comment, observation   ㈜ *remarkable*: 주목할 만
㈖ I decided to ignore his rude remarks.

remedy
[rémədi]
Ⓡ 4941/86800

n. v. 치료, 치료약, 구제책, 치료하다
Ⓣ 니(re)메디(medy 메디컬 센터 - 병원)에서 **치료**
㈜ treatment, cure
㈖ Shopping became a remedy for personal problems.

R

remind
[rimáind]
Ⓡ 4782/86800

v. 생각나게 하다, 상기시키다
- ⓣ re(다시, 뒤로) + mind(마음): 다시 마음에 있게 하다, 생각나게 하다
- ⊕ recall
- 파 reminder: 생각나게 하는 것 *remindful*: 생각나게 하는
- 예 Please remind me to post this letter.

remote
[rimóut]
Ⓡ 3285/86800

adj. 먼, 외딴
- ⓣ 리모(remote)콘(controller) 생각하면 됨, **멀리** 있는 화면을 조절하는 것
- ⊕ isolated, solitary: 외딴
- 예 It happened in the remote past, so no one worries about it any more.

removal
[rimú:vəl]
Ⓡ 4117/86800

n. 제거
- ⓣ 미국 사람들이 가장 싫어하는 친척은 **이모부(remove)** - 왜? 자꾸 **제거**하라고 하니까
- ⊕ exclusion, elimination
- 파 *remove*: 제거하다, 옮기다
- 예 The city is having problems with trash removal.

render
[réndə:r]
Ⓡ 8869/86800

v. ~로 만들다, 보답하다
- ⓣ 저번에 얻어먹었으니 보답으로 이번에 내가 **낸다(render)**, 서로 내는 것을 규칙으로 **만들다**
- 예 Depression can render a person helpless.

renew
[rinjú:]
Ⓡ 11319/86800

v. 갱신하다
- ⓣ re(다시, 뒤로) + new(새롭게 하다): 갱신하다
- ⊕ renovate 파 renewal: 재개
- 예 I forgot to renew my season ticket.

renounce
[rináuns]
Ⓡ 22366/86800

v. 권리를 포기하다, 부인하다
- ⓣ 챔피언 자리를 **내놓았스(renounce)**: 챔피언 **권리를 포기하다**
- ⊕ surrender
- 예 Gandhi renounced the use of violence.

✔ **renown**
[rináun]
Ⓡ 31162/86800

n. 명성
❶ 방송에 이름 **이 나온(renown) 명성**
㉮ fame, reputation
㉑ *renowned*: 유명한
㉖ Her renown spread across the country.

✔ **repair**
[ripéəːr]
Ⓡ 3865/86800

v. 고치다, 치료하다
❶ repair(뇌 빼어) **치료하다**
㉮ mend, fix
㉖ I really must get my bike repaired this weekend.

repay
[riːpéi]
Ⓡ 9912/86800

v. 보답하다
❶ re(다시, 뒤로) + pay(돈 내다): 보답하다
㉮ requite, recompense
㉖ How can I ever repay you for all your kindness?

repel
[ripél]
Ⓡ 24443/86800

v. 쫓아버리다, 불쾌감을 주다
❶ 니 패(repel) 쫓아버리다 - 너를 패서 **쫓아버리더라**... 불쾌하게
㉮ dispel, scatter
㉖ Magnets can both repel and attract one another.

repent
[ripént]
Ⓡ 28286/86800

v. 후회하다
❶ 이(치아) 뺀(repent) 것을 **후회하다**
㉮ regret
㉖ He repented (of his sins) just hours before he died.

✔ **repetition**
[rèpətíʃən]
Ⓡ 7584/86800

n. 반복
❶ repeat(반복하다) + tion(명사형 어미): 반복
   repeat는 학교에서 많이 들어보셨을 거예요
㉮ (re)iteration, repeat
㉑ *repeat*: 되풀이하다 *repeatedly*: 되풀이하여
㉖ His books are full of repetition.

replace
[ripléis]
ⓡ 2863/86800

v. 대신하다, 바꾸다
ⓣ re(다시, 뒤로) + place(위치시키다): 대신하다
㉠ replacement: 교체
㉠ The factory replaced most of its workers with robots.

reply
[riplái]
ⓡ 2349/86800

v. 응답하다
ⓣ 어떤 글에 **리플(reply)**달다 - **응답하다**
㉠ respond, answer
㉠ I replied that it was 12 o'clock.

repose
[ripóuz]
ⓡ 23291/86800

n. v. 휴식, 쉬다
ⓣ 건강이 **나빠져(repose)휴식**
㉠ rest, repose
㉠ She reposed on the sofa.

represent
[rèprizént]
ⓡ 2209/86800

v. 나타내다, 대표하다
ⓣ **예쁘리 젠(represent)** - 젠는 예뻐서 우리 반을 **대표한다**
㉠ stand for, symbolize
㉠ *representation*: 표시
  representative: 대표자, 대표하는
㉠ I sent my husband to represent me at the funeral.

reproach
[ripróutʃ]
ⓡ 19253/86800

v. 비난하다
ⓣ 이 선물 **니 풀었지?(reproach)** 하며 **비난하다**
㉠ reprove, blame
㉠ His mother reproached him for not eating all his dinner.

reproduce
[rì:prədjú:s]
ⓡ 9773/86800

v. 번식하다
ⓣ re(다시, 뒤로) + produce(생산하다): 다시 생산해 내다 - 번식(증식)
㉠ propagate, breed
㉠ *reproduction*: 재생, 번식
㉠ Salmon return to the stream to reproduce offspring.

reprove
[riprú:v]
® 81696/86800

v. 비난하다, 꾸짖다
❶ 니 풀어봐?(reprove) - 너는 문제 못 풀면서 왜 그러냐고 **비난하다**
㊌ blame, reproach
例 The teacher gently reproved the boys for not paying attention.

✔ **republic**
[ripʌ́blik]
® 2325/86800

n. 공화국
❶ R, O, K - Republic Of Korea에서 republic은 공화국
例 The Republic of Korea shall be a democratic republic.
(대한민국은 민주공화국이다.)

✔ **reputation**
[rèpjətéiʃən]
® 2649/86800

n. 평판, 명성
❶ 그 분 **평판**이 어때? 다른 애들이 **나빴데셔(reputation)**
㊌ fame, repute, name 파 repute: 평가하다
例 The hotel has a good reputation.

✔ **request**
[rikwést]
® 2249/86800

v. n. 요청하다, 요구
❶ re(다시) + quest(탐색, 찾다): 다시 필요해서 찾다, 요청하다
㊌ demand, ask
例 The boss refused our request to leave work early.

✔ **require**
[rikwáiə:r]
® 1486/86800

v. 요구하다, 필요로 하다
❶ 이건 반드시 **있과이어(require)** - 필요하다고 **요구하다**
㊌ claim, demand
파 *required*: 요구되는 *requirement*: 요구, 필요
例 Skiing at 80 miles per hour requires total concentration.

✔ **rescue**
[réskju:]
® 3851/86800

v. 구조하다
❶ 구조대가 사람들을 **구조**하러 **나섰구(rescue)**
㊌ relieve, save
例 The lifeboat rescued the sailors from the sinking boat.

R

research
[risə́:rtʃ]
® 322/86800

n. v. 연구, 연구하다
❶ re(다시) + search(조사하다): 자꾸 조사해 보는 것이 연구
㋈ study, investigation ㋐ *researcher*: 연구원
㋐ His researches in the field of disease prevention produced unexpected results.

resemble
[rizémbəl]
® 10411/86800

v. ~을 닮다
❶ 이젠 볼(resemble) 수록 닮았다
㋈ alike, take after
㋐ You resemble your mother very closely.

resent
[rizént]
® 14459/86800

v. 분개하다
❶ 성질 여전(resent)하다는 소리에 **분개하다**
㋈ enrage
㋐ *resentful*: 분개한 resentment: 분개, 원한
㋐ He resented his boss for making him work late.

reserve
[rizə́:rv]
® 3446/86800

v. 예약하다, 남겨 두다
❶ 자리를 리저 버(reserve)릴까봐 미리 **예약하다**, 비축하다
㋈ book ㋐ reservation: 예약, 보류
㋐ These seats are reserved for the elderly and women with babies.

reside
[rizáid]
® 16706/86800

v. 살다, 존재하다
❶ 그 집에서 니(너)자데(reside) - 그 집서 **사나봐**
㋈ dwell, live
㋐ *residence*: 거주, 주거 resident: 거주자
    residential: 거주에 관한
㋐ The family now resides in southern France.

resign
[rizáin]
® 7134/86800

v. 사임하다
❶ 이 자린(resign)그만 둔다
㋐ resignation: 사직
㋐ She resigned as director.

✔ resist
[rizíst]
ⓡ 4309/86800

v. **저항하다, 견디다**
❶ 조용하라고 한 대 때리자 re(다시) + sist(stand의 뜻, st가 들어
가면 거의stand를 줄인 말): 다시 일어서다 - 저항하다(때리면 넘
어져야지 자꾸 일어서니까 저항)
㊞ withstand
㊟ resistance: 저항 *resistant*: 저항하는, 저항자
㊐ The soldiers resisted (the enemy attacks) for two days.

resolute
[rézəlùːt]
ⓡ 21241/86800

adj. **결심이 굳은, 단호한**
❶ 내 **절루 트**(resolute) - 내 **절대루** 이번엔 **트**집 잡지 않을게 - **결
심이 굳은**
㊞ determined, decisive ㊟ resolution: 결의(안), 결심
㊐ She is a resolute competitor.

✔ resolve
[rizálv]
ⓡ 4715/86800

v. **용해하다(녹이다) 결심하다**
❶ re(다시, 뒤로) + **solve(잘부**- 잘게 부수다): 다시 잘게 부수다(용
해하다), 잘 보(resolve)이기로 결심
㊞ melt, dissolve
㊐ She resolved that she would never speak to him
again.

✔ resort
[rizóːrt]
ⓡ 4049/86800

n. v. **휴양지, 의지하다, 다시 분류하다,**
❶ 대개 휴양지 호텔에 무슨 리조트라는 말 많이 쓰지요? 대개 휴
양지가면 이 좋다(resort - 여기 좋다)하며 감탄합니다. re(다시) +
sort(종류, 분류)의 뜻이면 재분류한다는 뜻이 됩니다
㊞ rely, depend: 의지하다
㊐ Every summer our family goes to a resort.

✔ resource
[ríːsɔːrs]
ⓡ 3512/86800

n. **자원**
❶ re(다시) + source(원천, 출처, 공급원): 기름 떨어지면 다시 자원
을 찾아야 함
㊟ *resourcefulness*: 자원이 풍부함
㊐ Britain's mineral resources include oil, coal and gas
deposits.

R

respect
[rispékt]
® 1752/86800

v. n. 존경하다, 측면
❶ re(다시) + spect(보다 - 어원편): 존경스러워서
㉮ esteem, venerate
㉯ *respectable*: 존경할 만한 respectful: 존경하는
㉠ New teachers have to earn/gain the respect of their students.

respiration
[rèspəréiʃən]
® 25920/86800

n. 호흡
❶ re(다시) + spir(숨 쉬다 - 어원편 참조): 호흡
㉮ breath, breathing
㉠ Her respiration was slow and difficult.

respond
[rispánd]
® 2791/86800

v. 응답하다
❶ 니서반대(respond) - 너는 반대라고 **답하다**
㉮ answer, reply
㉯ *response*: 응답 *respondent*: 응답하는, 응답자
responsiveness: 응답함
㉠ To every question, he responded "I don't know."

responsibility
[rispànsəbíləti]
® 1102/86800

n. 책임
❶ 니 스폰지 빌렸지?(responsibility) 책임져!!!
㉮ obligation, duty ㉯ *responsible*: 책임이 있는
㉠ She takes her responsibilities as a nurse very seriously.

rest
[rest]
® 602/86800

n. v. 휴식, 나머지, 쉬다
❶ 근무 안나가고 내쉬었다(rest) - 근무 안가고 집에 있었다 - **휴식**했다
㉮ repose, respite
㉯ restless: 가만히 있지 못하는, 불안한 *restful*: 휴식을 주는
㉠ The doctor told him that he should rest for a few days.

restore
[ristɔ́:r]
® 4936/86800

v. 복구하다, 회복하다
❶ re(다시) + store(저장하다): 없어진 것을 다시 저장하면 복구하다
㉮ return, rehabilitate
㉯ *restorer*: 원상복구자 *restoration*: 회복, 복구
㉠ The badly neglected paintings have all been carefully restored.

✔ **restrain**
[ristréin]
®️ 12259/86800

v. 제한하다
❶ 니 썼 들어인(restrain) - 너 썼다가 들어오라고 제한하다
⊕ restrict, limit
📝 Growth in car ownership could be restrained by increasing taxes.

✔ **restrict**
[ristríkt]
®️ 6604/86800

v. 제한하다
❶ 니 썼드릭(restrict) - 너 거기 서있어! 하고 **제한**하다
⊕ restrain, limit 📃 *restriction*: 제한
📝 Having small children really restricts your social life.

✔ **result**
[rizʌ́lt]
®️ 420/86800

n. v. **결과, 초래하다**
❶ **결과**는 니 **졌다(result)**
⊕ consequence, effect
📝 I tried to repaint the kitchen walls with disastrous results.

✔ **resume**
[rizú:m][rèzuméi]
®️ 8728/86800

v. n. **다시 차지하다, 이력서,**
❶ re(다시) + sume(줌): 다시 준다는 말은 다시 **차지**할 수 있다는 말. 내 이력서 **주메(resume)**
📝 Please resume your seats, as the performance will continue in two minutes.

✔ **retail**
[rí:teil]
®️ 4154/86800

n. **소매**
❶ re(다시) + tail(꼬리): 도매상에게 사서 다시 꼬리(이윤)를 붙여 판매 - 소매
⊕ wholesale 📃 *retailer*: 소매상인
📝 The job is open to applicants with over two years' experience in retail.

retain
[ritéin]
®️ 3588/86800

v. **보유하다, 간직하다**
❶ 주신 것 있데인(retain) - 준 것 잘 **간직하다**
⊕ possess, hold
📝 She has lost her battle to retain control of the company.

retire
[ritáiə:r]
ⓡ 6628/86800

v. 은퇴하다, 물러나다
ⓣ 니퇴해야 (retire) - 니 은퇴해야
ⓢ turn in
ⓟ *retiree*: 은퇴자 *retirement*: 은퇴 *retired*: 은퇴한
ⓔ He is due to retire as chief executive next year.

retort
[ritó:rt]
ⓡ 21120/86800

v. 말대꾸하다
ⓣ 니 또또(retort) 말대꾸야?
ⓢ talk back
ⓔ "That doesn't concern you!" she retorted.

retreat
[ritrí:t]
ⓡ 5972/86800

v. 물러가다, 후퇴하다
ⓣ 리 튀릿(retreat): 니 튀어라 - 후퇴해라
ⓢ withdraw, recede
ⓔ When she came towards me shouting, I retreated.

reunification
[rijù:nəfikéiʃən]
ⓡ 15924/86800

n. 재 통일
ⓣ re(다시) + uni(하나) + fic(만들다) + tion(명사형 어미): 다시 하나로
만듦 - 재 통일
ⓢ reunion
ⓔ Reunification is our first and most important task.

reunion
[ri:jú:njən]
ⓡ 10624/86800

n. 재결합
ⓣ re(다시, 뒤로) + union(연합, 하나 됨)
ⓔ We will have a family union on June 6th.

reveal
[rivί:l]
ⓡ 3462/86800

v. 드러내다, 폭로하다
ⓣ re(다시) + veal(보일): 다시 보이게 되다, 드러내다
ⓢ expose, disclose ⓟ revelation: 폭로
ⓔ He was jailed for revealing secrets to the Russians.

revenge
[rivéndʒ]
ⓡ 6737/86800

n. v. 보복, 보복하다
ⓣ 니 벤쥐(revenge) - 너가 칼로 벤 쥐는 쌀 훔쳐 먹은 것에 대해
쥐에게 보복
ⓢ retaliation, reprisal ⓟ *revengeful*: 복수심에 불타는
ⓔ She wants revenge against her enemies.

revenue
[révənjù:]
® 2467/86800

n. 소득, 세입
❶ 니 버뉴? (revenue) - 너 돈 버니? **수입** 있니?
㊛ income, earnings
㈜ Government revenues fell dramatically.

reverence
[révərəns]
® 16966/86800

n. v. 존경, 존경하다
❶ 니 벌었어(reverence)! - 니가 돈을 많이 벌어서 **존경**스러워
㊛ veneration, esteem
㈜ She has great reverence for her professors.

reverie
[révəri]
® 24875/86800

n. 환상
❶ 내 벌이(reverie) - 내 돈 벌이 가 커지는 **환상**
㊛ fantasy, illusion
㈜ He was lost in reverie until he suddenly heard someone behind him.

🏆 **reverse**
[rivə́:rs]
® 3815/86800

adj. v. 반대의, 거꾸로 하다
❶ re(다시, 뒤로) + verse(돌다): 뒤로 놀다 - 반내의
㊛ opposite, contrary
㈜ She reversed the car into the parking space.

✔ **review**
[rivjú:]
® 1058/86800

v. n. 다시보다, 복습하다, 복습
❶ re(다시) + view(보다): 다시 보다
㈜ Let's review what has happened so far.

✔ **revise**
[rivа́iz]
® 13664/86800

v. 수정하다
❶ re(다시) + vise(봐야지): 다시 봐야지 - **수정**하려고
㊛ amend, modify ㈜ *revision*: 개정
㈜ His publishers made him revise his manuscript three times.

revival
[rivа́ivəl]
® 6273/86800

n. 부활
❶ re(다시) + viv(살아있음 - 어원편 참조): 부활
㊛ rebirth, resurrection ㈜ revive: 부활하다
㈜ Fashions from the 1970s are enjoying a revival.

R

✔ **revolt**
[rivóult]
Ⓡ 8319/86800

n. **반란, 불쾌감**
[T] 반란으로 독재 정권을 **내 몰다(revolt)**
[유] rebellion, insurrection
[파] ***revolution***: 혁명 revolutionary: 혁명적인
revolutionize: 혁명을 일으키다
[예] Troops were called in to crush/put down the revolt.

revolve
[riválv]
Ⓡ 25678/86800

v. **회전하다**
[T] **이 볼 봐(revolve)** - 이 공 봐! **회전한다**
[유] rotate, turn
[예] The Earth revolves around the sun.

✔ **reward**
[riwɔ́:rd]
Ⓡ 4346/86800

n. v. **보수, 보답하다**
[T] **이월 달(reward)보수**는 내일 줄게
[유] remuneration, recompense
[예] There's a reward for whoever finishes first.

✔ **rhyme**
[raim]
Ⓡ 14225/86800

n. **운율**
[T] **라임(rhyme)** - 도레미파솔라 중 **운율**은 라임
[예] I couldn't think of a rhyme for "Buffalo".

✔ **rick**
[rik]
Ⓡ 10992/86800

n. **볏가리, 더미**
[T] 볏 가 **리(rick)**
[유] large stack, pile
[예] Rick means a stack in the open air.

✔ **rid**
[rid]
Ⓡ 3480/86800

v. **없애다, 제거하다**
[T] 없애 버 **리다(rid)**
[유] remove, exclude
[예] That cream got rid of my skin rash.

riddle
[rídl]
Ⓡ 14950/86800

n. **수수께끼**
[T] 유괴된 어린 **리들(riddle)** 사건은 **수수께끼**
[유] puzzle, enigma
[예] Scientists may have solved the riddle of Saturn's rings.

✔ **ridiculous**
[ridíkjələs]
[R] 4515/86800

adj. **우스꽝스러운, 어리석은**
[T] **니들이 꿀(꿀)해서 - ridiculous** 니들이 꿀꿀거리며 돼지 흉내 내서 **우스운**
[유] absurd, foolish
[파] *ridicule*: 비웃음, 비웃다
[예] Do I look ridiculous in this hat?

✔ **righteous**
[ráitʃəs]
[R] 20737/86800

adj. **정직한, 올바른**
[T] right(바른, 오른쪽, 권리) + eous(형용사형 어미): 올바른
[유] honest, upright
[파] *right*: 올바른, 오른쪽, 권리
[예] He was regarded as a righteous and holy man.

✔ **rigid**
[rídʒid]
[R] 5480/86800

adj. **굳은, 엄격한**
[T] 다 **리 짓(rigid)** 고 (시멘트가) **굳은**
[유] strict, severe, stern: 엄격한
[예] I was rigid with fear.

riot
[ráiət]
[R] 7259/86800

n. v. **폭동, 폭동을 일으키다**
[T] 탐관 오 **리 였다(riot)**고 백성들이 **폭동**을 일으키다
[유] disturbance, uprising
[예] Inner - city riots erupted when a local man was shot by police.

✔ **ripe**
[raip]
[R] 9681/86800

adj. **익은, 성숙한**
[T] 군대갈 **라 입(ripe - 나이)** - 군대 갈 나이는 **성숙한**
[유] mature
[파] *ripen*: 익다, 원숙하다
[예] Those bananas aren't ripe yet - they're still green.

✔ **risk**
[risk]
[R] 835/86800

n. **위험**
[T] **위험**한 투자는 어 **리 석(risk)** 어
[유] hazard, jeopardy
[예] In this business, the risks and the rewards are high.

R

✔ ritual
[rítʃuəl]
® 5457/86800

n. adj. 종교 의식, 의식의
❶ 종교의식 에서 우리 **취(ritual) 춤**
📖 *rite*: 의식
📝 The priest will perform the ritual.

✔ rivalry
[ráivəlri]
® 11332/86800

n. 경쟁
❶ 라이벌(rival)생각하면 될 듯
🔄 competition, contest 📖 *rival*: 경쟁자
📝 There's such rivalry among/between my three sons.

✔ riverfront
[rívə:rfrʌnt]
® 순위외/86800

n. 도시의 강변지대
❶ river(강) + front(앞)
📝 I used to live at the riverfront.

✔ roam
[roum]
® 18360/86800

v. 방랑하다, 배회하다
❶ 건달 놈(roam)과 어울리며 **배회하다**
📝 The lion roamed in search of prey.

✔ roar
[rɔ:r]
® 9408/86800

v. 짐승이 으르렁거리다, 소리치다
❶ 짐승이 목 로아(roar - 놓아)으르렁거리다, 목 로아(roar)**소리치다**
🔄 growl, snarl
📝 We could hear the lions roaring at the other end of the zoo.

✔ rob
[rɑb]
® 5378/86800

v. 빼앗다, 강탈하다
❶ 랍(rob)뿐 놈들이 내 돈 **빼앗았어**
🔄 plunder, loot
📝 My wallet's gone! I've been robbed!

robust
[roubʌst]
® 8988/86800

adj. 튼튼한
❶ 이 단어는 **로버트(robot)** 생각하면 쉽게 튼튼함을 연상할 수 있음
🔄 healthy, strong
📝 He looks robust and healthy enough.

✔ **rod**
[rɑd]
[R] 5698/86800

n. **막대, 회초리**
[T] **로(r)**하면 **아(o)**빠가 **든(d)**다: 노하면(화나면) 아빠가 드는 것은 **회초리**
[유] whip: 회초리
[예] He was given a fishing rod for his birthday.

✔ **role**
[roul]
[R] 530/86800

n. **역할**
[T] 마당놀이 에서 각 배우 들이 **놀(role) 역할**
[유] part
[예] What is his role in this project?

✔ **roll**
[roul]
[R] 2976/86800

v. n. **구르다, 둥글게 만 것**
[T] 빵집에서 파는 맛있는 둥근 **롤(roll)** 빵
[유] tumble
[예] The dog rolled over onto its back.

✔ **rot**
[rɑt]
[R] 10620/86800

n. v. **썩음, 썩다**
[T] 그대로 방치해서 **놨(rot)둠** - 방치하면 **썩음**
[유] decay [파] ***rotten***: 썩은, 부패한
[예] The fruit had been left to rot on the trees.

rotate
[róuteit]
[R] 18029/86800

v. **회전하다, 회전시키다**
[T] 도로에서 **로타리(rotary)** 생각하면 **회전**하면서 도로가 나있음. rotate도 같은 어원에서 나온 말
[유] revolve, turn [파] rotation: 회전
[예] Rotate the handle by 180° to open the door.

✔ **rough**
[rʌf]
[R] 2789/86800

adj. **거친, 대략의**
[T] 터프(tough), 러프(rough) 등 전부 거친이라는 뜻 철자가 비슷하기 때문에 기억하기가 어렵지 않아요!!!(개콘 버젼으로)
[유] harsh
[파] ***roughly***: 거칠게 ***roughness***: 거침
[예] My hands get very rough in the cold.

R

✔ **route**
[ru:t]
[R] 1814/86800

n. **길, 노선**
[T] 이 **길** 밖에는 **루트(route)**가 없어 라는 말 할 때 루트는 길
[유] line: 노선
[예] I live on a bus route so I can easily get to work.

routine
[ru:tí:n]
[R] 3007/86800

n. **틀에 박힌 일상적인 일**
[T] **루 뛴(routine** - 하루 종일 뛴) **틀에 박힌 일**
[예] There's no fixed routine at work - every day is different.

✔ **row**
[rou]
[R] 1961/86800

n. v. **줄, 열, 배를 젓다**
[T] 일렬 로(row) **줄**서라. **노(row)를 젓다**
[유] line, rank
[예] We had seats in the front row of the theatre.

✔ **rub**
[rʌb]
[R] 8921/86800

v. **문지르다, 비비다**
[T] **rub**(love라고 생각하면) - 사랑한 사람들끼리 반가워 문지르다
[유] scour, scrub
[예] She yawned and rubbed her eyes sleepily.

✔ **rude**
[ru:d]
[R] 7147/86800

adj. **무례한**
[T] 모르는 사람에게 **누드(rude)** 라고 말하면 **무례한**
[유] impolite, discourteous [파] ***rudely***: 무례하게
[예] He's a very rude man.

ruin
[rú:in]
[R] 8144/86800

n. v. **파멸, 망치다**
[T] **누인(ruin** - 누를 끼치는 것인): 누를 끼쳐 **파멸**의 위기
[유] destruction, wreck
[예] Her injury ruined her chances of winning the race.

✔ **rumor**
[rú:mə:r]
[R] 9234/86800

n. **소문**
[T] **누 뭐(rumor** - 누가 뭐하는 지 **돌아다니는 말**)
[유] hearsay, gossip
[예] There are rumors that they are making a new film.

run
[rʌn]
[R] 418/86800

v. **달리다, 경영하다**
[T] run이 '달리다'라는 뜻을 가진 것은 모두 아는 뜻이고 회사도 잘 달려야 경영을 잘하는 것이므로 '경영하다'의 뜻이 있다는 것 기억하세요
[유] manage, operate
[예] Keep clear of the machines while they're running.

rural
[rúrəl]
[R] 1647/86800

adj. **시골의**
[T] 엄마야 **누나(rural)야** 강변 살자. 여기서 강변은 서울의 강변역이 아니라 강 **변두리(시골)**임
[유] country, remote [반] urban
[예] The area is still very rural and undeveloped.

rush
[rʌʃ]
[R] 3751/86800

v. n. **돌진하다, 돌진, 붐빔**
[T] **러쉬(rush)** 아워(hour)라는 말 - **붐비는** 시간 아시죠?
[유] dash
[예] We were rushing to catch the bus.

rustle
[rʌ́səl]
[R] 21433/86800

v. **(나뭇잎이, 비단, 종이가) 바스락거리다**
[T] **나슬(rustle)** - **나**뭇잎이 **슬**쩍 바**스락**거리다
[예] This tree rustled in the wind.

rusty
[rʌ́sti]
[R] 12226/86800

adj. **녹슨**
[T] **rusty(록스티)** - **녹이 슨** 티
[예] She has a rusty car.

ruthless
[rú:θlis]
[R] 9513/86800

adj. **무자비한**
[T] ruth(동정) + less(~이 없는): 동정심이 없는. **ruth(로써** - 인간으**로써** 가진 자비, 동정)
[유] pitiless, cruel
[예] Some people believe that to succeed in this world you have to be ruthless.

R

sacred
[séikrid]
® 5901/86800

adj. 신성한
❶ **시이 크리도(sacred) - 신이 그리도 신성한**
⊛ holy, divine c.f) *sacrifice*: 희생(하다), 제물
예 The burial site is sacred ground.

saddle
[sǽdl]
® 8624/86800

n. 말의 안장
❶ **서들(saddle)**있지 말고 **안장** ㅋ
예 I got into the saddle.

safe
[seif]
® 1471/86800

adj. n. 안전한, 금고
❶ **세입(safe - 세금으로 받은 돈)은 안전한 금고에 보관해야 함**
⊛ secure 파 *safety*: 안전 *safely*: 안전하게
예 In some cities you don't feel safe going out alone at night.

sagacious
[səgéiʃəs]
® 72593/86800

adj. 현명한, 영리한
❶ **(수)석 애 이셨어(sagacious** - 앞에 수 자를 붙이면 수석한 애 였어): **영리한**
⊛ wise, intelligent
c.f) sage: 성인, 현명한 *saint:* 성스러운 사람
예 They were sagacious enough to avoid any outright confrontation.

sail
[seil]
® 5122/86800

v. n. 항해하다, 돛
❶ **세일(sail - 세계 일주) 위해 항해하다**
예 This ship will sail from New York for San francisco.

sake
[seik]
® 2989/86800

n. 위함, 이익
❶ **세익(sake - 세상의 이익)**
예 Please do it, for David's sake.

salmon
[sǽmən]
® 5532/86800

n. 연어
❶ **연어**의 **삶은(salmon)** 자기가 태어난 곳, 찾아가는 삶
예 Might I suggest a white wine with your salmon?

380

salute
[səlúːt]
® 13828/86800

n. v. **인사, 인사하다**
❶ 설루 (salute) 인사하다: 설을 맞이하여 **인사하다**
㉠ greet: 인사하다
㉫ The soldiers saluted the colonel.

sane
[sein]
® 15561/86800

adj. **제정신의**
❶ 세 인(sane - 세상 인간): 일반적인 세상 인간은 **제정신**
㉠ sober ㉻ insane
㉫ In the doctor's opinion he was sane at the time of the murder.

✔ sanitary
[sǽnətèri]
® 16174/86800

adj. **위생의**
❶ 새 너털이(sanitary): 새 하얗게 너가 털어 **위생적인**
㉠ hygienic ㉴ *sanitation*: 공중위생
㉫ Cholera thrives in poor sanitary conditions.

✔ sash
[sæʃ]
® 21146/86800

n. **(여성과 어린이) 장식용 허리 띠, 창틀**
❶ 띠 샀어(sash)
㉫ She was sashed at the waist.

✔ satellite
[sǽtəlàit]
® 4963/86800

n. **인공위성**
❶ 새 떠 라잇(satellite) - 새처럼 떠서 라잇(빛)비추는 **인공위성**
㉫ The World Cup was transmitted around the world by satellite.

satire
[sǽtaiəːr]
® 19637/86800

n. **풍자**
❶ 장관이 강남에 투기로 땅을 **샀대여(satire)**: 빗대어 비판하는 것의 **풍자**
㉠ sarcasm, innuendo
㉫ Her play was a biting/cruel satire on life in the 80s.

✔ satisfied
[sǽtisfàid]
® 2786/86800

adj. **만족한**
❶ 셋이서 파이 들(satiesfiied) 고 **만족**
㉴ satisfactory: 만족한 *satisfy*: 만족시키다 *satisfaction*: 만족
㉫ Some people are never satisfied!

S

saucer
[sɔ́:sə:r]
ⓡ 14369/86800

n. 접시
❶ 접시에 음식을 **쏟아서(saucer)**먹지
예 I gave my dog a saucer of milk.

savage
[sǽvidʒ]
ⓡ 6463/86800

adj. 야만스러운
❶ **야만스럽게** 남의 물건을 **쌔비지(savage)** - 쎄비지는 훔치지 라는 말의 속어
ⓢ barbarous, uncivilized
예 He was the victim of a savage attack.

save
[seiv]
ⓡ 1432/86800

v. 절약하다, 구하다, 덜어주다
❶ **세이브(save)**라는 말은 많이 쓰는 말
ⓢ economize, spare
예 Wearing seat belts has saved many lives.

scale
[skeil]
ⓡ 1351/86800

n. 눈금, 저울, 지도의 축척, 규모
❶ 이 영화는 **스케일(scale)**이 달라 - **규모**가 다르다는 말
ⓢ balance: 저울
예 This map is large scale (= things are shown in detail).

scan
[skæn]
ⓡ 9353/86800

v. 자세히 조사하다, 회화 - 대충 훑어보다
❶ 스캐너로 **스캔(scan)**하면 **자세히** 나옴
ⓢ inspect, scrutinize
예 I scanned through the booklet but couldn't find the address.

scandal
[skǽndl]
ⓡ 5409/86800

n. 추문
❶ **스캔들(scandal)**났다는 말은 **추잡한 소문**
ⓢ ill fame
예 Some magazines contain nothing but scandal and gossip.

scanty
[skǽnti]
ⓡ 27592/86800

adj. 부족한
❶ **소(s - 한자로 작은) + 캔티(canty)** - 캔디가 적은, 부족한
ⓢ insufficient, scarce
예 The camera's scanty instructions left me somewhat confused.

scar
[skɑ:r]
ⓡ 12384/86800

n. 상처, 흉터
❶ 남을 **슥 까(scar)** 면 - 슥 때리면 **상처**가 남아요
⊕ wound, injury
예 That burn will leave a nasty scar.

✔ scarce
[skɛə:rs]
ⓡ 8640/86800

adj. 부족한, 드문
❶ 쑥 **캐어서(scarce)** - (쑥이) **부족한**
⊕ scanty, insufficient
파 scarcely: 거의 ~않다, 겨우 *scarcity*: 부족
예 Food and clean water were becoming scarce.

✔ scare
[skɛə:r]
ⓡ 10609/86800

v. 위협하다
❶ 깡패가 **써끼야(scare)**!욕하며 **위협하다**
⊕ menace, threaten
파 *scared*: 겁먹은, 두려워하는 *scary*: 무서운
예 Sudden noises scare her.

✔ scatter
[skǽtə:r]
ⓡ 15087/86800

v. 흩어버리다, 흩뿌리다
❶ 공부하는데 초딩들이 밖에서 떠들어 조용해 **씨끼들(scatter)이!**
하며 **흩어버리다**
⊕ strew; disperse 파 *scattered*: 뿔뿔이 흩어진
예 The soldiers came in and scattered the crowd.

✔ scenery
[síːnəri]
ⓡ 8429/86800

n. 풍경, 무대 배경
❶ scene(장면) + ery(모아놓은 것): 장면을 모으면 풍경이 됨
⊕ landscape 파 *scene*: 장면, 광경
예 They stopped at the top of the hill to admire the
scenery.

✔ scent
[sent]
ⓡ 7160/86800

n. 냄새
❶ s(smell) + cent(센다): 냄새 샌다
⊕ smell, odor
예 The flower has a wonderful scent.

S

scheme
[ski:m]
ⓡ 825/86800

n. 계획
🅣 s(새해) + cheme(켬) - 새해에 켬 - 새해 **계획** 세움
🅢 plan, project
🅔 There's a new scheme in our town for recycling plastic bottles.

✔ scholar
[skálə:r]
ⓡ 9016/86800

n. 학자
🅣 schol(스쿨 - 학교) + ar(사람): 학교에 있는 사람
🅟 *scholarship*: 장학금 *school*: 학파, 훈련하다
　　scholarly: 학자다운
🅔 She's a renowned scholar of African - American history.

scissors
[sízə:rz]
ⓡ 12220/86800

n. 가위
🅣 **가위**질하면 **찢어져(scissors)**
🅢 shears, clippers
🅔 Could you pass me the/those scissors, please.

✔ scold
[skould]
ⓡ 37973/86800

v. 꾸짖다
🅣 그 점수로는 **스쿨 다(scold)** 다녔다고 부모님이 **꾸짖다**
🅢 rebuke, reprove
🅔 His mother scolded him for breaking her favourite vase.

scope
[skoup]
ⓡ 2849/86800

n. 범위, 보는 것(시야)
🅣 telescope(멀리 있는 것을 보는 것,tele - 먼)라는 단어에서 힌트를 얻을 수 있어요
🅢 range, sphere
🅔 I'm afraid that problem is beyond/outside the scope of my lecture.

✔ score
[skɔ:r]
ⓡ 2460/86800

n. 숫자20, 득점, 악보
🅣 **수코어(score)**가 점**수** 얻는 것이라는 것은 다 알지요? 또 **수코어**가 **수 20**이라는 뜻이 있어요
🅢 point: 득점
🅔 He lived to be three score years and ten (= until he was 70 years old).

scorn
[skɔːrn]
® 13532/86800

n. 경멸
❶ 이런 **소 꾼(scorn)** - (꾼이라는 말은 대개 어떤 분야를 잘 하는 사람의 안 좋은 말투이므로) 하며 **멸시**하다
㊐ contempt, slight, disdain
㊐ She has nothing but scorn for the new generation of politicians.

scratch
[skrætʃ]
® 7274/86800

v. 긁다, 할퀴다
❶ s(슥) + cratch(긁어취) - 살짝 **긁었지**
㊐ claw
㊐ Be careful not to scratch yourself on the roses.

scream
[skriːm]
® 6860/86800

v. n. 소리치다, 비명
❶ **시끄럼(scream)!**하며 **소리치다**
㊐ shout, yell
㊐ A spider landed on her pillow and she screamed.

script
[skript]
® 6117/86800

n. 손으로 쓴 글
❶ **손으로 글 썼그립(script)**
㊐ handwriting
㊐ Do you know post scripts?

scrub
[skrʌb]
® 11980/86800

v. 세게 문지르다
❶ **슥갈아(scrub)**보다 - 슥슥 **문지르다**
㊐ I scrubbed a floor in the morning.

scrutiny
[skrúːtəni]
® 6220/86800

n. 자세한 조사
❶ 죄 없다면서 경찰이 자세히 **조사**한다니까 그 기세가 **수그러드니?(scrutiny)**
㊐ I'd never faced that kind of scrutiny before.

sculpture
[skʌ́lptʃəːr]
® 5787/86800

n. 조각
❶ scul(석고) + pture(붙여): 석고 붙인 **조각상**
㊐ engraving, carving
㊐ Tom teaches sculpture at the local art school.

seal
[si:l]
® 5642/86800

n. v. 바다표범, 봉인, 봉인하다
❶ sea(바다) + l(leopard - 표범), 실(seal)로 꿰매서 새지 않게 봉인 해주세요
예 Seal the package (up) with sticky tape.

search
[sə:rtʃ]
® 1643/86800

n. 수색, 조사, 찾다
❶ 써치 라이트(search light)는 잘 찾기 위해 설치(search) 해 놓은 거예요
㊙ investigation: 조사
예 The police searched the woods for the missing boy.

seashell
[si:ʃel]
® 80337/86800

n. 바닷조개
❶ Sea(바다) + shell(껍질): 바다에있는 조개 껍질
예 Definition of seashell is the empty shell of a small sea creature.

seaweed
[síːwìːd]
® 19289/86800

n. 해초, 미역
❶ sea(바다) + weed(잡초) - 바다 잡초는 해초
예 I like Korean seaweed.

seclude
[siklúːd]
® 순위 外/86800

v. 격리하다
❶ se(따로 분리해서 - 어원편 참조) + clude(닫다 - 어원편 및 앞의 단어들 참조): 따로 분리해서 닫다, 격리하다
㊙ isolate, separate
예 He secluded himself in his room to study for the exam.

secret
[síːkrit]
® 1788/86800

n. adj. 비밀, 비밀의
❶ 시끄럿(secret)비밀이야
㊙ mystery, confidence 파 secretly: 비밀로 c.f) secretary: 비서
예 So what's the secret of being a good cook?

section
[sékʃən]
® 517/86800

n. 부분
❶ sect(분할하다 - 어원편 참조) + tion(명사형 어미)
㊙ part, portion c.f) segment: 부분
예 Does the restaurant have a non - smoking section?

secure
[sikjúə:r]
ⓡ 2188/86800

adj. v. 안전한, 안정된, 안전하게하다
❶ 과일은 **씻구어(secure)**먹어야 **안전한**
㉦ safe ㉣ *security*: 안전 *securely*: 확실히
㉫ That ladder doesn't look very secure to me.

seed
[si:d]
ⓡ 4949/86800

n. 씨, 종자
❶ **씻(seed): 씨**
㉫ Sow the seeds(= put them in the ground) about 3cm deep.

seek
[si:k]
ⓡ 1875/86800

v. 찾다, 추구하다
❶ **색(seek): 수색의 索 - 찾다**
㉦ pursue c.f) *seeker*: 수색자
㉫ "Are you actively seeking jobs?" she asked.

seem
[si:m]
ⓡ 568/86800

v. ~으로 보이다
❶ **심(seem) - 마음 심, 마음으로 그렇게 보이다**
㉦ appear, look
㉣ seeming: 겉으로의 *seemingly*: 겉보기에는
㉫ He's 16, but he often seems (to be) younger.

seize
[si:z]
ⓡ 10192/86800

v. 붙잡다, 의미를 파악하다
❶ **seize(시조)의 의미를 파악하다**
㉦ catch, grasp
㉫ I seized his arm and made him turn to look at me.

seldom
[séldəm]
ⓡ 5334/86800

adv. 좀처럼 ~않다, 드물게
❶ **살다(seldom) 보면 드물게 보는 일들이 있다**
㉦ rarely, hardly
㉫ Now that we have a baby, we seldom get the chance to go to the cinema.

select
[silékt]
ⓡ 3153/86800

v. 고르다
❶ **이거 쏠래(select)! 하고 내가 고르다**
㉦ choose, pick ㉣ selection: 선택, 선발
㉫ How do you select people for promotion?

S

selfish
[sélfiʃ]
® 9096/86800

adj. 이기적인
❶ self(자신) + ish(형용사형 어미): 자신을 위한, 이기적인, 영어로 물이 뭔지 아삼? - 셀프
㉮ egocentric, egotistic
㈎ *self*: 자기 *selfless*: 이기심 없는
㈖ She's interested only in her own selfish concerns.

semester
[siméstər]
® 47202/86800

n. 학기
❶ C 맞었다(semester) - 성적은 학기 마다 나온다
㉮ term, session
㈖ I took 15 credits this semester.

senior
[síːnjər]
® 1230/86800

n. 연장자
❶ 나보다 손위여(senior): 연장자
㉮ elder
㈖ She was his senior in rank.

sense
[sens]
® 425/86800

n. v. 감각, 의미, 느끼다
❶ sense(감각)있는 여자
㉮ sensation, feeling
㈎ sensation: 감각 senseless: 무분별한
　 sensible: 분별있는 *sensitive*: 민감한
　 sensibility: 감각 *sensitivity*: 감성 *sensory*: 감각의
㈖ Did you get any sense of how they might react?

sentence
[séntəns]
® 1774/86800

n. v. 문장, 판결(하다), 선고(하다)
❶ 문장이라는 뜻은 아실테고 감옥에서 얼마 산단서(sentence - 감옥에서 얼마 산다는 글 - 판결)
㉮ condemn, adjudge: 판결하다, 선고하다
㈖ He is serving a 10 - year sentence for armed robbery.

sentiment
[séntəmənt]
® 9873/86800

n. 감정
❶ 감정 상치만(sentiment) - 감정이 상하지만
㉮ feelings, emotion ㈎ sentimental: 감상적인
㈖ I don't think she shares my sentiments.

separate
[sépərèit]
ⓡ 1113/86800

v. adj. **분리하다, 분리된, 개별적인**
❶ se(따로 분리하여) + parate(빨았다) - 빨래를 따로 분리하여 빨았다
⊕ split, detach
㉕ separation: 분리 *separately*: 단독으로
㉒ I try to keep meat separate from other food in the fridge.

sept
[sept]
ⓡ 19389/86800

n. **씨족**
❶ 쎕 다(sept) - 셋다 같은 **씨족**
⊕ clan
㉒ Sept is a branch of a family.

sequence
[síːkwəns]
ⓡ 2387/86800

n. **연달아 일어남, 순서**
❶ 책 **시리즈** 대로 **세권사**(sequence) - 1권, 2권, 3권 **연속**으로 세권 사
⊕ series, succession
㉒ Is there a particular sequence in which you have to perform these tasks?

serene
[siríːn]
ⓡ 18698/86800

adj. **고요한, 평온한, 화창한**
❶ **고요한** 곳에 **사이렌**(serene)
⊕ calm, tranquil
㉒ She has a lovely serene face.

serious
[síəriəs]
ⓡ 797/86800

adj. **진지한, 심각한**
❶ **진심**이 **실리었어**(serious)
㉕ *seriously*: 진지하게 *seriousness*: 진지함
㉒ There were no reports of serious injuries.

sermon
[sə́ːrmən]
ⓡ 13062/86800

n. **설교**
❶ **설문**(sermon - 설교 문)
⊕ preaching
㉒ Today's sermon was on the importance of compassion.

servant
[sə́:rvənt]
Ⓡ 4705/86800

n. 하인
❶ serve(봉사) + ant(사람) - 봉사하는 사람
㊉ domestic(n) 파 *serve*: 봉사하다 *service*: 봉사
예 The wealthy family had servants to clean and cook for them.

session
[séʃən]
Ⓡ 2284/86800

n. (의회, 법정) 개회 중, 기간, 시간, 모임
❶ 의회가 **셨션(session)** - 장이 선 것처럼 의회와 법원이 섰다는 것은 **개회 중**
예 The UN Security Council met in emergency session to discuss the crisis.

settle
[sétl]
Ⓡ 3571/86800

v. **정착하다, 해결하다**
❶ 새 터(settle - 새 장소)에 **정착하다**
㊉ domiciliate: 정주시키다
파 *settlement*: 정착, 해결 settler: 정착민
예 We need to settle this question once and for all.

severe
[sivíə:r]
Ⓡ 2198/86800

adj. **엄격한**
❶ 남의 것 **세비여(severe)?(훔쳐?)** - **엄한** 처벌
㊉ strict, stern 파 *severely*: 엄격하게
예 There is expected to be a severe frost tonight.

sew
[sou]
Ⓡ 19123/86800

v. **바늘로 꿰매다, 수놓다**
❶ **수(sew)를** 놓다 - **바늘로 꿰매다**
예 She made a beautiful skirt just by sewing two pieces of material together.

sewage
[sú:idʒ]
Ⓡ 8393/86800

n. 하수, 폐수
❶ 이게 **내려온 水(물)이지?(sewage** - 물이지?)
㊉ waste water
예 Some cities in the world do not have proper facilities for the disposal of sewage.

shabby
[ʃǽbi]
[R] 12461/86800

adj. 초라한, 누더기 걸친
[T] **차비(shabby)? - 초라한, 누더기 걸친** 걸인이 차비?좀 줘
[유] miserable, seedy
[예] He wore a shabby old overcoat.

✔ **shade**
[ʃeid]
[R] 5438/86800

n. 그늘, 색조
[T] **쉐이다(shade** - 쉬다 혹은 색이다) - **그늘**에서 쉬다 혹은 **色(색)**이다
[유] color tone: 색조 c.f) *shadow*: 그림자, 그늘
[예] The sun was hot, and there were no trees to offer us shade.

shallow
[ʃǽlou]
[R] 5596/86800

adj. 얕은
[T] **쉘(水 - 한자로 물) + 로우(low -** 낮은): 물이 낮은 - **얕은**
[반] deep
[예] Fry the onions in a shallow pan.

✔ **shame**
[ʃeim]
[R] 4191/86800

n. 부끄러움, 치욕
[T] 지금 몇 **쉐임(shame)?** - 나이가 몇 세임? **부끄러움**을 알아야지
[유] indignity, humiliation
[파] *shameless*: 부끄러움을 모르는
[예] It's a great shame that the concert had to be cancelled.

✔ **shanty**
[ʃǽnti]
[R] 29738/86800

n. 오두막, 판자집
[T] **싼티(shanty)**나는 판자집, **오두막**
[예] Shanty is a small house, usually made from pieces of wood or metal, in which poor people live, especially on the edge of a city.

✔ **shape**
[ʃeip]
[R] 1496/86800

n. v. 모양, 형성하다
[T] **새 입(shape) 모양**은 어떻게 생겼는지요?
[유] form, appearance
[예] Our table is oval in shape.

S

share
[ʃɛəːr]
® 723/86800

v. n. 나누다, 공유하다, 몫
❶ 당신도 써여(share)!: 같이 쓰는 것은 공유
㊦ divide, distribute
㉥ Bill and I shared an office for years.

shed
[ʃed]
® 4073/86800

v. 흘리다, 떨어뜨리다
❶ 눈물 따위가 세다(shed - 새다) - 눈물 흘리다
㉥ I shed tears.

sheer
[ʃiəːr]
® 4161/86800

adj. 옷이 비치는 (얇은), 섞이지 않은(순전한)
❶ 오렌지와 설탕이 섞이지 않아 시어(sheer). 또, 옷이 얇아서 시원(sheer)
㊦ diaphanous, transparent
㉥ She wore a dress of the sheerest silk.

sheet
[ʃiːt]
® 2390/86800

n. 침구의 커버, 종이의 장
❶ 침대 쉬트(sheet)
㉥ She has put clean sheets on my bed.
  A single sheet of paper.

shelf
[ʃelf]
® 5557/86800

n. 선반
❶ shelf(셔ㅍ) - 선반: 발음이 비슷함
㉥ She made a shelf so that objects can be stored on it.

shelter
[ʃéltəːr]
® 5263/86800

n. 피난처, 주거 시설, 보호 시설
❶ 쉴 터(shelter): 쉬는 곳은 피난처, 주거시설
㊦ refuge
㉥ We made a shelter from branches.

shepherd
[ʃépəːrd]
® 6474/86800

n. 양치는 사람
❶ 발음해보면 쉽(sheep - 양) 보다(pherd) - 양보는 사람
㉥ Shepherd is a person whose job is to take care of sheep and move them from one place to another.

✔ shield
[ʃi:ld]
ⓡ 6244/86800

n. v. **방패, 보호하다**
❶ 군인이 **방패**가 되어 국민이 편히 **쉴다(shield - 쉬고 살다)**
㊌ buckler
예 She shielded her eyes from the sun with her hand.

✔ shift
[ʃift]
ⓡ 2469/86800

v. n. **이동하다, 바꾸다, 변화, 교대**
❶ 선택과목 어떤 게 **쉴다(shift)**면 전부 그 과목으로 **바꾼다**
㊌ convert, vary: 바꾸다
예 I shifted the bag to my other shoulder.

shiver
[ʃivə:r]
ⓡ 14067/86800

v. **(추위나 다른 흥분으로) 떨다**
❶ **수이(추위) 벌(shiver) - 추위로 벌벌 떨다**
㊌ tremble, quiver
예 In the biting wind I shiver against the cold.

✔ shoot
[ʃu:t]
ⓡ 4000/00000

v. **발사하다, 싹이 트다**
❶ 축구경기에서 **슛(shoot)**, 영화촬영에서 슛(shoot)은 아는 거고 **싹**이 **슈욱(shoot)**하고 드다
㊌ discharge, fire
예 If he's not armed, don't shoot.

✟ shore
[ʃɔ:r]
ⓡ 4629/86800

n. **바닷가**
❶ **(shore - 슈왈)**발음하면 **바닷가** 파도 소리 연상
㊌ seaside, coast
예 You can walk for miles along the shore.

✟ shortage
[ʃɔ:rtidʒ]
ⓡ 5341/86800

n. **부족, 결핍**
❶ short(짧은, 부족한) + age(명사형 어미): 부족
㊌ deficiency, lack
예 The long hot summer has led to serious water shortages.

shortcoming
[ʃɔ:rtkʌmiŋ]
ⓡ 41813/86800

n. **결점**
❶ short(부족한) + coming(생기는, 오는): 부족해서 생기는 결점
㊌ weakness, drawback
예 Like any political system, it has its shortcoming.

S

✓ shortcut
[ʃɔ́:rtkʌ̀t]
[R] 55162/86800

n. **지름길**
[T] short(짧은, 부족한) + cut(자르기): 길을 짧게 자르기 - 지름 길
[예] I know a shortcut to town through the back streets.

✓ shorten
[ʃɔ́:rtn]
[R] 20042/86800

v. **짧게 하다**
[T] short(짧은) + en(~하게하다): 짧게 하다
[예] I've asked him to shorten my grey trousers.

✓ shot
[ʃɑt]
[R] 1257/86800

n. v. **발포, 시도하다,** shoot**의 과거, 과거분사**
[T] 나이스 **샷(shot)**이란 말 **시도**를 잘 했다는 뜻
[유] try, attempt: 시도하다
[예] Let's take another shot at the puzzle.

✓ shout
[ʃaut]
[R] 5392/86800

v. n. **외치다, 외침**
[T] **샤우팅(shout)**창법이란 말 들어보셨을 것 같아요. **소리 지르는** 창법이죠
[유] cry, exclaim
[예] There's no need to shout at me.

shovel
[ʃʌ́vəl]
[R] 19616/86800

n. v. **삽, 삽으로 푸다**
[T] **샵을(shovel)**들고 **삽질하다**
[유] spade, scoop
[예] Would you give me a hand shovelling the snow away from the garage door?

shrewd
[ʃru:d]
[R] 11722/86800

adj. **빈틈없는, 영리한**
[T] 없어지면 **새로 다(shrewd)**만들어 놓는 **빈틈없는** 사원
[유] sharp, keen
[예] She's shrewd about her investments.

✓ shrink
[ʃriŋk]
[R] 13465/86800

v. **(천이) 오그라들다**
[T] 뜨거운 물에 빨자 **小량(shrink)**이 됨 - **작아 짐**
[파] ***shrinkage***: 수축
[예] The sweater shrank when it was washed.

✔ **shrug**
[ʃrʌg]
®️ 11230/86800

v. **어깨를 으쓱하다**

🕊 소율더(shoulder - 줄여서 shr)가 위(u)로 가(g): 어깨가 위로 가서 으쓱하다

영화에서 보셨을텐데 대개 두 손바닥을 같이 보이죠. 미국인들의 감정 표현 방식으로 놀라움, 당황, 등의 감정을 나타냅니다

예 He just shrugged his shoulders.

---

shy
[ʃai]
®️ 6300/86800

adj. **수줍어하는, 부끄럼 타는**

🕊 **부끄럼** 많이 타는 **小 아이(shy - 작은아이)**

🐦 bashful, coy

예 He gave her a shy smile.

✔ **sideboard**
[sáidbɔ̀:rd]
®️ 19043/86800

n. **음식 얹는 작은 탁자**

🕊 찬장 말고 **옆(side)에 음식 얹는 판(board)**

예 Sideboard is a piece of furniture with a flat top and cupboards at the bottom, usually used for holding glasses, plates, etc.

✔ **sidewalk**
[sáidwɔ̀:k]
®️ 32557/86800

n. **인도, 보도**

🕊 side(옆) + walk(걸어가다): 옆으로 가는 길 - 인도

🐦 footpath, pavement

예 Bicycles are not allowed on the sidewalk.

---

siege
[si:dʒ]
®️ 7899/86800

n. v. **포위 공격, 포위하다**

🕊 둘러**싸지**(siege) - 포위하다

🐦 surround, encircle: 포위하다

예 The city is in a state of siege.

✔ **sigh**
[sai]
®️ 6386/86800

n. v. **한숨, 한숨 쉬다**

🕊 **사이**(sigh) - 세상사는 사이(sigh)에 **한숨** 쉰다

예 He sighed with relief when he saw that he passed the test.

S

sight
[sait]
[R] 1529/86800

n. 시각, 조망
[T] **sight(시야 트** - 시야가 트이는): **조망**
[유] vision, eyesight
[예] She regained sight in her left eye.

signature
[sígnətʃə:r]
[R] 6695/86800

n. 서명
[T] sign(싸인) + nature(넣어 줘): 싸인 넣어줘. 영어로 유명인에게 받는 싸인은 autograph라고 합니다. 주의하세요
[유] autograph, John Hancock
[예] There is a place for your signature at the bottom of the form.

significance
[signífikəns]
[R] 2169/86800

n. 의의, 중요성
[T] sign(싸인) + fic(만들다 - 어원편 참조) + ance(명사형 어미): 남의 싸인을 만드는 일은 중대한 일
[유] meaning, sense
[파] ***significant***: 중요한, 의미있는 signify: 나타내다
[예] The discovery has great significance to researchers.

silence
[sáiləns]
[R] 1725/86800

n. 침묵
[T] **싸 일 (sil)** + ence(명사형 어미) - **침묵**에 싸일
[유] reticence, taciturnity
[파] ***silent***: 침묵하는 ***silently***: 잠자코
[예] We sat there in dead silence.

silly
[síli]
[R] 3331/86800

adj. 어리석은
[T] **설 리(silly)** 근 (설익은) - **어리석은**
[유] foolish, stupid
[예] The idea does seem a bit silly.

similar
[símələ:r]
[R] 521/86800

adj. 비슷한
[T] **심어라(similar)** - 심으면 **비슷한** 것이 나옴
[유] analogous, akin
[파] ***similarity***: 유사(점) ***similarly***: 마찬가지로
[예] Our cats are similar in size.

✔ **simplify**
[símpləfài]
Ⓡ 14601/86800

v. 단순화하다
❶ simple(간단한) + ify(만들다): 간단하게 만들다
㈜ *simple*: 단순한 *simplicity*: 단순함
simplistic: 단순화한 *simply*: 단순히
㈖ Microwave ovens have simplified cooking.

simulate
[símjəlèit]
Ⓡ 19656/86800

v. 모의 실험하다, 흉내 내다
❶ sim(ilar)(비슷한) + ate(동사, 형용사형 어미):
비슷하게 하다, 흉내 내다
㈜ imitate, copy
㈖ The model will be used to simulate the effects of an earthquake.

✔ **simultaneous**
[sàiməltéiniəs]
Ⓡ 9591/86800

adj. 동시의
❶ 싸인 물 트니 어서 (simultaneous) - 쌓인 물을 트니 어서 **동시에** 쏟아짐
㈜ concurrent ㈜ *simultaneously*: 동시에
㈖ The two gunshots were simultaneous.

sin
[sin]
Ⓡ 5723/86800

n. (종교적, 도덕적) 죄
❶ 神(sin) 이 하지 말라는 것은 **죄**
㈜ vice
㈖ He thinks a lot about sin.

✔ **sincere**
[sinsíə:r]
Ⓡ 11591/86800

adj. 성실한, 진실한
❶ 신실해(sincere): 신실한은 진실하고 **성실한**
㈜ truthful, honest ㈜ *sincerity*: 성실
㈖ Please accept our sincere thanks.

✔ **singular**
[síŋgjələ:r]
Ⓡ 11787/86800

adj. 단독의
❶ single(싱글 - 단독) + al(형용사형)에서 나온 말
㈜ *single*: 단 하나의
㈖ In the phrase "his car is red," the word "car" is a singular noun.

sinister
[sínistəːr]
[R] 8989/86800

adj. **조짐이 불길 한**
[T] **신이(sini-) 섰다(ster):** 뭔가 인간에게 벌을 내릴 듯 한 - **불길한**
[유] ominous, unlucky
[예] There was something sinister about him.

✔ **sink**
[siŋk]
[R] 4485/86800

v. n. **가라앉다, 부엌의 물 버리는 곳**
[T] **싱크(sink)** 대 생각하면 물 버리는 곳
[유] descend, be submerged
[예] The rock sank to the bottom of the pool.

sip
[sip]
[R] 13289/86800

n. v. **한 모금, 홀짝이다**
[T] **슢(sip)** - 스프를 **한 모금 홀짝이다**
[유] gulp, draft
[예] She sipped her coffee while she watched the sun rise.

✔ **site**
[sait]
[R] 1042/86800

n. **장소, 유적**
[T] 인터넷 **싸이트(site)**
[예] Buffalo, New York is the site of the accident.

✔ **situation**
[sìtʃuéiʃən]
[R] 608/86800

n. **위치, 장소, 입장**
[T] sit(앉다) + tion(명사형 어미): 현재 내가 앉아 있는 곳, 위치, 상황
[유] location, site
[파] ***situate***: (어떤 장소에) 놓다 ***situated***: 위치하고 있는
[예] He's in a bad situation.

skeleton
[skélətn]
[R] 9593/86800

n. **골격, 해골**
[T] **슥 깰러던(skeleton) -** 슥 깨질 것 같은 **뼈대**
[예] He hung a plastic skeleton on the door for Halloween.

✔ **skeptical**
[sképtikəl]
[R] 78720/86800

adj. **회의적인**
[T] **수갑찰까?(skeptical) - 의심을 품은**, 회의적인
[유] incredulous
[예] She's highly skeptical of the researchers' claims.

✔ skid
[skid]
Ⓡ 27954/86800

n. v. 미끄럼, 미끄러지다
❶ 차 사고 때 **스키드(skid)** 마크(mark) - **미끄러진**
㉠ The shuttle bus skidded on some ice and hit a car.

✔ skill
[skil]
Ⓡ 2804/86800

n. 능숙함, 기술
❶ 수(s - 秀 - 빼어난)**킬(kill): 능숙한** 킬러
㊌ proficiency, expertness ㉥ skillful: 능숙한
㉠ Cooking is a useful skill.

skim
[skim]
Ⓡ 30070/86800

v. 대충 읽다, 스쳐지나가다, 소득을 속이다
❶ **속임(skim)** - 속여 **대충 대충함**
㉠ She only skimmed the reading assignment.

✔ skin
[skin]
Ⓡ 1455/86800

n. 피부, 가죽
❶ **스킨(skin)** 로션은 **피부**를 보호하기 위해 바르는 것
㉠ Potato skin is very nutritious.

skip
[skip]
Ⓡ 10575/86800

v. 가볍게 뛰다, 빼먹다, 거르다
❶ s(수업을)ki(가볍게)p(빼먹다)
㊌ omit: 빼먹다, 거르다
㉠ They skipped her name.

skyscraper
[skáiskrèipə:r]
Ⓡ 42588/86800

n. 고층 건물
❶ **스카이 섰고라파(skyscraper)** - 하늘에 서 있고 싶어라 - **고층 건물**
㉠ A skyscraper is a boast in glass and steel.

✔ slam
[slæm]
Ⓡ 11983/86800

v. 꽝 닫다, 털썩 놓다
❶ 농구에서 **슬램(slam)** 덩크 슛(꽝 하는 슛)
㉠ He slammed the door in my face.

slang
[slæŋ]
Ⓡ 19276/86800

n. 속어
❶ **슬 냄(slang)** - 친구랑 슬슬 내는 말 - **속어**
㉠ 'Chicken' is slang for someone who isn't very brave.

slant
[slænt]
[R] 23930/86800

n. v. **경사, 비스듬하다**
[T] 바로 **서란다(slant) - 비스듬히** 서있는 사람보고 바르게 서란다
[유] slope
[예] She slanted her hat a little to the right.

slave
[sleiv]
[R] 7610/86800

n. **노예**
[T] **술래이 봐(slave** - 술래 봐) - **노예**를 술래에 비유
[파] slavery: 노예 제도
[예] He treats her like a slave.

✔ **sled**
[sled]
[R] 56037/86800

n. **썰매**
[T] 눈에 **쏠려 다(sled)**니는 **썰매**
[예] Sled is a vehicle usually on runners for transportation especially on snow or ice.

sleeve
[sli:v]
[R] 7303/86800

n. v. **소매, 소매를 달다**
[T] **s(손) + leeve(립어):** 손이 옷 입어 - 손 입는 곳은 **소매**
[유] arm
[예] The sleeves are too long for me.

slender
[sléndə:r]
[R] 8482/86800

adj. **가느다란, 호리호리한**
[T] **늘씬한** 여자 보고 **설렌다(slender)**
[유] thin, slim
[예] She has a slender figure.

✔ **slight**
[slait]
[R] 3163/86800

adj. **약간의, 가벼운**
[T] **술 라이트(slight)** - 술을 **가볍게** 한
[파] slightly: 약간, 조금
[예] There is a slight chance of rain.

slim
[slim]
[R] 6006/86800

adj. v. **호리호리한, 가늘게 하다**
[T] **호리호리함**에 눈길이 **쏠림(slim)**
[유] slender
[예] She looked slim and fit for her age.

slip
[slip]
ⓡ 3818/86800

v. n. 미끄러지다, 전표
❶ 슬리퍼(slipper) 생각하면 됨
㉮ slide, glide
㉘ She slipped on the ice.

slope
[sloup]
ⓡ 5533/86800

n. v. 경사, 경사지다
❶ 스키장의 **슬로프(slope)는 경사**
㉮ slant
㉘ His handwriting slopes to the left.

slumber
[slʌ́mbə:r]
ⓡ 27237/86800

n. v. 선 잠, 꾸벅꾸벅 졸다
❶ 보초가 **조느라** 설렁 **설렁 봐(slumber)**
㉮ nap, snooze
㉘ She slumbered for hours while the train rolled on.

sly
[slai]
ⓡ 10957/86800

adj. 교활한
❶ **sly(殺 - 살 아이) - 사람을 죽인 교활한** 아이
㉮ cunning, foxy
㉘ He's a sly old devil - I wouldn't trust him with my money.

smart
[smɑ:rt]
ⓡ 4528/86800

adj. 똑똑한, 쿡쿡 쑤시는
❶ 학교 **秀(수 - 성적) 말(smart) 아 놓은 똑똑한**
㉮ clever, bright
㉘ Poodles are said to be smart dogs.

smooth
[smu:ð]
ⓡ 3049/86800

adj. 부드러운
❶ **스무드(smooth)하게 부드럽게 넘어간다는 말**
㉮ soft, tender ㉙ *smoothly*: 매끈하게
㉘ The milkshake was smooth and creamy.

snap
[snæp]
ⓡ 8357/86800

v. 덥석 물다, 짤깍 소리를 내다
❶ 스냅 샷을 기억하시고 - (덥) **석(s) + 냅다 (nap)** 물다
㉘ She broke the stick over her knee with a loud snap.

snare
[snɛə:r]
® 29912/86800

n. 덫, 함정
❶ 그 여자는 **덫**에 빠질 정도로 **순해여(snare)!**
⊕ trap, gin
例 The hunter took a fox in a snare.

sneer
[sniə:r]
® 20580/86800

v. 비웃다, 냉소하다, 깔보다
❶ 이름이 **순희여(sneer)?** - 뭔가 촌스럽다는 표정으로 **깔보다**
⊕ ridicule, scorn
例 She'll probably sneer at my new shoes because they're not expensive.

sneeze
[sni:z]
® 29439/86800

n. v. 재채기, 재채기하다
❶ 손이 **저(sneeze)**절로 가는 **재채기** - 예의 때문
例 She was constantly sneezing and coughing.

✔ soak
[souk]
® 13763/86800

v. 적시다, 빨아들이다, 스며들다
❶ **쑥(soak) 빨아들이다**
⊕ drench, dip
例 The oil soaked into the wood.

soar
[sɔ:r]
® 18375/86800

v. 높이 치솟다, (물가가) 급등하다
❶ 불꽃놀이를 **쏘아(soar) 높이 치솟다**
⊕ skyrocket, zoom
例 Stock prices are beginning to soar.

sob
[sɑb]
® 18033/86800

v. 흐느껴 울다
❶ 섭섭(sob)해서 흐느껴 울다
⊕ blubber, weep
例 "I hate you," she sobbed.

sober
[sóubə:r]
® 9811/86800

adj. 술 취하지 않은, 착실한
❶ 음주 측정기 **조바(sober)** - 음주 측정기 줘봐! 나 **술 안 취했어**
⊕ stable, sincere: 착실한
例 He is a sober, hardworking farmer.

✔ sociology
[sòusiálədʒi]
Ⓡ 4369/86800

n. 사회학
❶ socio(사회시어) + logy(학문, 이론, 말 - 어원편 참조): 사회학
[파] *sociologist*: 사회학자
[예] She has a degree in sociology and politics.

✔ soil
[sɔil]
Ⓡ 2409/86800

n. 흙, 토양
❶ 소일(soil) - 소가 일하는 곳은 흙
ⓨ earth
[예] The plant prefers a sunny area with well draining soil.

sojourn
[sóudʒə:rn]
Ⓡ 29457/86800

v. 머무르다
❶ 서 전(sojourn) - 서 (대)전에 **머무르다**
ⓨ stay
[예] She sojourns in several countries.

solace
[sáləs]
Ⓡ 22666/86800

n. v. 위안, 위로하다
❶ 쌀 넣었어(solace)하며 서민들 **위로하다**
ⓨ consolation, comfort
[예] Counselors did their best to solace the bereaved children.

✔ solar
[sóulə:r]
Ⓡ 5845/86800

adj. 태양의
❶ 빛을 쏘라(solar) 태양아!
ⓨ heliacal
[예] Solar panels provide a reliable long term solution.

✔ sole
[soul]
Ⓡ 3723/86800

adj. 오직 하나인
❶ 솔로(solo)와 같은 말
ⓨ single
[파] solely: 단독으로 *solitary*: 혼자의 *solitude*: 고독
[예] She was the sole survivor of the tragedy.

✔ solemn
[sáləm]
Ⓡ 11701/86800

adj. 엄숙한
❶ 살 엄(solemn): 살벌하고 **엄숙한**
ⓨ grave, serious
[예] He spoke in a solemn and thoughtful manner.

S

solid
[sálid]
®2695/86800

n. adj. 고체, 단단한
❶ 한쪽으로 **쏠리다(solid)** - 쏠리면 **단단해짐**
유 hard: 단단한 파 *solidness*: 단단함
예 Concrete is a solid material.

solution
[səlúːʃən]
®1489/86800

n. 해결, 용해
❶ **술 로션(solution)** 슬픔이 **용해**만 될 뿐 **해결**은 안 될 걸?
유 resolution, answer
파 *soluble*: 녹는 *solve*: 해결하다, 용해하다
예 Medication may not be the best solution for the patient's condition.

somehow
[sʌ́mhàu]
®2253/86800

adv. 어떻게든, 어쩐지
❶ 어떻게 **좀 하우(somehow)** - **어떻게든** 좀 하세요
예 It won't be easy, but we'll get across the river somehow.

somewhat
[sʌ́mhwɑt]
®2158/86800

adv. 약간
❶ some(약간) + what(왔): 약간 + 무엇 - 무엇이냐면 **약간**
유 slightly
예 Our work has progressed somewhat.

soothe
[suːð]
®20465/86800

v. 위로하다, 진정시키다
❶ 열심히 공부한 아들에게 성적이 **秀 다(soothe)**하면서 **위로하다**
유 comfort, console
예 The waiter tried to soothe the angry customer.

sophisticated
[səfístəkèitid]
®3677/86800

adj. 복잡한, 세련된
❶ sophi(지혜, 지식) + sti(서있다): 지식이 서 있는 복잡한
유 polished, refined: 세련된
예 Her knitting technique is more sophisticated than mine.

sore
[sɔːr]
®7626/86800

a. 아픈
❶ 벌이 **쏘아(sore) 아픈**
유 painful, aching, achy, afflictive, hurting, nasty
예 I have a sore leg.

sorrow
[sárou]
® 10390/86800

n. 슬픔
❶ 서러워(sorrow) - 슬픈가 보네
㊌ sadness, woe 팬 *sorrowful*: 슬픈
㉣ I felt sorrow at the death of my friend.

sort
[sɔːrt]
® 434/86800

n. v. 종류, 분류하다
❶ 분류해 놓으니 **수월타(sort)** - 수월하다
㊌ kind, class
㉣ What sort of car do you drive?

soul
[soul]
® 3162/86800

n. 혼, 정신
❶ 자동차 이름 **쏘울(soul)**은 **혼**이 담긴 작품
㊌ spirit
㉣ She suffered greatly while she was alive, so let us hope her soul is now at peace.

sour
[sáuə:r]
® 9359/86800

adj. (맛이) 신
❶ 맛이 **시워(sour)** - 맛이 **신**
㊌ acerbic, tart
㉣ The milk had turned sour.

source
[sɔːrs]
® 1127/86800

n. 원천, 출처
❶ source(쏠써 - 출처) - 발음 참 비슷하네!!!!
㊌ origin
㉣ His job is the family's main source of income.

souvenir
[sùːvəníər]
® 16620/86800

n. 기념품
❶ 여행가면 **기념품 수반 해여(souvenir)!**
㉣ When I went to the Super Bowl, I kept my ticket stub as a souvenir.

sovereign
[sávərin]
® 6651/86800

n. adj. 주권자, 주권을 가진
❶ 마음에 안 들면 **싸 버린(sovereign) 통치자**
㊌ ruler
㉣ We must respect the rights of sovereign states/nations to conduct their own affairs.

S

sow
[sou]
ⓡ 14773/86800

v. (씨를) 뿌리다
❶ s (씨)ow(우): 씨를 뿌리다
⊕ scatter
예 Every year we sow corn.

spacious
[spéiʃəs]
ⓡ 9418/86800

adj. 널찍한
❶ 널찍한 쇼파있었셔(spacious)
⊕ roomy, capacious 파 space: 공간, 우주
예 Almost all of the guests were able to fit into the spacious living room.

spank
[spæŋk]
ⓡ 65722/86800

v. (체벌로 손으로) 엉덩이를 찰싹 때리다
❶ 손(s)으로 빵(pank)엉덩이를 때리다
예 She spanked her child several times as a punishment.

spare
[spɛə:r]
ⓡ 3201/86800

v. adj. 절약하다, 여분의
❶ (용돈) 서 빼어(spare) 절약하다
⊕ economize, save 파 sparing: 알뜰한
예 Have you got a spare pen?

sparkle
[spá:rkəl]
ⓡ 15805/86800

n. v. 불꽃, 불꽃을 튀기다
❶ 스파크(sparkle) 튀긴다는 말 기억하면 되 셈
파 sparkling: 불꽃을 튀기는
예 The snow sparkled in the sunlight.

specialist
[spéʃəlist]
ⓡ 2420/86800

n. 전문가
❶ special(특별한) + ist(사람): 특별한 일만하는 사람
⊕ expert
c.f) specific: 구체적인, 특정한 specifically: 구체적으로
　　specificity: 특이성
파 specialize: 전문화하다 special: 특별한
　　specialization: 전문화 specially: 특별히 specialty: 전문
예 He saw a specialist for his foot problem.

species
[spíːʃi(ː)z]
® 1062/86800

n. 생물의 종
❶ 숲에셔(species) - 숲에서 다양한 **생물 종** 발견
예 There are approximately 8,000 species of ants.

spectacle
[spéktəkəl]
® 9657/86800

n. 광경, 장관
❶ spect(보다 - 어원편 참조) + cle(껄): 볼걸 장관
㊤ scene, sight
파 *spectacular*: 장관의 *spectator*: 구경꾼
예 We witnessed the extraordinary spectacle of an old lady climbing a tree to rescue her cat.

speculate
[spékjəlèit]
® 12243/86800

v. 깊이 생각하다
❶ spec(보다) + late(늦게로 생각): 늦게까지 깊이 생각하고 보다
㊤ ponder deliberate
예 She could only speculate about her friend's motives.

spell
[spel]
® 3877/86800

v. n. 철자로 쓰다, 한동안 지속
❶ 스펠링(spelling)이라는 말은 다 아실 테고 **spell(소뻴 - 소뼈) 한 동안 지속**해서 고아야 함
c.f) rainy spell: 우기
파 *spelling*: 철자법
예 I lived in London for a spell.

spend
[spend]
® 1375/86800

v. 돈을 쓰다, 시간을 보내다
❶ 스페인 다(spend)구경하는데 **돈쓰고 시간 보내다**
㊤ consume, expend
예 I spent $30 on his birthday gift.

sphere
[sfiəːr]
® 6085/86800

n. 구(球)형
❶ sphere(공, 구형 - 어원편 참조)
㊤ globe
예 All points on a sphere are the same distance from the center.

S

spice
[spais]
® 13655/86800

n. v. 양념, 양념하다
❶ 슢(s) 파있어(pice) - 스프에 파 있어 - 파로 **양념하다**
⊕ flavor, seasoning
예 Cinnamon, ginger and cloves are all spices.

spill
[spil]
® 11264/86800

v. 엎지르다
❶ 스플(spill) - 스프를 **엎지르다**
⊕ slop
예 I accidentally spilled coffee all over my new suit.

spin
[spin]
® 7488/86800

v. 실을 잣다, 뱅뱅 돌다
❶ s(실) + pin(뺀): 실을 자으려(뽑으려) 실을 뺀
⊕ twirl, whirl: 뱅뱅 돌다
예 I tried to stand up but the room was spinning.

❤ spirit
[spírit]
® 1591/86800

n. 정신, 마음, 영혼
❶ spir(숨 - 어원편 참조) + it(있): 숨이 있다 - 정신 한국군이 미군과
하는 team spirit 훈련
⊕ mind, soul 파 *spiritual*: 정신의, 영혼의
예 The spirits of long - dead warriors seemed to haunt
the area.

spit
[spit]
® 11716/86800

v. 침을 뱉다
❶ 서(s) 뱉(pit): 서서 **침을 뱉다**
예 Bob Ewell spat contemptuously right in the lawyer's
face.

❤ spite
[spait]
® 18681/86800

n. v. 악의, 괴롭히다
❶ 스파이 다!(spite)면 **악의를** 품은 간첩
예 She is jealous and full of spite.

✔ splash
[splæʃ]
® 10796/86800

v. (물을) 튀기다
❶ 서(s) 뿌려서(plash) - 서서 뿌려서 **물을 튀기다**
⊕ dabble
예 The baby splashed the water.

408

splendid
[spléndid]
® 4868/86800

adj. 빛나는, 훌륭한
❶ **숲 불란다(splendid)** - 숲이 불나서 **빛이 나는**
⊛ glorious
예 I have some splendid news.

split
[split]
® 2526/86800

v. 쪼개다, 나누다
❶ 나무를 s(세계)**뿌러(plit)** 쪼개다
⊛ cleave, divide
예 The board split in two.

spoil
[spɔil]
® 9580/86800

v. 망치다
❶ **섯뿌일(spoil): 섯** 불리 **일 망치다**
⊛ ruin, destroy
예 The fight spoiled the party.

sponge
[spʌndʒ]
® 11415/86800

n. 스펀지, 해면동물
❶ **스펀지(sponge)**는 일상에 자주 쓰이는 말 임
예 The bodies of sponges consist of jelly-like mesohyl sandwiched between two thin layers of cells.

sponsor
[spánsə:r]
® 8768/86800

n. v. 후원자, 광고주, 후원하다
❶ 짤린 **서판사(sponsor - 서씨 판사)를 후원하다**
⊛ supporter, patron
예 Our company is a sponsor of the race.

spontaneous
[spɑntéiniəs]
® 6924/86800

adj. 자발적인
❶ **스판 떼니 옷이(spontaneous): 스판** 옷은 **자발적**으로 늘어나는
⊛ voluntary
예 He's a guy who's spontaneous and fun.

spot
[spɑt]
® 2081/86800

n. v. 장소(현장), 반점, 발견하다
❶ **세파트(spot - 개**의 종류)가 **현장**에서 마약을 **발견하다**
⊛ place, point
예 I noticed some red spots on my arms.

S

spread
[spred]
ⓡ 1630/86800

v. n. 퍼지다, 퍼뜨리다, 확산
❶ 水(수) 뿌리다(spread) - 물 뿌리다, 퍼지다
ⓢ disseminate, diffuse
ⓔ The cancer has spread to her throat.

spring
[spriŋ]
ⓡ 1712/86800

n. v. 봄, 샘, 용수철, 튀어 오르다
❶ 샘이라는 뜻으로 솟뿌림(spring) - 솟구쳐 물을 뿌림, 봄, 용수철
이라는 뜻도 있음
ⓢ fountain: 샘
ⓔ The cushion has lost its spring.

sprinter
[sprintər]
ⓡ 22017/86800

n. 단거리 육상 선수
❶ 단거리 육상 선수가 총알같이 달리다가 결승점에서 섯버린다
(sprinter)
ⓔ Jamaica has a lot of world - class sprinters.

sprout
[spraut]
ⓡ 23809/86800

n. 싹
❶ s(슬슬) + pr(풀) + out(바깥으로): 슬슬 조그만 풀 같은 것이 밖
으로 나오면 싹
ⓢ bud
ⓔ The raspberry bushes began sending out sprouts in
early spring.

spur
[spə:r]
ⓡ 11585/86800

n. v. 박차, 격려, 박차를 가하다
❶ 이를 악물고 스펄(spur - 약간 원한이 섞인 욕을 내 뱉고) 두고
보자하며 복수에 박차를 가하다
ⓢ encouragement: 격려
ⓔ Rising consumer sales have the effect of spurring the
economy to faster growth.

square
[skwɛə:r]
ⓡ 1448/86800

n. 정사각형, 광장, 제곱
❶ 뉴욕의 time square(타임 스퀘어 - 광장)와 엠씨 스퀘어(MC^2) 생
각하고 기억하세요
ⓢ plaza: 광장
ⓔ Cut the brownies into squares.

squeeze
[skwi:z]
®️ 6985/86800

v. n. 짜다, 죄다, 압착
❶ 쎈(s) 퀴즈(queeze)내자 알아맞히려고 머리를 쥐어 **짜다**
㊌ wring
㈜ He squeezed the juice from the orange.

squirrel
[skwə́:rəl]
®️ 18001/86800

n. 다람쥐
❶ **다람쥐**처럼 도망 말고 **섯 거라(squirrel)**!!
㈜ There are so many squirrels in New State.

stable
[stéibl]
®️ 2862/86800

adj. n. 안정된, 마구간
❶ st(stand가 줄은 말) + able(~할 수 있는): 설 수 있는 - **안정적인**
㊌ firm, steady
㈜ Children need to be raised in a stable environment.

staff
[stæf]
®️ 405/86800

n. 직원
❶ sta(서 있는) - 서 있는 사람, 영화배우들이 상 받고 소감 말할 때 꼭 하는 말이 있다. "감독님 그리고 스탭 여러 분께 감사하다"고
㊌ employee, personnel
㈜ The entire staff has done a great job this year.

stage
[steidʒ]
®️ 583/86800

n. 무대, 단계
❶ 아기가 **섰대지(stage)**? 기어 다니다 **단계**가 돼서, 또 가수 **서태지(stage)**가 **무대**에서
㊌ step, phase: 단계
㈜ The actors walked out onto the stage.

stain
[stein]
®️ 11255/86800

n. v. 얼룩, 더러운 때, 더럽히다
❶ 순(s) 때인(tain) - 옷 이 순전히 때(얼룩) 인
㊌ blot, smear
㈜ She has a stain on her shirt.

stair
[stɛə:r]
®️ 13653/86800

n. 계단
❶ **계단**에 올라 **섯데여(stair)**
㈜ Go up the stairs and my office is on the right.

S

stake
[steik]
® 4107/86800

n. v. 말뚝, 내기(상금), 경계를 표시하다
❶ 숯 테이크(stake) - 숯(s)을 가져와서(take) 경계를 표시하다, 이 게임은 스테이크 내기야
⊕ post, picket
예 a poker game with high stakes.

stall
[stɔ:l]
® 7889/86800

n. 마굿간, 매점
❶ 마굿간에 말 뿐 아니라 소 도(stall)?
예 The horse lay in his stall.

standpoint
[stǽndpɔ̀int]
® 15426/86800

n. 입장, 관점
❶ stand(서있다) + point(요점, 점): 서서 보는 것 - 입장, 관점
⊕ viewpoint, angle: 관점
예 I never thought about it from that standpoint before.

staple
[stéipəl]
® 14189/86800
.

adj. n. 중요한, 중요 산물
❶ 스타 플(staple)레이어는 팀에 중요한
⊕ important, essential
예 The staple diet here is mutton, fish and boiled potatoes.

stare
[stɛə:r]
® 6336/86800

v. 빤히 보다, 응시하다
❶ 빤히 나를 보고 섰대여(stare)!
⊕ eye, watch
예 She stared out the window.

startle
[stá:rtl]
® 35991/86800

v. 깜짝 놀라게 하다
❶ 우리 집 앞에 스타틀(startle)이 나타나 깜짝 놀라게 했다
⊕ frighten, shock
예 I'm sorry that I startled you.

starve
[stɑ:rv]
® 16534/86800

v. 굶주리다
❶ 탐관오리의 수탈 봐(starve) - 수탈(강제로 빼앗음) 때문에 굶주리다
⊕ famish 파 *starvation*: 굶주림
예 Without food they would starve.

❤ state
[steit]
Ⓡ 215/86800

n. v. **국가, 상태, 말하다**
❶ United States (미 합중국), 밥은 **솥에 있(state)** 다고 **말하다**
⊕ country, nation
㈜ stately: 당당한 statement: 진술 statesman: 정치가
㈈ Happiness is the state or condition of being happy.

❤ static
[stǽtik]
Ⓡ 6224/86800

adj. **정적인**
❶ sta(stand - 서 있는) + ic(형용사형 어미): 그냥 서있는 정적인
⊕ quiet, calm ⊖ dynamic
㈈ Oil prices have remained static for the last few months.

statistics
[stətístiks]
Ⓡ 3010/86800

n. **통계, 통계학**
❶ **숫따 띠어서틱(statistic)** - 숫자들 떼어서 자료를 제시하는 것은 **통계**
㈜ statistical: 통계의
㈈ Statistics are an effective way of predicting things.

✓ statue
[stǽtʃu:]
Ⓡ 7470/86800

n. **상, 조소상**
❶ **섰댔쥬(statue)** - 서 있었데 **동상**이
㈜ stature: 키, 신장 *status*: 지위, 상태
㈈ They planned to put up/erect a statue to the President.

❤ steadfast
[stédfæ̀st]
Ⓡ 40174/86800

adj. **확고한**
❶ **스타다봤었다(steadfast)** - 스타다 내가 봤었다(내가 봤었다니 그 만큼 **확실한**)
⊕ firm, definite
㈜ *steady*: 꾸준한 *steadily*: 꾸준히
㈈ The group remained steadfast in its support for him.

✓ steal
[sti:l]
Ⓡ 7659/86800

v. **훔치다**
❶ 야구에서 도루 한다는 말 - **스틸(steal)**한다 함
⊕ rob, snatch
㈈ She was so poor she had to steal something.

S

413

steel
[sti:l]
ⓡ 2458/86800

n. adj. 강철, 강철의
❶ 축구 팀 포항 **스틸러**(steeler)스 생각하면 포항제철 팀이므로 **강철**(철자 e가 겹쳤으므로 더 단단한 강철이 된다고 기억하세요)
㉠ I bought a steel helmet yesterday.

steep
[sti:p]
ⓡ 5068/86800

adj. 가파른, 터무니없이 비싼
❶ **솟띠**(steep) - 솟아 있으면 **가파른**, 가격이 솟으면 **터무니없이 비싼**
⊕ sheer
㉠ The resort is set on a steep hill.

steer
[stiə:r]
ⓡ 10443/86800

v. 조종하다
❶ 차 **섰디여?**(steer) - 차를 정지하게 **조종하다**
⊕ handle, control
㉠ My car is very easy to steer.

stem
[stem]
ⓡ 6026/86800

n. v. 줄기, 유래하다
❶ 길거리에서 **샀뎀**(stem) - (길거리에서) **유래하다**
⊕ trunk, stalk
㉠ The melon is growing but its stem is shriveling.

sterile
[stéril]
ⓡ 13161/86800

adj. 메마른, 불모의
❶ **불모지**에서 **스타를**(sterile) 만들어 내다
⊕ barren, waste ⊖ fertile
㉠ The drug made us sterile couple.

stern
[stə:rn]
ⓡ 8293/86800

adj. 엄격한
❶ **秀(수) 딴**(stern) - **엄격**한 방식으로 공부해 수(수, 우, 미, 양, 가) 딴
⊕ strict, severe
㉠ The teacher gave us a stern look.

stick
[stik]
ⓡ 2317/86800

n. v. 막대기, 찌르다
❶ 치즈 **스틱**(stick) - 치즈를 넣어 튀긴 막대기 모양의 음식, 스틱은 **막대기**
⊕ cane ㉟ *sticker*: 찌르는 연장(막대기), 스티커
㉠ According to witness, the victim had been beaten with a stick.

✔ **stiff**
[stif]
ⓡ 5174/86800

adj. 뻣뻣한, 굳은
❶ 뻣뻣하게 섯(s)띠?(tiff) - 뻣뻣하게 섰지?
㈜ *stiffly*: 딱딱하게 *stiffen*: 뻣뻣하게 하다
㈀ My mother's back was stiff as a board.

stifle
[stáifəl]
ⓡ 20216/86800

v. 숨 막히게 하다
❶ 스타(st)입을(ifle)막아 **숨 막히게 하다**
㈜ suffocate, choke
㈀ I almost stifled in the heat of the Africa.

✔ **still**
[stil]
ⓡ 121/86800

adv. adj. 여전히, 더욱, 정지한, 그러나
❶ 소띨(still) - 소(s)는 여전히 떨띨(till)한
㈜ motionless, stationary: 정지한 ㈜ *stillness*: 고요
㈀ Do you still go to school?

✔ **stimulate**
[stímjəlèit]
ⓡ 6927/86800

v. 자극하다
❶ s(쎈) + timulate(침을 넣다): 쎈 침을 놓아 **자극하다**
㈜ excite, incite ㈜ stimulus: 자극 *stimulation*: 자극
㈀ The American economy was not stimulated by several actions.

sting
[stiŋ]
ⓡ 10305/86800

n. v. 쏘기, (동식물이) 침, 가시 등으로 쏘다
❶ 벌이 쏘(s)면 띵(ting)하다
㈀ He got stung by a bee.

stingy
[stíndʒi][stíɲi]
ⓡ 49252/86800

adj. 인색한, 벌이 쏘는
❶ 돈을 쓰디안지(stingy) - 돈을 쓰지 않는
㈜ miserly
㈀ The owner is so stingy that he didn't give me a raise.

✔ **stink**
[stiŋk]
ⓡ 19191/86800

v. n. 고약한 냄새가 나다, 악취
❶ 쏟디(st) 잉크(ink) - 잉크가 쏟아져 **냄새 나다**
㈜ stench: 악취
㈀ My mother told me that "Your feet stink!"

S

stir
[stə:r]
® 6291/86800

v. 휘젓다, 움직이다
❶ 숟(s)떠(tir) - 숟가락을 떠 휘젓다
예 Stir one spoon of sugar into the tea.

stock
[stɑk]
® 1277/86800

n. v. 줄기, 재고, 주식, 비축하다
❶ 쌓닥(stock) - 쌓다, 재고, stock market(주식 시장)
⊕ store, reserve
예 The MP3 is out of stock.
The supermarket is stocked with various items.

stockpile
[stákpàil]
® 30836/86800

n. 비축, 재고
❶ stock(재고) + pile(쌓다)
예 We have a stockpile of weapons and ammunition that will last several months.

stomach
[stʌ́mək]
® 3159/86800

n. 위, 배
❶ 솥다 먹(stomach) - 솥의 음식 다 먹은 위
⊕ belly: 배
예 The thief punched his stomach.

stoop
[stu:p]
® 22115/86800

v. 몸을 굽히다
❶ 솥뚜(stoop): 솥뚜껑에 몸 굽히고 밥하는 엄마
⊕ bend, bow
예 The doorway was so low that I had to stoop to go through it.

storage
[stɔ́:ridʒ]
® 3206/86800

n. 저장, 보관
❶ store(저장하다, 가게) + age(명사형 어미): 저장
⊕ keeping, preservation 파 *store*: 저장(하다)
예 My house is much smaller, so I had to rent additional storage.

stout
[staut]
® 10253/86800

adj. 단단한, 튼튼한
❶ (동네에) 튼튼한 다리가 섰다우(stout)
⊕ solid, firm
예 I have a stout heart.

straight
[streit]
[R] 1023/86800

adj. 곧은, 일직선의
[T] 섰데레이(straight) - 곧게 섰더란다
[유] upright
[예] He has short, straight hair.

straightforward
[strèitfɔ́:rwə:rd]
[R] 4358/86800

a. 정직한, 직접적인
[T] straight(똑바른) + forward(앞 쪽의): 정직한, 직접적인
[유] direct, clear - cut, forthright: 솔직한
[예] She was very straightforward with me.

strain
[strein]
[R] 3577/86800

v. n. 긴장시키다, 잡아당기다, 긴장
[T] 나를 긴장시킨 건 스트레인(strain - 스트레스인)
[유] tense: 긴장시키다 pull, draw: 잡아당기다
[예] As you get older, excess weight puts a lot of strain on the heart.

strait
[streit]
[R] 20802/86800

n. 해협
[T] the Straits of Dover - 도버해협, 해협은 좁고 긴 바다
[유] channel
[예] Do you know the Straits of Dover?

strategy
[strǽtədʒi]
[R] 1675/86800

n. 전략, 전술
[T] 전략이 좋아야 적을 쓰트러티지(strategy) - 적을 쓰러트리지
[유] tactics: 전술
[예] I'm working on new strategies to improve my GPA.

S

stream
[stri:m]
[R] 3556/86800

n. v. 개울, 흐름, 흐르다
[T] 水 들임(stream): 개울가에 모여 있는 것은 水 들임(물 들임)
[예] There's a lovely stream that flows through my garden.

strength
[streŋə]
[R] 1439/86800

n. 힘
[T] 어제 힘 좀 쓰더렝(strength): 너 어제 힘 좀 쓰더라
[유] power, might [파] *strengthen*: 강하게 하다
[예] He was deeply impressed by my strength.

strenuous
[strénjuəs]
® 15113/86800

adj. 열심히 노력하는

❶ 秀(수)또 내뉴? 어서(strenuous): 열심히 노력하니 수(성적표의 수)를 또 내니 어서?

예 My doctor advised me not to take any strenuous exercise.

❤ stress
[stres]
® 2080/86800

n. v. 압박, 강세, 강조하다

❶ 스트레스(stress) 받는다, 이 단어가 스트레스(stress - 강세)가 어디 있니?

㋐ accent: 강세 ㋙ *stressful*: 긴장이 많은

예 Table tennis is a very effective exercise for combating stress.

❤ stretch
[stretʃ]
® 3592/86800

v. n. 잡아당기다, 뻗음

❶ 스트레칭(stretching) 체육시간에 해보셨죠? 몸을 쭉 **잡아당겨** 줍니다

㋐ spread: 뻗음

예 I stretched out my hand to catch pillow.

✔ strict
[strikt]
® 4197/86800

adj. 엄격한

❶ 각서 썼더 릭?(strict) - 각서 쓰게 **엄격한**

㋐ severe, stern ㋙ strictly: 엄격히, 엄밀히

예 My high school teacher was very strict with me.

stride
[straid]
® 10022/86800

v. n. 성큼성큼 걷다, 성큼성큼 걷기

❶ 속(s)도(t)라이드(ride): 속도내서 버스를 라이드 하려고(ride - 타려고)**성큼 성큼 걷다**

㋐ stalk

예 I strode across the office towards her.

strife
[straif]
® 15860/86800

n. 투쟁

❶ 숱도(st)라이프(rife) - "밥 하는 것도 일생이냐?" 월급을 달라며 엄마가 **투쟁**하시다

㋐ fight, conflict

예 Civil strife has left this country's economy in ruins.

418

✔ strike
[straik]
ⓡ 1807/86800

v. n. **때리다, 인상을 주다, 타격, 파업, 야구의 삼진**
❶ 야구의 **스트라이크(strike)는** 잘 던진다는 **인상을 줍니다**
㊦ hit, beat
㈜ *strikingly*: 현저하게 *striking*: 현저한
㈎ I'm striking for a reduction in the working week.

✔ string
[striŋ]
ⓡ 3340/86800

n. **끈, 열**
❶ **실(s) + 뜨링(tring): 실**을 늘어뜨림
㊦ cord
㈎ I tied the books together with string.

✔ strive
[straiv]
ⓡ 14000/86800

v. **노력하다, 애쓰다**
❶ 자취생이 **솥(s)드라이브(trive): 솥** 뚜껑으로 드라이브하려고 **애쓰다**
㊦ endeavor
㈎ She always strives for beauty.

✔ stroke
[strouk]
ⓡ 4987/86800

n. v. **한 번 타격, 일 필, 뇌졸중, 쓰다듬다**
❶ 테니스 칠 때 **스트로크(stroke)한다는** 말이 **타격**한다는 말입니다, 뇌졸중도 갑자기 뇌가 타격을 입고 혈액순환 장애를 일으키는 병이죠
㈎ Nadal has a strong backhand stroke.

stroll
[stroul]
ⓡ 11160/86800

v. **한가롭게 거닐다**
❶ **숲(s) + 들을(troll): 숲** 들을 한가롭게 거닐다
㈎ Our couple strolled the streets of Buffalo New York.

✔ structure
[strʌ́ktʃə:r]
ⓡ 709/86800

n. **구조**
❶ 튼튼한 **구조** 덕분에 **섰더랬죠(structure): 구조**가 튼튼해야 설수 있다는 뜻
㊦ construction
㈜ structural: 구조상의
㈎ English structure is a piece of cake.

S

419

struggle
[strʌ́gəl]
Ⓡ 2286/86800

v. n. 애쓰다, 싸우다, 노력, 분투
❶ 썼더라 글(struggle): 싸우는 사람이 '투쟁'이라는 글 머리띠에 썼더라
㊌ strive, battle: 싸우다
㊐ Many women struggled for the right to vote.

stubborn
[stʌ́bəːrn]
Ⓡ 12429/86800

adj. 고집 센
❶ 소 도 본(stubborn)래 고집이 센
㊌ obstinate 파 *stubbornly*: 완고하게
㊐ I was a stubborn child when I was young.

stuff
[stʌf]
Ⓡ 1427/86800

n. v. 재료, 소지품, 채워 넣다
❶ 재료는 뭘 썼답(stuff)니까?
㊌ material(s), matter
㊐ There's sticky stuff all over the room.

stumble
[stʌ́mbəl]
Ⓡ 19206/86800

v. 넘어지다, 비틀거리다, 말을 더듬다
❶ 숲 덤불(stumble) 에 걸려 넘어지다
㊌ fall, tumble
㊐ I stumbled and almost fell.

stun
[stʌn]
Ⓡ 32324/86800

v. 기절시키다
❶ 사탄(stun)을 기절시키다
㊐ Incredible News stunned people throughout the Korea.

sturdy
[stə́ːrdi]
Ⓡ 11736/86800

a. 튼튼한
❶ 스트(st) 롱 하디(urdy)? - 튼튼하지?
㊐ I need a sturdy table.

subconscious
[sʌbkánʃəs]
Ⓡ 15551/86800

n. adj. 잠재의식, 잠재의식의
❶ sub(아래 - 어원 편 참조) + conscious(의식적인): 의식 아래있는 즉 잠재의식의
㊐ The love story was buried deep within my subconscious.

subdue
[səbdjú:]
Ⓡ 27330/86800

v. **정복하다, 복종시키다**
[T] sub(아래에) + due(두): 아래에 둔다 - 복종시키다
[유] conquer, subjugate
[예] They criticized the company for trying to subdue individual expression.

subject
[sʌ́bdʒikt]
Ⓡ 532/86800

n. adj. **주제, 과목, 지배를 받는, 복종하는**
[T] sub(아래에) + ject(쏘아둔 것): 아래에 놓여 있는 당면한 과제
[파] subjective: 주관적인 be subject to + 동사: ~하기 쉽다
[예] If you're interested in applied linguistics, I know an excellent University program on the subject.

sublime
[səbláim]
Ⓡ 16368/86800

adj. **웅대한, 숭고한**
[T] **숭고한** 정신을 가진 사람은 **써볼 아(사람)임(sublime)**
[유] noble: 숭고한
[예] Mountain Kumgang has sublime scenery.

submarine
[sʌ́bmərì:n]
Ⓡ 10999/86800

n. **잠수함**
[T] sub(아래) + marine(바다의): 바다 밑의 잠수함
[예] Nuclear submarine has been dispatched to Korean peninsula.

submit
[səbmít]
Ⓡ 6118/86800

v. **제출하다, 복종하다**
[T] sub(아래로) + mit(보내다 - 어원 편 참조) 제출하다, 복종하다
[유] present [파] submission: 제출, 복종
[예] He must submit his application before February 1st.

subordinate
[səbɔ́:rdənit]
Ⓡ 7765/86800

adj. n. v. **하위의, 종속의, 하급자, 하위에 두다**
[T] sub(아래) + ordinate(ordinary로 생각하면 보통의): 보통 보다 아래의 - **하위의**
[유] junior
[예] Your needs are subordinate to those of the company.

S

✔ **subscribe**
[səbskráib]
Ⓡ 13679/86800

v. **기부하다, 서명하다, 구독하다**
[T] sub(아래) + scribe(쓰다 - 어원편 참조): 아래에 쓰다, 기부하려고 서명하다
[파] ***subscription***: 기부, 구독
[예] The president subscribed $500,000 for the new school.

subsequent
[sʌ́bsikwənt]
Ⓡ 2344/86800

adj. **차후의**
[T] sub(아래) + sequent(연속의): 연속적인 것 그 다음의
[유] coming [파] subsequently: 후에
[예] Subsequent studies confirmed his invention.

subside
[səbsáid]
Ⓡ 31065/86800

v. **가라앉다, 진정되다**
[T] sub(아래에) + side(편들다): 아래쪽으로 가다, 가라앉다, 진정되다
[유] sink
[예] The laughter subsided in our class.

✔ **substance**
[sʌ́bstəns]
Ⓡ 4012/86800

n. **물질, 실체**
[T] sub(아래) + stance(서있음): 밑에 근본적으로 깔려있는 것은 물질
[유] material, matter [파] substantial: 실질적인
[예] The strange bag has several illegal substances.

✔ **substitute**
[sʌ́bstitjù:t]
Ⓡ 4565/86800

v. n. **대신하다, 대리인, 대용품**
[T] sub(아래에) + stitude(서 있다): 어떤 것이 문제가 있을 때 아래에 서서 대체하다
[유] replace [파] substitution: 대용
[예] Mr. Lee was substituted for Mr. Hwang in the first half of the match.

✔ **subtle**
[sʌ́tl]
Ⓡ 4631/86800

adj. **미묘한**
[T] **섭들(subtle** - 섭섭하게 들릴)섭섭하게 들릴지도 모르지만 하고 **미묘한** (감정을 섞다)
[유] delicate: 섬세한
[예] There is a subtle difference between two cars.

✔ subtract
[səbtrǽkt]
ⓡ 24361/86800

v. 빼다
❶ sub(아래) + tract(당기다 - 어원편 참조): 아래로 끌어당기면 하나가 빠짐
㊌ deduct, subduct ㉥ subtraction: 빼기
㉙ Nine subtracted from twenty equals eleven.

✔ suburb
[sʌ́bəːrb]
ⓡ 11741/86800

n. 교외, 도시 주변 주택지
❶ sub(아래) + urb(urban을 줄인 말로 도시의): 도시 아래있는 곳은 교외
㊌ outskirts ㉥ suburban: 교외의
㉙ Kenmore is a suburb of western New York.

succession
[səkséʃən]
ⓡ 4534/86800

n. 연속, 계승
❶ suc(=sub - 아래) + cess(가다) + sion(명사형 어미): 아래로 감, 계승
㊌ series
㉥ successive: 연속하는 successor: 후계자
㉙ Life was an endless succession of love and pain.

✔ suck
[sʌk]
ⓡ 12268/86800

v. 빨다
❶ 쑥(suck) 쑥 빨다
㉙ A vacuum cleaner sucks up water as well as dirt.

✔ suddenly
[sʌ́dnli]
ⓡ 841/86800

n. 갑자기
❶ 갑자기 왜 서두니(suddenly)? - 서두르니?
㊌ all of a sudden, on a sudden, abruptly
㉥ *sudden*: 갑작스런
㉙ The accident happened so suddenly that I didn't remember it.

✔ suffer
[sʌ́fər]
ⓡ 2825/86800

v. 고통을 겪다
❶ 슬(s)프고 아퍼(uffer); 슬프고 아프다
㊌ agonize
㉙ I suffered from asthma when I was in America.

S

✔ sufficient
[səfíʃənt]
Ⓡ 1732/86800

adj. **충분한**
[T] **suf(아래에) + fic(만들 다):** 아래에 대체해서 만들 것이 있는 충분한
[유] enough [반] short, insufficient
[파] ***sufficiently***: 충분히
sufficiency: 충분한 상태
[예] What is sufficient evidence to convict him?

suffrage
[sʌ́fridʒ]
Ⓡ 13502/86800

n. **투표, 투표권**
[T] **사표라지?(suffrage):** 내가 **투표**한 게 死표라지?(사표는 낙선한 후보에게 던진 표)
[유] ballot, vote
[예] There were black women for fought for suffrage in the past.

✔ suggest
[səgdʒést]
Ⓡ 1149/86800

v. **제안하다, 암시하다**
[T] **써(su) + ggest(제시**하다**):** 써서 **제시하다**
[유] propose [파] ***suggestion***: 제안
[예] Could you suggest where I might find a cheap airplane ticket?

suicide
[sú:əsàid]
Ⓡ 4707/86800

n. v. **자살, 자살하다**
[T] **sui(자기 자신 - 어원편 참조) + cide(죽이다 - 어원편 참조):** 자기를 죽이다 - **자살하다**
[유] self - murder
[예] A lot of suicides occur in Han river.

✔ suit
[su:t]
Ⓡ 2021/86800

n. v. **소송, 정장, 적합하게 하다, 어울리다**
[T] **suit(수트) - 수트라는 말은 정장**이라는 말로 일상에서도 많이 쓰는 말. 수트가 잘 어울리네. **소트(suit) - 소송을 트다** 등으로 기억하면 좋겠어요
[유] clothes: 옷, lawsuit, case: 소송
[파] ***suitable***: 알맞은, 어울리는 suitcase: 여행 가방
[예] You go well with dark suit.

✔ **suit**
[suːt]
[R] 2021/86800

n. v. **소송, 옷 한 벌, 적합하게 하다**
[T] 멋진 **수트(suit - 옷)**를 입은 젊은 오빠
[예] Young guy wore a dark blue suit.

sullen
[sʌ́lən]
[R] 17685/86800

adj. **시무룩한**
[T] 나이가 **서른(sullen)**인데 애인이 없으니 **시무룩한**
[유] gloomy, moody
[예] I'm sick and tired of sullen skies.

✔ **sum**
[sʌm]
[R] 2289/86800

n. v. **총계, 총계하다, 요약하다**
[T] 수학의 S(총계)와 **써머리(요약)** 생각할 것
[예] I'll get $100,000 from the company when I retire, which is a large sum.

✔ **summary**
[sʌ́məri]
[R] 3295/86800

n. adj. **요약, 요약한**
[T] 얼굴 사진이 사람을 요약한 것 처럼 **소머리(summary)는** 소를 **요약한 것**
[유] outline: 요약, brief, succinct: 요약한
[파] *sum*: 합계, 금액, 요약하다 *summarize*: 요약하다
[예] The policeman hand in a summary account of the accident to judge.

✔ **summit**
[sʌ́mit]
[R] 3603/86800

n. **정상, 수뇌부**
[T] **summit (수하 밑)** - 수하들이 밑에 있는 **수뇌**
[유] apex
[예] The seven summit talks will be held in Jeju.

summon
[sʌ́mən]
[R] 13973/86800

v. **소환하다**
[T] **summon(소 만):** 발음이 비슷하므로 소만**(소환)하다**로 기억
[유] convene
[예] The president summoned a commander back to the White House.

S

✔ **sundae**
[sʌ́ndei]
ⓡ 81853/86800

n. 과일과 시럽을 얹은 아이스크림
❶ 맥도날드에서 파는 **선데(sundae) 아이스크림**
예 Macdonalds sell sundae ice - cream.

✔ **sundial**
[sʌ́ndàiəl]
ⓡ 30216/86800

n. 해시계
❶ sun(태양) + dial(시계의 **문자반)**: 태양이 돌아가는 것
예 Sundial is an instrument to show the time of day by Sun.

✔ **sunspot**
[sʌ́nspàt]
ⓡ 58809/86800

n. 태양의 흑점
❶ sun (태양) + spot(점)
예 Sunspot is a dark spot that sometimes appear on the surface of the Sun.

superb
[su:pə́:rb]
ⓡ 4176/86800

adj. 훌륭한, 멋진
❶ super(최고, 지나친, 위에서, 뛰어난, 표면의 - 어원편 참조) + b: 최고의, 뛰어난
⊕ excellent, magnificent, marvelous,
예 I'm a superb student.

✔ **superbly**
[su:pə́:rbli]
ⓡ 13527/86800

ad. 훌륭하게, 멋지게
❶ superb(최고의, 훌륭한) + ly(부사형어미)
예 Seoul symphony orchestra played superbly.

superficial
[sù:pərfíʃəl]
ⓡ 8457/86800

adj. 표면적인, 피상적인
❶ super(표면의, 최고의) + fic(만들다) + cial(형용사형 어미): 표면을 만드는 - 피상적인, 혹은 **표면을 사포로 피셔(superficial)**로 암기
⊕ surface
예 They showed us a superficial analysis of the results.

superfluous
[su:pə́:rfluəs]
ⓡ 17892/86800

adj. 여분의
❶ super(최고의, 표면의) + flu(흐르는) + ous(형용사형 어미): 좋은 것이 흘러넘치는, 여분의
⊕ extra
예 My homework was spoiled by superfluous mistakes.

superior
[səpíəriər]
ℝ 3940/86800

adj. n. **우월한, 윗사람**
❶ super(최고의) + ior(이야): 최고야, 우월한
㊉ excellent ㊀ inferior ㉡ superiority: 우수
㉢ This book is the work of a superior English teacher.

superstition
[sù:pərstíʃən]
ℝ 18069/86800

n. **미신**
❶ super(지나친) + sti(서있다) + tion(명사형 어미): 지나친 것이 마음에 서있는 - **미신**
㉡ superstitious: 미신적인
㉢ Many people believe in the old superstition that the number 4 is unlucky in Korea.

supervise
[sú:pərvàiz]
ℝ 11518/86800

v. **감독하다**
❶ super(위에서) + vise(보다 - 어원편 참조): 위에서 일 잘하는 가 보다, 감독하다
㊉ oversee ㉡ supervisor: 감독
㉢ The professor supervised mid - term exam.

supply
[səplái]
ℝ 1064/86800

n. v. **공급, 공급품, 공급하다**
❶ 술 풀라이(supply): 술을 풀어라 - 술을 **공급**하다
㊉ furnish, provide
㉡ *supplement*: 보충하다 *supplier*: 공급자
㉢ Electric power is supplied by National grid in America.

support
[səpɔ́:rt]
ℝ 289/86800

v. **지지하다, 부양하다**
❶ sup(아래에서) + port(나르다): 아래에서 (돈을 벌어, 마음으로) 나르다 - 부양하다, 지지하다
㊉ brace, sustain ㉡ *supporter*: 지지자
㉢ He doesn't support government.

suppose
[səpóuz]
ℝ 945/86800

v. **가정하다, 추측하다**
❶ 만일을 가정하여 sup(아래) + pose(놓아두다): 가정하다
㊉ assume, guess
㉢ Do you suppose that Mr. Kim will marry so - young?

S

suppress
[səprés]
® 10523/86800

v. 억압하다
❶ sup(아래) + press(누르다): 아래로 누르다, 억압하다
⊕ overpower
예 The egyptian uprising could not be suppressed by government.

✔ **supreme**
[səprí:m]
® 2910/86800

adj. 최고의
❶ supreme(수 풀입): 秀(수 - 성적) 맞은 사람이 풀이한 것이므로 **최고의**
⊕ highest
예 This case will be treated in supreme court.

✔ **surf**
[sə:rf]
® 16717/86800

n. v. 밀려오는 파도, 파도타기 하다
❶ 서핑(surfing - 파도타기)하다, 인터넷 서핑은 인터넷 검색이라는 뜻
예 Many people can hear the roar of surf in east sea.

✔ **surface**
[sə́:rfis]
® 1132/86800

n. 표면
❶ sur(위 - 어원편 참조) + face(얼굴): 표면
⊕ exterior ⊖ interior
예 Be careful of icy surfaces in winter.

surge
[sə:rdʒ]
® 1132/86800

n. v. 큰 파도, 큰 파도가 일다, 급등하다
❶ 큰 파도가 다 쏠지(surge)
⊕ wave
예 There have been surges in house prices in Korea.

✔ **surgeon**
[sə́:rdʒən]
® 6840/86800

n. 외과 의사
❶ 외과의사가 칼을 주니 환자를 다 **썰 전(surgeon)** - 칼로 다 썰어 수술하는 **외과의사**
c.f) *physician*: 내과의사(칼 안주니까 *삐졌션*)
예 Erie county general hospital has lots of well - known surgeons.

surmount
[sərmáunt]
Ⓡ 41454/86800

v. 극복하다
❶ sur(위) + mount(산): 산위에 있으면 이미 어려움을 극복하고 올라간 것이므로 **극복하다**
⊕ overcome, conquer
例 I managed to surmount all difficulties to graduation.

✔ **surpass**
[sərpǽs]
Ⓡ 33459/86800

v. 보다 낫다, 능가하다
❶ sur(위) + pass(통과하다): 원래 통과선 보다 위로 통과하다, 능가하다
⊕ Excel
例 This English vocabulary book's success has surpassed my expectations.

✔ **surplus**
[sə́:rplʌs]
Ⓡ 4164/86800

n. 나머지, 잉여
❶ sur(위) + plus(더): 위에 더 있음 - 나머지, 잉여
⊕ remainder, residue ⊖ deficit
例 The Korea's deficit in travel business rose in the last six month.

✔ **surprise**
[sərpráiz]
Ⓡ 1920/86800

v. n. 놀라게 하다, 놀라운 일
❶ 설 프라이즈(surprise) - 내가 설에 프라이즈(상)받는 일은 사람들을 **놀라게 한다**
⊕ wonder, amazement, astonishment
派 *surprising*: 놀랄만한 *surprisingly*: 놀랄 정도로
例 It is no surprise that I receive Summa Cum Laude.

surrender
[səréndər]
Ⓡ 6647/86800

n. v. 항복, 항복하다
❶ 싸우다 죽느니 **살렌다(surrender)**면서 **항복하다**
⊕ yield
例 The protestants surrendered after one month of fighting.

✔ **surround**
[səráund]
Ⓡ 11564/86800

v. 둘러싸다
❶ sur(위) + round(둘러싸다): 위에 둘러싸다
⊕ encircle, enclose
派 *surrounding*: 둘러싸고 있는 *surroundings*: 환경
例 Justin bieber was surrounded by lots of fans.

survey
[sə:rvéi]
Ⓡ 1264/86800

n. v. 조사, 조사하다
ⓣ 강도에게 **살 베이(survey)**게 된 것 **조사**하다
ⓢ research
예 A majority of the people surveyed said that the president did well.

survival
[sərváivəl]
Ⓡ 3071/86800

n. 살아남음, 생존
ⓣ sur(위) + viv(생생한, 살아있는 - 어원편 참조): 살아서 위로 올라 오다 - 생존
ⓐ extinction 파 *survive*: 살아남다 survivor: 생존자
예 A physician told her that she had a 50: 50 chance of survival.

suspect
[səspékt]
Ⓡ 3195/86800

v. n. 의심하다, 용의자
ⓣ sus(sub - 아래) + spect(보다): 아래를 보며 자꾸 의심하다, spect (보다의 뜻으로 앞에서 언급)
ⓢ distrust, doubt: 의심하다 파 suspicious: 의심스러운
예 The police are chasing a suspect of murder.

suspend
[səspénd]
Ⓡ 12582/86800

v. 매달다, 보류하다
ⓣ sus(아래) + pen(매달리다): 아래에 매달려있다, 매달다, 보류하다
ⓢ delay, postpone, discontinue
파 suspension: 일시적 중단 suspense: 불안
예 Shuttle service has been suspended for the day because of snowstorm.

suspicious
[səspíʃəs]
Ⓡ 5674/86800

adj. 의심스러운
ⓣ 그 담배 **사서피셨소(suspicious)**? 뭔가 담배에 대해 **의심하고 있는**
ⓢ distrustful, suspect 파 *suspicion*: 의심, 혐의
예 The robber's behavior was very suspicious.

sustain
[səstéin]
Ⓡ 6076/86800

v. 떠받치다, 유지하다
ⓣ sus(아래) + tain(유지하다 - 어원편 참조)
  혹은, **서서 대인(sustain - 큰 사람)**떠받치다
ⓢ maintain 파 *sustainability*: 지속가능성
예 She seems to find it easy to sustain relationships with colleague.

✔ **swallow**
[swálou]
® 8107/86800

v. n. 삼키다, 제비
❶ 물을 **술로(swallow) 삼키다**, 제비 설로(swallow) 그저께(까치는 어제께)
예 When I swallow water, my throat hurts.

sway
[swei]
® 13467/86800

v. n. 흔들리다, 동요하다 흔들다, 흔들림
❶ 집단에서 **소외(sway)되어 흔들리다**, 동요하다
예 The attorney are trying to sway the judge.

swear
[swεər]
® 7667/86800

v. 맹세하다, 욕하다
❶ **맹세컨대** 다음에 꼭 **秀(수 - 성적))에여(swear)!**
㊀ take an oath: 맹세하다, curse: 욕하다
예 I swear that I don't swear again.

sweat
[swet]
® 5748/86800

n. v. 땀, 땀을 흘리다
❶ **스웨터(sweat)겹겹**이 입고 **땀**나다
㊀ perspire
예 I swear a lot when I play table tennis.

✔ **sweep**
[swi:p]
® 6825/86800

휩쓸다, 쓸다, 청소하다
❶ 축구감독 홍명보의 위치는 **스위퍼(sweeper)**
　 공이 오면 뻥하고 내질러 **청소하는** 역할이었죠
㊀ wipe out
예 She wants to sweep her living room.

swell
[swel]
® 10179/86800

v. n. 부풀다, 부풀리다, 팽창
❶ **써(s)웰(well) -** 잘 쓴다고 **부풀려** 말하다
　 (안 좋으면서)구입한 오디오 잘 쓴다고 부풀리다
㊀ expand
예 My broken arm swelled badly.

✔ **swift**
[swift]
® 6009/86800

adj. 빠른, 신속한
❶ 좋은 회사는 **수위부터(swift) 신속한**
㊀ fast, quick, rapid ㊀ slow 파 *swiftly*: 신속히
예 I received a swift response from the school.

swing
[swiŋ]
ⓡ 4408/86800

v. n. 흔들다, 흔들리다, 휘두름
ⓣ 야구 선수들이 배트를 **휘두르면 스윙(swing)**
예 I walked briskly along the path swinging my arms.

sword
[sɔ:rd]
ⓡ 5388/86800

n. 검, 칼
ⓣ **썰다(sword): 칼**로 썰다
ⓨ knife, blade: 칼 날
예 The pen is mightier than sword.

symbolize
[símbəlàiz]
ⓡ 34374/86800

v. 상징하다
ⓣ symbol(상징) + ize(만들다): **상징하다**
ⓨ represent, stand for
퓨 *symbol*: 상징 *symbolic*: 상징하는
예 What does this character symbolize?

symmetry
[símətri]
ⓡ 8318/86800

n. 균형, 조화
ⓣ sym(함께, 같은, 합성 - 어원편 참조) + metry(측정): 측정했더니 양쪽이 같음 - **균형**
ⓨ balance ⓝ asymmetry
예 The result of regular exercise was the symmetry of my body.

sympathetic
[sìmpəθétik]
ⓡ 5267/86800

adj. 동정적인
ⓣ sym(함께, 같은) + pathy(마음) + ic(형용사형 어미): 같은 마음을 가진, 동정적인
퓨 *sympathize*: 동정하다 *sympathy*: 동정, 공감
예 She comes across as a more sympathetic character in the film.

symphony
[símfəni]
ⓡ 8172/86800

n. 교향곡
ⓣ sym(함께, 같은) + phony(소리): 교향곡은 여러 악기가 같은 소리를 냄
예 The next concert in the series will feature the boston symphony orchestra playing the top show tunes of 2000.

symptom
[símptəm]
® 10396/86800

n. 증세, 징후
❶ 心부텀(symptom) - 심장부터 **증세**가 나타남
예 He's complaining of all the usual flu symptoms - a high temperature, headache and so on.

synthetic
[sinθétik]
® 8598/86800

adj. 종합적인, 합성의
❶ syn(합성, 함께) + thetic(편의상 세팅이라고 기억): 함께 세팅된 - 합성의
예 That organic farm doesn't use any pesticides or synthetic fertilizers.

❖ **systematic**
[sìstəmǽtik]
® 4877/86800

adj. 조직적인
❶ system(체계) + ic(형용사형 어미): 체계적인, 조직적인
파 *system*: 체계
예 We've got to be a bit more systematic in the way that we approach this task.

✔ **tablet**
[tǽblit]
® 14166/86800

n. 알약
❶ 물약 말고 **알약 타블래(tablet)**?
예 I need a sleeping tablet because of insomnia.

tactful
[tǽktfəl]
® 21137/86800

adj. 재치있는, 요령있는
❶ tact를 텍트(tact)를 테크(tech)로 생각 + ful(가득찬): 기술로 가득찬 - **요령있는**
파 tact: 재치, 요령
예 It was tactful of her not to criticize me in front of my boss.

✔ **tag**
[tæg]
® 9397/86800

n. 꼬리표
❶ 백화점에 가면 상품들이 내 **꼬리표** 좀 **떼가!(tag)**하고 기다린다
예 Look at these price tags.

✔ **tailor**
[téilə:r]
® 12580/86800

n. 재봉사
❶ **테일러(tailor)**주는 사람 - 당신 옷의 테가 어떻게 나올지 일러주는 사람은 **재봉사**
예 The tailor folded up his cloth and hurried away.

taint
[teint]
® 32041/86800

n. v. 더럼, 더럽히다
❶ 때 인(tain) + t(티셔츠): 때로 찌든 T셔츠가 **더러움**
예 His reputation was permanently tainted by the financial scandal.

✔ tale
[teil]
® 4152/86800

n. 이야기
❶ 전태일(tale) 열사 **이야기**
예 She told me some beautiful tales abou her life.

✔ talent
[tǽlənt]
® 4160/86800

n. 재능
❶ TV **탈렌트(talent)**는 연기 **재능**이 있는 사람
사실 미국에서는 TV personality라 함
예 Her talent for music showed at an early age.

✔ talkative
[tɔ́:kətiv]
® 28276/86800

adj. 말이 많은
❶ talk(말) + tive(많은 - 철자 ful과 tive는 꽉찼다는 말)
파 *talk*: 말하다
예 She's a lively, talkative person.

tame
[teim]
® 14105/86800

adj. v. 길이든, 길들이다
❶ 아기 젖을 떼임(taim) - 밥에 **길들이기** 위해
예 After a few months' contact the monkeys become very tame.

✔ target
[tɑ́:rgit]
® 1512/86800

n. v. 과녁, 목표, 목표로 삼다
❶ 대통령상을 **타겟(target)**다는 **목표**
예 I had four shots but I didn't even hit the target.

✔ task
[tæsk]
® 1111/86800

n. 일, 임무, 과업
❶ desk에서는 공부하고 **task**에서는 일
예 Our first task is to review the budget.

❤ tax
[tæks]
ℝ 593/86800

n. 세금, 무거운 부담
❶ 세금 얼마 뗐어(tax)?
예 The decision was made to raise taxes.

❤ tear
[tiə:r][tɛə:r]
ℝ 6337/86800

n. v. 눈물, 찢다
❶ 흙탕물이 **티어(tear)눈물**이 나고 점수가 나빠성적표를 **떼어(tear) 찢었다**
예 I tore my skirt on the chair as I stood up.

✔ tease
[ti:z]
ℝ 16971/86800

v. 놀리다
❶ 친구들이 내게 물이 **튀자(tease) 놀렸다**
예 I was only teasing, I didn't mean to upset you.

tedious
[tí:diəs]
ℝ 10746/86800

adj. 지루한
❶ 수업이 **지루해서** 공부가 **더디었어(tedious)**
예 The trouble is I find most forms of exercise so tedious.

telegram
[téləgræm]
ℝ 15864/86800

n. 전보
❶ tele(멀리 있는 - 어원편 참조) + gram(기록, 그림): 멀리있는 사람에게 기록을 남김, 전보
예 In the old times people used telegrams to communicate with each other.

✔ telegraph
[téləgræf]
ℝ 6343/86800

n. 전신
❶ tele(멀리 있는) + graph(쓴 것, 그린 것 - 어원편 참조): 멀리 있는 사람에게 쓴 것 - 전신
파 *telegraphic*: 전신의
예 The news came by telegraph.

❤ telescope
[téləskòup]
ℝ 11676/86800

n. 망원경
❶ tele(멀리 있는) + scope(보다): 망원경
예 The rings of Saturn can be seen through a telescope.

T

temper
[témpə:r]
ⓡ 6000/86800

n. 기질, 기분, 화
❶ 화날 때 쓰는 떼(억지) 퍼 (temper)담고 있는 것이 **기질, 화**
派 *temperament*: 기질 temperance: 절제, 금주
예 He is in a pleasant temper.

temperate
[témpərit]
ⓡ 12826/86800

adj. 기온이 온화한, 절제하는
❶ 떼 버렸데(temperate) - 떼를 부리지 않고 버린 - **절제하는**
派 *temperature*: 온도
예 He is a temperate man.

temple
[témpəl]
ⓡ 4136/86800

n. 사원, 절
❶ 댐 풀(temple) - damn은 저주 ple은 풀다
저주를 푸는 곳은 **사원, 절**
예 Mother went to a temple to worship.

temporary
[témpərèri]
ⓡ 2595/86800

adj. 일시적인, 임시의
❶ tempo(시간, 박자, 속도 - 어원편 참조) + ary(형용사형 어미): 시
간적인, 일시적인
派 *temporarily*: 일시적으로
예 The ceasefire will only provide a temporary solution
to the crisis.

tempt
[tempt]
ⓡ 15642/86800

v. 유혹하다
❶ 탐(temp)타(t): 탐(탐욕)을 탄(얻을 수 있다)다고 **유혹하다**
派 temptation: 유혹
예 The offer of a free car stereo tempted her into buying
a new car.

tenant
[ténənt]
ⓡ 3570/86800

n. v. 집, 토지를 빌린 사람, 임차하다
❶ 월세 안내면 보증금에서 **떼는(tenant)사람**
예 A tenant is now leasing the apartment.

tend
[tend]
ⓡ 1665/86800

v. 향하다, 경향이 있다(tend to), 돌보다
❶ 아이들은 닌 **텐도(tend)하는 경향이 있는**
派 *tendency*: 경향, 추세
예 She tends to shout.

✔ tender
[téndə:r]
Ⓡ 4806/86800

adj. 고기가 부드러운, 상냥한
❶ 고기가 **부드러워** 빨리 **탄다(tender)**
예 What you need is some tender loving care.

✔ tense
[tens]
Ⓡ 5910/86800

adj. 긴장한
❶ tens(당긴 - 어원편 참조): 옆으로 당기면 긴장한
파 *tension*: 긴장
예 She was very tense as she waited for the interview.

✔ term
[tə:rm]
Ⓡ 788/86800

n. v. 용어, 기간, 조건, 관점, 끝(한계), 이름을 짓다
❶ 어떤(term - 어떤) 용어로 저 뜻을 설명할 수 있을까? 텀(term - 기간)을 두고 생각해봐!
예 He received a prison term for drunk driving.

✔ terminal
[tə́:rmənəl]
Ⓡ 4542/86800

adj. n. 말기의, 종점(끝)
❶ 고속버스 **터미널(terminal)**은 **종점**
파 *terminate*: 끝내다
예 She has terminal cancer.

terrace
[térəs]
Ⓡ 4584/86800

n. 테라스
❶ 밖으로 이어지라고 **터놨어(terrace): 테라스** - 실내에서 길이나 정원 쪽으로 터놓은 곳
예 For sale: large three - bedroom house with adjoining terrace and garden.

✔ terrible
[térəbəl]
Ⓡ 2160/86800

adj. 무서운, 심한, 터무니없는
❶ 테러는 볼(terrible) 수록 무서운
파 terribly: 무섭게, 매우
예 I have a terrible cold.

✔ terrific
[tərífik]
Ⓡ 9378/86800

adj. 빼어난, 대단한, 맹렬한
❶ 둘이 빼(terrific): 둘이 빼어난
파 *terrify*: 겁나게 하다
예 I had a terrific time.

T

territory
[térətɔ̀:ri]
ⓡ 3078/86800

n. 영토, 영역
➊ terri(땅 - 어원편 참조): 땅, 영토
[예] Guam is a U.S. territory.

testify
[téstəfài]
ⓡ 15664/86800

v. 증명하다, 입증하다
➊ test(시험) + ify(만들다): 시험해서 결과를 만들다, 증명하다
[예] She testified before Congress today.

testimony
[téstəmòuni]
ⓡ 8660/86800

n. 증언, 입증
➊ test(시험) + mony(결과, 상태, 동작 - 어원편 참조): 시험 보는 상태, 증언
[예] The jury heard 10 days of testimony.

✔ **text**
[tekst]
ⓡ 1339/86800

n. 문서, 본문
➊ 텍스트(text - 문자) 메시지를 보낸다, 텍스트 북(textbook - 교과서)을 펴라 등을 생각하면 암기가 쉬워짐
c.f) *textbook*: 교과서
[예] Can we see the full text of your speech before Tuesday?

textile
[tékstail]
ⓡ 8714/86800

n. 직물, 옷감
➊ 떼 스타일(textile) - 옷감 떼서 스타일 맞게
[예] They import fine silk textiles from China.

✔ **theme**
[θi:m]
ⓡ 2585/86800

n. 주제, 테마
➊ 이야기의 테마(theme - 주제)라고 많이 들 이야기 함, 발음조심 하세요 - 씸
[예] A constant theme in his novels is religion.

theology
[θi:álədʒi]
ⓡ 6506/86800

n. 신학
➊ theo(神 - 어원편 참조) + logy(학문, 말, 이론): 신에 관한 학문, 신학
[파] theological: 신학의
[예] He has an interest in theology and pastoral work.

✤ **theory**
[θíːəri]
Ⓡ 748/86800

n. 이론
❶ 이것들을 무슨 **이론**이라 **쓰리**(theory)? - 이것들을 무슨 이론이라 쓸까?
파 *theorize*: 이론화하다
예 There is no evidence to support such a theory.

✔ **therapy**
[θérəpi]
Ⓡ 4468/86800

n. 치료법
❶ 아로마(aroma) **쎄라피**(therapy)
예 Joining a dance club is a therapy for loneliness.

✔ **thereafter**
[ðɛəræftəːr]
Ⓡ 5471/86800

ad. 그 후
❶ there(거기) + after(후): 그 후
예 She left the Seoul area in 80 and settled in Busan area shortly thereafter.

✤ **therefore**
[ðɛəːrfɔːr]
Ⓡ 392/86800

conj. 그러므로, 그래서
❶ 이건 **되었고**(therefore) **그래서**? 다음 것은?
예 We were unable to get funding and therefore had to abandon the project.

✔ **thermometer**
[θəːrmámitəːr]
Ⓡ 23841/86800

n. 온도계
❶ thermo(열, 온도 - 어원편 참조) + meter(측정);온도를 측정함 - 온도계
예 The thermometer says it's almost 80 degrees outside, but it doesn't feel that hot.

✤ **thick**
[θik]
Ⓡ 2136/86800

adj. 두꺼운, 뚱뚱한
❶ **씩씩**(thick)한 남자를 생각하면 근육이 **두꺼운**
예 She has thick, curly hair.

✔ **thigh**
[θai]
Ⓡ 8331/86800

n. 넓적다리
❶ **넓적다리**에는 살이 **쌓이**(thigh)네
예 He operated his thigh at Asan medical center last year.

thin
[θin]
® 1951/86800

adj. 얇은, 야윈
❶ 날 씬(thin)한 것 생각하면 **얇은, 야윈**
예 This is a thin book.

thirst
[θəːrst]
® 13909/86800

n. 목마름
❶ **水를 샀다(thirst) - 목이 말라 수(물)를 샀다**
파 *thirsty*: 목마른, 갈망하는
예 I've got a terrible thirst after all that running.

thorn
[θɔːrn]
® 11955/86800

n. 가시
❶ 가시가 **쏜(thorn) - 가시**가 손에 박혔네
예 A thorn defends the rose, harming only those who would steal the blossom.

thorough
[θə́ːrou]
® 6588/86800

adj. 완전한, 충분한
❶ 이 **쌀로(thorough)** 집 식구 먹기에 **완전한**
파 thoroughly: 완전히
예 The investigator will have to be thorough.

thoughtful
[θɔ́ːtfəl]
® 9693/86800

adj. 사려 깊은
❶ thought(생각) + ful(꽉 찬): 생각을 많이 한, 사려깊은
파 *thought*: 생각 *thoughtfully*: 사려 깊게
thoughtfulness: 사려 깊음
예 That's very thoughtful of you.

threat
[θret]
® 1813/86800

n. 위협
❶ **수류(threat)탄 으로 위협**
파 *threaten*: 협박하다
예 The threat of jail failed to deter him from petty crime.

thrift
[θrift]
® 20745/86800

n. 절약
❶ 남은 떨이라고 버리지 말고 **떨이부터(thrift) 절약**
파 thrifty: 검소한
예 Through hard work and thrift they sent all of their children to college.

440

thrive
[θraiv]
ⓡ 12410/86800

v. 번영하다, 잘 자라다
❶ **쓰라이브(thrive - 드라이브)** 하니 여친과 만남이 **번영 해진다**
㉠ These plants thrive with relatively little sunlight.

throb
[θrab]
ⓡ 24651/86800

n. v. 고동, 맥박, 심장이 뛰다
❶ **뜨랍(throb)** - 심장이 뛰고 **맥박**이 뛰라
㉠ The pain has changed to a dull throb.

throne
[θroun]
ⓡ 6198/86800

n. v. 왕좌, 왕위에 앉다
❶ 세계 탁구를 휩 **쓸어온(throne)** 중국이 **왕좌**에 앉다
㉠ The king sat on his throne.

throng
[θrɔ(:)ŋ]
ⓡ 17978/86800

n. v. 군중, 떼 지어 모이다
❶ 돈을 다 **쓸엉(throng)** 그럼 돈이 **떼지어 모인다**
㉠ Shoppers thronged the mall for the sales.

✔ throughout
[θruːáut]
ⓡ 798/86800

adv. 전체에 걸쳐
❶ through(여기 저기) + out(완전히): 여기 저기 완전히 전체에 걸쳐
㉠ The house is painted white throughout.

thrust
[θrʌst]
ⓡ 4180/86800

v. n. 밀어내다, 밀기
❶ 다른 강자들을 내가 다 **쓸었었다(thrust)** - 강자들을 **밀어냈다**
㉠ She thrust the papers at me (= towards me).

✔ thump
[θʌmp]
ⓡ 16834/86800

v. n. 탁치다, 탁 치기
❶ **쌈보(thump - 싸움 잘하는 사람)** 가 **탁 치다**
㉠ She thumped me in the face.

✔ tickle
[tíkəl]
ⓡ 23202/86800

v. 간질이다
❶ **티끌(tickle)** 같은 조그만 것으로 날 **간질이다**
㉠ She tickled my feet and I laughed.

tide
[taid]
® 4724/86800

n. 조수, 흐름, 풍조
❶ **흐름**(풍조, 바닷물의 흐름)을 **타다(tide)**
예 The tide is out.

tidy
[táidi]
® 6805/86800

adj. 단정한
❶ 저 타이(넥타이)면 **단정한 타이지(tidy)**?
예 The house was clean and tidy.

tie
[tai]
® 3248/86800

v. n. 묶다, 결합하다, 끈, 속박, 동점
❶ 타이(tie)라는 말은 일상에서도 많이 씁니다, 넥타이는 묶는 것, 묶으면 결합하는 것 또 묶는 것은 끈이고 스포츠에서 타이는 동점 등
예 I tie my hair back when it's hot.

tight
[tait]
® 2861/86800

adj. 단단한, 옷 따위가 긴, 엄격한
❶ 옷이 **타이트(tight)**하다 - **단단한**, 긴
파 *tightly*: 단단하게
예 I can't untie the knot - it's too tight.

timber
[tímbə:r]
® 13010/86800

n. 재목, 목재
❶ 뗌 벌(timber)木 - 벌목(나무를 떼고) **목재** 만듦
예 These trees are being grown for timber.

timely
[táimli]
® 13010/86800

adj. 시기적절한
❶ time(시간) + ly(형용사형, 부사형 어미)
예 She always responds to my requests in a timely fashion.

timepiece
[táimpì:s]
® 58060/86800

n. 시계
❶ time(시간) + piece(조각): 시간을 조각내서 보는 것은 시계
예 Students need timepiece for punctuality.

timid
[tímid]
® 15602/86800

adj. 겁 많은, 소심한
❶ 티미(timi)하고 띨(d - 멍청)해서 **겁 많고 소심한**
예 She's very timid and shy when meeting strangers.

442

tin
[tin]
ⓡ 4255/86800

n. 주석(금속 원소), 깡통
❶ 깡통이 틴(tin)
예 I have a tin of sardiness.

tiny
[táini]
ⓡ 1868/86800

adj. 아주 작은
❶ Tico라는 자동차 아세요? Tiny + Cozy(작고 아늑한)의 앞 자를 딴 차 랍니다
예 The computer chips were tiny.

tip
[tip]
ⓡ 3611/86800

n. 끝, 팁, 조언
❶ 여기 쓴 T가 암기 tip의 T자랍니다. 팁은 조언, 봉사료, 끝 이라는 뜻이 있습니다
예 There's paint on the tip of your nose.

tissue
[tíʃuː]
ⓡ 4221/86800

n. 조직, 화장지
❶ 화장지 좀 띠었슈(tissue)? 코 파게 ㅋㅋㅋ
예 His face is covered with scar tissue where he was badly burned.

toe
[tou]
ⓡ 9369/86800

n. 발가락
❶ 아기가 손가락 뿐 만 아니라 **발가락 도우(toe)** 닮았네!
예 I stubbed (= knocked) my toe on the edge of a bed.

token
[tóukən]
ⓡ 7933/86800

n. 표시, 증거
❶ 옷이 작으니 **또 큰(token)** 증거이자 **표시**
예 It doesn't have to be a big present - it's just a token.

T

tolerable
[tálərəbəl]
ⓡ 19895/86800

adj. 참을 수 있는
❶ 딸낳 블(tolerable) - 요즘 딸을 낳아도 **참을 수 있는**(오히려 딸을 선호, 효도한다구 선호)
파 tolerant: 관대한 *tolerate*: 관용하다
예 At their best the conditions in these prisons are scarcely tolerable.

toll
[toul]
® 19895/86800

n. 통행세
❶ 톨게이트(toll gate) - 고속도로 가면 어느 지역에 진입하기 전 통행세 받는 곳
예 He's just got a job collecting tolls at the start of the motorway.

tomb
[tu:m]
® 9797/86800

n. 무덤
❶ 사람을 묻어 둠(tomb)
예 They explored the historic graveyard and saw tombs that dated back two centuries.

✔ **tongue**
[tʌŋ]
® 3680/86800

n. 혀, 말
❶ 아기 보고 말 좀 터 엉?(tongue)
예 English is my native tongue.

✔ **tool**
[tu:l]
® 4006/86800

n. 도구
❶ 금광 뚫(tool)을 도구
예 A free low - interest credit card can be a useful budgeting tool.

torch
[tɔ:rtʃ]
® 7416/86800

n. 햇불
❶ 자유 여신상이 자유의 햇불을 들쥐(torch)!
예 She shone the torch into the dark room.

torrent
[tɔ́:rənt]
® 16933/86800

n. 급류, 억수
❶ 급류에 또랑(torrent)이 넘치는
예 Heavy rainfall turned the river into a rushing/raging torrent.

✔ **torso**
[tɔ́:rsou]
® 18297/86800

n. 머리, 손, 발이 없는 몸통 조각상
❶ 월가의 돌 소(torso) - 돌로 된 상
예 He made a torso in the art class.

torture
[tɔ́:rtʃə:r]
Ⓡ 7774/86800

n. v. 고문, 고문하다
❶ 또 쳐(torture)! 고문하다
㈜ torment: 고통, 괴롭히다
㉘ He revealed the secret under torture.

✔ **touch**
[tʌtʃ]
Ⓡ 1539/86800

v. 접촉하다, 감동시키다
❶ 접촉하다는 뜻은 아실 것이고 마음에 **닿치**(touch? - 마음에 와 닿는 것은 감동시키다
㉘ That paint is wet - don't touch (it).

✔ **tough**
[tʌf]
Ⓡ 2982/86800

adj. 질긴, 힘든, 강인한
❶ 사람이 **터프**(tough)한 것은 **강인한** 것이고 고기가 터프하면 질 긴, 미적분이 터프하면 힘든, 어려운의 뜻
㉘ Children's shoes need to be tough.

✔ **toward(s)**
[tɔ:rd]
Ⓡ 6018/86800

prep. ~을 향하여
❶ to(~를 향하여) + ward(~쪽으로): ~을 향하여
㉘ She stood up and walked towards him.

✔ **townie**
[táuni]
Ⓡ 순위외/86800

n. 마을 주민
❶ 타운(마을)에서 온 이(townie)
㉘ Many townies walked into the village pub.

✔ **trace**
[treis]
Ⓡ 3956/86800

v. n. 추적하다, 자국
❶ 범인이 들어 있어 (trace)경찰이 **추적하다**
㈜ *track*: 자국, 흔적, 통로, 뒤를 쫓다
㉘ The phone company were unable to trace the call.

✔ **trade**
[treid]
Ⓡ 471/86800

n. v. 무역, 거래하다, 교환하다
❶ 야구선수들 트레이드(trade)하는 것은 돈 **거래**를 하는 것
㉘ Seventy per cent of the country's trade is with Europe.

T

trade-off
[treid-ɔ:f]
® 순위외/86800

n. 협정, 교환거래
❶ trade(거래) + off(밖에서): 밖에서 거래하는 것은 협정
예 Political Trade offs between parties.

tradition
[trədíʃən]
® 1989/86800

n. 전통
❶ 각 나라가 **들여두신**(tradition - 보존하는)것은 **전통**
파 *traditional*: 전통의
traditionally: 전통적으로
예 Switzerland has a long tradition of neutrality.

tragedy
[trǽdʒədi]
® 4654/86800

n. 비극
❶ 뜰에 서 뒤(tragedy)진 것은 **비극**
파 *tragic*: 비극의
예 His life was touched by hardship and personal tragedy.

trail
[treil]
® 5638/86800

v. n. 질질 끌다, 흔적, 자국
❶ 장사가 **두 레일**(trail)의 기차를 **질질 끌다**
예 He left a trail of muddy footprints behind him.

trait
[treit]
® 15608/86800

n. 특성
❶ **또렷**(trait)**한 특성**
예 His sense of humor is one of his better traits.

traitor
[tréitə:r]
® 17336/86800

n. 배반자
❶ 저 **배반자 틀에 있다**(traitor - 형틀에 있다)
예 The leaders of the rebellion were hanged as traitors.

tranquil
[trǽŋkwil]
® 15465/86800

adj. 조용한, 평온한
❶ **조용한 뜰 안 길**(tranquil)
예 The hotel is in a tranquil rural setting.

✔ transact
[trænsǽkt]
® 45704/86800

v. **집행하다, 거래하다**
🌐 trans(횡단, 초월, 변화의 뜻 - 어원편 참조) + act(행동): 왔다 갔다 거래하다
📘 *transaction*: 처리, 거래
📝 The sale was transacted in conditions of the greatest secrecy.

transcend
[trænsénd]
® 22685/86800

v. **초월하다**
🌐 trans(횡단, 변화, 초월) + scend(오르다 - 어원편 참조): 초월하다, 능가하다
c.f) descend: 내리다
📝 The best films are those which transcend national or cultural barriers.

transcribe
[trænskráib]
® 32376/86800

v. **베끼다**
🌐 trans(횡단, 초월, 변화) + scribe(쓰다): 이쪽에서 저쪽까지 다 쓰다 - 베끼다
📝 Tape recordings of conversations are transcribed by typists and entered into the database.

✷ transfer
[trænsfə́:r]
® 1493/86800

v. **이동하다, 갈아타다**
🌐 trans(횡단, 초월, 변화) + fer(나르다 - 어원편 참조): 이쪽에서 저쪽으로 나르다, 이동하다, 갈아타다
📝 We were transferred from one bus into another.

✔ transform
[trænsfɔ́:rm]
® 7373/86800

v. **변형하다**
🌐 trans(횡단, 초월, 변화) + form(형태): 형태를 바꾸다
📘 *transformation*: 변형
📝 The reorganization will transform the British entertainment industry.

transient
[trænʃənt]
® 12588/86800

adj. **일시적인**
🌐 trans(횡단, 초월, 변화) + ent(형용사형 어미): 변화하는 동안의 - 일시적인
📝 A glass of whisky has only a transient warming effect.

T

transit
[trǽnsit]
® 7760/86800

n. 통과
ⓣ trans(횡단) + it(가다 - 어원편 참조): 횡단하여 감, 통과
㉴ transition: 변천, 과도기
㉖ The question is whether road transit is cheaper than rail.

translate
[trænsléit]
® 10134/86800

v. 번역하다, 옮기다
ⓣ trans(횡단, 초월, 변화) + slate(쓰랬데): 이쪽에서 저쪽으로 옮겨 쓰랬데 - 통역하다
㉴ translation: 번역 translator: 번역하는 사람
㉖ She works for the EU, translating from English into French.

♥ transmission
[trænsmíʃən]
® 5421/86800

n. 전달, 전도
ⓣ trans(횡단, 초월, 변화) + mission(보냄): 이쪽에서 저쪽으로 보냄 - 전달
㉴ *transmit*: 보내다, 전달하다
㉖ We apologize for the interruption to our transmissions this afternoon.

transparent
[trænspéərənt]
® 8742/86800

adj. 투명한
ⓣ trans(횡단, 초월, 변화) + parent: 양쪽 다 보이는
㉖ Her blouse was practically transparent!

transplant
[trænsplǽnt]
® 11499/86800

v. 이식하다
ⓣ trans(횡단, 초월, 변화) + plant(심다): 이쪽에서 저쪽으로 심다 - 이식하다
㉖ The plants should be grown indoors until spring, when they can be transplanted outside.

♥ transport
[trænspɔ́:rt]
® 1208/86800

v. n. 수송하다, 수송
ⓣ trans(횡단, 초월, 변화) + port(나르다): 이쪽에서 저쪽으로 나르다 - 수송하다
㉴ *transportation*: 운송
㉖ The company will arrange transport from the airport.

✔ trap
[træp]
® 4865/86800

n. v. 덫, 가두다
❶ 틀엡(trap - 틀에) 가두다
예 The fox got its foot caught in a trap.

✔ trash
[træʃ]
® 19141/86800

n. 쓰레기
❶ 더러워 씨(trash)!: 더러운 것은 쓰레기
예 There's only trash on the television tonight.

❖ travel
[trǽvəl]
® 1417/86800

v. n. 여행하다, 여행
❶ 돌아볼(travel): 돌아보는 것은 여행
c.f) *traveler*: 여행자
예 I travel to work by train.

treachery
[trétʃəri]
® 19443/86800

n. 배반, 반역
❶ 현 왕조에 틀어져리(treachery) - 반역
현 왕조와 틀어졌으면 **반역**
예 Corley said she was standing down as a leader because of the treachery of her own colleagues.

treason
[trí:zən]
® 14042/86800

n. 반역
❶ 정권에 틀어진(treason) - 반역
예 He is guilty of treason.

✔ treasure
[tréʒə:r]
® 7205/86800

n. 보물
❶ 보물을 틀어쥐어(treasure)
예 Stories about pirates often include a search for buried treasure.

❖ treat
[tri:t]
® 2618/86800

v. 다루다, 치료하다, 대접하다
❶ 트루잇(treat): 다루있 - **다루다**
파 *treatment*: 처리, 치료, 대우
예 He treated his wife very badly.

treaty
[trí:ti]
ⓡ 2031/86800

n. 조약
❶ 둘이 했디(treaty): 둘 이상의 국가 간 하는 약속, **협정**
㉰ We've signed a treaty with neighbouring states to limit emissions of harmful gases.

✔ tremble
[trémbəl]
ⓡ 16692/86800

v. 떨다
❶ 떨림 불(tremble):떨다
㉰ When he came out of the water, he was trembling with cold.

✔ tremendous
[triméndəs]
ⓡ 4307/86800

adj. 거대한, 굉장한
❶ 트리 만 됐어(tremendous) - 나무가 만 그루가 되었어 - **거대한**
㉴ *tremendously*: 굉장히
㉰ You won? That's tremendous!

✔ trend
[trend]
ⓡ 3511/86800

n. 경향, 추세
❶ 같은 또렌데(trend) 생각하는 **경향**(추세)이 같음
㉰ There's been a upward trend in sales in the last few years.

trespass
[tréspəs]
ⓡ 15863/86800

v. n. 침해하다, 침해, 죄
❶ 들에서 팼어(tresspass): 남을 들에서 패면 **죄**
㉰ I hope this is a public footpath and we're not trespassing on someone's land.

✔ trial
[tráiəl]
ⓡ 1599/86800

n. 시도, 시련, 재판
❶ 또라이 야(trial) - 또라이가 겪는 **시련** 한쪽이 **틀어야(trial)** 재판을 한단다
㉰ Trial by jury is a fundamental right.

✔ tribe
[traib]
ⓡ 8710/86800

n. 부족
❶ tri(숫자 3 - 어원편 참조) - 옛날 세 부족을 하나의 부족으로 치던 것에서 유래함
㉴ *tribal*: 부족의
㉰ The wedding joined the two tribes together.

trifle
[tráifəl]
ℝ 15706/86800

n. 사소한 일, 소량, 조금
🅣 tri(셋) - 숫자가 그리 크지 않은, 사소한, 소량
🅟 trifling: 사소한
🅔 There's no reason to argue over such trifles.

✔ **trigger**
[trígə:r]
ℝ 7717/86800

n. v. 방아쇠, 일으키다, 방아쇠를 당기다
🅣 은행 털이가(trigger) 방아쇠를 당기다
🅔 Smoke triggered the fire alarm.

✔ **trim**
[trim]
ℝ 8438/86800

v. 정돈하다, 손질하다, 머리, 수염등을 정돈하다
🅣 이것은 손질한 트리임(trim)
🅟 *trimly*: 깔끔하게
🅔 We trimmed the Christmas tree.

✔ **trip**
[trip]
ℝ 2204/86800

n. v. 짧은 여행, 발이 걸려 넘어지다
🅣 돌입(trip) - 돌이 들어와 걸려 넘어지다
Have a good trip! 하면 좋은 여행 되셈!
🅔 The dancers tripped off the stage.

✔ **triple**
[trípəl]
ℝ 9131/86800

adj. v. 3배의, 3배로 하다
🅣 tri(셋) + ple(접다 - 어원편 참조): 세배로 접다, 세배로 하다 triangle(삼각형)생각해 볼 것
🅔 The number of one - parent U.S. households reached 10.1 million in 1991, nearly triple that of 1971.

✔ **triumph**
[tráiəmf]
ℝ 4568/86800

n. v. 승리, 환호, 승리하다
🅣 둘 아이 엄포(triumph) - 바둑왕전에서 더 이상 둘 아이 없(이) (축)포 터트리다 - 승리
🅟 *triumphantly*: 의기양양하게
🅔 The match ended in triumph for the French team.

✔ **trivial**
[tríviəl]
ℝ 7616/86800

adj. 하찮은, 사소한
🅣 tri(셋) + via(길 - 어원편 참조): 삼거리 길 - 옛날 삼거리 길에 나가면 사람도 만나고 사소한 것들을 다 볼 수 있었다는 것에서 유래한 단어
🅔 Sexual harassment in the workplace is not a trivial matter.

T

troop
[tru:p]
® 10713/86800

n. 군대
❶ troop(트루루루룹); 기관총소리 - **군대**
예 All troops will be withdrawn by the end of the year.

tropical
[trápikəl]
® 4683/86800

adj. 열대의
❶ 더워피갈(tropical) - 더워 피서 갈 **열대의** 기후
예 The Amazon river basin contains the world's largest tropical rainforest.

troublesome
[trʌ́blsəm]
® 12435/86800

adj. 골치 아픈
❶ trouble(골치 거리) + some(약간): 골치 아픈
c.f) *trouble*: 고생, 시끄러운 일
예 the troublesome news that there will be more cuts in the school budget.

truce
[tru:s]
® 12327/86800

n. 휴전
❶ tru(troop - 군대라고 생각) + ce(서): 군대가 싸움을 하다가 서다 - 휴전
예 There's been an uneasy truce between her and her parents for the past several months.

trunk
[trʌŋk]
® 8122/86800

n. 나무의 줄기, 코끼리 코, 여행가방
❶ 코끼리 코는 드르렁 코(trunk), 짐을 담는 트렁크(trunk) 열어
예 This is trunks of elms.

trustworthy
[trʌ́stwə̀:rði]
® 23149/86800

a. 신뢰할 수 있는
❶ trust(신뢰) + worthy(가치가 있는): 신뢰할 만 한 가치가 있는
예 He is trustworthy.

tumble
[tʌ́mbəl]
® 14616/86800

v. 엎드러지다, 공중제비를 하다
❶ 덤블링(tumble - 공중제비) 한다는 말 아시면 암기가 쉬울 것임
예 He lost his balance and tumbled over.

tumult
[tjú:mʌlt]
ⓡ 31758/86800

n. 소동, 떠들석함
❶ 춤을(tumult)추느라 **소동**, 떠들썩함
㈎ The financial markets are in tumult.

✔ tune
[tju:n]
ⓡ 5130/86800

n. v. 가락, 곡조, 맞추다, 조정하다
❶ 현악기는 연주하기 전에 **튜닝(tuning** - 음 조정)을 합니다. 미국 방송을 들으면 stay tune(다른 데로 돌리지 말라)이라는 말도 자주들을 수 있어요
c.f) *tuning*: 조율
㈎ He was humming a tune as he dried the dishes.

twilight
[twáilàit]
ⓡ 13153/86800

n. 해 뜨고 지기 전의 어스름
❶ twi(둘 - 어원편 참조) + light(빛): 빛이 두 개이면 어스름(밝지도 어둡지도 않음)
㈎ The sun set and twilight fell.

✔ twinkle
[twíŋkəl]
ⓡ 20724/86800

v. 반짝이다
❶ 토인 칼(twinkle)이 **반짝이다**, 팅클 수퍼스타
㈎ Stars twinkle in the night sky.

✔ twist
[twist]
ⓡ 6339/86800

v. 비틀다
❶ 몸을 **비틀며** 추는 춤 **트위스트(twist)** 이 단어도 들어보셨을 거예요
㈎ The antenna was twisted out of shape.

✔ twofold
[tú:fòuld]
ⓡ 19044/86800

a. 이중의
❶ two(둘) + fold(겹): 두 겹의
㈎ A twofold increase in spending is not good.

✔ typical
[típikəl]
ⓡ 2085/86800

adj. 전형적인
❶ type(타입, 형) + ical(형용사형 어미): 타입이 정해진, 전형적인
㈎ *typically*: 전형적으로
㈎ It was his typical response.

tyranny
[tírəni]
ⓡ 16131/86800

n. 폭정, 학대
❶ 한국은 독재자의 **폭정**이 멀하니?(tyranny)
예 He was dedicated to ending the tyranny of slavery.

✔ ultimate
[ʌ́ltəmit]
ⓡ 3637/86800

adj. 최후의, 궁극의
❶ ultim(마지막 - 어원편 참조) + ate(동사형, 형용사형 어미): 마지막의, UFC는 Ultimate Fighter Championship 줄임
파 *ultimately*: 궁극적으로
예 Their ultimate fate has not yet been decided.

✔ ultraviolet
[ʌ̀ltrəváiəlit]
ⓡ 19086/86800

adj. 자외선의
❶ ultra(~외, 초과 - 어원편 참조) + violet(보라색, 자색): 자색 바깥의, ultraviolet rays(자외선)
예 We cannot see ultraviolet light in atmosphere.

unacceptable
[ʌ̀nəkséptəbəl]
ⓡ 6158/86800

adj. 받아들이기 어려운
❶ un(부정어) + accept(받아들이다) + able(할 수 있는); 받아들일 수 없는
예 Some of her ideas were unacceptable to other people.

✔ unanimous
[juːnǽnəməs]
ⓡ 11914/86800

adj. 만장일치의
❶ unus (하나 - uni의 옛 형태) + animus (마음): 마음이 하나인
파 *unanimously*: 만장일치로
예 The judges made a unanimous ruling.

✔ unavoidable
[ʌ̀nəvɔ́idəbəl]
ⓡ 13012/8680

adj. 피할 수 없는
❶ un(부정어) + avoid(피하다) + able(할 수 있는): 피할 수 없는
예 The accident was unavoidable.

unaware
[ʌ̀nəwéər]
ⓡ 6375/86800

adj. 알지 못하는
❶ un(부정어) + aware(알고 있는): 알지 못하는
예 I was quite unaware of the problem.

✔ **unbearable**
[ʌnbɛ́ərəbəl]
® 13997/86800

adj. **참을 수 없는**
❶ un(부정어) + bear(참다) + able(할 수 있는): 참을 수 없는
예 The heat was unbearable.

unbroken
[ʌnbróukən]
® 15880/86800

adj. **파손되지 않은**
❶ un(부정어) + broken(깨진): 깨지지 않은
예 This record I set is still unbroken.

✔ **uncertain**
[ʌnsə́:rtn]
® 4286/86800

adj. **불명확한**
❶ un(부정어) + certain(확실한): 확실하지 않은
예 The time of departure is still uncertain.

uncertainty
[ʌnsə́:rtnti]
® 4021/86800

n. **불확실**
❶ un(부정어) + certainty(확실함): 불확실함
예 There is some uncertainty about the company's future.

✔ **unchanging**
[ʌntʃéindʒiŋ]
® 21207/86800

adj. **변하지 않는**
❶ un(부정어) + changing(변하는): 변하지 않는
예 Let me state my unchanging enmity for trappers who capture animals with the cruel leg - hold trap.

❤ **uncomfortable**
[ʌnkʌ́mfərtəbəl]
® 5610/86800

adj. **불쾌한, 편안치 않은**
❶ un(부정어) + comfortable(편안한)
예 These shoes are really uncomfortable.

✔ **uncommon**
[ʌnkámən]
® 9533/86800

adj. **드문**
❶ un(부정어) + common(흔한): 흔하지 않은
예 It's not uncommon for people to become ill when they travel.

U

unconscious
[ʌnkánʃəs]
® 5575/86800

adj. 무의식의, 깨닫지 못하는
❶ un(부정어) + conscious(의식적인): 무의식적인
파 *unconsciously*: 무의식적으로
예 She was hit on the head by a stone and knocked unconscious.

uncooperative
[ʌnkouápərèitiv]
® 36136/8680

adj. 비협력의
❶ un(부정어) + co(함께) + operative(운영하는): 협력하지 않는
예 I found him rude and uncooperative.

uncover
[ʌnkʌ́vər]
® 17176/86800

v. 폭로하다, ~의 덮개를 벗기다
❶ un(부정어) + cover(덮다): 덮개 열어 폭로하다
예 Police uncovered a criminal plot.

undaunted
[ʌndɔ́:ntid]
® 27956/86800

adj. 굽히지 않는, 용감한
❶ un(부정어) + **daunted(돈뜯어)** - 돈 안 뜯었어 하며 **굽히지 않는**
예 The firefighters were undaunted by the dangerous conditions they faced.

underestimate
[ʌ̀ndəréstəmèit]
® 13316/86800

v. 과소평가하다
❶ under(아래의, 열등한, 보다 조금 - 어원편 참조) + estimate(평가하다): 과소평가하다
예 Never underestimate your opponent!

undergo
[ʌ̀ndərgóu]
® 9864/86800

v. 겪다, 받다
❶ under(아래의, 열등한, 보다 조금) + go(가다): 아래로 가다, 겪다
예 She underwent an operation on a tumour in her left lung last year.

undergraduate
[ʌ̀ndərgrǽdʒuiit]
® 9814/86800

n. 대학생
❶ under(아래의, 열등한, 보다 조금) + graduate(졸업생): 졸업하지 않은 학생
예 Most undergraduate take four years to earn a degree.

underground
[ʌ́ndərgràund]
ⓡ 3848/86800

adj. n. 지하의, 지하도
❶ under(아래의, 열등한, 보다 조금) + ground(땅)
예 Moles live underground.

undertake
[ʌ̀ndərtéik]
ⓡ 4767/86800

v. 떠맡다, 착수하다
❶ under(아래의, 열등한, 보다 조금) + take(손에 잡다): 떠맡다
예 Students are required to undertake simple experiments.

undifferentiated
[ʌ̀ndifərénʃièitid]
ⓡ 27033/86800

a. 차별받지 않는
❶ Un(부정어) + differentiated(차별하는)
예 I was moved by undifferentiated policy.

undoubtedly
[ʌ̀ndáutidli]
ⓡ 3748/86800

ad. 확실히
❶ Un(부정어) + doubted(의심 있는) + ly(부사형어미): 의심하지 않고
예 I will pass the exam undoubtedly.

unemployed
[ʌ̀nemplɔ́id]
ⓡ 3377/86800

adj. 실직한
❶ un(부정어) + employed(고용된): 실직한
예 He's been unemployed for over a year.

unemployment
[ʌ̀nemplɔ́imənt]
ⓡ 1605/86800

n. 실업
❶ un(부정어) + employment(고용): 실업
예 My unemployment lasted about six months.

unexpected
[ʌ̀nikspéktid]
ⓡ 4165/86800

adj. 예기치 않은, 뜻밖의
❶ un(부정어) + expected(기대한): 기대치 않은
파 unexpectedly: 예기치 않게
예 I'm sad that she's leaving, but it was not unexpected.

unfair
[ʌnfέər]
ⓡ 4424/86800

adj. 불공평한
❶ un(부정어) + fair(공정한): 불공정한
예 It's unfair for them to be allowed to leave early if we can't.

U

457

unification
[jùːnəfikéiʃən]
Ⓡ 8864/86800

n. 통일

❶ uni(하나 - 어원편 참조) + fic(만들다) + tion(명사형 어미): 하나로 만듦

예 The Republic of Korea shall seek national unification.

uniform
[júːnəfɔ̀ːrm]
Ⓡ 3545/86800

n. adj. 제복, 같은 모양의

❶ uni(하나) + form(형태): **형태가 같은 유니폼**

예 I love a man in uniform!

unify
[júːnəfài]
Ⓡ 25060/86800

v. 통일하다

❶ uni(하나) + ify(만들다): 하나로 만들다

예 The creation of the national railroad system unified the country.

✔ union
[júːnjən]
Ⓡ 548/86800

n. 연합, 조합

❶ uni(하나): 하나로 된 연합

예 She joined the teachers' union.

❥ unique
[juːníːk]
Ⓡ 2320/86800

adj. 유일한, 독특한

❶ uni(하나) - 하나 밖에 없는

파 *uniqueness*: 유일무이

예 Humans are unique among mammals in several respects.

❥ unit
[júːnit]
Ⓡ 923/86800

n. 한 개의 단위, 단일체, 부대

❶ uni(하나) - 하나로 된 편제, unity의 변형

예 The family is the basic unit of society.

❥ unite
[juːnáit]
Ⓡ 11930/86800

v. 결합하다

❶ uni(하나) - 하나 되다, United States - 연합 주

예 Students united to protest the tuition increase.

unity
[júːnəti]
ⓡ 3310/86800

n. 통일
❶ uni(하나) + ity(명사형 어미): 하나 됨, 통일
예 Every day, my grandma prays for unity among her feuding family members.

✔ **universal**
[jùːnəvə́ːrsəl]
ⓡ 3521/86800

adj. 우주의, 전 세계의, 보편적인
❶ uni(하나) + verse(돌다): 하나되어 돌다 - 우주
파 *universe*: 우주, 세계 *universally*: 보편적으로
예 Food is a subject of almost universal interest.

✔ **unjust**
[ʌndʒʌ́st]
ⓡ 13184/86800

adj. 부정한, 불공평한
❶ un(부정어) + just(정당한): 부정한
예 The convict received an unjust sentence.

✔ **unless**
[ənlés]
ⓡ 917/86800

conj. ~하지 않는다면
❶ 숙제 **하지 않는 다면** 엄마가 **혼냈어(unless)**
예 You can't get a job unless you've got experience.

✔ **unlike**
[ʌnláik]
ⓡ 2164/86800

prep. ~와 달리
❶ un(부정어) + like(~와 같이): ~와 달리
예 Unlike the owl, bats cannot see very well.

unlimited
[ʌnlímitid]
ⓡ 8937/86800

adj. 한없는, 무제한의
❶ un(부정어) + limited(제한된): 무제한의
예 Membership gives you unlimited access to the facilities.

unload
[ʌnlóud]
ⓡ 20869/86800

v. 짐을 부리다
❶ un(부정어) + load(짐을 싣다): 짐을 부리다
예 Could you help me unload the car?

✔ **unlock**
[ʌnlák]
ⓡ 20538/86800

v. 자물쇠를 열다
❶ un(부정어) + lock(잠그다): 자물쇠를 열다
예 Could you unlock the door for me?

U

unlucky
[ʌnlʌ́ki]
® 11150/86800

adj. 불운한

❶ un(부정어) + lucky(행운의): 불운의

예 Some people think that 13 is an unlucky number.

✔✔ unmanned
[ʌnmǽnd]
® 37089/86800

a. 사람이 타지 않은, 사람이 없는

❶ Un (부정) + manned(사람이 탄)

예 This restaurant is unmanned after 10 p.m.

✔ unpleasant
[ʌnplézənt]
® 5902/86800

adj. 불쾌한

❶ un(부정어) + pleasant(기쁜): 불쾌한

예 The weather is so unpleasant here.

unpopular
[ʌnpápjələr]
® 9576/86800

adj. 인기가 없는

❶ un(부정어) + popular(인기 있는): 인기 없는

예 I was unpopular in high school.

unprecedented
[ʌnprésədèntid]
® 7711/86800

adj. 선례가 없는

❶ un(부정어) + precedented(선례 있는): 선례가 없는

예 This level of growth is unprecedented.

✔ unpredictable
[ʌnpridíktəbəl]
® 9189/86800

a. 예상할 수 없는

❶ Un(부정어) + pre(미리) + dict(말하다) + able(할 수 있는)
- 미리 말 할 수 없는

예 Today's weather is unpredictable.

✔ unreal
[ʌnrí:əl]
® 15473/86800

adj. 실재하지 않는

❶ un(부정어) + real(진짜의): 실재하지 않는

예 The town seemed as unreal as a movie set.

unreasonable
[ʌnrí:zənəbəl]
® 7115/86800

adj. 비합리적인

❶ un(부정어) + reasonable(이유가 될 만한) - 비합리적인

예 It seems unreasonable to expect one person to do both jobs.

✔ **unrest**
[ʌnrést]
ⓡ 7544/86800

n. 불안
① un(부정어) + rest(휴식, 안정): 불안
예 The country has experienced years of civil unrest.

✔ **unsatisfactory**
[ʌnsætisfæktəri]
ⓡ 8431/86800

adj. 만족스럽지 못한
① un(부정어) + satisfactory(만족하는): 만족스럽지 못한
예 He was fired for unsatisfactory performance.

unsteady
[ʌnstédi]
ⓡ 21098/86800

adj. 불안정한
① un(부정어) + steady(안정된): 불안정한
예 He was a little unsteady on his feet.

✔ **unsuccessful**
[ʌnsəksésfəl]
ⓡ 7280/86800

adj. 성공하지 못한
① un(부정어) + successful(성공하는): 성공하지 못한
예 His last novel was unsuccessful.

untie
[ʌntái]
ⓡ 40000/86800

v. 풀다, 끄르다
① un(부정어) + tie(묶다): 풀다
예 He untied the package and opened it.

✔ **unwillingness**
[ʌnwíliŋnes]
ⓡ 16272/86800

n. 내키지 않음
① Un(부정어) + willingness(내킴, 기꺼이 함)
예 I am unwilling to go.

uphold
[ʌdphóuld]
ⓡ 14920/86800

v. 들어 올리다, 지지하다
① up(위) + hold(붙잡다): 위를 붙잡다, 지지하다, 들어 올리다
예 He took an oath to uphold the Constitution.

✔ **upper**
[ápər]
ⓡ 1878/86800

adj. 더 위의, 상부의
① up(위)의 비교급, 더 위의
예 Write your name on the upper left - hand corner of the page.

U

461

✔ upright
[ʌ́pràit]
® 6027/86800

adj. 똑바른
➊ up(위) + right(바른): 위쪽이 바른, 똑바른
예 Put your seat back in the upright position.

✔ uproot
[ʌprúːt]
® 39963/86800

v. 뿌리째 뽑다, 근절하다
➊ up(위) + root(뿌리): 뿌리를 위로 들면서 뿌리 뽑다
예 Many trees were uprooted by the storm.

✔ upset
[ʌpsét]
® 2994/86800

v. n. 뒤집어엎다, 뒤집힌, 전복
➊ 나쁜 놈들 내가 뒤집어 없앴(upset)다
예 Any mechanical problems would upset our plans of driving across the desert.

upside
[ʌ́psàid]
® 53564/86800

n. 위쪽
➊ up(위) + side(쪽): 위쪽
예 One upside to the new house is its location.

✔ upward
[ʌ́pwərd]
® 8907/86800

adv. 위쪽으로
➊ up(위) + ward(쪽으로): 위쪽으로
예 With an upward trend in inflation, you expect prices to rise.

✔ urban
[ə́ːrbən]
® 1861/86800

adj. 도시의
➊ 얼 반(urban - 얼굴이 반반)한 - 도시 티 나는
예 Green Belt is countryside next to urban areas where there is a risk that the openness will be invaded by urban sprawl.

✔ urge
[əːrdʒ]
® 5720/86800

v. n. 촉구하다, 충동
➊ 얼 줘(urge - 얼른 줘)얼른 달라고 촉구하다
예 I urge you to reconsider.

✔ urgent
[ə́:rdʒənt]
ⓡ 4052/86800

adj. **긴급한**
❶ 얼전(urgent - 얼릉줘): 빨리 달라는, **긴급한**
예 We've come to deliver an urgent message.

usefulness
[júːsfəlnis]
ⓡ 11073/86800

n. **유용성**
❶ use(사용) + ful(가득찬) + ness(명사형 어미): 꽉 차게 사용함, 유용성
파 useless: 소용없는 usage: 사용법, 관습
useful: 유용한 *use*: 사용
usable: 사용가능한 *user*: 사용자
예 Some people think this system of education has outlived its usefulness.

usher
[ʌ́ʃər]
ⓡ 17759/86800

v. n. **안내하다, 수위**
❶ 어셔(usher) 옵쇼! 하고 **안내하다**
예 She ushered us into her office and offered us a coffee.

utensil
[juːténsəl]
ⓡ 68892/86800

n. **가정용품**
❶ 유 뗀 실(utensil) - 당신이 뗀 실은 **가정용품**, uti(여기서는 ute)는 사용하다의 뜻
예 In the drawer was a selection of kitchen utensils - spoons, spatulas, knives and whisks.

✔ utility
[juːtíləti]
ⓡ 6846/86800

n. **유용, (전기, 가스, 수도 등의) 공익설비**
❶ uti(사용하다) + ity(명사형 어미): 사용성, 유용함
파 utilize: 이용하다
예 Notify the utility if there's an outage.

✔ utmost
[ʌ́tmòust]
ⓡ 11063/86800

adj. **최대한도의, 극도의**
❶ ut(밖으로) + most(가장 많이): 많은 데다 또 밖으로 즉, 극도의
예 The situation needs to be handled with the utmost care.

U

utter
[ʌ́tər]
® 9163/86800

v. adj. 말하다, 완전한
❶ 語(어 - 말씀) 터(utter): 말을 트다 - 말하다
파 utterance: 말하기 utterly: 완전히
예 She sat through the whole meeting without uttering a word.

✔ vacant
[véikənt]
® 8037/86800

adj. 비어 있는, 공허한
❶ vac(비어있는 - 어원편 참조) + ant(형용사형 어미): 비어있는 혹은 어디 비었간(vacant)?
파 *vacuum*: 진공의 vacancy: 빈자리
예 The hospital has no vacant beds.

✔ vague
[veig]
® 5308/86800

adj. 애매한, 희미한
❶ vague(베이그): 애이구가 아니라 베이그면 발음이 애매하죠?
파 *vaguely*: 어렴풋하게 *vagueness*: 애매함
예 I do have a vague memory of meeting her many years ago.

vain
[vein]
® 13829/86800

adj. 헛된, 허영심이 강한
❶ 합격자 명단에서 베인(vain - 짤린) - 헛된
예 He was very vain about his hair and his clothes.

✽ valid
[vǽlid]
® 3894/86800

adj. 유효한, 타당한
❶ 발효다(valid) - 발효되면 유효하다 는 뜻
예 My way of thinking might be different from yours, but it's equally valid.

valley
[vǽli]
® 2155/86800

n. 계곡
❶ 산 계곡이 쉽게 보일리(valley) 없다
예 There was snow on the hill tops but not in the valley.

✽ value
[vǽlju:]
® 539/86800

n. 가치, 평가, 가격
❶ 그 사람 평가가 별루(value)다
파 valueless: 가치 없는 *valuable*: 가치 있는, 귀중품
예 What is the value of the prize?

464

vanish
[vǽniʃ]
® 14891/86800

v. 사라지다
❶ va(텅빈 - 어원편 참조): 텅 비어 있다, 사라지다
예 The child vanished while on her way home from school.

vanity
[vǽnəti]
® 13053/86800

n. 덧없음, 무익, 허영심
❶ 배 나왔디?(vanity) - 배 나와서 **무익함**
예 He wants the job purely for reasons of vanity and ambition.

vapor
[véipər]
® 11473/86800

n. 증기
❶ 발포(vapor)된 뒤 총구 보면 **김**이 난다
예 Poisonous vapours burst out of the factory during the accident.

✅ variety
[vəráiəti]
® 1176/86800

n. 다양성
❶ 새이 **다양하네, 보라였지(variety)?**
파 *various*: 다양한 *vary*: 다양하게 하다 *variation*: 변화
예 My life needs more variety.

✔ vase
[veis]
® 11366/86800

n. 꽃 병, 단지
❶ 꽃 병 vase(비었어)!
예 I put a vase of carnations on the table.

✅ vast
[væst]
® 2148/86800

adj. 거대한, 방대한
❶ 거대한 **배 세트 (vast)** - 거대한 함선 세트
파 *vastly*: 광대하게
예 A vast audience watched the broadcast.

✅ vegetable
[védʒətəbəl]
® 7181/86800

n. 채소
❶ 배추더블(vegetable): 배추는 **채소**
파 *vegetation*: 식물
예 The potato is the most popular vegetable in Britain.

vehicle
[víːikəl]
ⓡ 2392/86800

n. 탈것
❶ 비클 (vehicle)!: 비켜 큰일나 탈것이 나가신다
㈜ Have you seen his new car? It's a fine - looking vehicle.

veil
[veil]
ⓟ 11532/86800

n. v. 면사포, 베일을 씌우다
❶ 베일(veil)에 가려있다
㈜ She dropped a veil.

vein
[vein]
ⓡ 8568/86800

n. 정맥
❶ 베인(vein) - 정맥을 칼에 베인
㈜ Normally their valves should allow blood to flow only inwards from the superficial veins to the deep veins.

venerable
[vénərəbəl]
ⓡ 20470/86800

adj. (인격, 나이, 지위로) 존경할 만한
❶ 배우노라 블(venerable) - 나이 먹어도 배우는 분은 존경할 만한
㈜ The venerable old man was a cherished source of advice and wisdom for the villagers.

ventilate
[véntəlèit]
ⓡ 47787/86800

v. 환기시키다
❶ vent(~에 구멍을 내다 - 빈터에 구멍을 내다로 기억) + ate(동사형 어미): 환기시키다
㈜ She opened the windows to ventilate the room.

venture
[véntʃər]
ⓡ 3783/86800

v. n. 위험을 무릅쓰고 가다, 모험
❶ 벤쳐(venture)기업은 모험 가망성 많은 사업
㈜ We ventured out into the woods.

verbal
[vɔ́ːrbəl]
ⓡ 5238/86800

adj. 말의
❶ 벙어리가 말하려고 버 벅(verbal)댐: 말의
㈜ We gave only verbal instructions.

verify
[vérəfai]
Ⓡ 17135/86800

v. 증명하다, 확인하다
❶ 확인하려면 **보라 파일(verify)** - 확인하려면 봐 파일(문서)을
㉠ She verified her flight number.

verse
[vəːrs]
Ⓡ 5502/86800

n. 운문, 시
❶ (읊)**벌서(verse)** - 시를 읊었어
㉠ The epic tale was written in verse.

✔ **version**
[və́ːrʒən]
Ⓡ 1272/86800

n. 번역, 판
❶ **버전(version)**이라는 말은 많이 사용하는 말
㉠ I have an older version of the software.

✔ **versus**
[və́ːrsəs]
Ⓡ 7161/86800

prep. ~대(한국 대 일본)
❶ Korea **vs** Japan 이때 vs가 versus
㉠ Today's game is Korea vs Japan.

✔ **vertical**
[və́ːrtikəl]
Ⓡ 4607/86800

adj. 수직의
❶ **버티 칼(vertical)** - 칼이 버티고 서 있으려면 **수직**으로 있어야 함
㉠ She looked over the cliff and found she was standing at the edge of a vertical drop.

vessel
[vésəl]
Ⓡ 5587/86800

n. 배, 그릇
❶ **배 쓸(vessel)** - 배에 쓸 **그릇**
㉠ The remains of some Roman earthenware vessels were found during the dig.

vex
[veks]
Ⓡ 82884/86800

v. 짜증나게 하다, 괴롭히다
❶ **백써(vex)** - 선생님이 숙제 **백번써(vex)**라고 나를 **짜증나게 하다**
㉠ We were vexed by the delay.

via
[víːə]
Ⓡ 2179/86800

prep. ~을 경유하여, ~에 의하여
❶ 남자는 **비아**(via - 비아그라)**에 의해** 힘을 얻음
㉠ She flew to Los Angeles via Chicago.

v

vice
[vais]
Ⓡ 6338/86800

n. 악
❶ 바이스(vice) - 바이러스 생각하면 컴퓨터의 **악**
예 He thought gambling was a vice.

victim
[víktim]
Ⓡ 2545/86800

n. 희생자, 피해자
❶ 피튐(victim) - **희생자**들이 총에 맞아 피튐
예 The children are the innocent/helpless victims of the fighting.

view
[vju:]
Ⓡ 400/86800

n. 견해, 경치, 보다
❶ 뷔유(view) - 보여유 - 보는것은 한자로 **견해**
파 *viewer*: 시청자 viewpoint: 관점
예 In my view, her criticisms were completely justified.

vigor
[vígər]
Ⓡ 10573/86800

n. 활력, 정력
❶ 남성 활력소 비아그라는 vigor(활력) + Niagara(나이아가라)의 합성어인데 암튼 vigor는 활력
파 vigorous: 힘찬
예 They set about their work with youthful vigour and enthusiasm.

vile
[vail]
Ⓡ 16495/86800

adj. 비열한
❶ 봐 일(vile) - 봐 일본군이 얼마나 **비열한**지
예 This vile policy of ethnic cleansing must be stopped.

vineyard
[vínjərd]
Ⓡ 19440/86800

n. 포도밭, 활동무대
❶ *vine*(와인, 포도나무, 덩굴식물) + yard(뜰)
예 vineyard is a piece of land on which vines are grown.

violate
[váiəlèit]
Ⓡ 22395/86800

v. 위반하다
❶ 봐요 래잇(violate) - 봐요 늦었데요! 하며 **규칙위반**을 일러바치다
예 He was arrested for violating his parole.

✔ violent
[váiələnt]
Ⓡ 3372/86800

adj. **폭력적인, 격렬한**
❶ 비열한(violent) - 폭력을 쓰는 것은 비열한
㎩ *violence*: 폭력, 맹렬
㉠ The peaceful protest suddenly turned violent.

virtual
[vớ:rtʃuəl]
Ⓡ 7704/86800

adj. **실질상의**
❶ 봤지요(virtual)! 실제 존재를
㉠ The Web site provides a virtual tour of the stadium.

✔ virtue
[vớ:rtʃu:]
Ⓡ 4504/86800

n. **미덕, 덕행**
❶ 부모님 산소의 **벌초(virtue)**는 돌아가신 후라도 **미덕**인 것 같아요
㉠ Patience is a virtue.

✤ vision
[víʒən]
Ⓡ 2382/86800

n. **시력, 시각**
❶ vi(보다) + sion(명사형 어미): 보는 것
㎩ *visual*: 시각의 *visible*: 눈에 보이는 *visually*: 시각적으로
visualization: 보이게 함
㉠ She has very little vision in her left eye.

✤ vital
[váitl]
Ⓡ 2000/86800

adj. **생명의, 필수적인**
❶ 바이탈(vital - vita는 살아있는 - 어원편)—**바이타민(vitamin)** 생각
해도 우리 몸에 필수적인
㎩ vitality: 활력
㉠ The sciences are a vital part of the school curriculum.

✔ vivid
[vívid]
Ⓡ 6934/86800

adj. **생생한, 활기찬**
❶ viv(살아있는): 생생한, 살아있어서 서로 비비다
㎩ vividly: 생생하게
㉠ He gave a vivid description of the scene.

✤ vocabulary
[voukǽbjəlèri]
Ⓡ 6159/86800

n. **어휘**
❶ 부엌에 **불러리(vocabulary)** - 부엌에서도 **어휘**
외울 때 노래 부르듯 외워라
㉠ She has learned a lot of new vocabulary.

vocal
[vóukəl]
Ⓡ 8515/86800

adj. **목소리의**
Ⓣ voc(목소리 - 어원편 참조) + al(형용사형 어미): vocal이란 말 들어보셨죠? 목소리와 관련된 말
파 vocation: 직업, 소명 vocational: 직업의
예 The six principal roles in this opera have an average vocal range of two octaves.

vogue
[voug]
Ⓡ 12995/86800

n. **유행**
Ⓣ 옷 사려면 **유행**을 **보고(vogue)** 사시게
예 That style went out of vogue years ago.

volcano
[valkéinou]
Ⓡ 13200/86800

n. **화산**
Ⓣ **화산** 폭발하면 **볼게 있노?(vocano)**
예 The volcano last erupted 25 years ago.

✔ **volume**
[válju:m]
Ⓡ 1904/86800

n. **책, 권(券), 양, 소리 크기**
Ⓣ 볼륨(volume - 소리크기) 줄여라, vol 2는 두 번째 책이라는 뜻입니다
예 Can you turn the volume up?

✔ **volunteer**
[vàləntíər]
Ⓡ 7462/86800

n. v. **자원 봉사자, 자원하다**
Ⓣ **자원 종사자**들은 **발로 뛰어(volunteer)!**
파 ***voluntary***: 자발적인 voluntarily: 자발적으로
volunteerism: 자유지원제
예 It's a volunteer army with no paid professionals.

✔ **vomit**
[vámit]
Ⓡ 17953/86800

v. **토하다**
Ⓣ 역한 것 **보** (면) **밑(vomit)**으로 **토하다**
예 She came home drunk and vomited all over the kitchen floor.

✔ **vote**
[vout]
Ⓡ 1445/86800

n. v. **투표, 투표하다**
Ⓣ 한 표 라도 **보테(vote):** 투표, voter - 투표자
예 She was too young to vote in the national election.

vouch
[vautʃ]
® 31602/86800

v. 보증하다, 증인이 되다
❶ 내가 **봤지(vouch)!** (내가) **보증**한다
㊙ warrant
㉠ As a medical examiner I can vouch from experience that his death was accidental.

vow
[vau]
® 17849/86800

n. v. 맹세, 맹세하다
❶ 두고 **보오(vow)** 내 **맹세**코 담배를 끊으리다
㉠ The guerrillas vowed (that) they would overthrow the government.

vowel
[váuəl]
® 12982/86800

n. 모음
❶ vo(목소리 - voc의 변형) + wel(발음이 울 이므로, 우는 자음 아니고 모음) - 목소리 나는 것 중 **모음**
㉠ The vowels in English are a, e, i, o and u.

voyage
[vɔ́idʒ]
® 9112/86800

n. 항해
❶ 저기 섬이 **보이지(voyage)?** **항해** 때 하는 말
㉠ He was a young sailor on his first sea voyage.

vulgar
[vʌ́lgər]
® 13998/86800

adj. 천한, 상스러운
❶ 일본인들이 **빠가 (vulgar)**야로! 라고 하는 것은 **상스러운** 말
㉠ It was an extremely vulgar joke.

wage
[weidʒ]
® 2988/86800

n. 임금
❶ 왜 **이지(wage)?**: 왜 이것 만 주지?를 줄인 말, **임금**에 불만 없는 사람 없어요? 왜 이것만 주지?
㉠ The smaller shops pay very low wages.

❖ **wander**
[wándəːr]
® 9079/86800

v. 목적 없이 돌아다니다, 배회하다
❶ 완 달(wander - 완전 건달): 건달이 주변을 **배회하다**
㉠ We spent the morning wandering around the old part of the city.

V

want
[wɔ(:)nt]
® 151/86800

v. n. 원하다, 부족
❶ **부족**하니까 **원(want)**하죠
예 I want some chocolate.

ware
[wɛə:r]
® 17738/86800

n. 제품, 물품
❶ hardware가 철물, 철제품인데 착안하여 ware는 제품이구나, 로 생각할 것
파 *warehouse*: 창고
예 She sold her wares at the market.

warfare
[wɔ́:rfɛə:r]
® 8341/86800

n. 전쟁
❶ war(전쟁) + fare(추세, 상태): 전쟁
파 *war*: 전쟁
예 companies engaged in constant warfare for dominance in the market for home computers.

warmth
[wɔ:rmə]
® 4234/86800

n. 따뜻함
❶ warm(따뜻한) + th(명사형 어미): 따뜻함
파 *warm*: 따뜻한 *warmer*: 온열기
예 I could feel the warmth of the fireplace.

warn
[wɔ:rn]
® 6515/86800

v. 경고하다
❶ 까불면 **완(warn)**력 쓴다고 **경고하다**
파 *warning*: 경고, 경고의
예 Nobody warned me about the dangers.

warrant
[wɔ́(:)rənt]
® 6483/86800

n. v. 보증, 보증하다
❶ 문제 있으면 **와란(warrant)**! 문제 있으면 와라 내가 **보증**할게!
파 warranty: 보증서 예 I'll warrant he did!

waste
[weist]
® 1517/86800

v. n. 낭비하다, 쓰레기
❶ **왜이썼데(waste)**?: 왜이리 썼어? **낭비하다**
파 *wasteful*: 낭비하는, 헛된
예 Come on, let's get started - we've wasted enough time already.

weaken
[wíːkən]
Ⓡ 12885/86800

v. **약화시키다**
❶ weak(왜커 - 왜소하게 커서) + en(만들다): **약하게 만들다**
파 *weakness*: 허약함 *weak*: 허약한
예 The disease weakens the immune system.

wealth
[welθ]
Ⓡ 2597/86800

n. **부, 재산**
❶ 웰써(wealth - 웰 을 잘로 해석하면): 웰 써(잘 써) - **재산**, 부
파 *wealthy*: 부유한
예 Her personal wealth is estimated to be around $10 billion.

weapon
[wépən]
Ⓡ 4337/86800

n. **무기**
❶ 왜 폰(weapon)?: 왜 포는? **무기**로 가져왔어?
예 The pitcher's slider is his most effective weapon.

weary
[wíəri]
Ⓡ 8985/86800

adj. v. **피로한, 싫증난, 지치게 하다**
❶ 단어를 언제 다 **외우리(weary)**? - **지친**, 싫증난
예 I need to rest my weary eyes.

weave
[wiːv]
Ⓡ 14690/86800

v. **짜다**
❶ 내가 **짠** 스웨터 **입어(weave)**
예 This type of wool is woven into fabric which will make jackets.

web
[web]
Ⓡ 10182/86800

n. **거미줄, 망**
❶ www(world, wide, web) web은 거미줄, 망이라는 말로 많이 사회에서 많이 쓰임
예 We watched a spider spin a web between three tall grass stems.

weed
[wiːd]
Ⓡ 11731/86800

n. **잡초**
❶ sea weed(바다 잡초는 해초 - 김, 미역)
예 The vacant lot was covered with weeds.

weep
[wi:p]
® 13454/86800

v. 울다
➊ w(woman) + eep(이쁘): 여자는 울때 이뻐!
예 She sat down and wept.

✔ weigh
[wei]
® 9380/86800

v. 무게를 달다
➊ 웨이트(weight)트레이닝을 생각해 보세요
파 *weight*: 무게 예 How much do you weigh?

weird
[wiə:rd]
® 6713/86800

adj. 이상한, 기묘한
➊ 단어 **위얼다(weird)** - 단어 외웠다! 해야 하므로 발음이 **이상한**
예 Her boyfriend's a bit weird but she's all right.

❖ welfare
[wélfɛə:r]
® 2098/86800

n. 복지
➊ well(건강한, 잘) + fare(추세, 상태): 잘 있는 상태, 복지
예 The welfare of all the orphans was at stake.

well-being
[wélbí:iŋ]
® 23445/86800

n. 복지, 행복
➊ well(잘) + being(존재): 잘 존재 - **복지**
예 People doing yoga benefit from an increased feeling
of well - being.

whimsical
[hwímzikəl]
® 31782/86800

adj. 변덕스러운
➊ 마음이 **움직껼(whimsical)** 이는 - **변덕스러운**
예 It's hard to make plans with such a whimsical best friend.

whip
[hwip]
® 7819/86800

v. n. 채찍질하다, 채찍
➊ 휙(whip)하며 **채찍질**하다
예 The jockey whipped his horse.

whirl
[hwə:rl]
® 24192/86800

v. n. 빙빙 돌다, 빙빙 돌리다, 회전
➊ 월 풀(whirlpool - 소용돌이) 욕조 생각
- 물이 **빙빙 도는** 월풀 욕조
예 Clothes were whirling in the washing machine.

wholesale
[hóulsèil]
Ⓡ 8893/86800

adj. 도매의
❶ whole(전부의, 건강한) + sale(판매): 대량으로 사서 소매업자에게 넘기는 도매의
c.f) *wholesaler*: 도매업자 ㉠ retail: 소매(의)
예 Is that price retail or wholesale?

wholesome
[hóulsəm]
Ⓡ 19907/86800

adj. 건강에 좋은, 건전한
❶ whole(건강한) + some(형용사와 쓰여 ~하게 하는): 건강에 좋은, 혹은 홀썸(홀쭉)해야 건강한
예 He looks like a nice, wholesome, young man.

wicked
[wíkid]
Ⓡ 6663/86800

adj. 사악한, 심술궂은
❶ 친구 몰래 체육복을 벗기다(wicked): 사악한, 심술궂은, 원래 wicked는 wizard에서 유래
예 She played the part of the wicked stepmother in the play.

widespread
[wáidspréd]
Ⓡ 2980/86800

adj. 널리 퍼진, 광범위한
❶ wide(널리) + spread(퍼진): 널리 퍼진
예 There is widespread public interest in the election.

widow
[wídou]
Ⓡ 5142/86800

n. 미망인, 홀아비
❶ 외도(widow - 바람피우는 일)하면 남편, 부인중 한사람이 죽습니다. 미망인, 홀아비
예 Jane's husband died in June so she has been a widow for only a couple of months.

width
[widə]
Ⓡ 6451/86800

n. 너비
❶ wide(넓은)의 명사형
파 *wide*: 넓은 *widely*: 널리 *widen*: 넓히다
wider: 폭이 넓은, 헐렁한
예 What is the width of the table?

wilderness
[wíldə:rnis]
® 9186/86800

n. 황야, 황무지
❶ wild(황량한) + ness(명사형어미),wilder(길을 잃게하다) + ness: 황량한 곳, 길을 잃게 하는 곳
파 *wild*: 야생의, 황량한 *wildly*: 격렬하게
예 She enjoys hikes through the wilderness.

willing
[wíliŋ]
® 2466/86800

adj. 기꺼이 ~하는
❶ 엄마가 시키면 **얼룽(willing)**하는 - **기꺼이 하는**
예 He was a willing participant in the crime.

wipe
[waip]
® 8409/86800

v. 닦다
❶ 차에 달린 **와이퍼(wiper)**에 착안, 와이퍼는 비나 눈이 오면 차를 **닦아** 줍니다
예 Would you wipe the dishes?

wire
[waiə:r]
® 3919/86800

n. 철사, 전선
❶ 와이어리스 인터넷(wireless Internet - 무선 인터넷)에 착안하세요
예 There was a wire sticking out of the chair.

wistful
[wístfəl]
® 24055/86800

adj. 탐내는 듯한, 그리워하는
❶ **위시다풀(wistful**: wish - 소망이 ful - 꽉 찬): **탐내는 듯한**, 그리워하는
예 He had a wistful look on his face.

witch
[witʃ]
® 9901/86800

n. 마녀
❶ **위치(witch)**를 마술로 알아낸 **마녀**
예 Her mother - in - law is a bitter old witch.

withdraw
[wiðdrɔ́:]
® 5192/86800

v. 움츠리다, 철수(회수)하다, 돈을 인출하다
❶ with(함께) + draw(끌어당기다): 끌어 당기려면 몸을 **움츠려야** 함, 회수, 철수, 인출하다
파 withdrawal: 철수, 인출, 회수
예 She withdrew $200 from her checking account.

wither
[wíðər]
® 27697/86800

v. 시들다
❶ **휘들(wither):** 발음이 **시들**과 비슷하므로 그렇게 암기 해 볼 것
예 Grass had withered in the fields.

withhold
[wiðhóuld]
® 18262/86800

v. 승낙을 보류하다, 억제하다
❶ with(함께) + hold(붙잡아두다): 보류하다, 억제하다
예 She was accused of withholding evidence.

withstand
[wiðstǽnd]
® 12333/86800

v. 저항하다
❶ with(함께, 반대하여) + stand(저항하다): 저항하다
예 They withstood attacks from many critics.

✔ **witness**
[wítnis]
® 3625/86800

n. v. 목격자, 목격하다
❶ **봤다니스(witness):** w가 독일어에서는 'ㅂ' 발음 나므로 봤다니
스로 읽으면 **목격하다**
예 The defense called its first witness to the stand.

✔ **witty**
[wíti]
® 12522/86800

adj. 재치있는
❶ 재치있는 사람보고 **위트(wit)**가 넘친다고 하는 것에 착안, witty
는 **재치있는**
예 He was witty and very charming.

✔ **workload**
[wəːrkloud]
® 11526/86800

n. 표준 노동량
❶ work(작업) + load(짐) - 작업량
예 I carried my usual work load.

workout
[wə́ːrkàut]
® 30379/86800

n. 운동, 운동 경기 연습
❶ 권투 경기를 위한 연습에서 유래한 말로 work(일, 연습, 운동)
+ out(철저히)
예 The team had a good workout at practice today.

w

worm
[wə:rm]
® 10111/86800

n. 벌레
❶ 벌레가 기어옴(worm)
예 A worm will turn.

worship
[wə́:rʃip]
® 5035/86800

n. v. 예배, 예배하다
❶ wor(worth - 가치있는) + ship(형용사와 추상적인 뜻 만듦): 신을
예배하는 가치 있는 일
예 Worship services are held daily.

worth
[wə:rθ]
® 802/86800

adj. n. 가치가 있는, 가치
❶ worth(월세): 월세를 내면 내가 그 만큼 살 가치를 얻는
파 worthless: 가치 없는 worthwhile: 가치가 있는
예 I think this matter is worth our attention.

wound
[wu:nd]
® 4053/86800

n. v. 부상, 상처를 입히다
❶ 운다(wound)! 상처를 입어서
예 She suffered a knife wound to her thigh.

wrap
[ræp]
® 9577/86800

v. n. 감싸다, 두르다, 싸개
❶ 짜장면 시키면 랩(wrap)으로 감싸서 오지요
예 She wrapped a scarf around her neck.

wreck
[rek]
® 10441/86800

v. n. 난파하다, 난파선
❶ wr(water) + eck(neck): 물에 목만 내놓고 있는 배 - 난파선
예 I wrecked my mother's car.

wretched
[rétʃid]
® 10025/86800

adj. 비참한
❶ 죄인을 비참히 내치다(wreched), 내치다는 쫓아내다, 버리다의 뜻
예 The slums were filled with poor, wretched children.

wrinkle
[ríŋkəl]
® 39871/86800

v. 주름(지게 하다)
❶ 링클 케어(wrinkle care)라고 주름살 줄이는 것 TV에서 선전하
던데 참고하세요
예 Try not to wrinkle your trousers.

yawn
[jɔːn]
® 21642/86800

v. n. 하품하다, 하품
❶ 잠이 **와온(yawn) - 하품하다**
예 Students were yawning in class.

✔ **yearbook**
[jíəːrbùk]
® 31404/86800

n. 연감, 연보
❶ year(해) + book(책) - 년 마다 발간하는 책
예 We publish yearbook every year.

yearn
[jəːrn]
® 32170/86800

v. 그리워하다, 갈망하다
❶ 戀(연 - yearn) - 한자로 **그리워하다** e.g.) 연모
파 yearning: 그리워함, 그리워하는
예 Sometimes I just yearn to be alone.

✔ **yell**
[jel]
® 18106/86800

v. 소리치다, 외치다
❶ 여덟, 아홉, **열(yell)** 하고 **소리치다**
예 The crowd was yelling wildly.

✔ **yet**
[jet]
® 258/86800

adv. 아직, 벌써, 그럼에도 불구하고
❶ 예(yet)?: 아직이요?
예 Has the mail arrived yet?

✔ **yield**
[jiːld]
® 4125/86800

v. 생산하다, 양보하다
❶ 일다(yield) - **일** 하면 다 **생산**을 하게 됩니다
예 This soil should yield good crops.

✔ **youth**
[juːə]
® 1884/86800

n. 젊음, 청춘기, 젊은이
❶ 유쓰 호스텔(Youth Hostel - 젊은이들을 위한 숙박 시설)
예 He got into a lot of trouble in his youth.

Y

zeal
[ziːl]

Ⓡ 14541/86800

n. 열심, 열의

❶ **젤(zeal)열심히** 할 거야

예 Everyone has a zeal for money making.

zone
[zoun]

Ⓡ 3582/86800

n. 지대, 구역, 지구

❶ **D.M.Z**(demilitarized zone - 비 무장 지대)에 착안해서 기억해보세요

예 This stretch of coast has been designated a danger zone.

zoology
[zouálədʒi]

Ⓡ 27332/86800

n. 동물학

❶ zoo(동물, 동물원) + logy(학문, 말, 이론): 동물학
날 꺼내 **주(zoo)!!!! - 동물**들이 꺼내달라고 외치네

파 *zoological*: 동물학의

예 Zoology is the study of animals kept in a zoo.

어원정리

어근	뜻	예
a	～위(안)에, ～로부터	aside(옆에), aboard(배위에), akin(동족의)
a, ab, ap	분리, 이탈, 아래	abate(빼다)
a(an)	無(없는),反(반대되는), 非(아닌)	apathy(무관심), atheist(무신론자)
ac(ad,af,ag,al,ap), ob	～쪽으로, 대항하여	appease(진정시키다), oppose(반대하다)
acr	쓴, 날카로운, 신	acrimony(신랄함)
aero, air, avi	공기, 분위기, 비행기	aerohydroplane(수상비행기), aviator(비행사)
ag	움직이다, 행동하다	agitate(움직이다), agile(민첩한)
agog	선동가	demagogue(대중선동가)
agr	농사짓다, 경작하다	agronomy(농경법)
alb, cand	하얗다	album(앨범은 하얀색), candid(솔직한)
ali, allo, alter, ater, hetero	다른	alibi(현장부재 증명*bi는 다른장소.allonym(가명), alteration(변경)
ambi, amphi	둘 다, 여기저기	ambidextrous (양손을 다 쓰는)
amor	사랑, 친목, 우호	amity(친목), amiable(상냥한)
amphi, circum, peri	둘레, 여기저기	periscope(잠망경)
ann	1년 이하 (enn: 1년 이상)	anniversary(기념식)
ant, anti	반대	antipathy(반감), antonym(반대말)
an, ante, anti, ant, ex, fore, pr	前(앞)	anticipate(예상하다), ex-wife(전처), ancestor(조상)
aqua	물	aquarium(수족관)

어근	뜻	예
arch	우두머리 ,활모양의	anarchy(무정부상태) archery(궁술)
arch, prim, prin, proto	우두머리, 첫째	primordial(최초의)
ard, ter	사람	youngster(젊은이)
arm	무기	armory(무기고)
aster, astro	별	astrology(점성술), disaster(재앙)
aud, aus	듣다	auditorium(강당, 관람석)
auto, aut	스스로	autonomy(자치)

어근	뜻	예
band, bond, bund	묶다	contraband(밀수품), bandage(속박), bandage(붕대)
bar	막대, 장애물	embarrass(당황하게 하다), barrier(장애물)
baro	압력	barometer(기압계)
be,en, em, fic, fac, ify, ize, feit	만들다	enligthen(계몽하다)
bell	아름다운,전쟁	belvedere(전망대), embellish(과장하다)
bene, bon	좋은	beneficial(이득이 있는)
bibli	책	bibliomania(독서광)
bio	살아있는	antibiotic(항생물질), biography(전기), biologyy(생물학)
bi, di, du, diplo	둘(2)	bilingual(두개 국어의)
~bird,~box,~bug	~에 몰두한 사람	jailbird(죄수)
by	옆	by-product 부산물

어근	뜻	예
caco	나쁜	cacophony(음치)
calor	열	calorification(발열)
camera	방	bicameral(양원제의)
cant, chant	노래하다	chant(노래하다)
cap	머리, 중요한, 잡다	cabbage(양배추), capture(포획)
cap, ceive, cept, cip	잡다	anticipate(예상하다)
car, carn	살	carnival(사육제), carnivorous(육식성의)
cata	아래, 부정	catastrophe(파국)
cede, ceed, cess, vent, it, gress, amb	가다	antecede(선행하다), amble(걷다), process(과정)
celer	속도	decelerate(감속하다)
cent, hect, hecato	백(100)	hectogram(백그램)
cept,	받나, 집다	accept(받아들이다), reception(수봉)
chrom	색깔	chromosome(염색체)
chron	시간	chronology(연대기)
cide	죽이다	homicide(살인범), insecticide(살충제)
cise, sec, tomy	자르다	excision(삭제), pneumectomty(폐절제술)
civ	시민	decivilize(비문명화하다)
claim, clam, clum	선언하다	exclamation(외침)
clus	포함하다, 범위	inclusive(포함하는), conclusion(결론)
co(m,n,l,r)	함께, 서로, 같은	coworker(동료), common(공통의)
cogn ,gn	알다	prognosis(예감)
coni ,koni	먼지	pneumonoconiosis(진폐증)
contra	반대, 대항	contradict(반박하다), conterattack(반격)
corp	신체, 단체	incorporate(합병하다)

어근	뜻	예
cosmo	세계, 조화	cosmonaut(우주비행사)
counter, countra	반대	counterattack(반격)
cracy	지배하다, 다스리다	autocracy(독재정치)
cred	믿다	accreditation(신뢰, 신임장), credible(믿을만한)
cross	교차된	crosswalk(횡단보도)
cur, course, flu	흐르다	curriculum(교육과정)
cycl, cyclo, circle	원, 순환하는	encyclopedia(백과사전)

어근	뜻	예
de	아래로, 철저히, 떨어져서, 부정, 단순강조	detour(우회하다), depress(낙담시키다), descendant(자손)
dec	열(10)	Decalogue(십계명)
dent, don't	이빨	denture(의치), trident(삼지창)
derm, dermato	피부	dermatology(피부학)
dia, di	통하여, 사이에, 가로질러	diameter(직경), dialogue(대화), diagram(도표)
di, du, bi(twi-twist)	둘(2)	dual(이중의), bicycle(자전거), divorce(이혼하다)
dic	말	abdicate(퇴위하다, 포위하다)
dis, dif	반대, 떨어져서	disappear
doc, tui	가르치다	doctrine(학설), intuition(직관)
dodeca, duodec	열둘(12)	duodecimal system(십이진법)
dol	슬픔	condolence(애도)
dom	지위, 상태, 영역	kingdom(왕국)
dorm	잠자다	dormitive(최면성의)
dors	뒤	endorse(이서하다)
drome	달리다	hippodrome(마차경주장)
duc	이끌다	educe(추론하다), deduct(공제하다)
dyna	권력	dynasty(왕조)
dys	나쁜	dyspepsia(소화불량)

어근	뜻	예
e(ex)	바깥의	emit(내뿜다), exclaim(외치다), exceed(초과하다), export(수출하다)
endo, in, intra, intro	이내, 안쪽에	endoparasites(기생충), endoscope(내시경)
eo	아래	eolith(원시석기시대)
epi, ecto	~사이에,~위	epidemic(전염병)
equi, par, sym(n)	같은	equanimity(고요), synonym(동의어) parity(동등, 같은 값어치)
~esque, ~oid	~같은	picturesque(그림같은), hemoid(피같은)
eu	좋은	euphony(좋은 소리)
ex~, former~	前(전)	ex-wife(前부인) former president(전 대통령)
exter, extra, extro	바깥의, 넘어선	extrovert(외향적인), extraordinary(이상한), extroverted(외향적인)

어근	뜻	예
fac, fec, fic	만들다	magnificent(웅장한)
fer	나르다, 지니다	circumference(둘레), transfer(갈아타다)
fer, lat	가져오다, 낳다	fertilization(비옥화)
fide, feal, ferder	믿음, 신뢰	infidel(이교도, 회의론자)
fila, fili	실, 선	filature(실 잣는 기구)
fin, term	끝	definition(정의), determine(정의하다)
fix	고정시키다, 붙이다	suffix(접미어)
flex	구부러진	circumflex(굴절의)
for	반대하는	forbade(금지하다)

어원
정리

어근	뜻	예
forc, fort,	힘	fortify(강화하다)
fore	앞에	foresee(예견하다), forehed(이마)
fortuna	운, 기회	unfortunate(불운한)
frac, frag, fring	깨다	fragile(부숴지기쉬운)
frater	형제	fraternity(협동단체), fraternal(형제의)
ful	꽉 찬	artful(기교를 부린, 인위적인)
fum	연기	fumiduct(굴뚝)
fus	붓다, 녹이다	confuse(뒤섞다, 혼동다), fusion(용해)

G

어근	뜻	예
gamos, gamy	결혼	endogamy(동족결혼)
gen	생산하다	progenitor(조상, 원조)
germ	싹, 씨앗, 원천, 세균	germinate(싹이 트다)
gest	나르다, 띠다	digestion(소화)
graph, gram	쓰다, 그리다	biography(전기)
grat	만족, 감사	gratification(만족)
grav	무거운	gravitation(중력)
greg, mob, flock	무리	congregation(모임), gregarious(떼지어사는)
gyno	여자	gynous(여성미)

H

어근	뜻	예
hal, spir	숨 쉬다	inhale(숨을 들이쉬다)
hav, habit	살다	habitat(서식지)
helio	태양	heliocentric(태양중심의), heliofugal(태양으로부터 멀어지는)
hema, hemo	피	hemophilia(혈우병)

어근	뜻	예
hemi,semi, demi, med	중간, 반	hemisphere(반 구체)
hepta, sept	일곱(7)	heptachord(7음계)
her, hes	붙다	adhere(부착하다)
hexa, sex	여섯(6)	sexcentenary(600년제)
holo	큰	holocaust(대학살)
homo	같은 성질	homogenize(동질화하다)
hum, hom, anthrop	흙, 사람	homicide(살인)
hydr	물	dehydrate(탈수하다)
hypno	최면, 잠자다	hypnosis(최면상태)

어근	뜻	예
in, im	안에	indoor(실내의), influence(영향), insert(삽입하다)
infer, infra	아래	infrared ray(적외선)
intel	알고 생각하는 힘	intellectual(지적인)
inter, intra, intro	안에, 사이에	international(국제인), introvert(내향적인사람), interrupt(방해하다)
im, il, in, ir	부정의 뜻	illegal(비합법적인), inevitable(피할 수 없는) inconvenient(불편한)
ine	화학성분, 추상, 성질, 과학용어, 여성형 어미	caffeine(카페인), doctrine(교리), feminine(여자의), alkaline(알카린), heroine(여성영웅)
~ile	~하기 쉬운	docile(가르치기 쉬운), ductile(유순한)
it	가다	circuit(순회하다), exit(출구)
~itis	질병	appendicitis(맹장염)

J

어근	뜻	예
jec,	던지다, 놓다	rejection(거절), subject(주제), injection(주사)
join, jug, junct	참여하다, 결혼하다	conjugal(혼인의)
jud, jur, jus	판단하다, 올바른	jurisdiction(재판), justify(정당화하다), injury(부상)
junct	결합하다	disjunctive(분리하는)

K

어근	뜻	예
kilo, milli	천	kilowatt(천 와트)

L

어근	뜻	예
lapse	실수	collapse(붕괴하다)
lateral	면, 변	equilateral(등변의)
league, feder	연맹	colleague(동료)
leg	법	legal(합법적인), legitimate(합법적인)
lev	가볍게하다, 들어올리다	elevate(들어올리다), relieve(경감하다)
liber, liver	자유로운	equilibrium(균형)
lic	허용하다	license(면허증)
lig	묶다	oblige(의무를 지우다)
～ling, ～oid, ～let, ～le, ～kin, ～ele	작다	sparkle(작은불꽃), princekin (소공자), duckling(새끼오리)
liter, lit	글자, 쓰다	literal(글자 그대로)
lith	돌	lithograph(석판화)
loc	장소, 위치	locate(위치시키다)
loc, loq, log	말	soliloquy(독백), logical(논리적인)
logos	이성	illogical(비논리적인)

어근	뜻	예
logy	연구, 학문, 말	anthropology(인류학)
luc, lum, lus, lun, photo, radio	빛	elucidate(설명하다)
lude	극,曲	interlude(막간-극 사이)
lunar	달	lunatic(미치광이)

어근	뜻	예
macro, mag	크다	macroeconomy(거시경제)
mal, mis	나쁜, 부정의 뜻	malfunction(기능장애), malefactor(행악자)
mand	명령하다	countermand(반대하다, 취소하다)
mania	증세, 정신이상	megalomania(과대망상증)
manu, mana, mani	손	manuscript(사본)
mari, mer	바다, 웅덩이	submarine(잠수함)
mass	덩어리	mass production(대량생산)
mater, matri, matro	어머니, 결혼	matrimony(결혼)
med, mid	중간	mediterranean(지중해)
mega, magn	백만, 큰	megavolt(백만볼트), megalophonous(큰소리내는)
melan	검은	melancholy(우울한)
mem	기억하다	commemoration(기념물, 기념식)
meta	변화	metamorphosis(변화)
meter	측정하다	thermometer(온도계)
micro, min	작다.	microcosm(소우주)
migra	이동하다	immigration(들어오는 이민)
mini	줄이다	diminish(줄이다)
mis	잘못된, 나쁜, 부정	misbehavior(그릇된 행위)
miss, mit	보내다	transmit(전도하다)
mob, mot, mov	움직이다	promote(증진시키다)
mon	경고하다, 알려주다	admonish(충고하다)

어원
정리

어근	뜻	예
monger	장사꾼	ironmonger(철물상)
~mony	결과, 상태, 동작	testimony(증언), ceremony(의식)
mono, sol, uni	하나	solitude(고독)
monster, must	보여주다, 귀신	remonstrate(충고하다)
mor	죽음	moribund(죽을 정도의)
morph	형태	amorphous(형태가 없는)
multi, poly, myria	많은	multifarious(다방면의), polyglot(다국어를 하는 언어학자)
mut	변화하다	commutate(전환하다)
myria	만	myriapod(다족류)

어근	뜻	예
nasc, nat	태어나다	naturalization(귀화)
neur	신경	neuritis(신경염), *itis(질병)
new, nov, neo, nova	새로운	novice(초보자), neoclassic(신고전의)
nic, nec ,nox	해로운	obnoxious(불쾌한)
noc, nox	밤	noctograph(맹인용 필기구)
nom, norm, nem	자, 기준, 규칙	enormous(엄청난)
non, un	부정의뜻	nonquenchable(수습되지 않는, quench: 구별하다)
nona, novem, ennea	아홉(9)	nonary(구진법)
noun, nunci	선언하다. 경고하다	denunciation(공공연한 비난)
number	수	innumerability(무수히 많음, 셀 수 없음)
nym	이름	synonym(동의어), antonym(반의어)

O

어근	뜻	예
oct	여덟(8)	octagon(8각형)
odo	길	odometer(차의 주행거리계)
onym, nom, onomato	이름	nomination(지명)
oligo, pauci	적은	oligocarpous(열매가 적은)
omni, pan	모든	omnivorous(잡식의), pan-American(항공사 이름)
op, ob, oc, of	대항하다	offensive(공격적인), oppose(반대하다)
oper	작동하다	operative(작전상의)
orth	옳은, 똑바른	orthopedist(정형외과 의사)
oss, osteo	뼈	ossification(골화)
out	바깥, 보다 우세한	outwit(재치가 뛰어나다), outdo(~보다 뛰어나다)
over	과도한,~위의	overhear(엿듣다), overwhelm(압도하다), overwork(과로히다)

P

어근	뜻	예
pac, plais	기쁘게 하다	implacable(달랠 수 없는)
pan, panto, omni	전체적인	pansophism(박식)
para, par	옆, 변화, 막아줌	parasol(파라솔)
pater, patri	아버지	patricide(부친살해)
part	나누다	depart(떠나다), partial(편파적인)
pathy, cord, cardio, cour	마음, 심장	apathy(무관심)
ped, pod	발, 어린이	pedestrian(보행자)
pel, puls	밀다	compel(강요하다)
pen	지불하다, 매달리다	compensation(보상), pendulum(추), dependent(의존하는), expense(비용)

어원 정리

어근	뜻	예
penta, quint, quinque	다섯(5)	pentagon(오각형)
per	완전히, 계속적인	person(완전한소리), perennial(영구적인)
petro	돌, 바위	petroleum(석유)
phil	좋아하다	philander(여자 꽁무니를 쫓아다니다)
phone, phon(y),son(y)	소리	homophone(같은발음), microphone(마이크)
phobia	두려움	gynephobia(여성공포증)
pict	그리다	picturesque(그림같이 생생한), depict(묘사하다)
plex, ply, plic	접다, 겹치다	explicit(명백한), multiply(늘리다, 곱하다), complicated(복잡한)
plu, plur, plus	많은	plurality(대다수)
pneuma	숨, 폐, 성령	pneumoconiosis(진폐증), pneumonia(폐렴)
pop, dem	사람들	populicide(대량학살), epidemic(전염병)
port	나르다	report(보고하다), transport(수송하다)
portion	부분, 몫	apportion(배분)
pose, pon	놓다, 자세를 취하다	dispose(배열하다), deposit(예금하다), depose(퇴위시키다)
post	後(나중에),뒤에	posthumous(사후의), postpone(연기하다)
poten, potes, posse	힘	potentiality(잠재력)
prehen, pris	붙잡다, 받다	misapprehend(오해하다)
prim, prin, proto, prior	첫 번째, 원시의	primitive(원시적인)
pro	앞, 좋아하는	proclivity(취향)
~proof	~을 막아주는	soundproof(방음의)
pseudo, quasi	가짜	pseudonym(가명)
psych	정신	psycho analyst(정신분석학자)
punct	점	punctographic(점자의)
pyr, volcan, vulcan	불	pyromania(방화광)

Q

어근	뜻	예
quadr, tetr	넷	quadruple(네 배)

R

어근	뜻	예
rad	뿌리	radicle(작은 뿌리)
re, retro, ano, ana	다시, 뒤로, 위	retrospect(회고하다), anastrophe(도치법), recede(물러가다)
rect	똑바른, 옳은, 규칙	direction(방향)
ridi, risi	웃다	ridicule(비웃음)
roga, rog	요구하다	rogation(기도회)
rupt	깨지다	corrupt(타락한)

S

어근	뜻	예
sacr	신성한	desecrate(신성을 더럽히다)
sang, sangui	피	consanguinity(혈족)
sat	충분함	satisfaction(만족)
scend	오르다	descendant(후손)
scope, vis, vid, opti, ocul	보다	periscope(잠망경), oculist(안과의사)
scrib, scrip	쓰다	post script(추신)
script, scribe	쓰다	manuscript(원고)
se, apo	떨어져서(분리, 이탈)	separate(분리하다), apostate(변절한), secure(안전한)
sect	자르다	dissect(해부하다), section(절개)
sens sent	느끼다	sentiment(감상)
sign	표시하다	insignificant(중요하지 않은)
simil, simul, semble, seem	비슷하다	assimilate(동화하다)

어근	뜻	예
soph	지혜	sophist(지혜로운 자), sophistication(세련, 정교, 궤변)
spec, spic, vi	보다	introspect(반성하다)
sphere	둥근 모양	hemisphere(半球)
spir,hale	숨 쉬다	conspire(공모하다), exhale(숨을 내쉬다)
spond, spons	맹세하다, 대답하다	respond(응답하다)
sta, sti, sist	서있다	subsistence(존재)
stereo	고체, 입체	stereotype(정형)
struc	건설하다	reconstruction(재건)
sub. sus, hypo	아래	suffix(접미어), submarine(잠수함), hypotension(저혈압)
sui	스스로	suicide(자살하다)
sum	쓰다	consumption(소비)
super, over, hyper, ultra	上, 최고의, 지나친, 표면의(super)	hypertension(고혈압)
sur, super, ultra	위,~보다 더, 초월하여	surrealism(초현실주의), superiority(우수함), survive(살아남다)
syn, sym	함께, 동시에, 같은, 합성의	symphony(교향곡)

어근	뜻	예
tang, ting, tact, tig	만지다	semidetached(반쯤 떨어진)
tail	자르다, 붙잡다	tailor(재단사), maintenance(유지)
taxi	순서, 배열	taxidermist(박제사)
thermo	열	thermometry(온도측정)
tech	기술, 예술	technicality(전문성)
tele	멀리 있는	telescope(망원경)
tempo	박자, 속도, 시간	contemporary(동시대사람), temporary(일시적인)

어근	뜻	예
ten, tin, tain, tent	유지하다	retain(계속하다)
tend, tens, tent	쭉 펴다, 당기다	superintend(감독하다), tendon(힘줄), contend(겨루다)
ter, tri	셋	trivium(삼학-논리, 문법, 수사학)
terra, terri, geo	땅	territory(영토), geometry(기하학)
the, theo	神(신)	monotheism(유일신교)
~tive	~이 가득한	talkative(말 많은)
tor	비틀다	tortoise(거북이-다리가 뒤틀려 있음)
tom	쪼개다	atom(원자)
tox	독	antitoxin(항독소), intoxicated(술에 취한)
tract	끌다, 뽑다	attract(끌어당기다)
tract, trah	끌다, 당기다	extraction(뽑아내기, 적출)
trans, tra	횡단, 관통, 변화	transplant(이식하다), transport(운송하다)
tri	셋(3)	triangle(삼각형), trivial(사소한)
trib	지불하다, 기부하다	retribution(보복, 징벌)
typo	활자	typography(인쇄술)

어근	뜻	예
und, unda	넘치다	abound(풍부하다), surround(포위하다)
under	아래에, 열등한, 덜	underbody(하부), underestimate(과소평가하다)
uni	하나(1)	unification(통일), uniform(제복)
up	위로	upright(직립의), uphold(지지하다)
ultim	마지막	ultimately(궁극적으로)
ultra	초(超), 과(過), 외(外)	ultraviolet rays(자외선)

어근	뜻	예
verse	돌다	universe(우주, 세계)
va(c)	비어있다	vanish(사라지다), vacuum(진공의)
vag	떠돌아다니다, 방황하다	vagabond(방랑자)
vale, vali, valu	용기, 힘	valedictory(작별인사)
ver, vera, veri	진리, 사실	verdict(판결)
ver, veri	진짜	averment(주장, 단언), verdict(평결)
vers, vert	반대로 돌다	controversy(논쟁), convert(바꾸다)
vest	옷 입다	vesture(의복)
via	길	trivial(사소한)
vic	변화하다	vicissitude(변화)
vice	대신에 ,副(부)	vicegerent(대리인)
vis	보다	vision(시각), television
vita, viv, bio, eco	살아있음, 생활	vitality(활력)
viv, vit	살아있는, 생생한	vivid(생생한), vital(생명의)
voc, vok	목소리	vocation(직업), vocal(목소리의)
vol, rot	감다, 빙빙 돌다	rotate(회전하다), revolver(연발권총)
vor, vour	먹다	voracious(식욕이 왕성한)

어근	뜻	예
with, re, retro, palin	뒤로, 대항하여, 다시	withhold(보류하다), withstand(견디다)
wri, wro, wry	잘못된, 굽은	writhe(몸을 뒤틀다)
wright	세밀한 작업하는 사람	playwright(극작가)

찾아보기

찾아
보기

찾아
보기